Praise for Lance Secretan and *Managerial Moxie:*

"The first edition of *Managerial Moxie* was brilliant. This revised edition takes it to the next level."
—*Don Watt, President, The Watt Group*

"You will succeed only if your employees do and that is what Lance Secretan writes about."
—*John Myser, Group Vice President, 3M Company*

"Secretan has captured the keys to long-term success."
—*D. Campbell Deacon, Chair and Chief Executive Officer, Deacon Barclays de Zoete Wedd Limited*

"The finest business book I have ever read."
—*Russell J. Daigle, Vice President and General Manager, McAsphalt Industries*

"A thought-provoking and dynamic book that throws conventional management wisdom on its ear; sagacious ideas that motivate and inspire individuals to vitalize corporations by giving them a purpose, a heart, a soul and a conscience."
—*Michael Trueman, President, Architech Microsystems*

"I strongly recommend *Managerial Moxie* to any CEO. The template outlined in this book not only forms the basis for an excellent strategic planning session but it galvanizes the management team to break down traditional walls and create new shared goals for the entire team."
—*Keith Keindel, President, Spalding Canada*

"What a pleasure to read a management book that balances the big picture with hard take-aways—take your choice."
—*Tom Corcoran, Vice President Communications and Quality, IBM Canada Ltd.*

"Lance Secretan has given me a new word. 'Moxie' is a great way to describe not only Lance's personal success story but the no-nonsense management methods which he describes so well in his book."
—*Professor Charles Handy, London Business School,* *author,* The Age of Unreason

"More than just a 'how-to-manage' book, this is a 'how-successful-managers-think' book."
—*William J. Coke, Former President, Manpower Inc.* *of Canada*

"The author is a rare find—a natural writer on business topics with a wealth of experience in that area."
—*Ingrid Philipp Cook*

"The author knows what he is talking about and has presented his point of view in a straightforward manner. It would be a pleasure to work in a company that practiced his philosophies."
—*Lesley Jones*

Managerial Moxie

*The 8 Proven Steps to
Empowering Employees and
Supercharging Your Company*

Lance H. K. Secretan

Prima Publishing
P.O. Box 1260BK
Rocklin, CA 95677
(916) 786-0426

Developmental editing by Candace Demeduc
Copyediting by Lura Dymond
Production by Janelle Rohr, Bookman Productions
Typography by Bookends Typesetting
Interior design by Renee Deprey, Judith Levinson,
   and Michael Yazzolino
Jacket design by Kirschner-Caroff Design
Illustrations by Robert V. Kozinets and Cyndie C. H. Wooley

Library of Congress Cataloging-in-Publication Data

Secretan, Lance H. K.
   Managerial moxie : the 8 Proven Steps to Empowering
   Employees and Supercharging Your Company / by Lance
   H. K. Secretan.
        p.   cm.
   Includes index.
   ISBN 1-55958-159-X
   1. Industrial management.   I. Title.
   HD31.S365   1992
   658—dc20   91-31176
                                                   CIP

93 94 95 96 97 RRD 10 9 8 7 6 5 4 3 2 1

Printed in the United States of America

How to Order:

Quantity discounts are available from Prima Publishing, P.O. Box 1260BK, Rocklin, CA 95677; telephone (916) 786-0426. On your letterhead include information concerning the intended use of the books and the number of books you wish to purchase.

For

Jules Bowes (1932–1985)

Entrepreneur
Moxie Manager
Scholar
Friend
Brother

Contents

Preface

> If you're not in business for fun or profit, what
> the hell are you doing here?
>
> —Robert Townsend

You've picked up *Managerial Moxie* . . . and
now you're probably wondering what it's about and what
makes it different from all the other business bromides
crowding the shelves of your local bookstore.

Let me explain . . .

I always wanted to retire when I was 40, and when
the day came, I did. By "retiring," I mean "doing what
I love—which I don't call work anymore—and never giving a second thought to money or security." Of course,
I've been ten times as busy ever since!

What's contained between these covers are the
philosophies and techniques that I used to build a successful group of companies. This enabled me to "retire"
and go on to build several more businesses, which have
been and still are both fun and profitable.

What I have learned during my corporate journey
is that running a successful business is very simple; in fact,
the problem is that we constantly overengineer and over-
complicate managerial theory. There are two things—and
only two things—that any successful entrepreneurial executive must do:

1. Inspire and motivate employees
2. Find and keep customers for life

Please note, I said it is *simple* but I didn't say it is *easy!*
In these pages, I will describe these two imperatives that
inevitably foster corporate excellence, supercharge employees, and turn customers into "fans."

In 1967 I was asked to straighten out or shut down the ailing British operations of Manpower, the multinational company that pioneered the concept of providing temporary personnel to industry, commerce, and government. The company was founded in Milwaukee, Wisconsin, in 1948 when two lawyers, Elmer Winter and Aaron Scheinfeld, were trying to get out a legal brief and had to scrounge typing help from their friends to meet their deadline. Realizing that many business people frequently faced similar staff shortages, they started the company on a part-time basis while continuing their law practice. During those early days, the company nearly went belly-up twice. Only the merest suspicion indicated that the new company would pioneer a new industry and maintain world leadership that continues today. Even in the 1960s, the company was privately owned; most of its senior employees had been part of its genesis. The few token offices that existed in Europe and Canada were the result of fate, opportunity, and coincidence rather than any grand, global corporate strategy.

Before arriving in the United Kingdom, I was told that annual sales were $2 million. The daunting size of the task became clearer when we learned that sales were barely half that—the red ink in the preceding year had amounted to a $350,000 lake! I was reminded of John F. Kennedy's observation of a few years earlier: ''When we got into office, the thing that surprised me most was to find that things were just as bad as we'd been saying they were.'' I was only 27 and probably not up to the task, but youth made me blissfully unaware of most of my personal shortcomings.

Ten years later, Manpower's operations in the United Kingdom, Ireland, the Middle East, and Africa were well on their way to annual sales of $100 million, with profits to match. We were trading through more than 100 offices, which employed more than 70,000 full- and part-time staff. In the United Kingdom, training organizations used our company as a model for success. Our competitors imitated our service standards and marketing strategies. Major corporations emulated our employment practices, and the business press regularly watched and reported our progress.

Shortly after leaving Manpower, I started the MBA program in entrepreneurship at McMaster University in Hamilton, Ontario, and later taught the flagship course in entrepreneurship at Toronto's York University. I needed a text from which to teach that reflected my own experiences of the practical rather than the theoretical tricks of the game. Unable to find an appropriate text (although I looked at 150 different academic and popular business books), I wrote my own, *Managerial Moxie.* In its pages I reflected upon my exciting years at Manpower and tried to recapture the techniques that accounted for our turnaround and subsequent success. With the benefit of 20/20 hindsight, I saw that our strategy had been very simple.

We assembled a team of smart, aggressive executives and together made corporate magic by using the skills and techniques that I collectively call **managerial moxie.** These real-world skills and techniques are what this book is all about.

Although there is some theoretical content in the following pages, the main emphasis in *Managerial Moxie* is on practical experience and hands-on technique. Please persevere with the first two chapters—I think you will find that the theoretical information will set up the rest of the book for you.

I am grateful to my clients, an outstanding group of executives and their teams at some of the finest organizations in the world, where I have been refining my theories and learning from some very talented people since 1981. They include the top teams at Apple Computer, Bell Telephone, British Petroleum, Cyanamid, Digital Equipment, Equifax, Ernst and Young International, Four Season Hotels, IBM, Kraft General Foods, Mary Kay Cosmetics,

Mercantile & General Reinsurance, Northern Telecom, Royal Insurance, Spalding, and the Young President's Organization.

This completely revised and updated edition of *Managerial Moxie* reflects my own years of experience and augments my earlier ideas with the very latest leadership techniques, which are the result of a new age of management. All the skills and techniques cited in this book reflect my own experiences as a CEO as well as those of many high-octane corporate leaders whom I've watched revving their corporations to the max in Europe, North America, the Middle East, and Africa.

I was once told by a man wiser than he cared to admit that we become better at what we study. Consequently, he reasoned, if we study problems, we will become better at creating them. Conversely, if we study successes, we will become more adept at repeating them. On the strength of this wisdom, I have tried to distinguish between the "eye-candy" of trivial and cosmetic tricks on the one hand and the crucial criteria that account for corporate success on the other. These vital criteria are the subject of this book.

Managerial Moxie was written expressly for the executive who now occupies, or aspires to occupy, the top job—what James Thurber called "the catbird seat." It will appeal to modern leaders who reject management mumbo-jumbo—leaders who want to work with teams that aspire to being peerless. As a result, this book will probably unnerve nearly everyone who

♦ has an MBA
♦ went to Harvard
♦ likes tidy answers to complex problems
♦ is a management consultant
♦ hasn't heard of Professor Northcote C. Parkinson
♦ doesn't make mistakes
♦ thinks fun and profit are mutually exclusive

Like the American humorist Josh Billings, I have now lived long enough to take another, more careful look at things I was certain of the first time. In *Managerial Moxie* I closely examine established leadership theory in order to help leaders and would-be leaders achieve one of the greatest highs in the exciting world of business: guiding a corporation by means of its executive team to outstanding levels of achievement.

———◆———

It requires a very unusual mind to make an analysis of the obvious.

—Alfred North Whitehead

Acknowledgments

*T*o become a successful leader, you must first be selected from the ranks by an alert observer who can not only recognize potential but also provide the chance for it to be developed. I am grateful for being given this chance when I was just a greenhorn. Despite the scares I gave Mitchell Fromstein, Bill Pollock, Jim Scheinfeld, and Elmer Winter as I accidentally and deliberately broke the rules, I am delighted to report that we are all still on speaking terms! I also owe a special debt to two terrific human beings, Jim Shore and Aaron Scheinfeld (neither of whom, sadly, are with us today). They showed me how they wove their magic with people, while making tons of dough and having fun at the same time. I still miss them.

I owe a debt to my colleagues at Manpower in the United Kingdom. The chemistry that developed between us was the basis of our corporate success. This team included Lillian Bennett, William (Ken) Davidson, Harry Mottram, Mike Scott, Peter Turner, and a terrific group of entrepreneurial franchisees. Our experiments in designing and leading an exciting company were the basis for many of the ideas that form the heart of *Managerial Moxie.*

Over the years I have had the good fortune to benefit from the cerebral talents and innovative thinking of Robert Kozinets. When we first met, he was a gifted MBA student and I was his professor of entrepreneurship at York University in Toronto. Since then, we have collaborated on many projects, including three books and numerous consulting assignments. Our association has been a joy for me, both professionally and personally.

Candee Tremblay puts discipline, creativity, logistics, and friendship into my life for which I am very grateful.

Janelle Rohr, Candace Demeduc, and Lura Dymond wove their magic, Chicago-style, over my manuscript, leaving it much prettier than they received it.

What are friends and clients for if not to endure manuscripts during their formative stages? Thanks to the entrepreneurial Peter Aldrich (Aldrich, Eastman, and Waltch), Dave Blair (D. C. Blair and Associates), Ken Copeland (Digital Equipment), Tom Corcoran (IBM), D. Campbell Deacon (Deacon Barclays de Zoete Wedd), John De Shano (Levi Strauss), Aki Friedman (Manpower), Keith Keindel (Spalding Canada), Veronica Maidman (Equifax), Ted Matthews (Promanad Communications), Ross Morton (Manulife Financial), John Myser (3M Company), Dan Oberlander (Cunard Hotels), Peter Patterson (Mercantile & General Reinsurance), Dick Ploetz (Medtronic), Jonas Prince (Delta Hotels), David Rae (Apple Computer), Heather Reisman (Paradigm Consulting), Harry Schell (BICC Cables), Bob Busch and Tom Schmidt (Cyanamid), Gerry Schwartz (Onex), Hugo Sorensen (Triathalon), Barry Sullivan (First Chicago), Allan Sutherland (Derlan Industries), Michael Trueman (Architech Microsystems), Don Watt (The Watt Group), and John Young (Four Season Hotels) for generously contributing intellect and constructive criticism drawn from *both* brain hemispheres.

Most important, thank you, Tricia. This book, like everything else in my life, has the imprint of your love.

Lance H. K. Secretan
Cataract, Ontario, Canada, 1992

Worksheet:
The Managerial Moxie Index (A)

The enlightened leaders of successful organizations have managerial moxie. How do you rate? You don't need a Ph.D. to have managerial moxie or to determine whether your organization is run by managers with moxie. Just complete the Managerial Moxie Index (A) below to see how you rate.

1. If you were to ask ten different colleagues the purpose of your organization, would they all give the same answer?

    Yes _____   No _____

2. Can you lay your hands on copies of your corporate mission, statement of values, and vision statement in less than 10 minutes?

    Yes _____   No _____

3. In your organization, if you were asked what it is like around here and how you would like it to be around here, would your answer be the same for both questions?

    Yes _____   No _____

4. Could you and your team become rich if you consistently turned in outstanding results for your organization?

    Yes _____   No _____

5. Are you empowered with all the authority and responsibility you need to meet your professional goals successfully?

    Yes _____   No _____

6. Do you have a current job description (created within the last 12 months) that is thoroughly covered on less than one page?

    Yes _____   No _____

7. Does your organization subcontract its catering, cleaning, printing, temporary staff, travel, training, recruitment, maintenance, legal, advertising, public relations,

and security requirements to specialized outside firms?

Yes _____   No _____

8. Does your organization employ more sales, marketing, and service staff than administrators?

Yes _____   No _____

9. Do you know the names of your top 20 customers and the annual contribution they each make to your revenues?

Yes _____   No _____

10. Are your monthly operating statements intelligible, helpful, limited to five pages or less, and delivered to you within 3 working days of your month-end?

Yes _____   No _____

Total   **Yes** _____   **No** _____

Did you score less than 5 yes's? Don't despair! You will thoroughly enjoy reading *Managerial Moxie* and practicing the exercises it contains. More than 5 yes's? Congratulations! Your organization is run by enlightened leaders—you're lucky to be a member of an invigorating organization. You scored 8 or more? Wow! Your outfit is hot. Now consider the toughest challenge of all: How do you stay that way? Organizations at the pinnacle of success are the most susceptible to becoming bloated bureaucracies stuffed with paper-pushing mandarins. The best defense against standard operating procedures, rule books, and regimented decline is a regular regimen of managerial moxie!

A final suggestion for those who scored more than 8 yes's: Ask your closest colleagues to complete the Managerial Moxie Index (A) too; in a company with managerial moxie, every team member will possess a synthesized perception of their corporate environment, aspiration, and culture, so their responses should match yours—it's like asking an orchestra what the musical score is.

You will find another version of the Managerial Moxie Index at the end of Chapter 10 (the Managerial Moxie Index (B)). Its purpose is to help you use the material in this book to develop managerial moxie in your organization. You can do this by comparing the results of Index (A) with Index (B), measuring the gap, and designing an action plan to close that gap.

Note: The Managerial Moxie Index (B) should serve as the agenda for your next management meeting.

Chapter 1

What Is Managerial Moxie?

moxie \mäk-sē, -si\ *n* -s [from *Moxie,* a trademark for a soft drink] **1** *slang* : ENERGY, PEP, LIFE <he shook out of my grip, but there wasn't much [moxie] in it —P. W. Denzer> **2** *slang* **a** (1) : COURAGE, PLUCK <had plenty of [moxie] and was afraid of nothing> (2) : AUDACITY, NERVE <only in the outposts of the British Empire do males have the [moxie] to regularly wear shorts in mixed company —*Fortnight*> **b** : STAMINA, BACKBONE, GUTS <show that mob in the stadium that you've got the old [moxie] —*Saturday Rev.*>

—*Webster's Third New International Dictionary*

*M*anagerial moxie—a deceptively simple philosophy—characterizes the leadership of such highly successful organizations as Body Shop, John Deere, Dell Computers, Delta Airlines, Honeywell, K-Mart, Loblaws, Matsushita, Merck, Motorola, Mrs. Fields Cookies, Nissan, Nucor, Sony, Turner Broadcasting Systems, Wal-Mart, and W. L. Gore. The leaders of these companies combine compassion and imagination with results-based pragmatism; in short, they possess managerial moxie, which is based on eight principles:

1. **A sense of purpose.** A crystal clear understanding of the reason for the corporation's existence sets the foundation for the corporation's success.

2. **A climate for success.** By respecting the individual and emphasizing excellence, leaders establish a climate that encourages everyone (colleagues, employees, suppliers, profit partners, and associates) to create, nourish, and enjoy corporate success.

3. **Motivated people.** A people-centered approach romances uncommon performance from ordinary people, infusing the corporation with a can-do attitude.

4. **A team of superstars.** Getting the right people for executive positions builds superbly balanced and high-performing teams.

5. **Delegation and empowerment.** Diffusing authority, power, and responsibility throughout the organization at the appropriate levels results in high-quality decision making.

6. **Out-sourcing.** Assigning certain professional, service, and staff functions to specialists outside the corporation allows the corporate team to devote itself to what it does best.

7. **Dedication to customers.** A service-driven philosophy results in customer loyalty and long-term success.

8. **Judicious management.** Exercising judgment by comparing numbers as well as other factors is crucial to running a successful corporation.

All too often, however, our corporations are managed by executives whose reliance on worn-out management theories puts them sadly out of tune with the dramatic changes taking place in the contemporary corporate climate. In order to adapt their corporations to a rapidly changing environment, these executives institute incremental modifications. Unfortunately, they don't realize that breakthrough performance is achieved by breakthrough thinking—revolution, not evolution, is what's needed in an age of permanent white water.

◆

Consider the example of British Airways. For 6 months after I left Manpower in 1981, I continued to provide consulting services to the company. During that time I flew between the United Kingdom and my home in Canada 30 times, and each British Airways flight was about as much fun as gum surgery. The company had yet to discover customer service—the old cronies who occupied senior positions were busy running the airline for themselves rather than for the customers. The employees were sullen and frequently on strike for more pay or better working conditions; in fact, British Airways was the flying basket case of Europe, losing $200 million on revenues of less than $4 billion that year.

Then along came a new chairman, Lord King of Wartnaby, and a new CEO, Sir Colin Marshall. These two did something that the airline had never done before: They asked their customers what they would change and what services they would like. In response to the feedback from customers, King and Marshall launched Club Europe and Club World. Club Europe addressed the customer as a total traveler, not simply a flying passenger (a first in the airline industry). For example, it provided valet parking on the Paris/London and Amsterdam/London runs, orange juice before takeoff, and hot towels before meals. Club World gave business-class travelers more legroom, larger and more comfortable seating, more service, and—a big change—food that was edible. The fleet was replaced or refurbished, airport lounges were enlarged, check-in procedures were streamlined, first-class services were spruced up, special fares and services were introduced for passengers over 55—and most important, the corporate culture throughout the airline's worldwide operations was completely overhauled.

New marketing alliances were struck with Delta Airlines and United Airlines as well as Air New Zealand to provide a truly global network. The staff received new uniforms, and an award-winning $34 million advertising campaign was launched to tell the world about the remaking of the airline. In the decade that followed, British Airways doubled its revenues to $8 billion and stands today as a tribute to corporate leaders who practice managerial moxie—*inspiring and motivating employees and finding and keeping customers for life.*

———◆———

Incremental modifications don't work because nowadays the corporate environment, especially the needs of customers and the marketplace, change in revolutionary, not evolutionary, patterns. When the incremental-modifications scenario is played out in a stumbling organization, anxious shareholders or a predatory acquisitor will enter the scene and the old-style CEOs and other top management will exit. The new leadership will spend the next 10 years—note the long-term implications—healing the wounded organization. According to research conducted by Eugene Jennings of Michigan State University, average annual turnover for the top two executive positions in major U.S. corporations in the 1960s was about 3.5%. In the last decade, this rose to almost 10%. In recent years this unproductive scenario has been enacted over and over in countless head offices throughout the Western world—continuous musical chairs in the executive suite.

To avoid this wasteful turnover and to guarantee the continuous productivity and success of our corporations, we must revolutionize the way we lead and manage. To do this calls for a new look at how we think, learn, and create.

The Kuhnian Approach

Many of the great scientific philosophers have argued that knowledge grows incrementally, becoming more comprehensive and contemporary and therefore more relevant through a continuing process of adaptation.

Thomas S. Kuhn, the distinguished historian of science and professor emeritus at the Massachusetts Institute of Technology, has argued forcefully that knowledge is not merely a process of compounding additional theories, scientific breakthroughs, advances, and new rules. Instead, Kuhn maintains that a revolutionary process occurs within each evolutionary field of scientific knowledge. He argues that perceivable and identifiable theories emerge from different sources through a process of communication, until a dominant theory takes control. This new theory or series of beliefs eventually emerges as the ruling paradigm, which Kuhn defines as a "universally recognized scientific [achievement], that, for a time, provide[s] model problems and solutions to a community of practitioners." Scientific examples of Kuhn's theory may be found in the replacement of Aristotelian with Newtonian dynamics and of Ptolemaic with Copernican astronomy. Another example is supply-side economic theory, a paradigm that competes with an older one, Keynesian economics.

Kuhn asserts that when a field of knowledge (such as management science) reaches the paradigm stage, practitioners and academics indulge in what he calls "**normal science**," or the *practice* of the discovery. This usually consists of validating the paradigm—that is, perfecting it or testing its techniques or methodology.

This process provides feedback that confirms and re-inforces the paradigm and the beliefs held by its prac-titioners.

The continuation of normal science deepens the paradigm, fleshing out the detail and complexity of the associated knowledge. So far, so good. But what happens when paradigms no longer work?

When Paradigms Fail

Consider the Ptolemaic and Copernican paradigms in astronomy. Until 1543 the prevailing paradigm concern-ing our cosmos was that the Earth was the fixed center of the universe around which revolved the Sun, Moon, and stars. But the publication in 1543 of Copernicus's hypothesis that the Sun, not the Earth, was the center of our universe gave birth to a new paradigm.

An **anomaly of fact** is the means by which scien-tists can observe the unexpected, which in turn can lead to a discovery. If the discovery fits within the prevailing paradigm, it reinforces the paradigm. But if it challenges the paradigm, it may lead to the creation of a theoretical anomaly—and this may result in a theoretical and con-ceptual breakthrough. The Copernican revolution was just such a breakthrough.

Before this process is complete, a crisis will occur—awareness of the theoretical anomaly will have "violated the paradigm-induced expectations that govern 'normal science.'" The crisis will continue with a more or less ex-tended exploration of the anomaly; it will end only when the paradigm's theory has been adjusted, so that the anomalous has become the expected. Crises, Kuhn has found, nearly always precede a paradigm change.

In this respect, Kuhn's concept of a paradigm shift has much in common with **chaos theory.** The "crisis" that Kuhn describes is a point of "chaos," or turbulence, in the environment, in which the machinelike system of the old paradigm no longer works.

A study of six major companies in The Netherlands found that during such a chaotic, paradigm-changing environment, organizations begin to emphasize:

1. Self-organization, or empowerment
2. Complex culture
3. Simple structure
4. Emerging, proactive strategies

These four principles are crucial to the successful transition from a failing paradigm to a new one. As the British writer P. A. Hansson has pointed out, "small-scale chaos will either stabilize the situation or drive it to a new state."

The failure of normal science brings the crisis to a head. Kuhn goes on: "As in manufacturing, so in science—re-tooling is an extravagance to be reserved for the occasion that demands it. The significance of crises is the indication they provide that an occasion for re-tooling has arrived."

What holds for science and manufacturing holds for the art and science of leading and managing too. Corporate crises—like those of Dome Petroleum, Continental Illinois, Rolls-Royce, and Penn Central—indicated that the time was ripe for extensive managerial retooling. To retool, however, requires that we refashion our ideas on how we think, learn, and create.

Brain-Hemisphere Theory

In 1968 Dick Fosbury, a 6-foot 4-inch Oregon State University senior, made history. In the Mexico City Olympic games, he burst toward the high-jump bar with a few strides and then did something no Olympic athlete had done before: He flipped in midair, turned his back to the bar, and sailed over it head first, with his back to the ground. With the "Fosbury Flop," he cleared 7 feet 4¼ inches, won the gold medal, and changed forever the style athletes would use for the high jump. He later said that he did it this way because the traditional forms of jumping weren't giving him what he wanted.

Dr. Edward de Bono has argued that "you cannot dig a hole in a different place by digging the same hole deeper." We can't expect dramatic results from people and organizations if we simply continue to do *more of the same*. We need to dig a *new* hole, to learn *new* theories and practices of leadership so that we can build great organizations during the last decade of this millennium and beyond.

In the field of human creativity and learning, a vital new hole has been dug recently. It is called **brain-hemisphere theory.** Since so much has been written and so much misunderstanding created about this theory, it's worthwhile to reexamine it in some depth (especially important here because much of managerial moxie depends on the willingness of leaders to take advantage of the existing but underutilized potential of the right-brain hemisphere).

The discovery of brain duality can be traced back to 1844 when English physician A. L. Wigan determined that the brain's left hemisphere controls the motor action of the right side of the body and the right hemisphere controls the motor action of the left side of the body. More recently, however, and especially following Dr. Roger Sperry's seminal work at the California Institute of Technology (for which he won the Nobel prize in 1981), we have learned that the left side of our brain controls our logic mechanisms and our capacity to process information sequentially, to perform linear operations, and to be rational. It also controls our language skills. The right hemisphere, operating in a more holistic way, simultaneously processes information and ideas. Many forms of human communication, especially those that require a relational or contextual evaluation (for example, most of our emotions) are right-hemisphere functions. So too are our melodic skills.

Linguistic and technical activities tend to be processed by the left hemisphere; artistic and abstract activities are associated with the right hemisphere. I realize that this is a very crude generalization and that there are limitations to extrapolating these concepts to the world of business. But we *can* say that lawyers, bookkeepers, accountants, production engineers, and computer operators and programmers probably tend to favor left-hemisphere processing; sales staff, creative consultants, marketers, advertising executives, and entrepreneurs probably draw more heavily from their right hemispheres.

It is too early to arrive at definitive conclusions in this ground-breaking field. My speculations about the role and application of brain-hemisphere theory to the business world are therefore largely a product of the right side of my brain! But this fascinating subject holds many truths yet to be discovered. Those we already know—such as the participation, dominance, and competence of the different hemispheres—have the potential to yield fresh insights into how we inspire and motivate employees and find and keep customers—for life.

In many people the two hemispheres perform in a complementary manner, like the two blades of a pair of scissors. The ideal entrepreneurial executive, for example, demonstrates the characteristics of a "double-dominant," that is, an individual who is equally at ease using either hemisphere and who has highly developed capabilities in both. In many people, however, one hemisphere seems to be superior to, or dominant over, the other. This book will attempt to show how entrepreneurial leaders, who are already adept at left-hemisphere activities, can use the right hemisphere to build successful leadership teams and therefore great organizations.

To test your own left/right hemisphere preference, try *The Thaler Brain-Hemisphere Profile* at the end of this chapter.

CULTURE AND HEMISPHERE

Anglo-American patterns of thought are generally left-hemisphere dominated, and the use of the computer is probably accelerating this tendency. This left-hemispheric bias has its roots in Western religions, which tend to be rational in orientation, containing neat answers and specific directions. As a result, we are temperamentally inclined toward pragmatism. Our learning systems are highly ordered and our societies are governed by legalistic procedures. For example, the United States has more lawyers per capita than any other nation on earth and 70% of the world's total legal population, which each year launches 18 million new lawsuits. The American mind-set (an extreme case of the Western prototype) is represented by one lawyer for every 335 Americans, enjoying $90 billion in fees; the Japanese mind-set is at ease with one lawyer for every 9,000 Japanese. During the last decade, the number of lawyers in the United States has grown by 50%, to around 729,000. In addition, numbers and other systems of quantification are prevalent in every part of our society, dominating our economic and commercial environments.

In contrast, Eastern cultures often embrace religious and societal practices that display a right-hemispheric bias. Oriental religions, such as Hinduism, Taoism, and Buddhism, are more mystical than those of the West. Oriental philosophies are more esoteric and, for the Occidental at least, hard to grasp. Looking at the business success of Japan, South Korea, Singapore, and Taiwan, one can't help speculating that the key may lie in the ability of these nations' managers to draw on a more highly developed right-hemispheric bias in the development and application of managerial techniques. Adaptive skills, responsible for so much of Japan's postwar economic success, are best developed through "spatial" methods and approaches. "Linear" processes act like intellectual ruts from which fresh ideas or adaptations of old ones seldom emerge.

———◆———

The research of Harvard's Professor Robert Hayes into the manufacturing facilities of several large Japanese companies, including Toshiba, Sanyo, Yokogawa Electric, and Mitsubishi, led him to conclude that there was no "secret" to Japanese manufacturing success. Hayes quoted an old Japanese proverb to describe what he found: The nail that sticks up is hammered down. Hayes observed that all the nails had been hammered down by Japanese managers, whom he found to be fanatical about emphasizing the basics. The Japanese, Hayes wrote, put an equal emphasis on all aspects of manufacturing, from product design to distribution, the goal being perfect products and error-free operations. This, he found, was achieved by improving equipment design, inventory control systems, and worker skills through close cooperation at all levels. We all know leadership teams who do the same things—they're the ones with a holistic, long-term view based on people rather than things.

Matsushita Electric demonstrated these techniques in the United States when it purchased a TV assembly plant from Motorola. Under previous management the factory had been plagued with low productivity and poor-quality output. After 3 years under the new management, productivity increased by 30% and defects were cut to less than 4 per 100 TV sets leaving the factory—and all this was accomplished in Franklin Park, Illinois!

In an era when many people have no faith in business plans that project further than 8 quarters, Konosuke

Matsushita was unusual. He developed a corporate plan that spanned 250 years. And every day he consulted the 3,000-year-old Chinese oracle called the *I-Ching* (pronounced "Eee Jeng") to divine his business strategy.

When Konosuke Matsushita died in 1988, he was one of Japan's most eminent educators and industrialists, possessing four honorary university degrees and considered by many to be the father of modern Japanese management. The February 23, 1962, cover story in *Time* magazine devoted five pages to his managerial philosophy and success. However, when he started his business in 1909, he had only two employees and less than $50. From that he built the company into the 37th largest industrial corporation in the world (nearly $50 billion in sales in 1990), the 20th largest non-U.S. corporation, and the world's largest consumer electronics manufacturer. Known as Matsushita Electric Industrial Co. Ltd., it is more familiar to us through its brand-name consumer electronics: Panasonic, Technics, and Quasar. The company gained much press when it purchased the U.S. entertainment giant MCA in 1990 for over $6 billion.

As a young entrepreneur, Matsushita (which means "under the pine tree") watched a tramp drinking water from a tap in the street. Matsushita realized that although it took much energy and skill to bring the water to the tap, nobody gave it a second thought or worried about its scarcity. As he pondered the concept of low-cost abundance, he decided that the business leader's task is to make products and services widely available to humankind in order to improve its lot on this planet.

From this realization came *meichi,* or "our mission is enlightened." On May 5, 1932, he announced his dreams to a small group of senior staff: "With achievement of mental stability and the resourceful supply of goods, happiness of human being's life will be secured. . . . In order to achieve this mission, 250 years from hereafter, are set as the period for its achievement." He then went on to

divide the 250 years into ten time spans, further sub-
dividing these into tasks and achievements for generations
of future Matsushita Electric Industrial employees in order
to raise the living standards of humankind.

In a world where overachieving, MBA-toting, left-
brained stockbrokers, bankers, and analysts make fortunes
by offering nit-picking analyses of corporate balance
sheets four times a year, it comes as a welcome relief that
one can make pots full of money from the combination
of farsightedness and a humane vision. (If Donald Trump
were to announce to his staff that he was driven by a mission to be the solace of humanity, half the staff would
probably faint and the rest would hurl themselves out of
the Trump Tower.)

———————◆———————

It seems clear that if we can forgo our long-standing
tendency to dampen our right-hemisphere traits and
marry their creativity with our old left-hemisphere capability—and do it quickly—we could enjoy a much-needed
renaissance in the Western economies. Although the
science of management (left-hemispheric competency) has
long dominated our corporations, it's the art of leadership (right-hemispheric competency) that must come to
the fore, as Konosuke Matsushita demonstrated. The
balance of this book focuses on the art of leadership that
emanates from this right-hemispheric competence.

———————◆———————

*These, if ever, are the brave free days of
destroyed landmarks, while the ingenious minds
are busy inventing the forms of the new
beacons which, it is consoling to think, will be
set up presently in the old places.*

—Joseph Conrad

WORKSHEET 1-1:
THE THALER BRAIN-HEMISPHERE PROFILE (TBHP)*

> Our brains are seventy-year clocks. The Angel of Life winds them up once and for all, then closes the case and gives the key into the hand of the Angel of Resurrection.
>
> —Oliver Wendell Holmes

Brain-hemisphere research has led to many fascinating insights into how our behavior is influenced by our two brain hemispheres. Using the latest research findings, this profile was specially designed by the Thaler Corporation to reveal your own brain-hemisphere orientation.

INSTRUCTIONS

♦ Answer all the questions quickly and honestly.

♦ Mark the answer that comes closest to describing how you think or feel.

♦ Check the answer that comes to you first and feels "right."

SECTION 1

This section questions you about your physiological tendencies, your activities, and your perceptions in a scientific attempt to determine your own brain-hemisphere orientation. Since these are questions about personal tendencies, there is no need to try to guess what the "right" answer is. The right answer is the answer that is true for you.

1. The following four drawings depict four handwriting positions. Which comes closest to representing yours?

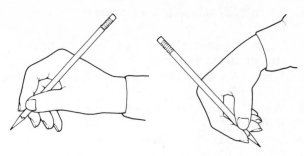

a. Upright right-hand position   b. Hooked right-hand position

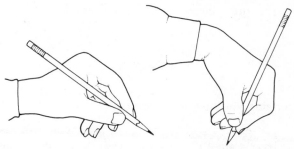

c. Upright left-hand position   d. Hooked left-hand position

2. While sitting comfortably, please clasp your hands together in a relaxed manner in your lap. Which of your thumbs is now on top?
   a. The left
   b. The right
   c. The thumbs are parallel

3. Visualize yourself standing upright at a starting line, about to take part in a speed-walking race. The gun goes off. Which foot did you mentally lead with?
   a. The left
   b. The right

4. Check off all the items below that describe you:
   a. I enjoy using clever and witty—even punny—language.
   b. I love to chat on the telephone.
   c. I can follow technical drawings (like diagrams and schematics) quite easily.

   d. When I am at a lecture or a meeting, I take a lot of notes.
   e. I approach problems by figuring out a methodical, step-by-step solution.
   f. Frequently, ideas come to me without any conscious effort.
   g. When I read, I vividly picture the characters and setting.
   h. I prefer fantasy stories to realistic stories.
   i. I can understand complicated written material (like legal documents) fairly easily.
   j. I rely quite heavily on first impressions.

SECTION 2

In this section, mark the one statement that comes closest to characterizing you or your behavior.

5. a. I can usually picture things in my mind with ease.
   b. I have some difficulty picturing things in my mind.

6. a. In conversation I am usually more comfortable being the listener.
   b. In conversation I am usually more comfortable being the speaker.

7. a. I can tell fairly accurately how much time has passed without looking at a wristwatch or clock.
   b. I find it difficult to tell how much time has passed without looking at a wristwatch or clock.

8. a. I like it better when social gatherings happen spontaneously.
   b. I prefer it when social gatherings are planned.

9. a. I would rather work in a group.
   b. I prefer to work alone.

10. a. I usually print when taking notes.
    b. I rarely print when taking notes.

11. a. I usually make decisions based on what feels right.
    b. I usually make decisions based on the information available to me.

12. a. I am better at remembering the words to songs.
    b. I am better at remembering the melodies and musical parts of songs.
13. a. I frequently have mood changes.
    b. I have very few mood changes.
14. a. I am very aware of body language and can accurately tell what people are feeling much of the time.
    b. I am not very concerned with body language; I listen a lot more to what people actually say.
15. a. I am good at remembering long numbers, like my driver's license or passport number.
    b. I am not very good at remembering long numbers.

SECTION 3

This section contains multiple-choice questions. For each question, check the one answer that comes closest to matching what you do or what you believe.

16. You've just bought your nephew a present that requires a lot of assembly. How do you approach the problem?
    a. I read the instructions carefully, check all the parts and their numbers, and then begin to assemble the present according to the written instructions.
    b. I skim the instructions, then follow them loosely, checking them when I need help.
    c. I look at what the assembled item should look like, try fitting a few parts together to get the feel of the finished product, and then begin assembling it.
17. Think about how you plan your day, how you do your work, and how you find out about things that interest you. How organized would you say you are?
    a. Very well organized; I plan everything out and then execute my plan.
    b. Fairly well organized; I do a bit of planning and then follow my plan.

    c. Not overly organized; I work within a general plan,
but I prefer to keep things flexible and spontaneous.

    d. Not very organized; I just allow the day to unfold.

18. You are faced with a difficult problem in your life or
your business. How do you approach a solution?
    a. I gather facts, list possible courses of action,
       prioritize the alternatives, and then make my
       decision.
    b. I try to get away from the problem for a while to
       think; maybe I'll take a walk or a swim and work
       out some ideas to discuss with others.
    c. I give the problem time to solve itself.
    d. I try to remember strategies that I used success-
       fully on similar problems in the past and then apply
       them to the problem at hand.

19. How often do you find yourself daydreaming?
    a. Frequently
    b. Occasionally
    c. Rarely
    d. Never

20. How often would you say you follow your hunches?
    a. Quite frequently
    b. Occasionally
    c. Rarely
    d. Never

21. Can you easily remember faces and names of people
you met a long time ago?
    a. Yes, I remember people's names and faces very well.
    b. I remember people's faces very well but often forget
       their names.
    c. I remember people's names very well but sometimes
       can't recognize can't recognize their faces.

22. How do you usually remember a name or the location
of a certain place?
    a. I try to see the information in my mind.
    b. I associate it with former information.
    c. I write myself notes.
    d. I verbally repeat similar words or names until the
       right one comes to me.

SCORING

Circle the number of points indicated for each answer you gave (be sure to count each response in quesiton 4).

SECTION 1

1. a. 1
   b. 4
   c. 5
   d. 2

2. a. 1
   b. 5
   c. 3

3. a. 4
   b. 2

4. a. 2
   b. 4
   c. 4
   d. 1
   e. 1
   f. 5
   g. 5
   h. 4
   i. 1
   j 2

SECTION 2

5. a. 5
   b. 1

6. a. 4
   b. 2

7. a. 1
   b. 5

8. a. 5
   b. 1

9. a. 4
   b. 2

10. a. 5
    b. 1

11. a. 5
    b. 1

12. a. 1
    b. 5

13. a. 5
    b. 1

14. a. 5
    b. 1

15. a. 2
    b. 4

SECTION 3

16. a. 1
    b. 3
    c. 5

17. a. 1
    b. 2
    c. 4
    d. 5

18. a. 1
    b. 3
    c. 5
    d. 2

19. a. 5
    b. 3
    c. 3
    d. 1

20. a. 5
    b. 3
    c. 2
    d. 1

21. a. 3
    b. 5
    c. 1

22. a. 5
    b. 3
    c. 1
    d. 2

Write your total score here   [   ] (X)

Write the number of questions you
answered here   [   ] (Y)

Divide X by Y (total score/number of
questions answered) and write number
here   [   ] (Z)

Z = your *brain-hemisphere dominance
quotient*

The range of Z is between 1 (completely
left-brain dominant) and 5 (completely
right-brain dominant).

BRAIN-HEMISPHERE DOMINANCE QUOTIENT: EXPLANATORY NOTES

1. In studies of handwriting positions, it was found that
   left-handers who hold their pencil in an upright handwriting position and right-handers who use a hooked
   handwriting position both have primary speech functions in their right hemispheres. The same research*
   showed that persons who have the upright right-handed
   writing style or the hooked left-handed position have
   primary language functions in the left hemisphere and
   thus have an advantage in language skills.

2. Hypnotists use the thumb-placement test to determine
   how easily a person can be hypnotized. People more
   comfortable with the right thumb on top are easier to
   hypnotize than those who prefer the left. Since right-
   dominants are more suggestible than left-dominants,
   this is also a test of hemisphere dominance: the right
   thumb on top shows right-brain dominance and vice
   versa.

3. The visualized speed-walk race is meant to simulate the
   real thing. The leg or foot that the runner leads with is
   opposite to the brain hemisphere that is dominant.

4. Right-dominants prefer visual information (charts, diagrams, maps) and have active imaginations and fantasy

*Jerre Levy. "The Mammalian Brain and the Adaptive Advantage of
Cerebral Asymmetry." *Annals of the New York Academy of Sciences*
299 (1977): 264–272.

lives; lefts like detail in sequential order, planned events, analyses, and written or verbal directions.

5. Since visualizing is a right-brain activity, those who can picture things in their minds with ease tend to be right-dominants.

6. Because lefts' verbal skills are more highly developed, they feel more comfortable being the speaker than the listener.

7. Lefts are much more conscious of time (as in planning, scheduling, etc.) than are rights—who are frequently apt to lose contact with the here and now. Hence an excellent time sense suggests left-brain dominance.

8. Because they prefer order, lefts are more comfortable with gatherings that are planned. Rights enjoy spontaneity in their social life.

9. Because they are very conscious of time, lefts become impatient with the time-consuming aspects of group work and thus prefer to work alone. Rights are less concerned with time passing and also enjoy the personal interaction of group work.

10. Printing is more pictographical than writing notes and is therefore liked by rights, because it is visual and because it is less structured.

11. Rights "feel" what is right, whereas lefts analyze and compare society's standards.

12. Appreciating and remembering music has been found to be primarily a right-brain activity, while remembering verbal information is a left-brain activity.

13. Both rights and lefts have mood swings, but rights feel their mood changes more strongly than lefts, who discipline themselves to control their mood swings.

14. Rights are more conscious of body language, emotional tone, and other subtleties of human communication than the left-dominants, who focus on the words and their meaning.

15. Because of their ordered minds, left-dominants remember numbers better than right-dominants. This is

similar to remembering any complex information, such as verbal material.

16. Since left-dominants are much more organized and sequential, they will follow instructions or rules very carefully. Right-dominants will take a more gestalt approach, seeing the whole as the sum of its parts.

17. Left-dominants tend to organize their day-to-day activities more than right-dominants; rights are more spontaneous.

18. Lefts tend to approach problem solving in a linear and ordered manner, whereas rights get a feel for the situation or may even wait to see what will develop.

19. Daydreaming (and night dreaming too) is a right-brained activity.

20. A positive attitude toward, and a use of, intuition is a characteristic of right-dominants.

21. Since rights are more visually than verbally oriented, they will tend to remember faces but not names. Lefts, being more verbal than visual, will remember names but not always recognize the faces to whom the names belong.

22. Left-dominants remember best by recording information, as in notes, or by verbalizing it. Rights prefer visual or emotional cues.

Chapter 2

The Graying of the Corporation

> It is a paradox that in our time of drastic rapid change, when the future is in our midst devouring the present before our eyes, we have never been less certain about what is ahead of us.
>
> —Eric Hoffer

*M*ost of us believe that leadership and managerial talent have been responsible for much of the success of our great entrepreneurial corporations. Why then do these same corporations often go into decline so soon after reaching the top? We will see that the paradox of failure within success is frequently a result of corporate growth—but it's not inevitable, if we can understand the crises that accompany corporate evolution.

———◆———

Look around. It is hard to ignore the malaise afflicting our large corporations and government bureaucracies. Notice how few people really enjoy their work (or even the people they work with). Like Charlie Chaplin in his famous film *Modern Times,* too many workers feel like cogs in a meaningless machine.

A recent survey of 11,000 employees in six industries (by Brooks International, a Florida-based consulting firm) found that only 24% of those surveyed felt secure about

23

their jobs, and a mere 36% believed that their senior executives could lead their companies in the right direction. A regular annual survey by Gallup repeatedly indicates that over 80% of those surveyed do not look forward to going to work on Monday morning.

Two-thirds of executives believe that their jobs are more stressful now than they were 10 years ago, according to a survey of 1,344 executives by Priority Management Systems; one-third think it will get worse by the year 2000. According to another study, executives who work 11 or more hours longer than the regular workweek are twice as likely to report being unhappy with their lives as those who work fewer hours. Yet only 5% of managers said they work the normal workweek or less. In addition, managers often feel frustrated because their carefully honed management techniques don't enable them to manage: They pull the managerial levers and press the executive buttons but the hoped-for results don't materialize.

Modern managers are caught in a paradox: Their work loads are growing along with the corporation; they must therefore work harder just to keep up. But because their old management methods are ineffective, they must spend additional time searching for and implementing new techniques—all of which results in excruciating work schedules. What happened to the heady dreams of the Industrial Revolution? Why haven't we reached the promised land of shorter workweeks and abundant leisure?

The answer lies in the demands of modern organizations whose very size creates problems. Somewhere along the way we began to equate "big" with "good," "big" with "success." But "big" has never been in our genes; we aren't programmed that way. Let me explain.

Our planet came into existence 4.6 billion years ago. To make this number more relevant, try to imagine Earth as if it were 46 years old (just drop all the zeroes). Although we don't know anything about the first 7 years and have only a very limited understanding of the middle years, we *do* know that flowers emerged when the planet was 42 and the dinosaurs and giant reptiles appeared a year ago. The planet was then 45. Modern man arrived 4 hours ago and the Industrial Revolution started a minute ago.

Most remarkable, it is only in these last 60 seconds that we have developed our large organizations. Before this, there were few large organizations of any kind; we lived in groups amounting to no more than 100 people—the average size of the human tribe. So for a scant 60 seconds, a mere fraction of our time on Earth, we have been trying to work naturally together in groups of unnatural size.

Ten thousand years ago, there were between 5 and 10 million of us scattered in small Neolithic settlements. This natural level endured more or less until we entered the 20th century, when human population growth exploded. By 1950 we had reached 2.5 billion; and we doubled our population in the ensuing years, so that by 1987 we numbered 5 billion. The United Nations Populations Division has projected a human swarm of 8.5 billion by 2025. Fortunately, this exponential growth is expected to ease after that, leveling out at around 10 billion by the middle of the next century.

Only in the last 200 years have humans created those two modern aberrations, the sprawling urban metropolis and the large corporate organization. But this fleeting moment in our evolution—a moment in which big has been considered best—is passing; we are attempting to return to our former, decentralized social patterns and structures.

It's not easy. The paradox is that modern executives, driven to create successful organizations, have gauged their success by the *size* of the structures they create. *But as the organization grows, the bureaucratic machinery starts to throttle the innovation, creativity, and zest that gave birth to the organization in the first place.* I call this process "the graying of the corporation." All too soon, the fresh and vibrant green corporation becomes stagnant, senile, and gray.

Of the companies that formed the original Dow Jones Industrial Average, only General Electric remains; more than 250 of the top companies of the mid-1940s have since disappeared. By 1990 37% of the companies who made the 1979 list of *Fortune* 500 Industrial Companies no longer existed in their previous forms.

Oh, some of our large organizations are a little better than others. Some are even relatively successful (although very few hearts soar at the thought of working for giant banks, large industrial companies, or unwieldy governments). But most of the old-time, large corporations are struggling.

Is anyone doing anything about this? The answer is yes—some organizations are reverting to structures that are about the same size as the tribes of our ancestors, structures that feel comfortable, consisting of about 100 people.

We see evidence of this all around us. Some of our largest companies are being broken up and dismembered into smaller units. This in turn has created the need for a wide range of innovative financing mechanisms (like junk bonds). It has ushered in an unprecedented wave of corporate acquisitions, leveraged buyouts, and public companies being purchased by their managers and turned into thriving, private businesses. Corporate raiders have acquired companies for less than their break-up value, dismembered them, and spun off the parts into independent, small-scale units. All this turmoil has already signaled the impending demise of the modern, publicly traded, widely held corporation as we know it, in a fundamental revision of the concepts of capitalism. It heralds the arrival of a new corporate paradigm.

During the 1980s, manufacturers shed hundreds of thousands of employees in the drive to streamline. Through the 1990s and into the next century, the service sector will follow suit. This will be much more painful than the downsizing that occurred in manufacturing because manufacturing employs only 30% of the work force, whereas the service sector employs 70%. Says Sandy Weill, CEO of Primerica: "The services simply have to become more efficient. We're going to see lots more restructuring." Some experts believe that there are still more dramatic reductions to come in the manufacturing sector and that corporate America remains overstaffed by 25%.

In the wake of this unprecedented, wide-ranging restructuring, the largest industrial corporations of the *Fortune* 500 have shed 3 million jobs in the last decade—200,000 in the last year alone. Of the middle managers who were casualties of these purges, 17% have not returned to the "graying" corporations but instead started their own new, freshly "greened" businesses.

In addition, with smaller permanent work forces, the formerly giant organizations are farming out their work to small specialists. This has created a boom in self-employment, in temporary and part-time work, and in partnerships. Over 25% of North Americans now count themselves among these new work groups (in this area, growth for women is even more dramatic than for men). During the last 5 years, the collective revenues of the *Inc.* 500 has blossomed from $563 million to $9.6 billion.

Along with these far-reaching changes in the service sector come additional changes in manufacturing. The microprocessor has enabled small firms to acquire capabilities of flexible manufacturing, automation, and robotics that were only available previously to large manufacturers. Rapidly growing numbers of small firms can now manufacture more product with fewer people while competing with large firms on service, price, quality, range, and customer satisfaction.

These profound changes are creating a new paradigm—a decentralized society—leading to what I call "the

Era of the Human Tribe." The big (and especially the publicly traded) corporation, like the dinosaur with the little brain and the large body, will eventually become extinct.

The purpose of this book is to help corporate leaders succeed and grow. To do this, we must first understand the paradox—how an organization goes from green to gray—so that we can avoid the pitfalls.

The Failure of Management Theory

Professor Harold Leavitt of Stanford University observed not long ago that "the decline of American management is closely correlated with the rise of the American business school," with its attendant worship of management theory.

Most management theorists believe that entrepreneurial corporations must inevitably change their management style to one that is "more sophisticated," defined as "professional management" by some and the "modern bureaucracy" by the more cynical. Here's how management theorist George Steiner describes this process:

> Companies at different stages of evolution tend to elicit different managerial and organizational styles. Often this means that those who have led the company at one stage may not be able to do so effectively at another; the probability that they will be replaced is high. In Stage I a company requires a single guiding executive who basically operates a "one man show." Such people tend to be authoritarian, to emphasize short-term thinking, and to have an operating orientation. . . . At Stage II a group of managers with functionally specialized duties replaces the entrepreneur. Thus, there is a requirement that the chief executive be able to work with other members of the manage-

ment team and utilize their talents effectively. . . .
The move into Stage III . . . calls for a general office
that maintains more or less loose-rein control over
operating units while stressing overall corporate
planning.

Is Steiner's view accurate? Is the evolution from
dynamic one-man show to groupthink inevitable? The left-
hemispheric thinking of many executives and academics
prevents them from seeing the flaws in this theory.

First, *all* companies—regardless of their age, stage,
and size—require a CEO who functions as a "single
guiding executive." However, it's a popular fallacy to
assume that this is the stereotypical CEO, driven by greed
and the desire for short-term gain, striking fear and
loathing into the hearts of the company's unfortunate
workers. Rather, strong and successful leaders are often
both innovative and compassionate, drawing heavily from
their right-hemispheric skills to lead, teach, inspire, and
motivate individuals in their companies to reach new
levels of excellence. Such singular leadership is a necessary
condition before any corporation can continue to add
value and grow.

Second, the assumption that the Stage I CEO is in-
capable of "work[ing] with other members of the management team and utiliz[ing] their talents effectively" is patent nonsense. If this were true, many so-called Stage I
companies would never reach Stage II or III. More accessible education, improved communications skills, and
more positive societal values have all helped shape capable
modern managers. Consequently, such managers are well
able to elicit synergistic results from teams of highly
motivated colleagues.

Third, may we all be protected from the "general office that maintains more or less loose-rein control over
operating units." I see no advantage in being managed by
the "office of the president." Such Orwellian ideas have

not enjoyed wide success, as demonstrated by the experience of corporations like General Electric, where such ideas were tried and discarded.

In a recent research project, I interviewed several CEOs who had founded their businesses or acquired them when they were small or faltering. All had fashioned major corporations from these humble beginnings ranging from $150 million to $2 billion. Among the many reasons these CEOs gave for their success, the five most important were:

1. Don't ever lose sight of the company's fundamental purpose, its skills, and its core business.

2. Remember that the CEO's main responsibility is not to run the company but to make decisions about *how* it should be run.

3. Stay flexible; be willing to adjust, radically if necessary, to changing environmental conditions.

4. Run a lean, keen—and green—corporate machine; executive-office and other support staff as well as plant and equipment should be kept to the minimum required for optimum performance.

5. Hire the finest people available and provide them with the best personal and professional development programs and communications so they can perform with maximum creativity.

Corporate Evolution

Professor Larry Greiner of the University of Southern California offers an alternative to Steiner's view of the dynamics of corporate evolution. He argues that corporations go through five distinct phases of development, each characterized by smooth periods that end with a management crisis. Greiner's theories fit neatly with those of Kuhn (discussed in Chapter 1). The five phases of growth are (1) creativity, (2) direction, (3) delegation, (4) coordination, and (5) collaboration. The end of each of the first four phases is signaled by (1) a crisis of leadership, (2) a crisis of autonomy, (3) a crisis of control, and (4) a crisis of red tape, respectively (see Figure 2-1). Greiner points out that each phase is strongly influenced by the previous one; creative managers can prepare for each phase and continue managing through the attendant crises.

Figure 2-1   The Five Phases of Growth

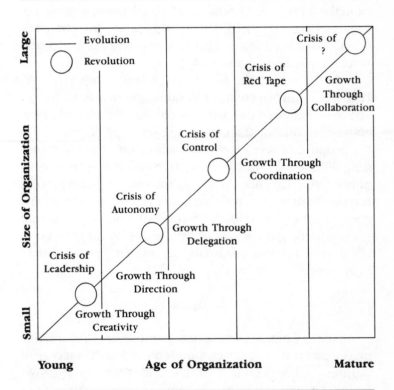

CREATIVITY AND THE
CRISIS OF LEADERSHIP

In Greiner's view, the first of the five phases is one of growth, during which the small, young company is creatively driven rather than managed in the conventional sense. This period is characterized by a highly entrepreneurial style of leadership and a total physical and emotional commitment to marketing the new product or service. Internal communication is frequent and informal. High work output and low rewards (but high potential capital yields) are the norm. Formal management approaches are disdained. During this phase the company is a highly sensitive structure that reacts as the customers react. But this does not last.

At the end of the first phase, a leadership crisis occurs. The informal communications systems are no longer effective because the work force has ballooned. New employees do not share the same sense of dedication to the product or service as those who were in at the beginning. Financing and administrative-control requirements burden the executives with unwelcome management responsibilities for which they have not been trained. The company begins to drift into confusion, and current management spends a lot of time yearning for the "good old days." Everyone eventually agrees that "professional" managers must be brought in.

————◆————

Apple Computer took just over 6 years to reach this phase. Steve Jobs, who cofounded his highly successful business with Steven Wozniak and $500 in a (now-famous) garage, built the corporation from zip to sales of over $1.5 billion in 1984 in the space of 8 breathless years. But before that achievement, the computer wunderkind managed to tangle up the management. Dealers as well as Apple executives were warring with the company.

If Steiner's theory were correct, Jobs's spiritual and executive leadership of Apple would have ended there. But it didn't. Jobs adroitly adopted a strategy that demonstrated his smarts as an entrepreneurial leader. He went out and hired the superstars necessary to *complement*—not *replace*—his skills at Apple. He brought in John Sculley, vice president in charge of marketing at PepsiCo, as president; and Floyd Kvamme, the former head of National Semiconductor's computer division, as head of marketing. Sculley removed 6 of the company's 15 top managers, trimmed the work force from 5,300 to 4,600, and froze hiring; merged five divisions into two; and centralized marketing and manufacturing for all Apple products. Del W. Yocum, a 6-year veteran with Apple, was put in charge of the Apple II division (responsible for Apple IIc and IIe computers). Meanwhile, Jobs took on two new assignments: the chairmanship of the company, and something that better matched his entrepreneurial strengths, the development and introduction of a new computer to fend off IBM's newly introduced and hot-selling PC (this enabled Apple to retain its status as the number-two computer maker). The happy result was the Macintosh, designed by one-time Apple repairman Burrell Smith and successfully introduced amidst a $15 million blaze of publicity on January 24, 1984. Jobs's growth strategy took advantage of his greatest skills: consultant, visionary, and guru to the organization. In 1984, sales rose 54% to $1.5 billion and earnings rose 600%.

John Sculley's power play ousting Jobs in favor of himself is now part of computer-industry folklore. Jobs left Apple in 1984 in sadness and anger. Prior to these musical chairs, a reorganized top-management team at Apple established a goal of displacing Digital Equipment from the number-two spot in the industry; but half a decade later, the new team without Jobs is struggling to hang on to sixth spot in a fragmented and fiercely competitive industry. An alliance with IBM, unthinkable a few years previously, is the latest twist in Apple's adaptation to the new realities.

The evolution from Phase 1 creativity to Phase 2 direction is what Stanley Davis has called "the distinction between the *function* of management and the *manager* as a person, or the succession from entrepreneurs to executives." The change is better made by *augmenting* the managerial capability of a founding visionary leader like Steve Jobs, not by *replacing* him with a professional manager like John Sculley; replacement is often a sure way to unglue a successful company. Worse still is the tendency by addled board members to press a host of unfamiliar, "professional-management" duties onto the founding entrepreneur—a strategy about as logical as appointing Jennifer Capriati or Monica Seles to the chairmanship of the Lawn Tennis Association at the peak of their careers! Star performers should exploit and continually develop their strong talents and capabilities, resisting the temptation to venture into activities and responsibilities for which they are technically, temperamentally, or functionally ill equipped.

Steven Wozniak, Apple's cofounder, left Apple in 1981 because he was uninterested in task-related goals and therefore unable to focus upon them for any length of time—and as the new company grew, so did the number of such tasks. (Wozniak, the designer of some of the most successful microcomputers in the world, wanted to concentrate on finishing his degree in computer sciences!) In June of 1983, Jobs persuaded Wozniak to return to Apple with the understanding that he would be free to devote all his time to designing new machines and additional features for old ones, rather than running the company. "I'm just a normal engineer," was Wozniak's understated comment on the situation. "I just wanted to sit down and do some nice peaceful projects." But Wozniak left the company again early in 1985, along with

Joseph Ennis, the lead designer of the company's hottest-selling product, the Apple IIc. Their ambition: to start a new business devoted to expanding the potential of videorecorders.

Inventing the world's first microcomputers and running a business are not the same thing. Unlike Jobs, Wozniak never wanted to run a company. As a brilliant engineer, he wanted to focus on projects from conception to completion. The modern organization needs both the Jobses and the Wozniaks, and the two can live together.

DIRECTION AND THE CRISIS OF AUTONOMY
In Greiner's model, the second phase of growth—the formalization of managerial practices and systems—is sustained through directive leadership. But when this goes too far, a second crisis occurs. As a result of over-centralization and the resulting lack of individual autonomy, employees find that they are closer to the market than is corporate management, and they therefore understand the market better than does management. Employees are torn between following corporate standard operating procedures and initiating their own creative decisions. Feeling unempowered, they become frustrated.

DELEGATION AND THE CRISIS OF CONTROL
According to Greiner's model, when the corporation slips out of control, a third crisis waits in the wings. At this stage, says Greiner, top management senses that it is losing control over a diversified, sprawling organization. Parochial attitudes and territorial jealousies break out. Senior management sparks the third crisis when it reasserts its control over its corporate domain.

———◆———

In 1955 Ray A. Kroc first met Dick and Maurice McDonald, two hamburger-hut operators in San Bernardino, California. Thirty-five years later, the company Kroc founded had parlayed this small beginning into a worldwide corporation holding the number-one position in the fast-food industry and becoming the 17th largest retailer in America. But critics felt that the company image was slipping; McDonald's seemed to be losing touch with the consumer. Though it feeds 6% of Americans every day and 1 out of every 15 Americans finds a first job there, McDonald's marketing strategy was becoming confused. The home microwave, deep discounts, and clumsy handling of issues raised by a public newly sensitized to nutrition and the environment slowed North American growth to a crawl. These telltale signs of corporate languor could be traced to the company's enormous size (there are more than 11,000 pairs of golden arches in over 50 countries). Ironically, as the 900-seat McDonald's opened in Moscow, back in America the average number of patrons per restaurant had been flat for 5 years. Even a huge annual advertising and promotion budget failed to kick-start the numbers.

COORDINATION, THE CRISIS OF RED TAPE, AND COLLABORATION

The fourth phase of growth is characterized by a return to centralization via a systems approach; that is, through the utilization of product groups, formal planning, staff control functions, centralized capital-allocation programs, centralized technical functions (like data processing and research and development), and company-wide profit-sharing programs. At the end of this phase, Greiner's model predicts that large companies will seize up in a crisis of red tape, to bring forth the fifth phase: a return to entrepreneurship, but of a more sophisticated, collaborative order than the first.

———◆———

The five phases of growth occur at different stages of a company's development and are correlated with the company's size, rate of growth, and maturity. For instance, if a small entrepreneurial company eschews growth altogether, it may delay the occurrence of phases 2–5 indefinitely. Alternatively, some phenomenally successful growth companies buck the trend—like Cogentrix (which develops and operates cogeneration facilities), founded in 1983 by George Lewis in Charlotte, North Carolina. The revenues of Cogentrix grew from $133,000 in 1985 to $201,869,000 in 1989, the first company ever to top the *Inc.* 500 list of fastest-growing companies 2 years in a row. Gateway 2000 of Sioux City, North Dakota, founded in 1985, has grown from 2 employees into a healthy firm of 700, manufacturing and selling low-cost personal computers through mail-order advertising. Gateway 2000's revenues zoomed from $101,000 to $70,574,000 in their first 5 years and climbed to $275 million the following year.

The one sure message to be gained from Greiner's five-phase growth theory is that the problems raised by the crises are predictable and can be resolved by creative leadership and management techniques. A corporate crisis does not have to be terminal. Although each phase may be more or less inevitable, the manager with moxie acquires the appropriate skills needed to steer safely through the shoals that, predictably, must be negotiated in any fast-growing corporation.

But if these leadership techniques are so perfect, one may ask, why do corporations periodically run off their evolutionary rails and hit the revolutionary skids? Part of the answer may be found in the antimony that exists within any corporation—the inherent conflict between its entrepreneurial and bureaucratic purposes.

The Corporate Push-Me/Pull-Me

Antimony means a contradiction or inconsistency between two apparently reasonable principles or laws; conclusions that are discrepant though apparently logical. Such an antimony exists between the *entrepreneurial* and *bureaucratic* purposes of most corporations. This is the "push-me/pull-me" of corporate life. Like fire and water, they seem destined for incompatibility. Table 2-1 illustrates this dilemma.

As the table shows, entrepreneurs and administrators often seek opposite aims and sometimes even contest each other for the same goal. Traditionally, the potential synergy of entrepreneurial and administrative needs is seldom realized. This is just as much a result of stereotypical thinking about both as it is of their competing ideologies. Still, the question remains: How do entrepreneurs with their high personal-achievement needs comfortably coexist with bureaucrats and their controlling natures? Remember the old saw, How do porcupines make love? The answer is the same: Carefully!

Organizations are complex structures in which the goals of lower levels are the means for achieving the goals of higher levels. But this chain often breaks down: The lower-level goals become the ends in themselves to those undertaking them. As a result, policies, procedures, and rules that were originally developed to help people achieve organizational goals assume an intrinsic value all their own. Soon, individuals at each level are perceived to be merely parts of a subsystem whose sole purpose is to meet its own functional goals. This invariably leads to organizational rigidity and a "not-invented-here" mentality among employees, who assume the personalities of drones.

Not surprisingly, the managerial inhabitants of bureaucracies look upon innovation as a threat to established order and consider adaptation to be an administrative

Table 2-1   The Push-Me/Pull-Me Syndrome

Entrepreneurial Drive *The entrepreneur* *wants . . .*	*Administrative Drive* *The corporate* *bureaucrat wants . . .*
Control	Control
Personal achievement and ego gratification	Enhancement of the corporate image through achievement
To honor and give credit to individuals	To honor and give credit to groups
Moderate risk	Risk avoidance
Motivation through feedback	Motivation through merit reward
Goal attainment through energy and activity	Results that conform to standard operating procedures
Organizational skill	Systems approaches
Individuals with an internal locus of control	The creation of a "corporate womb"
Mastery of the environment	Mastery of people
Informal communications	Formal communications
Lateral organizational relations	Vertical organizational relations
Participative, involved, open decision making	Formalized channels for decision making
Authority derived from task or leadership skills	Authority derived from hierarchy
An informal ethos	A formal ethos
Inspiration from individual leaders	Inspiration from the corporate image and culture
Flair, charisma, the opportunity to follow hunches	Systems and management science

inconvenience: Such bureaucrats are practicing the administrative version of Kuhn's "normal science." People—the heart of any dynamic and successful organization and the focus of successful, entrepreneurial leaders—are usually ignored by bureaucrats, who generally prefer to subordinate the individual to the organization.

Max Weber remarked that "once it is fully established, bureaucracy is among those social structures which are hardest to destroy." But until we are able to at least bend bureaucratic systems to our will, corporate success will elude us. We can tame the corporate push-me/pull-me by this guiding principle:

> *Appropriately* bend the rules in order
> to *exceed* customer's needs.

As Greiner's five-stage model demonstrates, after the bureaucratic organization lurches back and forth between centralization and decentralization, the corporation needs another entrepreneurial infusion to bring it back to life.

Sadly, some entrepreneurs feel that refashioning from the same old clay is just not worth the effort. For them, Donald K. Clifford of McKinsey and Co. says it all: "People who start small businesses love to do everything themselves, but when it gets to be highly complex, there's no way. You need a different kind of guy. If the entrepreneur is smart, he sells out and starts again." Despite such traditional assertions, however, less drastic solutions to the paradox are available.

The Square-Cube Law

The greening of the corporation is the essence of corporate regeneration. But this cannot be achieved without a clear understanding of the distinctions between big and small companies. The popular notion puts all organizations somewhere on a continuum between a megacorporation like General Motors, with nearly $130 billion in annual sales, and the downtown flower vendor. But big business is *not* a very large small business.

A great number of theories of organizational growth have been based on analogies drawn from other fields— biology, physics, and engineering, to name but three. Mason Haire has used a biological analogy to demonstrate the differences between large and small organizations. He points out that all organizational systems, like all living organisms, are regulated by the **square-cube law.** This law holds that as the volume of mass increases by a cubic function, the surface enclosing it only increases by a square function. As an example, the giant in *Jack and the Beanstalk* is a physical impossibility: If the giant had the same proportions as the average human and if, as the story suggests, he were ten times as large as Jack, his mass would be a thousand times bigger than Jack's (10^3), but his leg bones would only be a hundred times bigger (10^2)—so they wouldn't be able to support his weight! It's the same for any organization: The configuration and capability of a small company would buckle under the mass of a giant corporation.

◆

At Manpower we got in touch with all our senior managers and franchises at Christmas to thank them for their contribution during the year, to talk about their aspirations for the coming year, and to share the spirit and goodwill of the season. In Manpower's early days, we used to spend several weeks on the road visiting our offices and attending local Christmas parties. While it was great fun, the business's rapid growth soon turned this event into an alcoholic and geographic marathon, requiring several days to restore the sensibilities of senior management! Reluctantly, we adopted a less masochistic method of keeping in touch. We spent half-an-hour or so on the telephone during the last 2 weeks of December, catching up with everyone and exchanging seasonal greetings. But as each Christmas season rolled around, we increasingly needed our staff to brief us about personnel changes, time-zone differences, new divisions and locations, and other data to keep us from making it too obvious that our good intentions had been overwhelmed by our growth. This wasn't fun and it was wooden. So we reverted to traveling again, but with an important difference: We threw several large, regional Christmas parties and invited managers and staff from the local offices. Eventually, even this proved grueling, so we then divided the parties among ourselves. This worked well: Among us, we were able to visit everyone in our organization at this special time of year.

Although this example is tactical rather than strategic, it illustrates the need to adapt processes, even with the seemingly mundane yet vital issues of human interaction and communications. Often, it is necessary to introduce entirely new approaches, not merely resort to an incremental magnification of existing methods, as each new phase of growth is reached in the corporation. Meanwhile, management must keep sight of the original objective; in this case, staying close to the heartbeat of its most important asset—its employees.

———————◆———————

In the final decade of the 20th century, the greening of the large corporation is more likely to be achieved by emulating the entrepreneurial characteristics of smaller companies. Rather than continuing to grow, large companies may do better by spinning off portions of the company as soon as they reach a certain size, instead of growing them into one misformed giant who cannot stand up.

The relationship among corporate size, human resources, and corporate excellence was investigated in a study by the Chicago-based consulting firm A. T. Kearney, which selected 41 large manufacturers for their "general reputation, participation in prior Kearney research and recognition in recent books and publications on management excellence." To the research sample, Kearney then added 320 similar companies with annual sales of more than $250 million. The results showed that 26 of the 41 organizations outperformed the averages for their industries in growth of sales, profits, and stock value; but the researchers also found that in all 26 companies, "staffs are out of control in size, cost and most significant, contribution." Kearney's experience and research showed that "in general . . . [the] raw talent of the people in one company is not greatly different from the raw talent of another company. The difference comes in how that talent is used or allowed to work." Among the differences found were:

> The successful companies averaged 500 fewer employees per $1 billion of sales than the less successful ones (the cost of the benefits and salaries for these employees is equal to the average net profits on $1 billion of sales achieved by most companies).

> The successful companies had four fewer management levels than the less successful ones.

> The successful companies were more likely to consider results than numbers of subordinates when rewarding managers.

> The successful companies were less likely to penalize failures of managers who take entrepreneurial risks.

The Xerox Solution

Consider the example of Xerox. For years the inventor of the plain-paper copier owned the market worldwide.

Then it slowly but surely began to lag behind. Xerox went from an 18.5% market share in 1979 to 13% in 1981, bottoming out at 10% in 1984. Compared with the most efficient photocopier manufacturers in Japan, Xerox had nine times as many production suppliers; product lead times that were twice as long; and a production line that took five times longer to set up and had ten times the number of rejected parts and seven times more defects.

So what did then-CEO David Kearns and his leadership team do about this? After studying their leaner competitors, they wiped out the company's top-heavy decision-making structure; eliminated its matrix organizational system; decentralized authority from the president's office to the engineer responsible for each project; furloughed 17,000 employees; and cut the corporation's manufacturing costs by half. The Xerox leadership team, made up of 25 executives, designed and implemented a program called "Leadership Through Quality" (LTQ), a corporate-wide bootstrap effort that cost $125 million and consumed 4 million work hours. The leadership team learned the processes and concepts first and then shared these with their colleagues. The program's two core concepts were (1) customers must be satisfied, and (2) quality improvement is the job of every Xerox employee. These concepts were carried to the hearts and minds of Xerox employees through a process dubbed LUTI: learn, use, teach, and inspect. Part of the process involved *benchmarking,* a method of continuously measuring the firm's products and services against those of other outstanding companies. Involving 250 functional areas of the company, each benchmarking investigation takes between 9 and 12 months to complete and involves from three to six different companies monitored by teams of up to 12 employees. L. L. Bean became the benchmark for distribution, Federal Express for billing efficiency, and Cummins Engine Company for production scheduling. In the process of implementing LTQ, Xerox reviewed management role modeling, transition-team support, new standards and measurements, new reward and recognition programs for quality achievement to underscore the new philosophy, and wide and deep employee communications.

The efforts started to pay off—customer satisfaction increased by 40% and complaints decreased by 60%. In 1989 after 4 years of relentless efforts to dramatically increase quality and service, Xerox earned the prestigious Malcolm Baldrige National Quality Award. Today 94% of the company's employees state that customer satisfaction is their top priority. Xerox's quality drive has been deliberately inculcated into the firm's suppliers too; as a result, during the last 5 years, the quality of incoming parts has improved 13 times and the parts-reject rate on the assembly line has dropped from 10,000 per million to 350 per million. A new standard is being enjoyed: 99.9% of all incoming parts are now defect-free.

Paul Allaire, who was largely responsible for implementing the turnaround and has now succeeded Kearns as CEO, has kept up the pressure by introducing an unheard-of 3-year, "total-satisfaction" guarantee on all of the company's document-processing products—no hassle and no quibble. If a customer fails to be pleased with a product, he or she gets a new one that meets expectations. "Customers don't want their money back," says Allaire. "They want a product that works properly. This really puts power behind the rhetoric and shows people we are serious." The company seldom has to deliver on the guarantee.

A similar story was repeated after the Chessie and Seaboard railroads merged into the CSX Corporation. Before the merger, senior management was 200 strong; after the merger, this group downsized to just 27 senior executives and 14 support staff. The company now enjoys revenues of over $8 billion and operates in 20 American states and in Ontario, Canada.

An example directly the opposite of these success stories illustrates Parkinson's First Law: Work expands to fill the time available. Uncle Sam's army seems to have settled rather comfortably into the bureaucratic mire. Following the 1983 invasion of Grenada by U.S. troops, the army awarded 8,612 medals to its personnel, even though no more than 7,000 officers and enlisted men ever set foot on the miniature Caribbean island. Sounds like a bad joke, doesn't it? No doubt, rampant bureaucracy would be even more amusing if it weren't such a threat to the creation of jobs and the production of wealth.

———◆———

He who confronts the paradoxical exposes himself to reality.

—Friedrich Dürrenmatt

Chapter 3

Corporate Purpose

There is one quality more important than
"know-how" and we cannot accuse the United
States of any undue amount of it. This is "know
what" by which we determine not only how
to accomplish our purposes, but what our
purposes are to be.

—Norbert Weiner

*T*he development of a clear sense of purpose
starts with the corporate mission, which is fashioned from
the *real* needs of customers. From this are crafted the goals
and a statement of values. The vision statement pulls the
organization into the future. The sum of these components
is called corporate purpose.

———◆———

Have you ever marveled at the motivation and sense
of purpose of the leaders, managers, and staff of some
corporations? Why are these women and men so self-
assured? Why are they so committed to success? Why do
they work so hard and so well? What sets them apart from
the rest of the corporate pack? Part of the answer lies in
leaders who know what business they're in, where they're
heading, and what their goals and guiding principles are.
This is called **corporate purpose,** which consists of four
distinct but closely related components:

1. The corporate mission
2. The statement of values

47

3. The ALDO audit

4. The statement of vision

All businesses need solid philosophical under-pinnings. Weak corporations often seem to share two common characteristics: Their managements haven't clarified what business they're in; and their objectives, if any exist, lack focus. The first and most important task in the development of a new business—and a crucial task in revitalizing an ongoing one—is the establishment of corporate purpose, which shapes the corporate culture and becomes the guidepost for decision making. Its definition begins with the corporate mission.

The Corporate Mission and the Customer

Every employee in a business should be able to answer the question, What does your company do? The response —the statement of the **corporate mission**—must reflect the *customer need that the company seeks to satisfy;* it should not merely be a reiteration of the product or service produced. As Peter Drucker put it:

> To know what a business is we have to start with its purpose. Its purpose must lie outside of the business itself. In fact, it must lie in society since business enterprise is an organ of society. There is only one valid definition of business purpose; to create a customer.

I would go even further: *The purpose of a business is to find customers—and keep them for life.* Additionally, every employee in the organization should be able to answer this vital question with a succinct but detailed statement like this one from AT&T:

Our Mission is to apply the talents, knowledge, and skills of our people to make the company the global leader in enabling customers to reap the benefits of information technology.

Or this from Canadian National:

CN's Mission is to meet customers' transportation and distribution needs by being the best at moving their goods on time, safely, and damage free.

Contrast these with the mission statements of many organizations that use the mission to (1) describe *their* goals, not those of the customer; (2) articulate numerous self-serving platitudes; and (3) give the impression that their management is on the cutting edge.

Here are some examples that, sadly, are fairly typical of modern corporate mission statements:

Our mission is to continuously improve the company's long-term value to customers, employees, shareholders, and society. We will achieve our mission through the pursuit of total quality. We will follow a three-part strategy of efficiency, distinctive competence, and focused growth [Boise Cascade].

Chevron is an international petroleum company whose mission is to achieve superior financial results for our stockholders, the owners of our business. We will never be satisfied with the status quo— we will continuously strive to become better than the best.

Our mission is to become the leading personal products company in the United States, and the flagship company of Unilever's worldwide personal products business [Chesebrough-Pond's USA].

. . . which is nice if you are Unilever, the parent of Chesebrough-Pond's USA—but it doesn't say much about the company's role in adding value for its customers or exceeding their expectations in service and quality.

Would you have guessed that the next mission statement comes from a communications company?

> Our mission is to provide quality products and services to customers in responsive and innovative ways in order to create the highest possible value for our investors through long-term growth and profitability [U S West].

It's been said that if the Baldwin Locomotive Works had recognized that its business had changed from just making steam locomotives to making tractive power for railroads—and had included this concept in its corporate mission—it probably would still be in business. At the other extreme, you could say that a manufacturer of lead pencils is overstating its corporate mission if it defines itself as a maker of communications equipment!

CLARITY OF PURPOSE

Imagine that you can interview the members of your local symphony orchestra before a performance. You ask them, What music will you be playing? Suppose they all give different answers? How do you think the performance will sound?

If all this seems like a statement of the obvious, try "the symphony test" in your own organization:

1. Ask ten employees from various organizational levels what business they think the company is in.

2. If you have ten different answers (and you probably will), go back to your office and spend 15 quiet minutes attempting to come up with a better definition!

If a company's employees cannot readily identify the corporate mission, the company could be in serious trouble. Even if the members of the leadership team can offer identical mission statements when asked independently to do so—and you *should* ask them—if the rest of the employees can't, the company is still in trouble: The latter may all be reading from different scores and playing different tunes. This makes for dreadful corporate music! Such a failure may also signal a serious weakness in internal communications.

Let's look at an example. Suppose the mission of your general practitioner is "to be the most profitable general practitioner in North America, offering the lowest-cost health care through a nationally franchised system of offices from coast to coast." Would you visit this doctor with confidence? A doctor who takes the Hippocratic oath seriously would more likely have a mission of "helping the patient become well." When you visit your doctor, your need is "to feel well again." Notice how *the mission statement and the customer need reflect each other:* They are perfectly complementary. But when corporate mission statements do not include meeting the needs of customers, corporations can alienate customers instead of attract them.

We hear a lot about customer satisfaction, excellence, and customer service—some would even say too much. However, in my research and in my consulting, I have found that a great many organizations don't even bother to ask what the customer needs; they assume that they already know. But if they haven't asked the customer, they can't be sure that they *do* know.

Recently, I met with Ken, the president of an international insurance broker. We were talking about a multinational insurance company, another client of mine, with whom they place much of their business. I mentioned that the insurance company president, Bob, had told me he often met with the brokerage president. Ken quickly pointed out that these contacts had *always* been initiated by him, never the insurance company. As a result, his impression was that Bob and his company didn't really care.

If we want to know what the needs of our customers are, we have to sit down with them and ask them. No fancy Harvard research model is needed—just straight talk and, more important, lots of listening between the parties can make things happen. Managers are *not* experts on customer needs—the *only* expert is the customer.

In addition to addressing customer needs, it helps if the mission statement gives *employees* a clear picture. If it is ambiguous—such as "our business is service," which was used by AT&T for over 50 years—each employee might come up with a different interpretation, and this can obscure the firm's real purpose and competencies. For instance, "serving the beauty needs of North America's women" could mean anything from plastic surgery to diamond mining to cosmetics to prescription drugs to whale hunting and mink ranching.

---◆---

At the outset, Manpower's U.K. companies had no corporate mission statement. If one *had* existed, it might have read: "Manpower provides temporary staff for limited-time assignments and places employees in permanent jobs." Recognizing the need to redefine our current mission, we researched its relevance to our values, to our aspirations for the company, and most important, to the needs of our customers. What we found was sobering: Our employees thought the company's emphasis and priorities were ambiguous, so they felt rudderless in their day-to-day efforts. Our customers thought we were running two different businesses: an employment agency and a temporary-help service. They saw this as a conflict of interest and believed we would sell what was *easiest for us,* rather than what the customer needed: If we didn't have a suitable candidate for a permanent job, we'd recommend a temp. This negative image in the market rubbed off on our employees, further impairing their self-esteem.

Neither they nor our customers believed our purpose was to fill customers' needs.

By asking questions from the customers' perspective, we discovered what their needs really were: Our customers were not interested specifically in temporary staff; what they really wanted was to solve short-term work problems. When we understood this, we were able to redefine our corporate mission in terms of the *work needs of our customers.* We found that customers called us for a temporary typist or a secretary because they had typing or secretarial work that needed doing. In other words, the customers first defined their needs and then translated these, for *our* convenience, into *our* language; a backlog in the order-processing department became "please send me a data-input operator for 4 days." But surely it would make more sense to define the customer's work needs first and then tailor a solution to those needs? Closer questioning of our customers revealed that they often needed several people for a day rather than one person for a week; sometimes they required equipment and supervision as well as operators; and sometimes it was more desirable to undertake the work on our premises as well as on the customer's and charge contract prices for the work as well as hourly rates for the people on-site. Many of our customers, we found, believed that we should guarantee the quality of the work; accept the responsibility of meeting agreed-upon deadlines; and broaden our services to include the costs of statutory insurance, pensions, employee benefits, and income and payroll taxes. Almost without realizing it, we were redefining our business *and* an industry: The modern temporary-help business was being born, and it would develop into the second-fastest-growing industry in the world.

For 30 years the industry had remained virtually unchanged. No wonder Manpower and others like it were failing—because the rest of the world *had* changed: A boom had occurred in office work; the balance between men and women in the work force had shifted dramatically; more people wanted part-time work; the nonwage costs of employment had skyrocketed; labor legislation had virtually converted labor overhead into a fixed rather than a variable cost; and specialization of skills had become a feature of managing and leading a work force.

To update Manpower's relevance, we addressed these changes (and eventually led the market). Our new corporate mission reflected our fresh commitment to the customer:

> Manpower is a *work contractor,* meeting the short-term work needs of our individual and corporate customers, typically caused through work peaks, staff shortages, emergencies and special orders or projects, through the provision of our own employees.

To this could be added the qualifying statement: "The range of our work includes office, industrial, skilled, technical, and marketing tasks."

Note that the new corporate mission statement is brief—only 36 words—and clear. Most mission statements are so long and so full of irrelevant puffery that no one can understand *or* remember them! (Imagine what would happen if no one in the symphony orchestra could interpret or remember the score!) The key is to be concise (no more than 40, or better still, 20 words) and concrete (the meaning of the words should be plain).

◆

Because corporate strategy flows from the corporate mission, clarity is vital. However, such clarity is easier to achieve in a one-product or one-service company than in a conglomerate. Take the example of the former Beatrice Foods. Before acquiring the Esmark Corporation agglomerate (including Playtex foundation garments, the Swift and Hunt-Wesson food lines, Avis car rentals, and

Max Factor cosmetics), Beatrice already had 400 profit centers selling 9,000 different products. If you had asked an employee at the water cooler in Beatrice's head office what Beatrice Foods does, would she or he have said something about dairy products? Beverages? Nuts? Luggage? Chemicals? Agricultural products?

In an effort to rationalize its jumble of businesses, Beatrice decided to sell 50 of its subsidiaries that had sales of less than $90 million each. The company also brought in new management, eliminated various hierarchical levels, reorganized into six operating groups, trimmed the number of advertising agencies from 100 to 7, and sought buyers for slow-growing units. Beatrice also launched a special $29 million corporate advertising campaign to restore a clear sense of mission and identity (this was in addition to the $120 million that it was spending on support for its brand names). But these moves failed to reckon with changing demographics, such as altering tastes and a slowing of population growth. Beatrice never paused to identify and act on the needs of its customers. Its success rate for new product introductions plummeted to only 10%, and eventually Beatrice became a victim of the 1980s' takeover frenzy, succumbing to Kohlberg Kravis and Roberts.

The importance of the mission statement to unify the formulation and implementation of corporate strategy cannot be overstated. But because a corporation is no more than a legal entity, it does not "live" until the hearts and minds of its men and women give it life: The combined attitudes of the corporation's employees endow it with an apparent spirit and will of its own. So it's vital that *every* employee understand and subscribe to a clear definition of the corporate mission.

This was obviously a problem at Ralston Purina when R. Hal Dean, then chairman of Ralston and an avid hockey nut, bought the St. Louis Blues for $4 million—even though the National Hockey League team had a negative net worth of $8.5 million. Over the next 6 years, the team continued to lose money, to the tune of $19 million. A new CEO, William P. Stiritz, finally unloaded the team after much difficulty and expense. How did Ralston Purina get in such a mess? Not only because it was rare for *any* NHL hockey team to make money but because it was even more unlikely for a hockey team owned by a pet-food/fast-food/grocery business: There was no natural fit between Ralston's products and the endorsing powers of star hockey players.

———◆———

Although a business's complexity can make it difficult to achieve clarity of purpose—as we saw with Beatrice and Ralston Purina—it doesn't have to preclude it. Take Mead Corporation. It is one of the world's largest paper manufacturers; a leading paperboard and packaging producer; one of the biggest distributors of paper, packaging, and business supplies made by other companies; the largest maker of paper-based school and office supplies; and the developer of the world's leading electronic information-retrieval service for law, patents, accounting, finance, news, and business. In spite of its complexity, Mead's mission statement is simple—and clear: "Mission: To be number one in customer satisfaction." Mead's president, Steve Mason, puts it this way:

> It may be the shortest mission statement of all the *Fortune* 500 companies. We asked ourselves a simple question some time ago—How would we like Mead to be described 10 years from now? A good many thoughtful, intelligent answers were proposed, but this one had universal appeal: Mead is number one in customer satisfaction in all of its businesses.

Mason emphasizes that the corporate mission makes customer satisfaction a key strategy in every one of Mead's businesses. He goes on to say:

> It also requires that we look closely at our customers to identify those whose needs we can satisfy better than anyone else. But above all, this is a corporate mission which challenges each employee. Every one of us has customers. If we're in the woodyard, the pulp mill is our customer. If we're in the pulp mill, the paper mill is our customer. It may be the local printer or one of the world's great publishers. It may be a law firm, a toymaker, or a fourth-grader who buys a Mead notebook.

Although Mead's corporate mission statement is not perfect, it captures the spirit of the organization and makes it possible to integrate corporate values with corporate strategy.

Another client of mine, Northern Telecom, is the world's leading supplier of fully digital telecommunications switching equipment. It sells products in over 80 countries, operates more than 40 manufacturing plants and 21 research facilities, and employs over 60,000 people worldwide. Like Mead's, its mission statement is short and clear: "Exceeding our customer's expectations and setting the industry standard for quality and value."

The common denominator in both mission statements is the *customer.* Yet my research into the phrasing and definition of corporate missions shows that they tend to be extraordinarily self-centered; for example:

> Polaroid manufactures and sells photographic products based on inventions of the company in the field of one-step instant photography and light polarizing products, utilizing the company's inventions in the field of polarizing light. The company considers itself to be in one line of business.

All too rarely do we see the corporate mission couched in terms of the customers' interests and needs, as it is below:

> It's long been a business philosophy of General Portland [Cement Company] that "we manufacture and sell cement, but we market concrete." Our job as we see it is to manufacture top-quality cement and to work with our customers to develop new applications for concrete while expanding current uses.

Instead, mission statements often contain egocentric phrases, such as "to be the largest widget maker in the world," "to be the most profitable widget maker," "to be the best widget maker," "to be the most socially responsible widget maker," "to increase (a) earnings per share or (b) the value of the shares or (c) the return on stockholder's investment at International Widgets," and so on.

Harold Burson, chairman of Burson-Marsteller, one of the world's largest public-relations firms, doesn't mince words on this subject. In his firm's statement of values, he writes: "We exist solely to serve our clients." That says it all.

We should remember that profit is like oxygen— essential for our survival but not the point of the exercise. The *only* purpose of a business is to meet a customer need. All other statements, such as the attainment of specific profit objectives, are simply goals that can be achieved only when the needs of customers are consistently well met. Earning handsome profits is the means by which we measure how well we have been meeting the needs of our customers; because if we focus on customers and consistently exceed their needs, they will reward us with ever-increasing levels of profitability.

WRITING A MISSION STATEMENT
By answering *all* of the following questions, you can fashion a successful corporate mission statement:

1. Who is the customer?
2. What is the customer's need?
3. Who is the end user?
4. What is the end user's need?
5. How will you *uniquely* meet that need?

Let me use the corporate mission statement of my company, the Thaler Corporation, to illustrate the process.

1. *Who is the customer of the Thaler Corporation?*

A leader of other people. Our client list includes the corporate "who's who" of North America—leaders come to us because they are already good at what they do, and they know that we are at the leading edge of our field.

2. *What is the need of the Thaler Corporation customer?*

Because our clients are already very good at what they do, they don't need training or instructing. Rather, they are interested in learning the subtle techniques of doing what they already do well, so they can do it *even better.* Thaler's role is that of coach.

3. *Who is the end user of the Thaler Corporation's services?*

In our case, corporate leaders are the end users as well as the customers—although it can be argued that their employees, customers, and their customers are the ultimate end users of our services.

4. *What is the need of the Thaler Corporation end user?*

Since our end users are also our customers, their needs are the same as the customer's (see number 3 above).

5. *How will the Thaler Corporation* uniquely *meet that need?*

Much of our work is based on establishing strong values in the minds and hearts of private individuals and corporate teams as well as entire organizations. We have pioneered the concepts of value-centered leadership, and our process has become known by many as the *new value movement,* which is unique to our organization. But we also believe—and our clients tell us—that the establishment of strong values must help our client achieve what all great corporate leaders strive for:

To inspire and motivate employees.

To find and keep customers—for life.

By answering the above questions, we were able to devise the Thaler Corporation's mission statement (in only 17 words):

Coaching leaders of outstanding organizations to inspire and motivate employees and find and keep customers for life.

——————◆——————

Functional and divisional missions, equally customer focused, flow from the corporate mission. It helps for department and division managers to think of their particular mission statement as if it were a Ukrainian doll, housing several smaller dolls but itself fitting into a larger one. The functional and divisional missions describe how each area fits into and assists in the achievement of the corporate mission: The sum of all these minimissions equals the corporate mission. This "cascade effect" is important in an organization's design of strategic approaches. In the functional mission, the "customer" is defined as "the next person who gets your work."

At the end of this chapter, you will find worksheets to help you create your own corporate mission statement.

SETTING CORPORATE GOALS
Goals are the milestones along the path to fulfillment of the corporate mission. Every company needs goals. They

are dreams with deadlines. They define the specific performance, results, and standards that the activities of an organization are designed to produce. They provide for orderly growth; for measuring group and individual performance and identifying candidates for promotion; and for diffusing corporate control.

Defining goals is a constant process that involves the interaction of key management members—a process in which self-interest must be balanced with corporate interest. Few tasks so effectively put the collective executive nervous system through the wringer as the annual goal-setting process. In order to avoid the conflicts that often arise, you would do well to remember that consensus is always easier to achieve for *the long run;* the real disagreements tend to be about *the short run.* Everyone agrees that corporate revenues should grow by $10 million over the next 5 years; but not everyone agrees on how to split next year's $2 million increase! It follows then that more progress can be made (and fewer business friendships strained) if your team *first* reaches a consensus about long-term goals; *then* hashes out short-term goals. Done with sensitivity, this can result in a healthy interchange that allows goals to be set and then fine-tuned.

Good goals are S.M.A.R.T.: Specific, Measurable, Attainable, Relevant, and Trackable. They define a result to be achieved, not the act of getting there; they contain a deadline for achievement; and they represent a degree of realistic corporate "stretch."

The Value-Centered Leadership

Although the establishment of corporate values are as critical to successful corporate leadership as the corporate mission and goal-setting, many so-called rational corporate leaders find the idea of a statement of values beside the point. These left-hemisphere managers are more concerned with policies, operating procedures, budgets, and long-range plans. They forget—or choose to overlook—the fact that their employees are not mere cogs in the corporate machine: They are human beings with complicated needs.

Milton Friedman has argued that the social responsibility of business is to increase its profits. Other issues, states Friedman, are outside the mandate of the modern manager. For many, this is a dated notion—a left-hemispheric philosophy that is no longer valid. Most people operate from their right hemispheres just as often as from their left. As a result, they want to know where their company stands on issues that are important to them, their dependents, their friends, and their communities, not just how much money their company wants to make. In an age of uncertain and changing values, employees seek moral and philosophical benchmarks from the leaders of their organizations. Corporate leaders must be able to make unequivocal statements about the company's attitudes on equal employment opportunities, pay equity, sex and racial discrimination, women in business, minorities, doing business in high-risk or politically sensitive areas, facilitating payments, promotion, expansion, union relations, environmental issues, politics, quality and service, the community, profit, training, career development, competition, and so on. All these matters are vital to employees. A leadership statement on these topics helps to answer the question, How do the leaders in my company see the world? Further, it helps employees relate their own actions to the corporation's values.

Although the absence of a statement of corporate values is still commonplace, values can be a driving force in an organization. Along with the corporate mission, a statement of values can provide a sense of corporate self-concept. It is undeniable that organizations have an impact on people in a way that transcends individuals or groups of employees. Organizations have policies—they are or are not aggressive, competitive, or destructive to the environment; they may or may not "greet you with a smile." They also manufacture goods and create jobs and wealth. These are the actions of organizations, not individuals (although they are carried out by individuals). Values are implicit in these actions and contribute to the corporate self-concept as well as its image in the outside world. Today, when corporate values are increasingly important to the consumer, corporations would do well to think them through and act on them.

One of the best-known examples of the value-centered approach is Body Shop International, a chain of cosmetics stores founded in 1976 by a former British school teacher, Anita Roddick, which has grown into a half-billion-dollar, worldwide organization. Roddick visualizes her business as an agent for social change—the Body Shop's products are not tested on animals, all are biodegradable and packaged in reusable containers, and raw materials are bought almost exclusively from developing countries or economically disadvantaged regions of the world. The Body Shop does not advertise, preferring to build a profile by supporting environmental causes in collaboration with groups such as Greenpeace and Friends of the Earth.

———————◆———————

The intention of this section is to focus on *strengthening positive values,* but it should be pointed out that a clearly signaled set of negative values can be communicated just as effectively. For example, an internal memo to bond salesmen at failed Lincoln Savings and Loan instructed them on how to sell to elderly investors: "And always remember that the weak, meek and ignorant are always good targets." The top U.S. leveraged-buyout firm Kohlberg, Kravis and Roberts built a formidable business and incredible fortunes for the founders and investors by raising capital from pension funds to take over such companies as Beatrice Foods and RJR Nabisco. KKR strengthened the financing package through the sale of junk bonds to institutional investors, from which KKR obtained hefty consulting and introduction fees as well as handsome fees for managing the companies after their purchase. After laying off thousands of employees to force greater returns, the companies were sold back to the public, while KKR kept as much as 20% of the capital gain. Despite this bounty, Henry Kravis managed to persuade his first wife to settle for a mere $4 million; KKR attorney Richard Beattie kept his holdings in the firm a secret in order to avoid sharing his wealth with his partners; and when Kravis and Roberts's mentor and cofounder of KKR, Jerome Kohlberg, left the firm, he was forced to sue his former partners in order to recover the full value of several of his holdings, which they had arbitrarily reduced in value from 30% to 17.6%. His claim was honored by the courts while his revulsion with the practices, exorbitant fees, and flawed values of his former partners was vindicated.

THE STATEMENT OF VALUES

Because the CEO is the primary moral and intellectual force in the organization, the statement of values will be strongly influenced by the CEO's values. But because coalition building is a crucial part of corporate strategy—especially for an issue as vital as establishing values—the leadership team should develop the statement in conjunction with all employees. After all, these values will guide each employee's day-to-day decision making. By participating in the genesis of the statement of values, employees develop a stronger and more durable commitment to the company; they can then be counted on to defend it stoutly against all detractors.

In my work I see many value statements that are too vague or too ambitious—or both! One of my clients, for example, lists 51 values. No one could possibly remember them all, let alone *live* them.

At Thaler we limit our clients to three values (which are the subject of my book *The Way of the Tiger: Gentle Wisdom for Turbulent Times*):

The Three Keys of Work and Life

Mastery: Undertaking whatever you do in you personal and professional life to the highest standards of which you are capable.

Chemistry: Relating so well with others on a personal and social level that they actively seek to associate themselves with you.

Delivery: Identifying and meeting the needs of customers, both inside and outside the organization.

While recognizing that values are personal, we believe that any particular value falls under one of these broad headings. But it's not enough to list the values. To *live* them requires the adoption of certain behaviors and habits, called the "Core Values," that underpin the Three Keys. Mastery, chemistry, and delivery resemble a plowed field. The Core Values are the seeds we sow in that field.

The Core Values

Learning: To acquire greater *mastery,* we must learn from masters—in person and through their teachings. Mastery is never perfect, just as knowledge is never perfect. We must continuously learn in order to maintain mastery in all areas of our work and personal life.

Empathizing: To relate well with others—to achieve *chemistry*—we must not only be friendly with them, we must understand them as well. We can do this by imagining their feelings and thoughts; by putting ourselves in their place.

Listening: We cannot meet the needs of others—we cannot achieve *delivery*—if we don't know what their needs are. We can only find this out by asking and then listening to the answer. Listening is not merely "not talking." We must shut down our mental chatter to genuinely and nonjudgmentally listen to our customers. Then and only then can we hear the customer's needs; and only then will we be able to meet—and exceed—them.

Northern Telecom has developed a different set of core values, six very straightforward statements:

Excellence: We have only one standard—excellence.

Teamwork: We share one vision. We are one team.

Customers: We create superior value for our customers.

Commitment: We do what we say we will do.

Innovation: We embrace change and reward innovation.

People: Our people are our strength.

Frank Stronach, founder and CEO of Magna International, the Canadian auto-parts–industry pacesetter, has a set of clearly defined values (which appear to have evolved out of the many strong arguments he had with his father, an Austrian communist and labor radical). When 22-year-old Stronach, a qualified toolmaker, arrived in Montreal with $200 in 1954 and set up business, he often slept behind the lathe in his shop. Since then, he's built Magna into a world-class corporation. Among the specific values listed in Magna's Corporate Constitution, often called the "Magna Carta," are the following:

The majority of board members should be from outside the ranks of management

Allocation of 10% of profits to employee profit sharing

Allocation of 6% of profits to corporate management

Allocation of 7% of profits to research and development

Allocation of 2% of profits to charitable, cultural, educational, and political institutions "to support the basic fabric of society"

Distribution of 20% of profits to shareholders

Obtaining prior approval of the shareholders for the commitment of more than 20% of the company's equity to an unrelated business.

◆

Corporate self-concept is based on the leadership team's perception of how the corporate world and the world outside it will react to the corporation. Conversely, the *actual* reactions contribute to the self-concept. In turn, corporate self-concept shapes the quality and type of behavior displayed by executives and employees; once the statement of values is made public, it becomes very awkward for corporate leaders and their teams not to comply with it! Employees, suppliers, and customers want more than your written statement of values—they want your living commitment to them. As Francis of Assisi put it: "When you are walking somewhere to preach, be sure that your walking is the preaching." Now we say, Walk your talk. People want to know *how* you act, not just how you *say* you will act.

If the intrinsic argument for adopting a strong statement of values doesn't appeal to you, perhaps the financial argument will. When Jim Burke was the chairman of Johnson & Johnson, he credited the speedy decision to yank Tylenol off the shelves following the poisoning scare to his firm's potent values statement. He believed so strongly in the efficacy of written values statements that he commissioned a study of U.S. companies that had maintained such statements for at least one generation. His findings showed that during a period in which the GNP had grown 2 ½ times, the net income of those companies with written statements of values grew by 23 times! *Strong values help to create strong earnings.*

At the end of this chapter, you will find a draft statement of values that may help you develop your own.

The ALDO Audit

Vital though the corporate mission and values statements are, it is seldom wise to engrave them in stone. Like many aspects of strategic management, these statements need to be reappraised regularly. As society and the business environment change, relative corporate strengths and weaknesses change. As a result, statements of corporate mission and values must be retooled regularly. A sensitive leadership team will conduct employee-attitude audits regularly in order to compare internal signals with those from society and other organizations in the same field; then it will make adjustments accordingly. This continual feedback makes for a fresh, dynamic, and "in-tune" corporate character. This assessment process is called the **ALDO audit,** an acronym for the company's internal *A*ssets and *L*iabilities that corporate leaders must continually review in terms of external *D*angers and *O*pportunities in the environment that could affect future performance and market position. The environmental variables are illustrated in Figure 3-1.

———◆———

For years, the Walt Disney Company concentrated on producing wholesome family entertainment under the

Figure 3-1 The Environmental Variables in the ALDO Audit

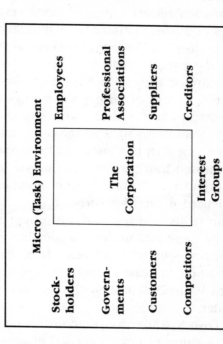

avuncular but wily eye of Walt Disney. Over time, consumer tastes changed but Disney corporate strategy didn't. Soon profits started to look very Mickey Mouse!

It's a cardinal rule of successful corporate strategists that environmental opportunities and dangers (competitive advances, changes in consumer tastes) must remain congruent with assets and liabilities (resources, talents, and capabilities); a good fit being a good strategy. Sometimes corporate heritage blurs judgment. Disney's "magic kingdom" had been so successful that the signals from the environment were brushed aside. But 3 years of declines in earnings, a $33 million loss in the film division, the eclipse of Disney's offerings to children by blockbusters like *E.T.* and *Star Wars,* and a sudden absence of TV hit shows signaled the end of an era. Disney required a major shift in strategy and went about it brilliantly. It formed Touchstone, a new movie label appealing to a broader and more mature audience, and recruited Richard Berger, formerly of Twentieth Century Fox, to run it. Its first successful offering, *Splash,* was followed by more hits under a leadership team led by Michael Eisner, who joined Disney from Paramount in 1984. The studio increased its share of the American box office from 3% to 20% and by 1990 had become the box office leader.

The Disney leadership demonstrated the kind of astute recognition of environmental change that is the essence of corporate strategy. As Miyamoto Musashi pointed out in *A Book of Five Rings,* strategy is "the capacity to see distant things closely and close things at a distance."

At the end of this chapter, you will find a thorough review of the ALDO audit, an explanation of the concepts involved, and a step-by-step outline of how to conduct your own in-house ALDO audit.

The Vision Statement

"Vision," Jonathan Swift said, "is the art of seeing the invisible." Essential to the leader's role is that of visionary. As my friend Robert Burns, a leading Canadian design and communications consultant, puts it, a leader pictures "a richly imagined future." His or her task is to get others to embrace the vision as their own, because they know that their best interests will be served by doing so. They will also be assured of something else—that the leader is looking forward not backward.

In their book *The Leadership Challenge,* James Kouzes and Barry Posner quote Lee Eisenberg, describing visionary leaders:

> While their contemporaries groped at the present to feel a pulse, or considered the past to discern the course that led to the moment, these [visionaries] squinted through the veil of the future. Not that they were mystics. They were much more worldly than that. For most of them, reality was pure and simple; what set them apart was a conviction that a greater reality lay a number of years down the pike.

There is a close relationship between *vision* and *passion.* Leaders who hold a dream of the future close to their heart have an uncanny way of making those dreams come true. T. E. Lawrence wrote:

> All people dream, but not equally.
> Those who dream by night
> in the dusty recesses of their minds
> wake in the day to find it was vanity.
> But the dreamers of the day
> are dangerous people,
> for they may act their dreams with open eyes
> to make it possible.

A vision statement does not need to be long or complicated. At Northern Telecom it is simply: "To be the world's leading supplier of telecommunications equipment by the year 2000." That means that they intend to jump five places in a decade; they call this statement "Vision 2000." Ask any Northern Telecom employee about the company's vision and you will always hear the same thing—they are *purposeful*.

Disney is another company with a crisp vision statement: "To make people happy."

A vision statement is a strategic tool that helps leaders transform organizations from the aspirations of today to the reality of tomorrow. It sets aside reason, owing as much to the heart as it does to the mind. Evocative, compelling, and exciting, it describes how things *could* be— the *possible* dream.

A vision statement is usually written at three levels:

1. **Material aspects:** How the organization will look in terms of its tangibles (technology, equipment, plant, process, patents, finance, and other "hard" assets).

2. **Human aspects:** How the organization will look in terms of its human resources (values, job satisfaction, experience, diversity, rewards, motivation, contribution and development, and other "soft" issues).

3. **Philosophical aspects:** What the organization's assumptions will be in terms of its relationship to humanity and to the Earth; how the organization would like to change the world.

Although there are other ways to create a vision statement, I believe the best is for the CEO to write the first draft and then share it with his or her immediate colleagues for feedback and development. To secure commitment to the statement from not only these colleagues but all concerned, the CEO should take the following four steps:

1. Communicate the rough draft of the vision statement to the leadership team and a small number of insiders as well as to a group of thoughtful outsiders, including customers, union representatives, suppliers, professional advisors, consultants, and government officials.

2. Listen to and act upon the feedback from this process to revise the vision statement. A vision statement is not truth but hope, and it should therefore receive the benefit of many constructive criticisms.

3. Consult all affected parties about the revised statement so that they can develop a sense of "ownership," resulting in a wide "buy-in." The new vision statement will work better if it is "owned" instead of being imposed.

4. Celebrate the introduction of the new vision statement with rituals of passage that mark the passing of the old way and attach fresh symbolism to the new vision statement, which enables people to emotionally "lock on" to it.

A vision statement should describe the leadership's aspirations regarding such aspects of the organization as:

How the organization will perform: profitability, size, locations, number of employees, revenues, costs, margins.

What business it will be in: products, lines, new businesses, acquisitions, mergers, geography, market segments, customer base.

How it will relate to its employees and how others will see it as an employer: rewards, security, promotion, professional development, organizational structure, freedom, opportunity.

How it will be viewed by its suppliers.

How customers will view it.

How its relationship with labor will develop.

How its relationship with government, regulators, and legislators will develop.

What its position will be on a range of relevant ethical issues.

What its leadership style, values, and culture will be: creativity, *Kaizen* (the Japanese concept of continuous improvement; see Chapter 9), quality, service, risk taking, empowerment, ownership, competition, the environment.

How its systems, technology, production processes, delivery, and marketing will change. How its behavior will change.

What distinctive marketplace advantages it will offer. What the value added will be for the customer.

How the organization will stand out.

How it will be perceived by the general public.

What passion will drive it.

This list is by no means intended to be exhaustive but merely to indicate the range of issues that can be usefully covered by a vision statement. Below are some guidelines for the introduction of the new vision statement.

♦ Ask people to develop their own personal vision, a dream of what they want to achieve in their lives. How does it fit the vision statement? How can the new vision statement help them to achieve their personal vision?

♦ A vision statement is inherently ambiguous. Many people will think of it as airy-fairy or "touchy-feely." Try to counteract this with built-in measurement criteria. Use benchmarks and tangible measures by which progress toward the vision can be gauged.

♦ Be careful to ensure that the vision "walks its talk." If it talks about empowerment, for example, avoid handing the vision to employees as a directive. If it describes a commitment to egalitarianism, demonstrate this through its introduction.

♦ Try not to rush things. The development of a new vision statement is intimidating. Be patient. Its introduction may take many months and its acceptance several years.

♦ Create an action plan. Develop a team to define the specific, tactical steps necessary to achieve the grand aspirations contained in the vision statement.

♦ Involve everyone; be sure that no one feels excluded from the process of vision development.

♦ Identify your "champions," those in the organization who will pioneer the new vision because they share your passion for it.

♦ Look for opportunities to demonstrate the new vision playfully and imaginatively—at staff functions, celebrations, corporate meetings, customer events, or meetings with outside parties.

♦ Determine how the organization can reward the behavior required to realize the new vision.

♦ Ask people outside your business to read the vision statement to see whether it is easily understood, appealing, and emotionally compelling.

♦ Make legends out of employees and customers whose actions exemplify the new vision. Re-create their deeds on video and circulate copies throughout the organization. Tape-record interviews with them and give copies to employees to listen to during their daily commute.

The Manager's Dilemma

Good corporate administration (strategy implementation) is pointless unless it follows good corporate entrepreneurship (strategy formation). This is because no organization can be successful if it is doing the wrong things, no matter how well the strategy is being implemented. The function of corporate administration must therefore be subordinated to corporate entrepreneurship, which is expressed in the corporate purpose.

Relating the results of the ALDO audit to the aspirations represented by the corporate purpose may reveal a **strategic gap,** usually defined as a shortage of resources and experience or in anticipated performance. Two choices are available to the strategist: altering the goals or correcting the shortages. Both options require planning.

Planning is a mysterious and often misunderstood subject. Strategic planning had its heyday in the mid-1970s. Roger B. Smith, former chairman of General Motors, is widely credited with the introduction of centralized strategic planning at GM in 1971. But after three "unsuccessful tries" at getting a centralized planning system to work, Michael E. Naylor, GM's general director of corporate strategic planning, observed: "Planning is the responsibility of every line manager. The role of the planner is to be a catalyst for change—not to do the planning for each business unit." Said Smith, "We got these great plans together, put them on the shelf, and marched off to do what we would be doing anyway. It took us a little while to realize that wasn't getting us anywhere." The disillusionment has been widespread. John F. Welch, chairman of General Electric, cut corporate planning staff from 58 to 33 and eliminated scores of planning jobs at lower levels in the organization. Eaton Corporation cut its planning team from 35 to 16, and similar purges have occurred at Rockwell International and USX. In a study of 15 medium-sized North American companies, Mansour Javidan of the University of Alberta found that half the CEOs were dissatisfied with the impact of planning on their companies and thought their planning staffs were unsuccessful. Research into French companies by Thomas Durand of the École Centrale des Arts et Manufactures has shown that many planners complained that their CEOs often arbitrarily altered strategic plans or shelved them altogether.

In another study, Larry Alexander of Virginia Polytechnic found that two-thirds of the 93 companies and 127 government agencies he studied failed to implement agreed-upon strategies because:

♦ Implementation took longer than expected
♦ Major, unexpected problems arose
♦ Major environmental changes occurred over which the company had no control (for instance, sudden increases in the costs of energy)
♦ Competing crises and activities within the organization absorbed and deflected management attention
♦ Coordination was sloppy

As this study confirms, part of the problem is that much corporate planning seems to take place in a time warp. For example, car makers simultaneously build gas guzzlers as Middle Eastern oil producers jack up oil prices; developers build suburban shopping centers as society becomes increasingly aware of the need for energy conservation; governments cut back on university funding as student applications rise; corporate management trims training, advertising, selling, and research budgets as profits and sales decline; corporations and governments increase borrowing as interest rates increase.

One reason for this time-warp effect is our inability to understand the important difference between *when we plan* and *when we do.*

Plans are often based on the operating environment of the organization as it is *now,* failing to take into account the possibility—indeed the likelihood—that by the time the plans are implemented, the operating environment will have changed. As GE's Welch put it:

> Strategy is trying to understand where you sit today in today's world. Not where you wish you were and where you hoped you would be, but where you are;

and where you want to be . . . assessing with
everything in your head the competitive changes, the
market changes that you can capitalize on or ward
off to go from here to there. It's assessing the realistic
chances of getting from here to there.

In other words, the ALDO audit must be time-sensitive
and the strategic-gap analysis must account not only for
resource deficiencies evident at the time but those that
will develop by the time the goals have to be met. This
is "the manager's dilemma."

G. Lynn Shostack, at the time a vice president in
charge of business planning at CitiCorp Bank, neatly illustrated a case of the manager's dilemma in the banking
sector:

Banks often devote significant resources to an activity
they call "new product development." The phrase
is so alluring that groups are regularly set up to create
these "new products." The realization seldom seems
to occur to such banks that they are not in the *product* development business at all. In fact, many banks
do not seem to have arrived at the insight that *things*
are not the basis for their industry. Even marketers
in such banks apparently do not understand that they
are engaged in perhaps the most difficult and dimly
understood realm of business endeavor—the development and marketing of financial services.

Part of the problem is that the first theories of
modern strategic planning were developed in a manufacturing context. Even among those of my clients who
operate organizations in telecommunications, retailing,
banking, hospitality, personal services, information technology, insurance, and broadcasting, there persists a
tendency to talk about "products."

The acceleration of change and the attendant difficulties associated with forecasting in our speeding world

virtually ensure that overly sophisticated long-range plans will not be achieved. Take, for example, the case of Texas Air.

————◆————

In 1975 the Civil Aviation Board began its campaign to deregulate the airline industry to make flying more affordable for more travelers. The following year Texas Air, led by a Harvard MBA, Frank Lorenzo, gained permission to lower fares by as much as 50% on certain low-density flights to 121 American cities. Lorenzo's strategic plan called for the creation of "critical mass" in the marketplace, and this led to the acquisition of Continental Airlines in 1982. Shortly afterward, Lorenzo put Continental into Chapter 11, fired the company's 12,000 employees, and rehired 4,000 of them at pay rates 40% to 60% less than they received previously (most were prepared to accept this in the inhospitable economic climate). This cut $250 million in operating costs, turned a $100-million loss into a $150-million profit over the following 3 years, and gave Lorenzo the lowest operating costs in the industry. But Lorenzo's plans called for continued growth, which led to the purchase of $1 billion of new aircraft; although the company was still in Chapter 11, this was financed by further debt. Lorenzo continued to implement his critical-mass plan by acquiring Eastern Airlines and People's Express. His fleet now consisted of 352 aircraft. But his plan started to seriously unravel when he attempted to implement its next stages: To further reduce costs, he moved to break the union at Eastern and transfer jobs to nonunion Continental. Employee morale plummeted and many Continental pilots defected to other airlines; customer dissatisfaction with safety and service rose dramatically; and the airline turned in an operating loss of $257 million. To offset the declining sales, the plan called for aggressive price cutting, which further aggravated the service, safety, morale, and image problems that Lorenzo's strategy had created in the first place. With planning and forecasting like this, dartboard projections could enjoy a renaissance! Today, Texas Air and Eastern are gone and Continental has again filed for protection under Chapter 11.

Fortunately, at American, United, and Delta airlines, something quite different has happened. These companies are committed to relatively *higher* labor costs and an "on" approach that helps to consistently win industry awards for service and quality.

---◆---

Another reason that strategic planning has become what *Fortune* magazine called "bedraggled" is that many managers invested their misplaced faith in the infallibility of planning for planning's sake, often becoming the victims of what Pearson Hunt called "the fallacy of the one big brain." Hunt wrote:

> The study and practice of business management . . . is seen whenever people act as if business problems were solved by a single entity having one big brain. All too often, we design schemes of analysis that assume that problems can be recognized, defined, analyzed, and solved by one brain of enormous capacity, which operates in a completely objective manner, searching for and comparing all possible alternatives in one thinking process . . . to arrive at the best possible answers.

Much of the planning that emanates from the left hemisphere is irrelevant, and the concept of the "rational" man or woman is obsolete. When it comes right down to managing, manage*ment* doesn't, manage*rs* do.

To lead and manage businesses effectively, therefore, we must arrange our strategies in some order, with simplicity and with the understanding that people will make decisions from different perspectives based on different judgments. Predicting these idiosyncratic reactions is an endeavor that has not yet yielded itself to management science, whatever the planners say. But holding in our mind's eye a sure picture of our corporate purpose (the reason for our existence today, the characteristics that will impel or impede us in achieving it, the values and principles that will guide us along the way, and our dreams of what we shall be tomorrow) enables us to become strategic thinkers rather than strategic planners—a subtle but superior alternative that sets direction and enables leaders and managers to shape the future of their organizations and react quickly to environmental changes. Said Napoleon, "Unhappy the general who comes on the field of battle with a system." He knew the value of keeping strategic options open!

Finally, written strategies are preferred to implicit ones. For one thing, strategies known only to the owner can be lost.

THE STRATEGIC LEADER
The most successful entrepreneurial leadership is strategic —but this can take many forms. Numerous researchers have confirmed what corporate leaders already know: managers and leaders plan by muddling with a purpose— by incrementally building their strategies, seizing opportunities, developing coalitions, and working their respective networks. The executive's classic response to the question, What do you do? will probably be a variation of the five words introduced into the lexicon of management science in 1916 by Henri Fayol, the French management theorist: *planning, organizing, directing, coordi-*

nating, and *controlling.* But as Professor Henry Mintzberg of McGill University has asked:

> When [a manager] is called and told that one of his factories has just burned down, and he advises the caller to see whether temporary arrangements can be made through a foreign subsidiary, is he planning, organizing, coordinating or controlling? How about when he presents a gold watch to a retiring employee? Or when he attends a conference to meet people in the trade? Or, on returning from that conference, when he tells one of his employees about an interesting product idea he picked up there?

Mintzberg studied CEOs in middle- to large-sized organizations and reviewed the research already done on the subject. He found that "managers are not reflective, regulated workers, informed by their massive [management information] systems, scientific and professional. The evidence suggests that they play a complex intertwined combination of interpersonal, informational, and decisional roles."

In a survey of 160 British middle and top managers, Mintzberg found that these managers only worked for half an hour or longer without interruption about once every 2 days. Further, 93% of the verbal contacts made by the CEOs in Mintzberg's study were arranged on an ad hoc basis.

From his studies, Mintzberg was able to report that executives work at a frenetic pace and that their activities are characterized by brevity, variety, and discontinuity. Not surprisingly, he found that managers prefer verbal means like telephone calls and meetings to formal planning sessions. Finally, Mintzberg exploded the long-standing myth that management was a science. He argued that how managers plan and make decisions remains a mystery. We might choose to say that these processes are the result of intuition and judgment, but these designations are really just labels to cover up our ignorance concerning the whole subject. Perhaps it was this difference between the theoretical and the real worlds of planning that Will Rogers had in mind when he observed, "Plans get you into things, but you got to work your way out."

Strategic planning (of which goals form a part) is a right-hemisphere activity; it is an *attitude* rather than a methodology. It focuses on the future and is instinctive, intuitive, subjective, inductive, idealistic, and emotional— it is one of the *arts* of leadership. (Compare this with operational planning, a left-hemisphere activity that focuses on today; it is objective, deductive, "scientific," linear, task and goal oriented, pragmatic, and political.)

Corporate Purpose

Collectively, the corporate mission, the statement of values, the ALDO audit, and the vision statement comprise the corporate purpose. A sound system for building and maintaining the corporate purpose is both a reactive and proactive feedback system. When you walk toward a door controlled by an electronic eye, the door appears to open in response to your approach. But actually the door is controlled by a sensory mechanism that is activated by your proximity to the door. The process of maintaining a clear corporate purpose works in the same way—it's activated by its environment and sensitive to changes in it. A corporate purpose that is truly sensitive to the environment will shape the collective state of mind of all the men and women who work for and come into contact with the organization.

Because the successful corporation is an environment-sensitive system based on feedback, it's alert to environmental changes, dangers, and opportunities; it uses this feedback to capitalize on corporate assets and to augment or correct liabilities. It defines goals and implements the policies, programs, budgets, and procedures by which they will be achieved. Using the ALDO audit, it monitors the entire process, ready to refine and modify the system when changes are detected that will affect the achievement of the corporate mission.

The job of the leadership team is to make the corporate purpose credible and appealing to all the organization's employees so that the widest possible commitment to corporate strategy is secured. This is accomplished by providing a clear explanation of the process to all team members. As employees gain an understanding of the corporate purpose, the cascade effect produces feedback that continues to play a role in the corporation's formulation of strategy.

The examples of how Beatrice and Ralston Purina lost focus of their corporate purpose demonstrate the same thing; the trick for corporate leaders is to ensure that there is a clear line of logical consistency running through the strategic-management process. The corporate machine hums when there is a synergistic fit among the corporate mission, the statement of values, the ALDO audit, and the vision statement. When the fit is good, nobody should be standing out in left field wondering what's going on.

◆

[As Chiang said to Jonathan Livingstone Seagull,] You will begin to touch heaven, Jonathan, in the moment that you touch perfect speed. And that isn't flying at a thousand miles an hour, or a million, or flying at the speed of light. Because any number is a limit, and perfection doesn't have limits. Perfect speed, my son, is being there. . . . To fly as fast as thought . . . you must begin by knowing that you have already arrived.

—Richard Bach

WORKSHEET 3-1:
CORPORATE MISSION
STATEMENT WORKSHEET

THE *CURRENT* CORPORATE, DEPARTMENTAL, OR FUNCTIONAL MISSION STATEMENT

First, write down the current corporate mission at your organization.

_____

_____

_____

Now, describe (in 20 words or less) how you would rewrite your corporate mission statement.

_____

_____

_____

Next, describe (in 20 words or less) the mission for your department or function.

_____

_____

_____

THE *NEW* CORPORATE MISSION
STATEMENT: PART 1

For your organization, division, department, or function, answer the following (in 20 words or less):

1. *Who is your customer?* Define your customers by their market segment: their types of businesses, revenues, geography, position titles, affiliations, buying patterns, etc.

_____

_____

_____

_____

_____

THE *NEW* CORPORATE MISSION
STATEMENT: PART 2

You have defined

1. *Who is your customer?* Define your customers by their
   market segment: their types of businesses, revenues,
   geography, position titles, affiliations, buying patterns,
   etc.

Now define for your organization, division, department, or
function, the following, (in 20 words or less):

2. *What is your customer's need?* Determine what your
   customers need from you and why.

_____

_____

_____

_____

_____

_____

THE *NEW* CORPORATE MISSION
STATEMENT: PART 3

You have defined

1. *Who is your customer?* Define your customers by their
   market segment: their types of businesses, revenues,
   geography, position titles, affiliations, buying patterns,
   etc.

2. *What is your customer's need?* Determine what your
   customers need from you and why.

Now define for your organization, division, department, or
function, the following, (in 20 words or less):

3. *Who is your end user?* Define the end users (as distinct
   from your customers) of your products or services by
   their market segment: sociodemographic group, affiliations, TV viewing habits, buying patterns, etc.

_____

_____

_____

_____

_____

THE *NEW* CORPORATE MISSION
STATEMENT: PART 4

You have defined

1. *Who is your customer?* Define your customers by their market segment: their types of businesses, revenues, geography, position titles, affiliations, buying patterns, etc.

2. *What is your customer's need?* Determine what your customers need from you and why.

3. *Who is your end user?* Define the end users (as distinct from your customers) of your products or services by their market segment: sociodemographic group, affiliations, TV viewing habits, buying patterns, etc.

Now define for your organization, division, department, or function, the following, (in 20 words or less):

4. *What is your end user's need?* Determine what your end users need from you and your customers and why.

_____

_____

_____

_____

_____

THE *NEW* CORPORATE MISSION
STATEMENT: PART 5

You have defined

1. *Who is your customer?* Define your customers by their market segment: their types of businesses, revenues, geography, position titles, affiliations, buying patterns, etc.
2. *What is your customer's need?* Determine what your customers need from you and why.
3. *Who is your end user?* Define the end users (as distinct from your customers) of your products or services by their market segment: sociodemographic group, affiliations, TV viewing habits, buying patterns, etc.
4. *What is your end user's need?* Determine what your end users need from you and your customers and why.

Now define for your organization, division, department, or function, the following, (in 20 words or less):

5. *How will you* uniquely *meet their needs?* Determine how you will meet the needs of your customers and end users in a way that distinguishes you from all the rest; detail the technology, philosophy, or process that you will employ.

_____

_____

_____

_____

_____

_____

THE *NEW* CORPORATE MISSION STATEMENT: COMPLETE STATEMENT

1. *Who is your customer?* Define your customers by their market segment: their types of businesses, revenues, geography, position titles, affiliations, buying patterns, etc.

2. *What is your customer's need?* Determine what your customers need from you and why.

3. *Who is your end user?* Define the end users (as distinct from your customers) of your products or services by their market segment: sociodemographic group, affiliations, TV viewing habits, buying patterns, etc.

4. *What is your end user's need?* Determine what your end users need from you and your customers and why.

5. *How will you* uniquely *meet their needs?* Determine how you will meet the needs of your customers and end users in a way that distinguishes you from all the rest; detail the technology, philosophy, or process that you will employ.

6. Putting it all together: For your organization, division, department, or function, take into account your answers in Parts 1 through 5 above and write your *new* mission statement (in 20 words or less):

_____

_____

_____

_____

_____

_____

Worksheet 3-2:
Statement of Values
Mastery, Chemistry, and Delivery
For

(Name of Your Organization)

INDIVIDUAL ASSESSMENT

Step 1: Best for Us

Please rank the 24 *values* shown on the next three pages, using the following scale:

5 = A *value* essential for us to continually achieve excellence
4 = Should have if possible
3 = Nice to have
2 = Not important
1 = Not desirable
0 = Irrelevant

Circle your evaluation in the left-hand column headed "Best for Us."

Step 2: How We Do It

Please rank the 24 *values* shown on the next three pages, using the following scale:

5 = A *value* that we practice every day
4 = This is our goal and it often happens
3 = We try hard but often fail
2 = Nice but not practical
1 = This never happens
0 = Irrelevant

Circle your evaluation in the right-hand column headed "How We Do It."

MASTERY
AT

_____

(Name of Your Organization)

_____

Best for Us		Mastery Values	How We Do It
0-1-2-3-4-5	A.	Our goals are clear and lead to excellence.	0-1-2-3-4-5
0-1-2-3-4-5	B.	We build on strengths rather than weaknesses.	0-1-2-3-4-5
0-1-2-3-4-5	C.	We invest significant time and resources in coaching and professional development.	0-1-2-3-4-5
0-1-2-3-4-5	D.	We create solutions rather than analyze problems.	0-1-2-3-4-5
0-1-2-3-4-5	E.	We build on new ideas instead of criticizing them.	0-1-2-3-4-5
0-1-2-3-4-5	F.	We choose simplicity over complexity or bureaucracy.	0-1-2-3-4-5
0-1-2-3-4-5	G.	We give people the best tools with which to do the job.	0-1-2-3-4-5
0-1-2-3-4-5	H.	Winning means doing whatever you do as well as you can; it does not mean destroying others.	0-1-2-3-4-5

CHEMISTRY
AT

_____

(Name of Your Organization)

Best for Us		Chemistry Values	How We Do It
0-1-2-3-4-5	A.	We put the interests of the team before individual egos.	0-1-2-3-4-5
0-1-2-3-4-5	B.	We make decisions affecting the individual with compassion and consideration.	0-1-2-3-4-5
0-1-2-3-4-5	C.	We tell the truth and we communicate clearly, at every level.	0-1-2-3-4-5
0-1-2-3-4-5	D.	Our actions always reinforce the self-esteem of others.	0-1-2-3-4-5
0-1-2-3-4-5	E.	People are more important to us than things.	0-1-2-3-4-5
0-1-2-3-4-5	F.	We support our people and praise them to success.	0-1-2-3-4-5
0-1-2-3-4-5	G.	We manage conflict rather than avoid it.	0-1-2-3-4-5
0-1-2-3-4-5	H.	We lead by inspiring and trusting, not by intimidating.	0-1-2-3-4-5

DELIVERY
AT

(Name of Your Organization)

Best for Us		Delivery Values	How We Do It
0-1-2-3-4-5	A.	The needs of our current and future customers come first, and we make clear decisions that are in their best interest.	0-1-2-3-4-5
0-1-2-3-4-5	B.	Our reward systems are tailored to the needs of individuals and linked to results and customer satisfaction.	0-1-2-3-4-5
0-1-2-3-4-5	C.	*Kaizen* (continuous improvement) is our everyday practice.	0-1-2-3-4-5
0-1-2-3-4-5	D.	We identify our customers' needs by listening to them regularly and without "filters."	0-1-2-3-4-5
0-1-2-3-4-5	E.	The needs of our internal customers are as important as those of our external customers.	0-1-2-3-4-5
0-1-2-3-4-5	F.	We proclaim our commitment to integrity, ethics, and truth—and we walk our talk.	0-1-2-3-4-5
0-1-2-3-4-5	G.	We are committed to "doing it right the first time."	0-1-2-3-4-5
0-1-2-3-4-5	H.	We value and encourage innovation and creativity that helps to exceed the needs of our customers.	0-1-2-3-4-5

TEAM ASSESSMENT

Step 3: Best for Us

Working together in teams of four, please discuss the individual rankings that were noted in Steps 1 and 2. Reach agreement on every one. Based on the team consensus, rate each of the 24 *values* defined on the previous pages using the following scale:

5 = A *value* essential for us to continually achieve excellence
4 = Should have if possible
3 = Nice to have
2 = Not important
1 = Not desirable
0 = Irrelevant

Your responses shoud reflect the *ideal* condition for your organization. Enter your *ratings* in the appropriate boxes under the heading "Best-for-Us Ranking" on the next page.

Step 4: How We Do It

Following Step 3 above, based on the team consensus, rate each of the 24 *values* defined on the previous pages using the following scale:

5 = A *value* that we practice every day
4 = This is our goal and it often happens
3 = We try hard but often fail
2 = Nice but not practical
1 = This never happens
0 = Irrelevant

Your responses should reflect the *actual* condition of your organization. Enter your *ratings* in the appropriate boxes under the heading "How-We-Do-It Ranking" on the next page.

TEAM TOTALS

Best-for-Us Ranking

	Mastery	Chemistry	Delivery
Team 1			
Team 2			
Team 3			
Team 4			
Team 5			
Team 6			
Team 7			
Team 8			
Totals	1. ___	2. ___	3. ___

How-We-Do-It Ranking

	Mastery	Chemistry	Delivery
Team 9			
Team 10			
Team 11			
Team 12			
Team 13			
Team 14			
Team 15			
Team 16			
	4. ___	5. ___	6. ___

THE CURRENT ORGANIZATIONAL
EFFECTIVENESS OF

(Name of Your Organization)

Please transfer totals 1 through 6 from the previous page to the appropriate boxes on this page. Calculate the differences between [A] and [B]. The result reflects the gap between the *values* currently practiced by you and your colleagues at your organization and those to which you aspire. Determine your organization's percentage of effectiveness by dividing [B] by [A].

	Mastery	Chemistry	Delivery
[A] Best for Us	1.	2.	3.
[B] How We Do It	4.	5.	6.
Difference			
Current Organizational Effectiveness [B]/[A]	%	%	%

Our goal is to agree upon the best values for us and to design and implement a program that will close the gap between what we do and what we aspire to do.

WORKSHEET 3-3:
THE ALDO AUDIT

A NOTE ON TERMINOLOGY

ALDO An acronym for the organization's *internal* (to be found within the organization) *A*ssets and *L*iabilities and *external* (to be found outside the organization) *D*angers and *O*pportunities.

Assets Those *internal* characteristics and assets of the company that can have a material and positive effect on strategy and impetus.

Liabilities Those *internal* characteristics and assets of the company that can have a material and negative impact on strategy and impetus.

Dangers Those *external* dangers and difficulties that represent significant impediments to the successful achievement of desired strategy.

Opportunities Those *external* trends and market characteristics that, properly exploited, could result in significant gain for the organization.

Degree The extent to which the noted characteristic is present; ranked on a 1–10 scale (1 = virtually nonexistent; 10 = existing in great amounts).

Relevance The extent to which the noted characteristic can positively assist in the meeting of the mission (assets and opportunities) or its potential damage (liabilities and dangers) ranked on a 1–10 scale (1 = virtually nonexistent; 10 = existing in great amounts).

Impact The correlation between degree and relevance.

Delta A fraction obtained by subtracting degree *(D)* from relevance *(R)* and multiplying the result by relevance *D*, i.e. *(R − D) × D*. The resulting number signals the degree to which an important *asset* does not exist in sufficient quantities to achieve substantial and relevant growth. The higher the negative value of *D* the greater the deficiency of a relevant *asset*.

INSTRUCTIONS FOR COMPLETING AN ALDO AUDIT

The initial objective of an ALDO audit is to identify the *A*ssets, *L*iabilities, *D*angers, and *O*pportunities (ALDO) of the organization. The ultimate objective is to set corporate strategy.

Before the ALDO Audit

1. Read Chapter 3, which describes how the ALDO audit works and its importance.

2. Hold a preliminary meeting with your immediate team. Ask them to identify the most important *assets* of your specific operation. Be careful not to criticize team members' contributions; instead, build on and elaborate them. Be sure that everybody participates. Avoid domination of the discussion by any individual. Write down *everybody's* comments on large sheets of paper set on an easel; tear off the pages as they are filled and hang them on the wall with masking tape. Complete the same procedure with *liabilities, dangers,* and *opportunities.*

   If you have time to hold a preliminary ALDO audit meeting, find time to ask the same questions informally every opportunity you get. It is vital that you bring a good sense of your team's input to the ALDO audit meeting.

3. If you have time, refine your lists by asking for your team's collective judgment on every single item. First, determine the degree of "frequency" or depth of each issue, and second, the "importance" (in the case of assets and opportunities) and the potential "damage factor" (in the case of liabilities and dangers). Assign a value based on a scale of 1–10. Delete any that are valued at less than 8.

4. To complete the exercise, consider the implications of your analysis. Use the wisdom, judgment, and experience of your team to identify the two or three most important strategic issues that emerge from this ALDO audit. When considering what is "strategic" and what is not, think in terms of the medium to long term and of major ALDO items that are vital to the future health and success of your operation.

   An inability to capitalize on perceived opportunities because of inadequate assets and an inability to defend yourself from perceived dangers because of the presence of internal liabilities represent what is called the **strategic gap.** It is the soft underbelly of the organization, the area of vulnerability that a competitor will search for and take advantage of. An intensive review of the strategic gap will lead to the identification of medium- and long-term strategies, called **strategic thrusts.** To determine these, identify the steps for acquiring the appropriate assets needed to take advantage of the identified opportunities. In addition, determine how to lessen your liabilities to ward off identified dangers.

During the ALDO Audit

1. Complete the following tables, using an easel and a large pad of paper, tearing each page off and hanging it on the wall as you fill each sheet.

2. After you have identified all the assets, liabilities, dangers, and opportunities, ask the entire ALDO audit group to rank them in terms of relevance and degree, as defined above. Use the discussion to create unanimous agreement—the process of consensus building is critical to a sense of shared ownership and vision.

3. Add the degree and relevance ranking numbers together, divide by 2, and place the resulting number in the impact column.

4. Place the impact numbers in the ALDO audit scattergram.

5. Rank the *assets* by the *delta* in ascending order, thus clarifying and suggesting actions required to address appropriate priorities.

6. Prioritize the impact rankings and remove anything below 8. Select the top five priorities that result and define them in the appropriate pages that follow. This is your foundation for defining the strategic gap for your organization.

ASSETS

	Degree (1–10)	Relevance (1–10)	Impact $\left(\dfrac{D + R}{2}\right)$	Delta $(R - D) \times D$
1.				
2.				
3.				
4.				
5.				
6.				
7.				
8.				
9.				
10.				
11.				
12.				
13.				
14.				
15.				
16.				
17.				
18.				
19.				
20.				

LIABILITIES

	Degree (1–10)	Relevance (1–10)	Impact $\left(\dfrac{D + R}{2}\right)$
1.			
2.			
3.			
4.			
5.			
6.			
7.			
8.			
9.			
10.			
11.			
12.			
13.			
14.			
15.			
16.			
17.			
18.			
19.			
20.			

DANGERS

	Degree (1–10)	Relevance (1–10)	Impact $\left(\dfrac{D + R}{2}\right)$
1.			
2.			
3.			
4.			
5.			
6.			
7.			
8.			
9.			
10.			
11.			
12.			
13.			
14.			
15.			
16.			
17.			
18.			
19.			
20.			

OPPORTUNITIES

	Degree (1–10)	Relevance (1–10)	Impact $\left(\dfrac{D + R}{2}\right)$
1.			
2.			
3.			
4.			
5.			
6.			
7.			
8.			
9.			
10.			
11.			
12.			
13.			
14.			
15.			
16.			
17.			
18.			
19.			
20.			

THE ALDO AUDIT SCATTERGRAM

	Assets	Liabilities	
10			10
9			9
8			8
7			7
6			6
5			5
4			4
3			3
2			2
1			1
0	0-1-2-3-4-5-6-7-8-9-10	0-1-2-3-4-5-6-7-8-9-10	0
	Dangers	Opportunities	
10			10
9			9
8			8
7			7
6			6
5			5
4			4
3			3
2			2
1			1
0	0-1-2-3-4-5-6-7-8-9-10	0-1-2-3-4-5-6-7-8-9-10	0

THE ALDO AUDIT STRATEGIC GAP

The Top Five Key Strategic Issues

Review the assets, liabilities, dangers, and opportunities. From those with the highest impact, select the *five* most significant key strategic issues. Fill out a Key Strategic Issue form for each issue, using the following pages.

KEY STRATEGIC ISSUE 1:

Resources Required	By When?	Who Is Responsible?

KEY STRATEGIC ISSUE 2:

Resources Required	By When?	Who Is Responsible?

KEY STRATEGIC ISSUE 3:

Resources Required	By When?	Who Is Responsible?

KEY STRATEGIC ISSUE 4:

Resources Required	By When?	Who Is Responsible?

KEY STRATEGIC ISSUE 5:

Resources Required	By When?	Who Is Responsible?

Chapter 4

Corporate Climate

A leader is a dealer in hope.

—Napoleon I

An organization should approach all tasks with
the idea that they can be accomplished in a
superior fashion.

—Thomas Watson, Jr.

*T*he skilled corporate leader creates a climate
for success—a corporate ambience that inspires and
motivates employees, who share a single vision that gives
real meaning to terms like *quality* and *customer service.*
Such a vision is the foundation for corporate success.

———◆———

For some weeks following a trip to Italy, I had been
carrying some left-over lira in my pocket. Part of Italy's
charm is the bulk of its money—it takes a thousand lira
to buy a newspaper or a cappuccino.

I was waiting for the opportunity to convert my
35,000 Italian lira into dollars when one day I found
myself near a bank and with 15 minutes to spare, I sub-
mitted myself to the humiliating ritual of lining up between velvet ropes, an offensive specialty of some banks.
As it turned out, 10 minutes passed before I realized that
I had been in the wrong line. So I joined the tail of the
correct line, eventually meeting the teller face to face. All

bank personnel were wearing yellow T-shirts imprinted with a locomotive and the inscription, Engineering the Switch.

Smiling at the teller, I asked, "What does 'Engineering the Switch' mean?"

"We've embarked on a marketing campaign to encourage customers from other financial institutions to switch to ours."

I waited for her to continue—but that was it! I thought she might suggest something like, "Can we interest you in opening an account with our bank? We'd really love to have you join our family so that we can show you how much better our service is and how well we would look after you as our customer? How can I help you?" But she didn't. In fact, she didn't say anything more at all. So I simply continued with my business.

"I have 35,000 Italian lira that I would like to change into dollars, please."

"Do you have an account with our bank?" asked the teller.

When I told her that I didn't, she replied, "Well, you have to have an account with our bank before we can change foreign currency for you."

Funny thing. I thought banks were places where they kept the money. I thought the general idea of a bank was to deposit or withdraw money or even exchange different kinds of it.

At this point, the manager overheard our strained conversation—between a potential customer and an employee who couldn't seem to care less.

"What's the problem?" he asked.

"There's no problem," I replied. "I simply want to change these 35,000 Italian lira into dollars. This is a bank, right?"

The manager asked me whether I had an account, and I politely told him I did not. He then told me what I had already heard from the teller: Because I didn't have an account, he couldn't change foreign currency into dollars for me. At least their customer-repelling style was consistent.

"Why not?" I asked with genuine innocence.

"Because it costs us money to make the exchange."

"I know that, but you're not going to give fair exchange—you will take a service charge, which I am perfectly happy to pay, and this service charge will cover your profit and the costs of foreign exchange. Am I right?"

"Yes, but I can't change your money here unless you have an account with our bank."

"Why not?"

And then came the numbingly bureaucratic, fail-safe answer that employees who don't care give to customers who are desperately trying to do business with them: "Because it's against company policy."

And so I witnessed, once again, another perfect example of a well-intentioned customer-training program that had reached the mind but hadn't touched the heart. The staff of this bank had been "trained": They were aware of the advertising campaign, how the promotion worked, what the logos and slogans meant—they even vaguely understood the grand plan behind it all. But nobody had given these employees *a reason for doing it*. No one had encouraged or empowered them to create their own ways of charming prospective customers into their branch. They had been given no incentive to romance customers into their branch because they would not be celebrated nor participate in the success nor share the rewards that new customers help to create.

I was writing a weekly newspaper column at the time this happened, so I decided to use this story in my column to advance my theories. As soon as it was published I received a call from the Manager, Quality of Service, Ontario Region.

"Very interesting article you wrote," he said. The praise sounded a little hollow but I thanked him anyway.

He paused, then asked, "Would you be kind enough to tell me the name of the bank you were writing about?"

"Of course," I responded. "It was yours."

He sighed. "I was afraid you were going to say that." Another pause. "Can I ask you another question?"

"Of course."

"What was the address of the branch?"

I told him. His sigh of relief was immediate. "Phew! That's not in my territory."

The bank employees had been trained—but training is for dogs. Real people don't want to be trained; they want to be inspired, motivated, and rewarded. Teaching the *process* of quality or customer service or innovation or even leadership is easy, but it will mean nothing if employees don't care. The real trick therefore is to create a **climate for success,** in which everyone wakes up in the morning wanting to be the best, wanting to turn customers into dedicated and loyal fans, wanting to be a part of a high-flying team that constantly strives to invent new and better ways to make dreams real. As Fritz Perls put it, "I don't want to be saved, I want to be spent."

———◆———

In 1979 Bernie Marcus and Arthur Blank were fired from their positions as president and controller of Handy Dan after the Texas-based home-center chain was taken over by a conglomerate. So they started The Home Depot in Atlanta, Georgia. Ten years later, The Home Depot had become the largest home-improvement retailer not only in the United States but in the world. It continues to maintain astonishing growth rates. Each store generates $28 million in sales, twice that of Building Square, its closest competitor. How do they do it?

Marcus and Blank look for employees who possess paradoxical qualities: creativity and independence as well as dedication to the vision and culture of the company. The Home Depot rewards people who can function individually *and* as team members. "Everyone within the team is different," says Don McKenna, vice president of human resources. "We need to allow them their individuality. Managers need to learn how to manage the different opinions they get."

This distinctive corporate culture is achieved by building on six key components:

♦ Hiring superstars
♦ Sharing ownership
♦ Empowering employees
♦ Minimizing bureaucracy
♦ Coaching ceaselessly
♦ Rewarding excellence

Buying decisions are made locally, and managers and staff have access to the details of the company's performance. Says McKenna, "If they're committed, there's nothing to be afraid of." All technical coaching takes place in the stores; every month in every store, 20 field-based human-resource managers help store managers run 16 coaching sessions. Once a month, Marcus and Blank as well as most of the leadership team run five separate 8-hour development programs, known as "belly-to-belly" sessions, which focus on the company's vision. Employees hear about company plans and prospects and are encouraged to challenge and contribute. Other interactive briefings, called "breakfast with Bernie and Arthur," are conducted monthly via satellite with each store. As one commentator put it, "Other companies have corporate strategies, The Home Depot has a religion."

———————◆———————

As we reviewed in Chapter 3, creating the corporate mission, closing the strategic gap, agreeing on a statement of values, and defining a corporate vision are the foundations of corporate purpose. But corporate purpose does not exist simply because it has been typed and circulated.

Too many organizations believe that putting something on paper makes it happen or that training someone changes their behavior. Many of us have participated in the heroic task of creating a corporate 5-year plan. After an elephantine pregnancy, the tome is born. Everyone admires its shiny covers, clever narratives, and stylish charts and graphs. Then it is consigned to the chief executive's personal library where it sits companionably with the efforts of previous years. The problem lies in corporate climate. To achieve corporate purpose, the leadership team must create a climate that fosters success.

The Climate for Success

In a speech to the British House of Commons in September 1941, Winston Churchill wryly remarked: "I see it said that leaders should keep their ears to the ground. All I can say is that the British nation will find it very hard to look up to the leaders who are detected in this somewhat ungainly posture."

In his own inimitable way, Churchill always strove to create the right climate for action. In an organization whose climate is set for success, employees know that their company both wants and intends to succeed. They see that top management wants and needs the employees' help to achieve corporate goals.

IBM, the number-one computer company in the world, credits its corporate climate with the astounding success of the organization. Its climate for success rests on three basic tenets, which were laid down by Thomas J. Watson at the time of the company's foundation:

1. Respect for the individual
2. The best customer service in the world
3. The pursuit of excellence

Any IBMers, past or present, anywhere in the world, can recite these three "basic beliefs" by heart. These beliefs run in the blood—and they run the company. They will keep IBM in the forefront of the industry. As Lincoln confided long ago: "It is difficult to make a man feel miserable while he feels worthy of himself."

At IBM, employees have been inspired to implement articulated goals. But all too often, employees in other organizations are encouraged to do nothing of the kind. The metaphor that I like to use is that of the sweeper in the sport of curling. The sweeper's job is to sweep the ice clean in front of the stone as it travels to the end of the rink. The sweeper's task is to *make it easier* for the person throwing the stone to reach the target. Likewise, the role of management is to make it easier—*not more difficult*—for the corporate team to reach its goals. But the heritage of management often thwarts this. We spend more time explaining why something cannot be done, as in the banking example earlier, than we do offering creative solutions to get it done. (At the end of this chapter, you will find a means for determining the corporate climate for your organization, called the Analysis of Cultural Tendency, or ACT.)

The Heritage of Contemporary Management Science

Modern management techniques are not very old. In 1886 Henry R. Towne, president of Yale and Towne Manufacturing, suggested that "management" be an independent field of inquiry; he and others who followed based their studies on management in manufacturing. In 1911

Frederick W. Taylor published his *Principles of Scientific Management*. The thinking of that bygone era is best summed up in Taylor's rather interesting appreciation of employer/employee relationships: "Now one of the very first requirements for a man who is fit to handle pig iron . . . is that he shall be so stupid and so phlegmatic that he more nearly resembles . . . the ox than any other type. . . . He consequently must be trained by a man more intelligent than himself." And this was just 80 years ago!

Many of the pioneers of scientific management believed that people were sophisticated machines. Machines, they reasoned, went faster if you squirted oil on them and so, they figured, people would go faster if you squirted money on them. Thus the concept of piecework was born. Ever since, the most widely accepted theories of managerial motivation have been based, more or less, on this line of thinking.

In 1927 Elton Mayo and Fritz J. Roethlisberger of the Harvard Business School conducted their famous productivity studies at the Hawthorne Plant of Western Electric. These pioneers attempted to apply to people the methodology that they had used so successfully with their machines. Much of the subsequent scholarship continued this trend. During the 1950s and 1960s, the volume of literature increased considerably; and although the emphasis shifted from work measurement to behavioral concepts, the analytical methodology remained much the same. Researchers knew that more work needed to be done in the area of behavior—especially motivational, leadership, and group behavior—but their approach was not new. Despite today's values and cultural adaptations, many modern managers still follow these mechanistic approaches to management. Given their first taste of managerial responsibility, they behave with diligent authoritarianism toward their "subordinates." Even ardent fans of participative management, upon scaling the heights of the corporate hierarchy, often revert to a Big Brother style.

The Art of Leading and the Science of Managing

In order to create a climate for success, the CEO must skillfully balance management and leadership—and not confuse the two. Leading and managing are like one hand washing the other; they are the complement of art and science, the left hemisphere and the right; they are harmoniously balanced in corporations run by men and women with moxie.

Asked to define jazz some years ago, the great trumpeter Louis Armstrong replied, "If you gotta ask, you ain't never going to get to know." In many ways, defining and understanding the concepts of leading and managing requires a similarly intuitive analysis.

Warren Bennis, professor of management and organization at the University of Southern California, believes that the difference between the two is that a manager is someone who does things right and a leader is someone who does the right thing. Bennis illustrates this maxim with the story of Robert Redford's meeting with a group of skeptical cinematographers when directing his first movie, *Ordinary People*. Although Redford was an accomplished actor, had produced pictures before, knew Hollywood and how to run a movie company, what did he know about camera work or directing a film?

Redford acknowledged his lack of experience but said he had a clear idea of how the movie should open. With that, he played a tape of the "Canon in D" by Pachelbel, told the cinematographers that the opening scene would portray a beautiful suburb, and asked them to jot down the images that came to mind as they listened to the music. Redford's leadership was apparent in that moment, and his movie went on to win several Academy Awards (including best picture and best director).

If managing is the *science* of planning, organizing, and controlling an organization, then leading is the *art* of motivating and developing people to achieve personal and organizational objectives. Managers obtain their authority by being appointed. Leaders earn their authority from those whom they lead. Although some of the authority and power in executive positions is situational, much of it results from the rapport between the leader and the led. Through this symbiosis and the mutual respect that results, followers acknowledge their willingness to support their leader.

Managers are concerned more with things; leaders more with people. Managers conserve; leaders encourage growth. Managers decide what must be done; they are primarily concerned with the goals of the organization. Leaders, on the other hand, align their employees' interests with their own; they maintain a high degree of sensitivity to the needs and goals of the individual.

The dictionary defines *to lead* as "to show the way" and *to teach* as "to show how to." Note the similarity of the two. Being a leader is synonymous with being a teacher.

The science of management is inert until a leader unlocks employee motivation to achieve goals. People who work for an outstanding leader seem to be of superior caliber than their counterparts in other organizations; their attitudes and operating results are consistently higher. Where managers are concerned with maintaining the status quo, leaders focus on changing the future. Where managers allocate resources, leaders create them.

Although mediocre companies can be quite well managed, it's only leadership that can transform such companies into great organizations. According to Henry M. Boettinger, writing in the *Harvard Business Review,* managers see the parts, but leaders see "a whole which is more than the sum of its parts, has something internal, some inwardness of structure and function, some specific inner relation, some internality of character or nature that constitutes that *more.*"

One of the essential distinctions between leading and managing is to be found in the subjective/artistic/right-hemispheric nature of leading and the objective/scientific/left-hemispheric nature of managing. Obviously, neither exists in total isolation of the other. Learning, understanding, and applying these dynamics is what managerial moxie is all about.

Because outstanding leaders are generally more interested in people than things, the art of the task more than its science is their chief concern. The results of this art—the leader in action—cannot be measured or appreciated by any more relevant means than the judgment and approval of people. The results of managership, on the other hand, can be measured and appreciated through measurement, analysis, and quantification.

Leadership is an acquired skill. It's tricky to teach and, although theoreticians can help, it's best learned from leaders themselves. With this in mind, I try to persuade people who are keen to assume the mantle of leadership to seek out a dynamic leader to work with. And it's the *individual* that counts here: a job with Lee Iacocca is not the same as a job with Chrysler! Such an experience, no matter how brief, provides a powerful learning experience.

The CEO and the Climate for Success

Our technological and affluent society dismisses the need for outstanding leaders in favor of committees and homogenized, technocratic, problem-solving approaches. We teach leadership skills by breaking these problem-solving approaches down into their components as if they were the original item. This is similar to explaining to an aspiring track athlete that Edwin Moses became the world's greatest hurdler by creating a breakthrough—by taking 13 strides between each barrier instead of the 14 or more taken by everyone else. Although this is technically correct, it misses the point: It analyzes the process instead of capturing the desire. The desire created the process, not the other way round. Likewise, management technique is not the same as the personal quality of leadership. Superficial and mechanical methods of conveying the subtleties of leadership to managers results in well-trained managers, not leaders. A leader is the best qualified mentor to transfer leadership skills.

Nearly all successful corporations are run by successful leaders. Often the most successful companies are no more famous than the names of their CEOs. What would the following companies have looked like without the inspiration of their famous current or former leaders?

In Australia

Rupert Murdoch	News Corporation Limited
Kerry Packer	Consolidated Press International

In Britain

Richard Branson	Virgin Group
Jimmy Goldsmith	General Occidental Investments
Lord James Hanson and Lord Gilbert White	Hanson Plc
David Ogilvy	Ogilvy Mather & Benson
Mary Quant	Mary Quant Group
Anita Roddick	Body Shop International
Tiny Rowland	Lohnro
Marcus Sieff and Derek Rayner	Marks and Spencer
Arnold Weinstock	General Electric

In Canada

Thomas Bata	Bata Limited
Laurent Beaudoin	Bombardier
Conrad Black	Hollinger
Edgar M. Bronfman	Seagram
George Cohon	McDonald's
James Connacher	Gordon Capital
Paul Desmarais	Power Corporation
Jim Pattison	The Pattison Group
Ted Rogers	Rogers Communications
Isadore Sharp	Four Seasons Hotels and Resorts
Dr. Paul Stern	Northern Telecom
Lord Kenneth Roy Thomson	Thomson Newspapers
Gaylen Weston	George Weston Limited

In the United States

Mary Kay Ash	Mary Kay Cosmetics
Warren Buffet	Berkshire Hathaway
Max De Pree	Herman Miller
Michael Eisner	The Walt Disney Company
Debbie Field	Mrs. Fields
Paul Fireman	Reebok International
William H. Gates III	Microsoft
Lee Iacocca	Chrysler
F. Kenneth Iverson	Nucor
Esteé Lauder	Esteé Lauder
Charles P. Lazarus	Toys R Us

(the late) William G. McGowan	MCI Communications
Roger Milliken	Milliken & Company
Thomas Monaghan	Domino's Pizza
Gordon E. Moore	Tandy
Robert N. Noyce	Intel
Ken Olsen	Digital Equipment
Dr. Anthony J. F. O'Reilly	H. J. Heinz
T. Boone Pickens, Jr.	Mesa Petroleum
James D. Robinson III	American Express
Frederick W. Smith	Federal Express
R. David Thomas	Wendy's International
R. E. (Ted) Turner	Turner Broadcasting
(the late) Sam Walton	Wal-Mart Stores
John F. Welch, Jr.	General Electric
Leslie Wexner	The Limited
John Young	Hewlett-Packard

These great corporations are distinguished by great leaders, who are uniquely responsible for shaping the climate for success.

The CEO creates the corporate climate, from which he or she fashions the climate for success. Professor Abraham Zaleznik astounded his teaching colleagues at Harvard when he suggested that the personality of the corporation's executives has far greater impact on corporate results than on its organization. And in a special report prepared for the Presidents Association, John Drake noted that:

> The personality of most organizations almost always has its origin in the style and personality of the most powerful individual in that organization—usually the chief executive officer. It may take many years for

his personality and behavior patterns to impact on the organization sufficiently that the company itself mirrors the CEO's make-up, but eventually, it occurs. . . . As close staff members mirror the CEO's behavior, others in the organization, in turn, observe these staff members, and gradually the mode of the behavior of the CEO permeates the organization.

The CEO for All Seasons

We all know that the Iacoccas, Murdochs, Turners, and Welches are outstanding leaders who have created the appropriate climate for success in their organizations. But how do they do this so much better than everyone else?

Although the tasks of general management are often described as planning, organizing, implementing, and controlling the strategic process, this definition seems to devalue the difference between the concepts of managing and leading by reducing something exciting and dynamic to a series of dreary banalities. Worse, it is far from being accurate. In his book *Management—Tasks, Responsibilities, Practices,* Peter F. Drucker suggests that "the top [executive] tasks require at least four different kinds of human being: the 'thought man,' the 'action man,' the 'people man,' and the 'front man.' Yet those four temperaments are almost never found in one person. Failure to understand these characteristics is a main reason why the top management task is so often done poorly or not at all."

This summary explicitly acknowledges the technical competence expected of the top executive while implicitly pointing out that leading is the only task that a top executive has time to accomplish. The CEO is the principal architect of the climate for success, and through the leadership team, it is the CEO's task to create and maintain the climate for success required to secure organizational and individual success.

It's not that top executives must be four people, but rather that they must operate at four levels simultaneously if they are to be leaders with moxie. If Drucker is right, most corporations need a CEO for all seasons.

BARRY SULLIVAN AT FIRST CHICAGO

What leaders do when creating the climate for success is best explained by example—take First Chicago's Barry Sullivan, who succeeded A. Robert Abboud as chairman of First Chicago in 1980. In his first 3 years, the former Chase Manhattan executive took a number of strategic steps designed to materially alter First Chicago's internal and external climate: He encouraged an open atmosphere and an approach based on teamwork, a collegial management style, and a new compensation system; he buttressed these changes with personal example.

Sullivan recruited 300 new executives, including 9 for the top leadership team (most of whom were added to the bank's marketing and customer-service functions); reorganized the bank into 145 strategic business units (SBUs); trimmed annual executive staff turnover from 12.7% to 5% in his first 4 years; and acquired American National Bank and Trust.

After a decade with Sullivan at the helm, the assets of First Chicago rose to $50 billion. This performance was set against a darkening market environment: U.S. bank failures increased from 10 in 1981 to over 70 in 1984 and international debt and bad loans threatened the industry. In addition, new entrants into the market—like Sears, Merrill Lynch, and American Express—were successfully competing for the industry's traditional customers.

Sullivan's personal style was clearly stamped on the events and the people at First Chicago. He was into everything from budgets to new service development to selecting the art for the bank's walls. He created a new corporate climate by changing the cultural emphasis—which energized the business, improved internal and external communications and management participation (for example, Sullivan instituted a system for managers to vote on issues), and sharpened the bank's efforts in marketing and customer awareness. The new climate for success prompted Vivian L. Blackman, one of the bank's corporate account officers, to remark, "I don't want to sound mushy, but there is a very positive attitude among people here. There is a lot of excitement."

Sullivan's success story emphasizes how vital it is for the CEO to create a climate in which employees can learn, grow, flourish, and be rewarded—materially *and* spiritually. The CEO must guide the company's human, physical, and financial resources into dynamic organizational units capable of attaining agreed-upon objectives, which provides a high level of satisfaction to those served (the external customers) and a significant sense of self-esteem and achievement to those rendering the service (the internal customers). Establishing the right climate for success by recognizing the difference between leading and managing is a cornerstone in the philosophy of managerial moxie.

DR. ANTHONY O'REILLY AT HEINZ

Since Tony O'Reilly took over H. J. Heinz, sales have doubled (from $2.9 billion to $6.1 billion in the year ended April 1990) and net profits have soared (from $143 million to $504 million), prompting *Chief Executive* magazine to bestow upon Tony O'Reilly its 1990 CEO-of-the-Year award.

When O'Reilly came to Heinz, he found a company that was successful but lethargic; it was avoiding growth, suffering from low quality, and faced with intensifying competition and rampant price cutting. Calling for a complete overhaul of the company's culture, O'Reilly embarked on a program of cost reduction, total quality management (TQM), and acquisition (purchasing other successful brands, ranging from pastries to dog food). He coordinated the advertising and marketing efforts of the 44 subsidiaries and boosted their budgets from 4.3% to 8.2% of sales. He built the Weight Watchers subsidiary at an annual clip of 20% to $1.333 billion (which O'Reilly says will be $3 billion by 1994) and increased the margins of Heinz every year since 1977. In fact, Heinz's catsup business, which sold nearly 600 million bottles last year (enough to circle the globe three times), enjoys a 21% profit margin, among the most profitable processed foods on the market. And as a result of a policy that enables employees to become significant stakeholders in Heinz's successes, they now own stock or options equal to 16% of equity; several top executives have become millionaires, including Tony O'Reilly, who owns Heinz stock valued at over $100 million.

R. DAVID THOMAS AT WENDY'S
Detractors of the importance of climate setting by the CEO should remember that corporations are not living, breathing entities—they are artificial constructs that enable us to undertake commercial transactions. The quality of a corporation's results depends upon the people who work under its aegis. The flair and dynamism of employees—their attitudes and self-concepts—become the corporate image and attitude. How the employees of a corporation *act* is how the customers, suppliers, and employees of the corporation see it to *be*.

Like many entrepreneurial leaders, R. David Thomas —who founded Wendy's in 1969—was a whiz at marketing and motivating people but a klutz at writing memos or dealing with lawyers and accountants. In 1982 at the age of 50, he decided to step aside as CEO while remaining senior chairman (a title he created so that others would have a greater sense of executive freedom). It was the right time, he felt, "to back off and let other people who were smarter than me do things." He loved the company that he founded and didn't want to damage it: "Here's a company I didn't want to screw up," he said (the famous "Where's-the-beef?" promotional campaign helped savvy managers drive profits to levels that would not be equaled for more than half a decade). But while Thomas invested in orange groves and car dealerships and played golf, things started to unravel. A deterioration in quality and service standards helped to erode sales for the next 2 years.

At this point, Thomas asked a former Wendy's franchisee, James Near, to take over as chief executive. Near agreed on condition that Thomas return full time to the company, not in an operational role but as chief cheerleader, quality guru, and corporate spokesperson. One of the first things Thomas did was to work with the advertising agency to create a new promotional campaign. The agency was so impressed with his grasp of the business and his skills of articulation that they built the campaign around his presence on television. Referring to his successful efforts as TV pitchman, *Advertising Age* described Thomas as "a steer in a half-sleeved shirt." While the sales of other hamburger chains remained flat, Wendy's sales jumped to over $3 billion and profits rose by 29% to $34 million.

Thomas now enjoys his celebrity status and Wendy's franchisees line up to get him to visit their locations, which he does for 35 weeks every year. His knack for creating a vibrant and exciting climate for success is summed up by Michael Welch, an owner of 11 Wendy's restaurants in Sarasota, Florida: "In a franchise company, you have to have someone who is inspirational. Who can do that better than Dave Thomas—the founder?"

WILBERT L. GORE AT W. L. GORE AND ASSOCIATES
Another company that has built a legendary reputation for a successful corporate climate is W. L. Gore and Associates—"associates" being the sobriquet that the late

chairman Wilbert L. Gore gave his employees when he founded the company in 1958.

Today, employees own 10% of W. L. Gore stock through an associate stock-option plan; some own shares valued at $100,000. To maintain a "family" atmosphere, Gore limits the size of its operating units to 200 employees. Says Frances Hughart, a veteran Gore associate, "We manage ourselves here. If you waste time, you're only wasting your own money." Gore once wrote a memo to an associate who referred to himself as a "manager," reminding him that at Gore, people manage themselves—they do not manage others.

Wilbert L. Gore developed his unique climate for success by fostering a culture built on four precepts: freedom, fairness, commitment, and the "waterline"—the notion that the organization resembles a ship on which all the associates earn their livelihood. Thus, any associate is empowered to make his or her own decisions, providing any negative impact will only affect the ship *above* the waterline. If an associate believes that a decision could impact *below* the waterline—that is, pose danger to other members of the ship—then he or she must consult with the relevant sources.

W. L. Gore and Associates represents a more extreme version of the unstructured, and therefore empowered, organization—an organization in which the traditional hierarchy has been replaced with the lattice structure, in which the governing principles are such intangibles as fairness, freedom, commitment, and discretion. The result is **unmanagement.** Gore discovered that those people who do not prefer a structured environment become highly motivated by W. L. Gore's climate for success—which encourages each member of the team to become a leader, committed to personal goals and standards that, if executed successfully, will result in organizational success.

ISADORE SHARPE AT FOUR
SEASONS HOTELS AND RESORTS

When the employees at the Inn on the Park in Toronto
went on strike during the depths of a bitter winter, senior
executives served the shivering employees with coffee and
pastries. As John Young, senior vice president of human
resources, pointed out at the time, "Before they went out
on strike yesterday, these people were our trusted, loyal
employees. The day after the strike ends, they will, once
again, be our loyal trusted employees. Therefore, walking the picket line or not, they still are." And the
employees responded with a mutual respect. "We are their
staff. They still looked after us," said an employee after
the strike was over. "When we came back in the door,
they treated us exactly the same, as if nothing had happened."

This climate for success is the direct result of, among
other things, the entry-level hiring policy established by
Isadore Sharpe when he founded the Four Seasons Hotel
chain in 1961. Unlike many other organizations, the principal hiring criterion at Four Seasons is based not on skills
but on attitude and personality—"style" as John Young
describes it. For example, a doorman whose previous experience was in sales was hired as the hotel's first person
to greet a guest because he was outgoing, upbeat, and articulate: "I consider my job a very great challenge. I consider myself an ambassador for this hotel. I also consider
myself an ambassador for this country. We get a lot of
visitors from the U.S." In Chicago, 15,000 applicants were
screened for 545 jobs to reach these same standards.

I recently ran a strategy meeting for all the sales and
marketing managers from all Four Seasons Hotels around
the world. They came from New York, the Caribbean,
Hawaii, London, Toronto, Vancouver, San Francisco—and
yet they spoke to each other as if they conversed every
day. I later discovered that this remarkably sharp group

of executives *did* speak to each other every day, whether it was in Houston, Los Angeles, Chicago, or the island of Nevis—about sales leads, corporate accounts to be won and shared, new sales or service techniques, rate changes, or company policies.

"Issy" Sharpe has built his business from a small hotel on Toronto's Jarvis Street to the world's largest operator of luxury hotels—23 of them hosting 20,000 guests every day—a feat that is done so well that he has been named "Corporate Hotelier of the World" by *Hotels and Restaurants International* magazine. Sharpe prefers to be considered a mentor than a boss, and one manager says that he "coaches rather than commands." Explains Sharpe, "We have no secret of success. There's no sophisticated way of doing things. It's just simple, common sense. You must have confidence in the employees that they will know what to do. Our [service] doesn't begin on an assembly line, but at the front desk. If we're the best in our field, that's why. It starts with me, it goes all the way down. The way we treat our employees is the way we treat our guests. If you're looking for the magic word, it's respect."

The success of the Four Seasons Hotel chain is based on a climate for success that starts with hiring people with the right attitude, then builds on that attitude to create a sense of teamwork dedicated to just one thing— providing the best hospitality in the hospitality industry —bar none. And it's achieved with employees like the doorman described earlier who says, "I'm so happy here it burns. I love the people. I love my bosses. It's nice to be able to work in a place where all the employees smile and greet each other in the lobbies and corridors."

SAM WALTON AT WAL-MART
He was the youngest Eagle Scout in Missouri, state champion high school quarterback, president of the student

council, Army officer, and president of a small-town five-and-dime. He was also the founder and chairman of America's biggest retailer and reputed to be America's richest citizen. But Sam Walton was a late starter: He didn't open his first Wal-Mart store until he was 44 and had to borrow from almost every bank in Arkansas to do it (eventually he owned a few banks of his own). And because the big distributors wouldn't call on him in Bentonville, Arkansas, he built his own distribution centers and over-the-road truck fleet (which is now one of the nation's largest).

Wal-Mart's 1,600 retail stores and 150 warehouse-membership stores (called Sam's Club) romped to the top spot in retail sales with revenues of nearly $33 billion, just topping those of K-Mart but doubling profitability ($2 billion versus $1 billion). The increased margins allow Wal-Mart to focus even more closely on pleasing customers and keeping costs down, creating a productivity loop: extra checkout lines for quicker service; "greeters" in every store; lower prices; bonuses for employees who achieve low shrinkage; more training; and the best information-distribution system in the industry, incorporating the latest satellite-based technology.

The greatest advantage Wal-Mart has over its competitors is its climate for success: "Be an agent for consumers, find out what they want, and sell it to them for the lowest possible price." This profound philosophy speaks volumes about what it feels like to be one of Wal-Mart's 350,000 employees.

Wal-Mart empowers its employees (also called "associates") to make the right decisions in the best interests of customers. Employees are provided with information about the performance of their department and company (costs, markups, overhead, profits) and the necessary power to make appropriate decisions on the spot. This empowerment encourages them to contribute their ideas; Sam Walton claimed that as a result 90% of the best ideas come from employees. Until Walton passed away in 1992, he and Wal-Mart's CEO, David Glass, as well as the rest of the leadership team, spent at least 2 days every week on the road listening to local store managers and associates. Like Four Seasons' Issy Sharpe, Wal-Mart's leaders believe in keeping as close to employees as they do to customers.

The failure of other retailers to adopt these principles prompted David Glass to predict recently that 50% of all retailers won't be around by the year 2000. He later corrected himself, suggesting that he may have been too conservative. He is probably right, considering that in 1990 25% of all retail sales in the United States were conducted by companies in various stages of bankruptcy.

Like Anita Roddick's approach at Body Shop International, Sam Walton involved the entire organization in causes. During the 1980s he championed a Buy-American campaign to encourage U.S.-made goods over imports; the company has reported that the initiative has so far resulted in the repatriation on $3.8 billion in goods and services and created or saved 100,000 American jobs. Now Wal-Mart is crusading for the environment. Says Glass, "I believe our environmental problems are ten times as bad as have been reported." Part of the campaign is to let customers know which suppliers make products or packaging that is friendly to the environment.

The CEO as Folk Hero

The way in which the outside world—the media and other opinion-makers—view a CEO's performance and character can significantly affect corporate climate and therefore employee motivation and results. Consider the case of Kerry Packer.

When Australia's richest entrepreneur married off his daughter Gretel in London in the summer of 1991, he staged a ceremony that the British press described as the most expensive (almost $2 million) nonroyal wedding in history. Among the guests were the international elite of corporate glitterati, including Sir James Goldsmith (Anglo-French), Jacob Rothschild (British), Conrad Black (Canadian), and Rupert Murdoch (formerly Australian, now American).

Said media baron Conrad Black, "He's, I guess, a sort of controversial guy in Australia, but of all those prominent Australian businessmen from the harum-scarum era of the '80s, he's virtually the only one who isn't dead or bankrupt." Black describes Packer's exploits with not a little admiration: "He sold his TV stations to Alan Bond for a billion dollars, and bought them back from receivers for half-a-billion dollars. Your grandmother may have told you when you were little that you could do a deal like that but no one ever expects you to do it." Commented Packer shortly after the deal with Bond, "Only one Alan Bond comes along in your lifetime—and I've had mine."

Today Packer's empire embraces sprawling cattle ranches, ski resorts, commercial developments, and companies in mining exploration, chemicals, and engineering. His TV stations claim 60% of Australia's viewing audience and his magazines 50% of the readership market.

But it's Packer's style that creates the climate for success in his organizations. In 1974, for example, Packer stunned the world of cricket by signing up the top players from the Australian cricket team as well as the British, West Indian, and New Zealand national teams to play in his World Series Cricket, which was televised exclusively by his TV network. He created another stir when he reportedly blew $20 million at the tables of London's Ritz Casino. Packer has subsequently denied this story, but it has never been clear whether he disputed the loss or the amount!

Packer is a force in Australia as well as in the international arena. He has particularly close ties to Australia's

Labor Party, and his friend Bob Hawke is Australia's prime minister. Some believe that these connections were not unimportant when the New South Wales Labor government awarded Packer, together with Rupert Murdoch, the license to Lotto, a lottery that is very popular among the gambling-crazy Australians and generates enormous cash prizes to winners.

After Packer suffered a near-fatal heart attack on the polo field in 1990, in gratitude for his life he paid half the cost of installing specialized cardiovascular equipment in every ambulance in New South Wales. Today his private jet is at the free disposal of Sydney's St. Vincent Hospital, which has become one of the world's leading centers for heart surgery and research.

Kerry Packer inspires people around him and throughout the world. He creates his own climate for success. Conrad Black describes him as "robust, opinionated, extremely wealthy, highly successful, colorful [and] swashbuckling," and adds, "But you know, what's wrong with that?"

Or consider the case of Sir Clive Sinclair, who won knighthood for inventing computers that Britons could, at last, afford. He is considered a hero in a nation committed to reviving entrepreneurial spirit: "He has given enormous confidence to everyone," said Kenneth Baker, Britain's former information technology minister. "He has proved that we don't have to lie back and let the Japanese roll over us."

Sinclair has been credited with the invention of the first pocket calculator, the first flat-screen television, and a practical electric car. His companies have sold, directly or under license, more computers than any other company in the world; invented a $200 satellite broadcast-receiver dish; and consistently been at the leading edge of technological innovation.

Sinclair's brilliant mind (he was president of Mensa in the United Kingdom) and his personal style and dynamism have made him a high-tech folk hero. He attracts high-flying scientists and inventors to his new company, Sinclair Research, which has shown consistent innovation and high-caliber performance in market sectors notoriously fraught with hazards. Although one of Sinclair Research's contributions—the C5, an electric car for the urban commuter that cost about $450 and could travel for about 20 miles before needing to be recharged—didn't succeed (in fact, the company folded with debts of 8 million pounds), Sinclair's reputation as an idiosyncratic genius survives. It is notable that most of the major international car companies are working on prototypes of electrically powered cars (Nissan is leading the way in electric-car battery technology).

CEOs can even assume an international role, if they are skilled enough and have developed the requisite following. Robert Edward Turner III, better known as Ted Turner—president and chairman of Turner Broadcasting Systems; founder of Cable News Network (CNN); owner of the Atlanta Hawks and the Atlanta Braves; winner of the America's Cup race; owner of three 5,000-acre plantations, an equally large island off the coast of South Carolina, a Big Sur beach house, and a 10,000-acre ranch in Monterey; recipient of nine honorary degrees; and husband of Jane Fonda—is a case in point.

Turner has been called many things: maniac, jerk, Clark Gable look-alike, visionary, profane, impulsive, optimistic. His flamboyance, brilliance, and contradictions have made him a hero on both the national and international stages. In 1976 he created the nation's first superstation (broadcasting one station across the country via cable). In 1980 he launched CNN, which became the worldwide channel of choice for those eager for the latest news of the 1991 Persian Gulf war.

After meeting Jacques Cousteau during the early 1980s, Turner became an activist in the international peace movement, founding the Better World Society, an international organization devoted to ending the arms race, preserving the environment, and limiting population growth. His genuine passion for the cause of peace persuaded Prince Sadruddin Aga Khan, Jimmy Carter, Russell Peterson, and Gro Harlem Brundtland (former prime minister of Norway) to serve on its board. He organized the Goodwill Games, an off-year, Olympic-style competition held for the first time in Moscow in 1976, which, by some accounts, was an important component in the process of advancing the thaw in the Cold War and selling the concept of capitalism to the Russians. He instituted "World Report," a forum in which he has discussed world peace with the presidents of Nicaragua and Costa Rica as well as with Iranian and Iraqi diplomats. Why has this passion for peace captured his heart? "I just care. I'm deeply concerned. We're destroying the planet, that's all. We can save it. We just have to be the best that we can be, rather than the worst," says Turner, and he carries his associates with him. This passion powers his organization as well as his network of contacts around the world, creating and nourishing his climate for success.

All great organizations distinguish themselves this way—with passion and deeply held beliefs that touch the hearts of employees, customers, and the public alike. The shaping of an appropriate climate for success at Turner Broadcasting and CNN through the impact of actions and beliefs emanating from the CEO is a rare but extraordinary achievement. Its value in enhancing the self-esteem and self-image of the company's employees has therefore been critical in the attainment of their high performance and service levels.

Whether CEOs operate as corporate leaders or as folk or national heroes, their personal values and their commitment to realizing their organization's goals are the keys to their corporation's ultimate destiny and a vital component in creating a climate for success.

The Leader as Manager

The scientific tools of management are merely sterile concepts until they are ignited by the art of leadership that motivates and creates the climate for success. And understanding and applying the crucial distinction between leading and managing is the touchstone for setting corporate climate. The sociologist Max Weber gave us the idea that charismatic leaders launch, build, or reinvigorate new enterprises, but administrators eventually assume the management of them. Therein lies the reason for the rise and decline of great corporations.

———◆———

For the most part our leaders are merely
following out in front; they do but marshal us
the way that we are going.

—Berger Evans

WORKSHEET 4-1:
THE ANALYSIS OF
CULTURAL TENDENCY (ACT)

Corporate North America's hottest buzzword today is *corporate culture*. A veritable swarm of management consultants and gurus perform their patented litmus tests to determine the current status of an organization's cultural climate.

You can administer your own test of corporate climate with the Analysis of Cultural Tendency (ACT) matrix (Figure 4-1), which gives a visual representation of an organization's culture. The vertical scale (labeled "Commitment to People") measures the level of concern declared and demonstrated for fellow human beings by the corporate leadership team. The horizontal scale (labeled "Commitment to Results") measures the level of concern the leadership team declares and demonstrates for performance and results. The matrix is divided into four quadrants, or squares, which represent four different types of corporate culture. Each square is calibrated from 0 to 10.

Paternalistic: This quadrant represents a corporate culture in which management is so dedicated to people and their welfare that any balancing concern for corporate performance is overshadowed. Management is dedicated to ensuring that everyone feels part of a big, happy family; it avoids conflict and ranks the welfare of people above all other considerations.

Darwinian: This quadrant represents the law-of-the-jungle culture. Darwinians look out for number one because they believe that only the fittest can survive. Managers see employees as cannon fodder, simply the means to corporate ends. In the Darwinian culture, when you're hot, you're hot; and when you're not, you're not.

Political: This quadrant represents a culture dedicated neither to people nor to results. There are no rules, so employees must invent them. Since management recognizes no virtue in either empathy or performance, only political in-fighting ensures survival and promotion. In a vacuum of values, people spend their energy on political games, which by their very

142

Figure 4-1 The ACT Matrix

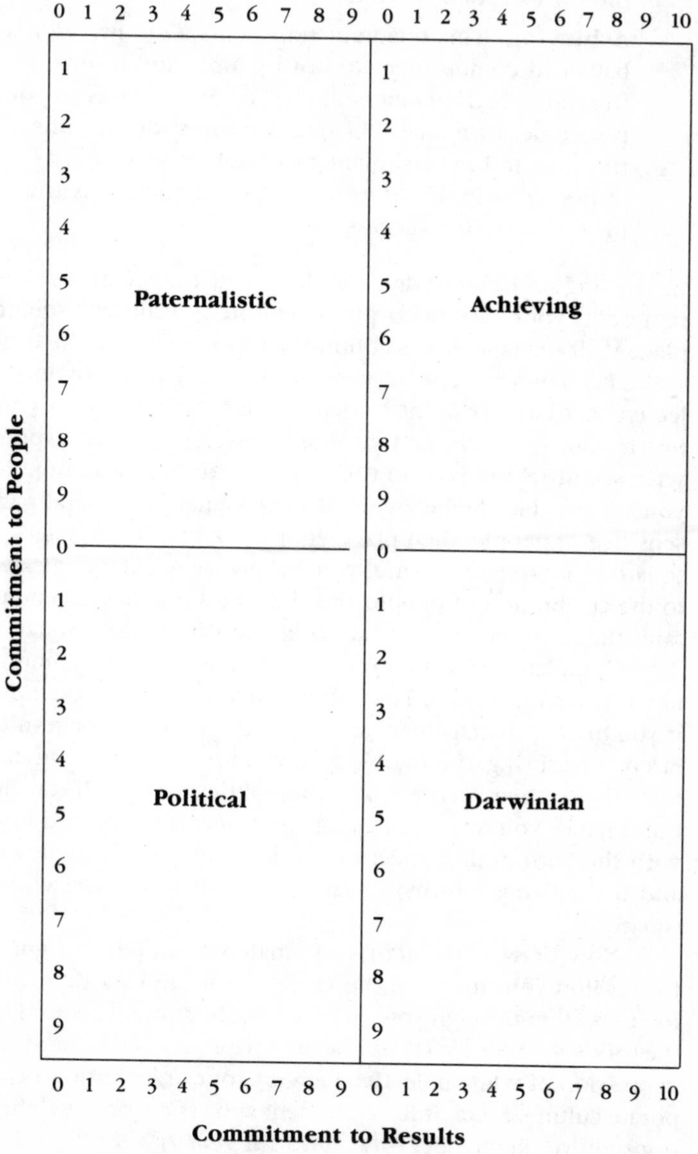

	0 1 2 3 4 5 6 7 8 9	0 1 2 3 4 5 6 7 8 9 10
Commitment to People	1 2 3 4 5 **Paternalistic** 6 7 8 9 0	1 2 3 4 5 **Achieving** 6 7 8 9 0
	1 2 3 4 5 **Political** 6 7 8 9	1 2 3 4 5 **Darwinian** 6 7 8 9
	0 1 2 3 4 5 6 7 8 9	0 1 2 3 4 5 6 7 8 9 10

Commitment to Results

nature are defensive and self-serving. Mayhem is the unhappy result as everyone stabs each other in the back in their frenzy to make themselves look good in the eyes of their masters.

Achieving: This quadrant represents a culture with a balanced commitment to both people and results; to the individual members of the team as well as to corporate performance. This culture most ideally suits the care and nourishment of customer service, entrepreneurship, innovation, and excellence. It is the ideal climate for success.

Using *subjective* judgment, determine the square that best represents your current corporate culture. Within that square, place your management's commitment to people on the 0–10 scale. Remember, we want your *subjective* views, not an objective analysis; we want to determine how you *feel* in your heart, your stomach, and your subconscious! Try to express what scientists call your top-of-mind reaction. If, for example, you believe that the behavior of management is generally insensitive to people, then place your mark at 0 in the Political square. If, on the other hand, you feel management is dedicated to the celebration of people and their personal development, rank the corporate culture at 10 in the Paternalistic square.

Complete the same exercise for management's commitment to results (which is the horizontal scale). For example, if you believe management displays little concern for results, rarely measuring them objectively and seldom giving fair rewards for them, score a 0 in the Political square. If, on the other hand, you feel that management seems concerned *only* with the bottom line (meeting budgets, keeping costs down, and maximizing returns), then score a 10 in the Darwinian square.

Now draw a line across the matrix from left to right at the level of your mark on the vertical scale and another from top to bottom through your mark on the horizontal scale. Mark the spot where the two lines intersect. This position is the visual expression of your subjective view of your organization's corporate culture. Study it for a moment and reflect on the definitions above. Remember, *perception is reality*.

After you have determined which culture most closely represents that of your organization, gather your team around you and ask them to plot the corporate culture using the same techniques described above. Don't disclose your own view at this stage. Remember, *their* observations should be objective and instantaneous too. Your staff will be guarded if they suspect that you'll reward undue frankness with a posting to the North Pole. To encourage scrupulously honest input from your team, offer them a copper-bottomed guarantee that their candor will not be met with reprisals or criticism. (I have conducted this experiment in hundreds of seminars all over the world. Usually, 50% of the respondents select the Achieving square and the other 50% select the other squares.)

Next, ask your staff: What kind of culture would you like to see around here? How can we build a climate for success? Almost everyone will respond by choosing the Achieving culture.

Finally, ask your staff two things: (1) What do you think we need to do to close the gap between the culture that you believe we have and the culture that you would like, so that together we can build a climate for success? (2) Please help me close the gap.

You must be sincere in your efforts to secure the input of your team members. You must convince them that you have a genuine interest in their welfare and in the performance of the organization as a whole. If they believe you, they will be eager to cooperate.

Outstanding organizations owe much of their success to a shared vision and a common set of beliefs and values that glues their people together. From this solid foundation, team spirit and corporate magic soar. It's called the *climate for success*.

Chapter 5

The Motivated Team

A man cannot be comfortable without his own approval.

—Mark Twain

An organization that builds a truly motivated team is rewarded with outstanding performances by everyday people. And we all play a role in building and nourishing that "can-do" attitude with our colleagues, suppliers, and customers which makes an organization hum.

---◆---

One of my clients is in the agricultural chemical business. A very small window of opportunity exists at the beginning of each growing season to apply herbicides and fertilizers. Any snags resulting from application must be fixed quickly. In these circumstances conventional wisdom holds that the sales representative will need to deal with irate farmers, so they are taught how to deal with irate farmers.

But these assumptions can be challenged. Let's pretend that Mother Theresa has joined our sales team. After receiving a call from an irate farmer, Mother Theresa drives out to his farm in her Ford F-150 pickup truck. As she jumps out of the truck the farmer comes striding across the field toward her and notices that the representative is Mother Theresa. Does he hurl expletives at her? Does he vent his anger? Of course not. Although the farmer is the same person, with the same problems, *we* have changed, and therefore we have changed the farmer's behavior. The behavior of others is neither a given nor separate from our own. We can do more than merely react to the behavior of others: We can dramatically and positively change and influence it. We call this phenomenon motivation.

Where motivation is concerned, corporate teams are similar to other "teams," such as those in the fields of sports and music. As we discussed in the last chapter, creating the climate for success is one requisite of leadership. Another is **motivation.** The successful corporation, like the successful sports team or symphony, is *motivated.* Corporate leaders need to know:

1. What inspires individuals to extraordinary achievements

2. What factors account for a highly motivated corporate team

3. How to sustain an exceptional level of individual motivation, thereby maintaining excellent corporate performance

Many modern motivation theories are merely mechanical devices that seek to answer questions like these by treating people as objects, to be exploited and manipulated. But people are not objects, and any attempt to understand them as such—and more important, to change their behavior as such—will fail.

Half-Empty or Half-Full?

We can divide people into two great camps: They are either pessimists or optimists—they either perceive the glass to be half-empty or half-full. Of course, this applies to executives as well: They are either pessimistic or optimistic—or as the social scientists like to say, they're either **Hobbesian** or **Lockean**. These terms are derived from Thomas Hobbes (1588–1679) and John Locke (1632–1704), two English philosophers. Hobbes postulated a social conflict so profound that peace and order could be achieved only under the iron rule of an all-powerful "Leviathan"; Locke believed in a natural social order so nearly perfect that it required a government of only minimal powers and functions.

Hobbes believed that man was inherently evil, greedy, selfish, power seeking, and violent. Locke, on the other hand, believed that man was essentially benign and his antisocial traits a result of malevolent conditioning.

Hobbesian leaders (a virtual oxymoron) have no chance of successfully building the motivated team so necessary to corporate success. Their negative views of the human race—of their employees—preclude their ability to bring out the best in people. Indeed, they would view this as an impossible and fruitless task. All our modern theories of human behavior and our motivational techniques are either useless or downright dangerous when placed in the hands of Hobbesian executives, because they have a high need to exert power, and they meet goals by extracting no more than mechanical compliance from their subordinates. It is the Hobbesian power broker that Eric Hoffer had in mind when he observed that "our sense of power is more vivid when we break a man's spirit than when we win his heart. . . . It is when power is wedded to chronic fear that it becomes formidable." But Baltasar Gracián had the Lockean personality in mind when he pointed out that "the sole advantage of power is that you can do more good."

Leaders with a Lockean, half-full outlook have a high need for achievement; they meet this need by inspiring exceptional performance from their teams. Researchers have found that the dominant motive of most successful, large-corporation executives is the need for power, whereas the dominant motive for entrepreneurial leaders is the need for achievement (see Chapter 11 for a review of this subject). In this distinction lies one of the keys to why entrepreneurial leaders inspire employees and corporate bureaucracies do not.

THE RIGHT STUFF

There is widespread agreement that altering a fundamental belief system is like pushing a car uphill with a rope—it's possible in theory but impossible in practice. We often seek environments that reinforce our ideas, and corporate leaders do the same. Those with Hobbesian outlooks will find it painfully difficult—maybe even impossible—to achieve a Lockean view. Not everyone can be a leader of this sort. In fact, not everyone can be a leader.

Although Western culture would have us believe otherwise, not aspiring to leadership positions is not an admission of weakness or incompetence. We play a pointless game of "chicken" when we assume that all managers are required to lead, as if it were some sort of rite of passage in which they must learn the appropriate "techniques" for leadership. It's dangerous to assume that everyone can acquire leadership skills. Moreover, this assumption ignores the damage done to real people by managers who pretend to lead. Just as we don't require all students of music to become conductors or all painters to become directors of art colleges, we should not expect all managers to become leaders. Some people are temperamentally better equipped to be leaders than others; executives who can recognize this and act upon it do everyone a favor. The characteristics necessary to leadership include high intelligence, emotional maturity, persistence, conscientiousness, extroversion, and inner direction.

Motivational Theories

Many conventional theories of motivation assume a "perfect-state" scenario that says all people will respond to a range of stimuli—in a corporate context, react to supervisory directions and management styles—in certain predictable ways. Behind this is the notion that all humans pass through a hierarchy of needs. Perhaps many do, but since we cannot even agree on what those hierarchical needs are, it seems wise not to be too dogmatic about their universal application. For example, social psychologists Abraham Maslow and Paul Sites identified human needs in quite different ways.

Maslow's Hierarchy of Needs

Self-actualization (personal fulfillment)

Recognition (as an individual)

Status (identity with a group)

Safety (security, health)

Physiological (food, shelter, warmth)

Sites's Human Needs Requiring Fulfillment

Sense of control (rather than mere reaction)

Meaning (deduced from consistent response)

Development and appearance of rationality (avoiding inconsistent response from others)

Distributive justice (matching experience and expectations)

Recognition (to provide approval and encouragement)

Security (to avoid withdrawal from response and stimulus)

Stimulation (to help develop language, customs, and skills)

Consistent response (to help in learning consistent behavior)

Maslow developed his ideas in the 1950s; Sites developed his in the 1970s. Although better versions of these conceptions have not yet emerged, we cannot assume that even if these ideas were right in their day, they apply to the values or describe the needs of contemporary employees. Much has changed. For example, Maslow's notion that the human hierarchy of needs is capped by self-actualization is the product of an era of hedonists—the "me generation." But such self-serving individualism, which contributes so little to the general well-being of the community, belongs to the era of Michael Milken and Donald Trump; it has much less relevance to today's values and therefore little merit as a motivational theory for the new millenium.

The Optimum-Potential Theory

We all have the potential to display genius. One might view this as an **optimum-potential theory.** In fact, if every craft and occupation were cross-referenced with every known skill or talent, we should all find that particular talent that is uniquely suited to our personal and intellectual capabilities. That we haven't the means to do this commits most of us to careers (and therefore lives) of imperfection and sometimes even misalignment. Rockefeller, Picasso, Isaac Newton, Thomas Watson, Nijinsky, and Shakespeare are a few examples of those fortunate enough to find the perfect match between latent skill and professional aspiration. This is what the optimum-potential theory is all about. Genius might be simply defined as being the unusual but coincidental discovery of a perfect fit between aspiration and talent—a unique fit that lies dormant in each and every one of us. People who love what they do have reached that blissful state.

Matching individual talents and aspirations with organizational and task needs is the mark of successful, modern corporate leaders. Such leaders seek to light that potential fire of genius within the belly of each employee. The great leader is a great motivator, and the greatest motivation is often achieved by a leader who shows others how to discover and capitalize on their potential.

THREE LEADERSHIP ATTITUDES

Before you can create your own motivated team, you should be aware of three managerial attitudes that you'll probably encounter at the blueprint stage (see Table 5-1).

First, meet the **traditional manager,** the most Hobbesian of the bunch. He or she can usually be found supervising a disgruntled and unmotivated group of employees, who are totally preoccupied with getting out of the department or the company.

Next, meet the **human relations manager,** usually a "reformed" Hobbesian with a passable but unspectacular track record in interpersonal skills and people management. This individual believes that all people have similar motivational urges and aspirations. Human relations managers emphasize the employees' contribution and sense of usefulness to the organization.

Finally, there's the **human resources manager,** a true Lockean. These individuals are more consultants and coaches than managers. They constantly seek better motivational techniques, theories, and ideas. Moreover, they're too sensitive to the emotions and aspirations of people to be mechanical or patronizing (unfortunate traits of human relations types). Human resources managers view members of their team as individuals possessing untapped and often unidentified resources. Their leadership

Table 5-1 Patterns of Leadership Attitudes

Traditional Model	Human Relations Model	Human Resources Model
Assumptions	**Assumptions**	**Assumptions**
1 Work is inherently distasteful to most people.	1 People want to feel useful and important.	1 Work is not inherently distasteful. People want to contribute to meaningful goals that they have helped establish.
2 What they do is less important than what they earn for doing it.	2 People desire to belong and to be recognized as individuals.	2 Most people can exercise far more creative, responsible self-direction and self-control than their present jobs demand.
3 Few want or can handle work that requires creativity, self-direction, or self-control.	3 These needs are more important than money in motivating people to work.	
Policies	**Policies**	**Policies**
1 The manager's basic task is to closely supervise and control his subordinates.	1 The manager's basic task is to make each worker feel useful and important.	1 The manager's basic task is to make use of his "untapped" human resources.
2 He must break tasks down into simple, repetitive, easily learned operations.	2 He should keep his subordinates informed and listen to their objections to his plans.	2 He must create an environment in which all members may contribute to the limits of their ability.

3 He must establish detailed work routines and procedures, and enforce these firmly but fairly.

Expectations
1 People can tolerate work if the pay is decent and the boss is fair.
2 If tasks are simple enough and people are closely controlled, they will produce up to standard.

3 The manager should allow his subordinates to exercise some self-direction and self-control on routine matters.

Expectations
1 Sharing information with subordinates and involving them in routine decisions will satisfy their basic needs to belong and to feel important.
2 Satisfying these needs will improve morale and reduce resistance to formal authority—subordinates will "willingly cooperate."

3 He must encourage full participation on important matters, continually broadening subordinate self-direction and control.

Expectations
1 Expanding subordinate influence, self-direction, and self-control will lead to direct improvements in operating efficiency.
2 Work satisfaction may improve as a "by-product" of subordinates making full use of their resources.

Source: Raymond Miles, "Leadership Attitudes Among Public Health Officers," *American Journal of Public Health*, Vol. LVI, No. 12. Reprinted with permission.

styles are highly consultative because they respect the opinions of those they *lead* (rather than manage). The consequence is an atmosphere of trust, leading to high team morale.

Assembling Your Own Motivated Team

Although the first prerequisite for assembling a motivated team is the presence of a Lockean leader, the second is the understanding that motivation is **people centered,** *not* task centered. Our left-hemisphere preoccupation with the task rather than with the human being doing it is one of the single largest impediments to unlocking human potential.

If people feel that they are being treated as a means to an end, as mere cogs in the corporate machine (the squirt-money-on-them-they'll-go-faster school of management), they will respond accordingly—that is, minimally. But if they believe that their leaders are genuinely interested in them, their problems, their lives, and their dreams, they will reward their leaders with outstanding performance and friendship. Mary Kay Ash, the architect of the worldwide cosmetics firm that bears her name, puts it simply: "Praise people to success!"

Motivation, then, requires a right-hemisphere focus from the corporate leader, and it's such a rarity that it is instantly identifiable.

For an organization to be successful, its needs and those of its employees should always overlap. The greater the overlap, the more highly motivated the employee will be. The larger the gap, the less motivated the employee. The process of achieving the powerful effects of such an overlap is started by considering the needs of the employee first—a totally unconventional approach, which I call the **motivational-circle theory.**

Figure 5-1 The Motivational-Circle Theory: Synthesizing Corporate and Employee Needs

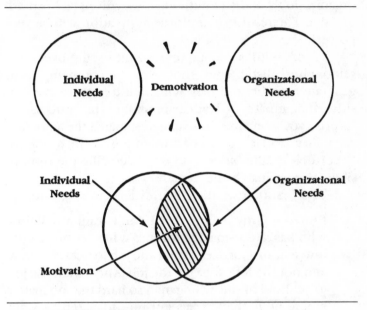

THE MOTIVATIONAL-CIRCLE THEORY

Think of the needs of the individual as one circle and the needs of the organization as another (see Figure 5-1). Traditionally, employees are told what their responsibilities are and what rewards they will receive if they successfully execute them. But this only recognizes the needs in one of the circles—those of the organization. A more enlightened approach is to start the process in the other circle, by asking employees to describe their needs. Let us suppose that an employee, Dave, describes his financial goals and a number of others, such as a company-sponsored program to upgrade skills and a 6-month sabbatical in 3 years. In this way you are now informed about the needs and the motivators of Dave, which puts you in a better position to describe the responsibilities that you feel would fairly justify these rewards. Through negotiation you will be able to strike a contract, and the needs of both circles—the organization's and the individual's—will have been addressed. The resulting employee motivation will be very powerful.

Faced with such an opportunity, employees are seldom unrealistic. They know that the company has to generate a profit, and they will want to reward the sensitive and empathetic leader. Sometimes this process can surprise you—you may have underestimated the ambition, capability, and capacity of the employee in question. Nevertheless, all you need to do is describe the responsibilities that match the demand.

The U.S. industrialist Charles F. Kettering said:

> I often tell my people that I don't want any fellow who has a job working for me. What I want is a fellow whom a job has. I want the job to get the fellow and not the fellow to get the job. And I want the job to get hold of this young man so hard that no matter where he is the job has got him for keeps. I want that job to have him in its clutches when he goes to bed at night, and in the morning I want that same job to be sitting at the foot of his bed telling him it's time to get up and go to work. And when a job gets a fellow that way, he's sure to amount to something.

In other words, Kettering wanted his employees to be inspired.

The Motivation Check

Prospective employees look for motivational signals in your company when they read your recruitment advertisements, call your switchboard, converse with your support staff, attend the first employment interview, and meet other corporate staff members. They want to know whether your organization and its leadership represent an opportunity for them to experience the motivation that Kettering described. Would-be employees are quick to pick up the scent of the answer to the burning question, What is it like around here?

Besides employees, people outside the corporation try to gauge its motivational spirit. The corporate leader with moxie ensures that a motivating, employee-centered ethos reaches out to the corporation's farthest contact point. Union members, suppliers, customers, the media, competitors, industry associations, political groups, relatives and friends of employees, and many others have a stake in whether the spirit is friendly or hostile.

I try to determine this whenever I acquire a new client. I always ask a lot of questions and meet as many people in the organization as possible so I can get up to speed quickly. I also set in motion a quick litmus test, so that I can learn more about the organization and get a behind-the-scenes perspective.

Some time ago, I was doing some consulting on corporate strategy for a major international organization. Shortly after our first meeting, I gave the president some feedback about how I perceived the company. He was amazed. He couldn't understand how I picked up on the corporate climate so quickly. My secret is to look at four key things.

What is the condition of the washrooms? It might seem an odd place to measure corporate climate, but the corporate can is one of the first places I visit. What I want to know is whether management respects its employees by giving them the best facilities possible. If I find a dirty washroom where the soap dispensers are empty, the toilet paper is of the lowest grade, and the faucets and basins are the chintziest on the market, then I know that management is cheap, cutting costs and corners where the public can't see. But if management makes the washrooms bright and airy, invests in deodorizers, keeps the soap dispensers filled, provides a hygienic hand-drying system, supplies a copy of the daily newspaper, puts a rose in a vase somewhere, and otherwise decorates the facilities, then I know the management cares enough to pay attenti onto even the smallest things. If you want to take your washroom research one step further, occupy a stall for 30 minutes to find out what people really talk about when they think no one is listening! Whenever I address a conference, I scoot out as fast as I can to the washroom, after I finish signing books and selling tapes. Hidden in this private space, I obtain instant feedback on what people *really* thought about my presentation. Only once did I get hoist by my own petard—I forgot to shut off my wireless microphone!

What are they saying about the competition?   Companies in trouble usually blame the competition; they make themselves feel better by criticizing their competitors. In a demoralized organization, people will say, "Oh, their product is not as up-to-date as ours, and they have terrible problems with delivery. Our prices are better than theirs, and I hear staff turnover and morale are really bad over there." The well-motivated organization will probably say something like, "You know, the one thing I've always admired about them is the attention they pay to writing really good user's manuals. In most areas I think we are superior to them, but in this particular aspect I think we have something to learn from them. We're working on new user's manuals that will eventually be better than theirs." The well-known platform speaker Zig Ziglar says that when you point a finger at someone, three point back at you. Excessive criticism of the competition is a sure sign of insecurity.

What is the reception area like?   There are two kinds of corporate reception areas: those that intimidate and repel and those that embrace and welcome. The former tend to be hostile, cold, ugly, and unfriendly. They are staffed by the unwilling and uncaring, who lack telephone technique and regard visitors as an unwelcome intrusion into their lives and their novels. These reception areas are undecorated, crudely finished, and utilitarian. On the other hand, the warm and friendly reception area is staffed by one of the most talented (and well-paid) people in the organization. This is the person who has the responsibility for making the very first (and often therefore the longest lasting) impression on visitors. There are flowers, carpets, a visitor's telephone, comfortable furniture, reading material, comfort facilities close to hand, and refreshments. Companies that care for customers will invest in them—and they know that everybody who enters their reception area is a potential customer, even if they are not visiting the organization for that reason. Companies that declare that they are customer-driven but provide inferior reception facilities are hypocrites.

How do they answer their telephones? A company that pays attention to the needs of its customers knows that callers don't want to be kept waiting—so it establishes a policy that ensures that no telephone in the entire organization will be left unanswered after two rings. Nor will it allow the telephone to be answered with anything sloppy, such as, "ABC Widget Company, please hold," . . . click. Instead, it coaches all employees in the art of telephone friendship—because callers can hear smiles just as well as frowns. A caller's telephone number is taken early on in the conversation, in case they accidentally get disconnected. Employees are coached to promote the organization, its services, and products and to listen for buying signals and clues. It invests in state-of-the-art telephone equipment that allows call transfers, call waiting, call forwarding, and teleconferencing to occur quickly and effectively.

Whenever I see that management has not coached its people in telephone technique, I realize that it hasn't made a really serious commitment to the needs of its employees and customers. And whenever I see an overworked and harassed switchboard operator, with dated equipment, I know that both employees and callers are suffering unnecessary stress—and that management hasn't considered their needs. I therefore conclude that this is an organization run by inconsiderate managers.

Motivation from Unlikely Sources

It's easy to see how employees can be motivated by those friendly to the company—but not-so-friendly sources can be motivational too. For example, Manpower's chief accountant often met with his counterpart in another company in our industry to exchange ideas and technical information. After a number of these encounters, he confided his view of the competition to me: He was convinced that we had nothing to fear from them because, as he said at the time, "We're dedicated and committed to our goals, we have a corporate purpose, we're a strong team, and we're passionate about what we do. But they're just doing a job." The contrast between Manpower's philosophy and strategy and those of a competitor acted as a powerful motivator for this man.

Another source of motivation is corporate image. At a planning meeting with our advertising agency, the agency chief wanted to know the purpose of the proposed campaign. We responded that not only did we want to increase our revenues and attract new customers, we also wanted our public and our employees to be associated with *award-winning campaigns,* advertising that would be talked about. We wanted our employees to bathe in the sun of successful advertising—and that's what we got. Our ads were framed and hung proudly on walls all over the world—even by our competitors!

Being seen as the "best-of-the-breed" is a motivational turn-on for our team and a demoralizing embarrassment for the other companies in the industry. Winning the advertising industry's most coveted awards helped us to gain a psychological advantage, keeping our competitors off balance by forcing them to react—and it's tough to score goals when you are defending your own goal.

Even when they appear threatening, outsiders can be motivating. In 1986 C.P.C. International was a conservative marketer of corn-based products and other grocery items, including Skippy peanut butter, Hellman's mayonnaise, and Thomas' English muffins. The company invested most of its excess cash flow in modernizing its plants, and it turned in a satisfactory but unimaginative performance. But when Ronald O. Perelman came along and posed a takeover threat, C.P.C. was galvanized into action. It sold off its low-margin commodity business to concentrate on its higher-margin grocery lines. It used the capital from the sale to rejuvenate its brands, acquire over 100 new ones that complemented them, boost advertising expenditure by 50%, and extend existing lines. Sales took off, passing $5 billion for the first time. Return on equity moved from the 19% of the mid-1980s to 32.5%, and the value of C.P.C. stock tripled. Better management, a sharper focus, and a refreshed leadership approach were the result of what at first appeared to be a dire threat.

All too often we consider motivation only in terms of employees. But we can be motivated by outsiders as well—and our motivation can play a pivotal role in winning the confidence of new customers and building the business. Therefore, to motivate your team, consider your competitors and any other external contacts, especially those that appear hostile. In this way, managers with moxie exploit the potential of the external environment to contribute positively to corporate motivation.

Staying "Up" When You're "Down"

Occasionally, it seems that all the news is bad. In periods like this, it's a real challenge to keep your team motivated. But it's vital to excise motivational rot quickly, and at almost any cost, because a severely demoralized corporate staff will suffocate and neutralize all other corporate attributes, leading to atrophy and ultimately to the destruction of the corporation. The CEO is responsible for maintaining corporate strategies that keep motivation strong at all times, even in the face of catastrophe.

Consider the now-famous case of Tylenol. In 1982 seven people died after taking Extra-Strength Tylenol capsules purchased at stores in the Chicago area. The product had been poisoned, and panicky purchasers deserted Tylenol (one of Johnson & Johnson's top money makers) in droves. It was widely predicted that the company would have to remove Tylenol permanently from the market. But instead, the company dealt with this catastrophe with cool and sensitive pragmatism. It redesigned the package to make it tamper-proof, agreed to take back unused product, and offered incentives when the repackaged product was launched. As a result, the company's market share rebounded to its leading position. Many people had written Tylenol off after the horrible events in Chicago, but companies with moxie, like Johnson & Johnson, motivate customers to maintain their loyalty and employees to dig the company out of holes when the occasion demands it.

The chance to exert leadership often arrives unannounced. In the wee hours of March 24, 1989, 25 years to the day after the Alaska earthquake, the supertanker *Exxon Valdez* ripped open her hull on Bligh Reef, spewing 1.26 million barrels of oil into the chilly waters of Alaska's breathtakingly beautiful Prince William Sound. The state government's prediction that the salmon harvest would climb from 13 million to 43 million fish in the 1989–1990 season was dashed on that reef, and half of Prince William Sound's 15,000 sea otters received a death sentence. The *Exxon Valdez* became the latest member of an infamous family of names that includes Bhopal, Chernobyl, *Amoco Cadiz,* and Three-Mile Island.

Why did it happen? became the question asked by many—but was it the right question to ask? Accidents like these will continue to happen, although let's hope infrequently. It goes with our energy-hungry life-style. The real question is, Why was it handled the way it was? The problem wasn't any shortage of money, equipment, or facilities.

Corporate culture is maddeningly difficult to define and more difficult still to foster. Yet the *Exxon Valdez* tragedy exposes the critical role an organization's culture plays in shaping the outcome of events and maintaining a motivated team. The fundamental beliefs and values of the leadership team directly shape a company's reaction to unexpected crises. One must surmise that the largest oil company in the world had no prior deeply held passion for or financial commitment to the safety and well-being of the community of Valdez, the $83-million salmon-fishing industry, or the wildlife of Prince William Sound.

The real problem was not money but *motivational will*. Alyeska, a consortium of seven oil companies (Exxon, British Petroleum, Arco, Mobil, Unocal, Amerada Hess, and Phillips Petroleum), had all the facilities necessary to control the spill. Although the seven partners had an agreement with the Alaskan government to put up booms to trap the oil within 5 hours, Alaska governor Steve Copper said, "There was almost nothing on the sea for the first 18 hours." During that Saturday and Sunday, the oil spill was no larger than 4 square miles; by Monday 70 mile-an-hour winds prevented planes carrying dispersant until the afternoon, and the spill grew to obscene proportions.

Many corporate Neros fiddle with bureaucracy and paper shuffling while a crisis burns. Others pursue a damn-the-torpedoes attitude, taking whatever action they believe to be in the best interests of their community, regardless of the risk to their own careers.

Some corporate management teams read the vibes of their environmental and social constituents with such sensitivity that they develop contingency plans to protect against potential crises. The reaction of Johnson & Johnson to the Tylenol scare in 1982 is a copybook example of a motivated team operating at its best under pressure. If Lawrence Rawl (the CEO of Exxon) and his management team had immediately executed such a plan, the *Exxon Valdez* disaster would have been news for only 24 hours instead of for years. But Rawl kept his head down for an entire week after the spill. When he eventually did communicate with the media, he didn't even visit Valdez.

What kind of attitude does Exxon have toward the selection, quality, motivation, and training of its key people? The 42-year-old captain, Joseph Hazelwood, could not legally drive a car because of drunken-driving convictions—but Exxon management deemed him capable of commanding a $125 million tanker the size of three football fields. When the *Exxon Valdez* foundered on Bligh Reef, the vessel was being steered by the third mate Gregory Cousins (who had no license to navigate through those waters) because, it is alleged, Hazelwood was too intoxicated to steer the tanker. Hazelwood (who had entered an Exxon alcohol-abuse program in 1985 and had subsequently been reinstated as a captain of Exxon's tankers) was indicted shortly after the oil spill on three misdemeanor charges of intoxication at the time of the accident. According to transcripts of audiotapes between the U.S. Coast Guard and the *Exxon Valdez,* the captain may have worsened the spill by attempting to rock the tanker off the reef. When asked what he would now do differently, Rawl responded, "That man would not be piloting the ship. There's no question that there was bad judgment involved in even putting a person with a critical skill back in that kind of work. It is pretty clear that [we] have to tighten those things up." Some empathetic corporate management teams display their thoughtfulness and concern for environmental and social issues *before* rather than after crises. And when Rawl was later asked if he learned something from the Tylenol and Perrier recalls, he replied flippantly, "We tried to recall the oil but it didn't hear us."

The key questions to be asked about the *Exxon Valdez* disaster are: Were Exxon's leaders purposeful in the face of bureaucracy? Did they have workable and effective plans to protect the community in which they lived and worked from any likely disaster? Did they show that they cared? Did they have first-class programs to select, screen, coach, and motivate people? In other words, did they lead? And did they provide the motivational climate for others to lead? These are the things we call corporate culture and, as we have seen, they shape events.

◆

All companies go through periods when the wheels seem to come off the corporate machine. At Manpower we had our share over the years: a team of technicians kidnapped in Northern Ireland; thieves who blasted their way through our Stoke-on-Trent office with a shotgun; our Cape Town office firebombed; violent riots in our Iranian offices followed by nationalization; the kidnapping and disappearance of our Nigerian franchisee. In almost all these cases, the responsibility for dealing with the problem belonged exclusively to the local managers, who rose superbly to the occasion. (Top management kept in close touch, acting as a sounding board for local management.) In discussions after the dangers had passed, our managers observed that hands-on crisis management was a unique experience builder. Additionally, because Manpower's leadership demonstrated unquestioningly their total confidence in the company's employees, the staff was heartened—and further motivated. The Tylenol case is taught at hundreds of business schools around the world as a model of preparation and cool action taken in the face of danger—and being motivated and self-assured were the keys.

Remuneration as a Motivator

The very first thing I would do as the new CEO of most organizations would be to throw out any system of salary levels and compensation planning. Remuneration is earned by individuals, not by levels; individuals are motivated one at a time, not in job-level classifications. The reward package or remuneration program is an integral and major part of creating a motivated team. As the late Frederick Herzberg pointed out, the absence of what he called "hygiene factors" (organizational policy and rules; management style and controls; retirement and sickness policies; and pay and recognition of status) would impede motivation. Although their absence is frequently demotivational, they are *not* the most effective motivators. What works better are the *motivation factors,* and these tend to be nonfinancial (*achievement:* making a meaningful contribution; *recognition:* praise and feedback; *advancement:* growth and new challenges; *interest:* practicing skills and using intelligence; and *responsibility:* authority for a task or goal). The rules are simple.

Link pay to performance only.   Performance is the *only* criterion on which to make judgments concerning the levels of, or changes to, compensation. Age, seniority, nepotism, number of dependents, union parity, qualifications, exam results, and other artificial norms are the bane of motivational efforts.

Too frequently, there is scant relationship between performance and rewards. The CEO of General Dynamics, William Anders, announced a loss of $578 million for 1990 and a plan to lay off 27,000 employees while simultaneously being awarded an incentive option package that, in 4 short months, earned him $4 million in paper profits plus an opportunity to double his $800,000 salary if the company's stock rose to $10. In 1990 Robert C. Stempel, chairman and CEO of General Motors, took a drop in pay from $1,400,000 to $1,000,000, as a slap on the wrist for creating $4 billion in losses at the company he leads. But when the members of the California Public Employees Retirement System learned that the compensation of ITT's CEO, Rand V. Araskog, had been boosted by 103% (to $11.4 million) in 1990, just as the firm's profits plunged 67% in a quarter, they blew a fuse: As owners of 1.15 million shares in the company, they felt they had a right to close the gap between compensation and reward and threatened to vote against the reelection of the firm's directors unless they received a satisfactory explanation. Across the state, others are balking at these exorbitant and undeserved rewards. The Bank of America froze executive salaries. After his company's earnings plunged 43%, L.A. Gear's chairman, Robert Y. Greenberg, volunteered to work without pay until the bottom line improved satisfactorily. At Bank of America, at least, linking pay with performance appears to be working: It is now the most profitable bank in the industry.

In the book he cowrote with Shintaro Ishihara, *The Japan That Can Say No,* Sony Chairman Akio Morita asserts that "the income gap between American and Japanese business executives is astounding." Describing how American executives get fired for ruining their corporations but are rewarded with fabulous separation payments, he laments the lack of connection between performance and reward: "Even though the corporation may stall or crash, the executive is equipped with his 'golden parachute' and is thereby guaranteed to land safely and comfortably," a practice he describes as an "outrageous system."

One-third of all U.S. firms whose white-collar employees enjoy some form of bonus or incentive program report that they *don't work*. This, I believe, is because we reward *A* and expect *B*. By this I mean that we frequently reward for length of service, position, title, attaining objectives, reaching sales targets, making budget, reducing expenses—but almost never for customer service, quality, or building long-term relationships and partnerships with customers—the kinds of actions that fashion great organizations over the long run. GTE's California unit spent $170,000 to train its customer-service representatives to emphasize service over speed; yet the company continued to evaluate its employees according to the time they took to handle each call!

The kind of remuneration programs I like best—and the kind we design for our clients—are those which are determined, to a large degree, by the company's customers. When employees know that their remuneration will not be determined exclusively by the company but by the person who is the reason for the company's existence—the customer—everyone gets the message. The customer knows the company intends to take care of the customer as a precondition of taking care of its employees. **Customer-based compensation programs** (CBCs) reflect a true customer-driven philosophy. And employees understand that their rewards are inextricably tied to customer satisfaction. This represents true relevance in remuneration goals. Everyone now "gets it," and quality and customer service cease to be merely the latest buzzwords. Under this system, when employees ask their customers how they can exceed their needs and then successfully do so, everyone wins. (For more about CBCs, see Chapter 9.)

Provide the kinds of compensation the employee wants. Compensation is not a synonym for cash. The term should describe any reward the employee wants and that the company is legally able to provide. If you want to motivate an employee and that employee wants wire wheels on the company car, three lunches a week at the Pierre, and a subscription to the *New Yorker* and *Popular Mechanics*—providing the tax man is happy—we should happily comply. The accounting gets a little messy, and the payroll department will squawk at such administrative inconveniences. But the company's payroll program was not designed to meet the administrative needs of the payroll department staff, it was designed to meet the remuneration needs of the most important asset of the organization—its employees. You must first find the right compensation system(s) and then, as with every other matter, adjust administration and staff functions to fit. This is sometimes called the **cafeteria approach** to compensation, because employees are able to select options from a wide menu provided by the firm. Motivators love it; bureaucrats abhor it.

Since employees disperse their remuneration individually, as they see fit, compensation should be tailored to each employee's individual requirements. It is intriguing that we are so eager to customize our products and services so that they precisely meet (or better still, exceed) the needs of external customers but consider it unnecessary to treat our internal customers—our employees —in exactly the same way. Every single human has a unique pattern of motivation. No standard compensation plan can cover this diversity. Therefore, it stands to reason that there should be as many remuneration programs as there are employees—and the standardized salary-level system, together with the "one-size-fits-all" incentive program, should be consigned to the round file.

Avoid employee stress over personal finances.   Employees worried about money will be counterproductive: This can affect company morale and ultimately customer service and quality. Prudent and caring leaders offer professional counseling services to employees with financial problems or aspirations. Clearly, team members pull their weight better when they are concentrating on what they are doing rather than on the spiraling costs of their mortgages.

Institute a profit-sharing program.   Perhaps one of the explanations for corporate America's anemic profits is the lack of any real *sense of ownership* on the part of their CEOs. Recent data shows that the chief executives of America's 120 largest companies own a feeble 0.037 of their employer's stock. *All* employees, not just the CEO, should be able to—indeed encouraged to—obtain a financial interest in the organization through profit sharing, so that they have a stake in the future success of the corporation. The opportunity to acquire long-term wealth should be part of the attraction.

Negotiate a risk/reward ratio with each employee. For example, in a commission-only agreement, the reward should be proportionately higher, since the company has no fixed salary overhead and the employee is taking most of the risk. Conversely, employees who do not share in the fortunes of the corporation (up and down) take fewer risks and cannot expect the same proportional rewards as those who do.

Offer creative systems of remuneration.   Employees will reward and respect leaders who offer creative options. Some imaginative approaches include encouraging managers and other employees to undertake work at home on a fees-for-services or assignment basis rather than wages and entering into subcontracting arrangements with employees on a project-by-project basis.

Another option is a value-added remuneration program, which is one of the fairest methods of encouraging employees to participate in the fortunes of the company. A well-conceived value-added compensation plan is one that is made accessible to *all* employees, involves them in the determination of corporate budgets, and ultimately establishes and then achieves the company's planned revenue. The amount of the added value to be paid to the employees is subject to negotiation; however, there should be only one corporate-wide formula that applies to everyone, from the CEO to the janitor. The company's revenues should be published regularly, so that all employees know where they stand. Staff and management should be asked to frequently submit suggestions for increasing the added value. (See Chapter 10 for a more detailed discussion of value-added theories and their application.)

Executives are beginning to realize that reward systems work best when aligned with corporate objectives. In a study of 200 chief executive officers, compensation specialists Towers, Perrin, Forster, and Crosby found that only 37% of the CEOs' remuneration was accounted for by base pay; other incentives accounted for 54% and the remaining 9% came from benefits. Another study, undertaken by Hewitt Associates, showed that a handsome 52% addition to base pay was earned by the *Fortune* 500 CEOs receiving bonuses.

The importance of remuneration as a motivating tool is often downplayed by management practitioners and academics alike, but the evidence suggests that rewards of all kinds are vital as a spur to creativity. It is well documented that achievement is a greater motivator than money for most entrepreneurs (we shall review this more thoroughly in Chapter 11), but this does not mean that financial rewards are unimportant. Most entrepreneurs probably appreciate the opportunity to decide this issue for themselves.

In the 1980s we saw many CEOs receiving exorbitant amounts of money. In 1982 Frederick W. Smith, chairman of Federal Express, was paid no salary but instead received "bonuses" to the tune of $414,000 and "long-term income" amounting to $51,130,000, for a whop-

ping total of $51,544,000. In the same year, Chairman
Charles P. Lazarus and Executive Vice President W. John
Devine of Toys R Us earned $43,773,000 and $15,431,000,
respectively—hardly the sort of numbers paid to executives who are not motivated by money! In 1984 the
total compensation for some of the leading entrepreneurial lights continued to be impressive: $22.8 million for
T. Boone Pickens, Jr. of Mesa Petroleum and $18.1 million
for Humana's David A. Jones. In 1990 Time Warner's
Steven J. Ross earned $78.1 million, UAL's Stephen M. Wolf
scooped up $18.3 million, Apple Computer's John Sculley
earned $17.7 million, and Reebok's Paul B. Fireman pulled
down $14.8 million. T. J. Rogers, founder and CEO of
Cypress Semiconductor, runs a company in which
everyone gets the same bonuses, "from the receptionist
to myself"; and compared to the previous examples of
largesse, Rogers is a piker—he is paid $250,000 in salary,
adding, "When I look at overpaid executives, I feel like
a New England Protestant minister watching Jimmy Swag-
gart on TV." Jugi Tandon, founder of Tandon Corporation, the leading U.S. manufacturer of disk drives for
microcomputers, boasts that he has 60 millionaires working for him, one of whom was a former assembly-line
worker whose stock is now valued at several million
dollars. Tandon himself owns a significant portion of Tandon equity—and after indulging his penchant for fancy
automobiles (11 cars including a Rolls-Royce and a Lam-
borghini) on his 20-acre estate, he retires to his 30-room
mansion at the end of the day. Clearly, money does
motivate some people! (Interestingly, Tandon epitomizes
the cafeteria system of remuneration.)

But concern over the lavishness of compensation at
the top of America's major corporations is being heard
more frequently every day. The total 1990 compensation
of Time Warner's Steven J. Ross was 2½ times greater than
the combined earnings of 600 employees laid off in the
magazine division, earning him the sobriquet "The Prince

of Pay." In 1980 the average CEO in the largest companies earned $624,996, 42 times the pay of the ordinary worker. Ten years later this had mushroomed to $1,952,800, or 85 times that of the factory worker!

Change in Compensation 1980–1990

CEO	up 212%
Teacher	up 95%
Engineer	up 73%
Factory worker	up 53%
Earnings per share of Standard and Poor's 500	up 78%

In Table 5-2 research conducted by Sibson shows how wage disparities grew in the United States during the 1980s.

Table 5-2   Growing Wage Disparity

	CEO Total Compensation	White-Collar-Worker Index	Hourly-Production-Worker Index
1979	100	100	100
1980	118	109	109
1981	135	120	119
1982	153	131	127
1983	157	140	132
1984	185	149	137
1985	207	158	142
1986	224	167	147
1987	250	177	153
1988	279	186	157
Compound Annual Increase	**12.1%**	**7.2%**	**5.2%**

In contrast, in 1927 the average Japanese CEO earned more than 100 times the total compensation of an entry-level college graduate but by 1989 this had dropped to less than 8 to 1. Says Ralph V. Whitworth, president of the United Shareholder's Association, "We're getting more letters from shareholders expressing outrage over pay. With profits falling, executive pay is getting a new focus." The message is that although a handsome executive-remuneration package is a key motivational factor for a great number of people, if not handled sensitively by the leadership team, it can turn into a *de*motivator for the rest of the employees. The implication for the firm's fortunes down the road (and therefore the compensation of the leadership team) is obvious.

THE REMUNERATION EQUATION

When an employee and his or her manager agree on a compensation plan, they also agree on the results that the company expects in return. The terms of this agreement are negotiable, but once agreement is reached, a moral contract exists. The company is not morally entitled to reopen the negotiations unless both sides of the agreement are up for reconsideration. If the results achieved exceed the bargain that has been struck, the compensation should be adjusted in order to maintain the integrity of the risk/reward ratio. This is done not simply by increasing the employee's pay, but by recognizing the employee's achievements and performance and offering the cafeteria selection of compensation options. This course of action forces corporate leaders to review employee performance regularly if they are to stay abreast of results. It also requires executives to review the achievements of employees, thereby providing and obtaining valuable feedback. In this way, corporate leaders maintain equilibrium between income and reward, and employees experience a sense of fairness and recognition.

Leadership 101

Throughout this book I have argued that we over-complicate the art of leadership. I like to illustrate the *simplicity* of leadership (note that I did not say *easiness*) with an exercise I call "Leadership 101."

First, consider this question: How do you lead a great organization? As with all elegant ideas, the answer is astonishingly simple.

Suppose somebody were to ask you to describe your perception of the ideal organization, the perfect environment in which to work. I suspect you would probably respond with something like the following:

To work with fun, interesting, and caring people

To work in an attractive, well-equipped, and friendly environment

To do work that has meaning (for me personally) and honor (in the eyes of the public)

To understand how my work makes a difference in the lives of customers; to be directly connected with the joy of that achievement

To work in a culture that encourages and rewards outstanding quality

To be appreciated and respected by management

To work with leaders who listen

To be praised for positive contributions

To be inspired, stretched, and motivated

To be paid fairly

To be freed from unnecessary bureaucracy and trivial politics

To be a member of a team characterized by mutual trust and integrity

To enhance self-esteem through work

To receive the coaching, development, and tools necessary to excel

To wake up in the morning feeling enthusiastic about work and raring to go

To be offered appropriate opportunities as they occur

Almost anyone would produce a list that was similar. Which tells us that followers have an exceedingly good grasp of what they want from their leaders.

Now the question is, Why aren't leaders listening? Let's try another question: What would your employees answer if asked the same question? A similar wish-list, don't you think? So it really is this simple—leadership is the art of inspiring your employees and providing them with the same motivational environment that you seek from your own leader.

You may well be thinking that it just isn't this easy— that we must consider many other factors, like taxation, legislative imperatives, salary levels, comparable practice in the market, and so on. Of course, it is necessary to work within some parameters, but let's choose the right ones. When it comes to leadership and motivation, *the employee is the customer.* With external customers, we build our destinies on identifying needs and then exceeding them. Why wouldn't we do the same with internal customers? Leadership, it seems, is no more than asking people to describe the ideal components of their occupations, the nature and characteristics of the people with whom they work, and the raison d'être for their tasks—and then meeting or, better still, exceeding these aspirations, just as we strive to do with external customers.

Fine-Tuning the Motivated Team

Corporations are like sport cars: A little fine-tuning of the engine—the motivated team—is essential if it is to be maintained in tip-top running order. Next is a selection of

additional creative, workable ideas honed from experiences at Manpower and consulting assignments to
help build your motivated team.

1. Treat the *personnel department* with circumspec-
tion to prevent the buildup of a bureaucratic empire that
can impede the task of the operating executive. CEOs *are*
the personnel department. In enlightened organizations,
they acquire advanced skills as highly knowledgeable
human resource managers, and they regularly upgrade
these skills.

2. In order to satisfy some rather obscure rationale,
many companies operate a policy of *mandatory retirement* for employees of a certain age. In this way, companies lose some of their most experienced, skilled, and
wise employees. Retirement policies based on age should
be abolished for something more selective, so that companies don't lose valuable employees wholesale.

3. Many companies operate a system of *salary levels.*
As suggested earlier, this archaic system is intended only
to make administration easier—it has nothing to do with
motivation. A more enlightened approach to salary policy,
reviewed earlier, is to steer just this side of anarchy,
customizing the entire reward program within an inch of
its life, using the widest array of creative remuneration
options available.

4. Christmas and "thirteenth-month" bonuses are
another anachronism, an invention of the Dickensian era
that should have accompanied Ebenezer Scrooge to the
grave. As we said earlier, performance (largely determined
by the customer), not paternalism, is the only fair criterion by which to determine remuneration.

5. *Derecruiting* (also known as "out-placement")
is a contemporary euphemism for *firing,* with the aid of
a management consultant! Firing of any kind is painful,
and a company should do its best to avoid it—first, by
attempting to hire the right people; then, by helping them

to adapt and grow. Regular appraisals and reviews are essential for keeping things on track; if things get off track, employee counseling will do much to get things back on the rails. If this doesn't work, the employee should first be reassigned and then given time to find a new job before being let go. Finally, the employee's manager should discuss with his or her manager ways to avoid this situation in the future. For the fired employee's manager, this may involve additional coaching in human resource management skills. What can *never* be considered a viable alternative is to voice a commitment to people as the corporation's most important asset and then to shut down operations and indiscriminately terminate large numbers of people. One of my clients whose payroll grew too large called a meeting of the international leadership team. Addressing them, the CEO said, "We need to reduce our head count by 10,000, and I believe that we cannot achieve this by laying off any employees. After all, you made the decision to hire them; therefore, it's your responsibility, not theirs, and it is unfair that they should shoulder the pain. Therefore, I am asking you to solve the problem another way." This galvanized the leadership team into an unprecedented series of initiatives involving creative ways to use the company's existing human resources. Although endangered these days, continuous employment policies like the one in the example and those at IBM and many other enlightened companies promote mutual trust and increase mutual integrity, both vital ingredients of motivation. Such corporate values also encourage executives to treat human assets with greater respect, altering their view of people from being an easily disposable commodity to being long-term assets.

   6. *Downward mobility* is a contemporary euphemism that means "assignment to a dead-end job." A powerful demotivator is the sad spectacle of yesterday's star in the undignified role of has-been. In such a case, be straight with the employee and work to design a sensitive

program of reassignment. The effect may well surprise you: The employee concerned may be rejuvenated by your concern and everyone else inspired by your sensitivity.

7. *Restrictive covenants* (also called "noncompete agreements") are used by many companies to keep an employee from competing with them after he or she leaves. But corporate motivation is not enhanced by bringing big legal guns to bear on former comrades. According to Jack W. Schuler, former chief operating officer of Abbott Laboratories, as a condition of receiving a severance, his former employer required him to sign an agreement that barred him from working for a competitor anywhere in the world for 6 years. The company agreed to revise the time restriction to 2 years, prompting Judge Edwin M. Berman to note that this was "an admission [on the part of Abbott] that it was too far-reaching." More and more courts are throwing out such cases in favor of the defendant, making plaintiff companies look both foolish and heartless in the eyes of their employees. Says one Abbott executive, "It's disturbing that the board could force one of the country's top health care executives out of his job and then fight to keep him from going back to work."

8. It's probably wise to avoid *matrix management* (a management system that combines both vertical and horizontal or diagonal reporting relationships; employees often have to report to two different people). To paraphrase Samuel Johnson, this approach is another instance of the triumph of hope over experience. The initial euphoria that greeted its introduction has long since been replaced by mistrust. It's great if you are trying to put a man on the moon or build the World Trade Center, but in the world of mere mortals (where such megaprojects are only things that we read about in the papers), it has severe limitations. I have worked with large global corporations where the decision-making process has completely seized up because of matrix management—too many sign-offs, too many bosses, too much paper, too little empowerment.

9. *Employee attitude surveys* are very useful, if conducted by a totally independent professional. If you're really serious about listening to your team and getting unbiased feedback, you'll find the use of employee attitude surveys invaluable for three reasons. First, employees are aware that the leadership team is interested in their views; second, they can participate in shaping their work environments; and third, they can contribute to the creation of synthesis between personal and corporate needs. At United Technologies, the Readiness to Compete Survey is sent to 7,000 workers, including 500 middle managers. Respondents are asked to rank on a scale from 1 to 5 the degree to which ten obstacles pose a danger to the firm's competitiveness. Some of the obstacles include: management complacency, indifference, or lack of urgency; management not being committed to change; reactionary rather than proactive management style; ineffective immediate supervisors. Says Senior Vice President Franklyn Caine, "No one person is smart enough to know what is going on in every part of a company this big."

10. *Employee appraisal* of the leadership team is a rigorous test of corporate climate and is being adopted by a growing number of enlightened organizations, including Amoco, Cigna, Continental Bank, Dupont, and Johnson & Johnson. This technique is for leaders who really want *to listen* to their employees, so that they can learn how to better accomplish their leadership responsibilities.

11. The best people you're likely to hire are those *recommended by your own team*. Who else is as motivated as they are? Who else is as familiar with the corporate culture and what it takes to succeed in this environment? By asking them to recommend their friends or contacts and paying them what a headhunter would cost you, you are giving your employees a vote of confidence. They know that you want them to introduce people to

your company who are as good as they are. (See Chapter 6 for more discussion on the topic of recruitment bonuses.)

12. Everyone should have an *exit plan,* a plan that spells out how and when you plan to leave the organization and elicits the corporation's practical help in effecting the move. Employees are concerned about their long-term future, but it is unusual for executives to address this. Those who do so encourage a heightened sense of security and loyalty among employees and therefore achieve higher levels of motivation. No matter when you're going or why, everyone wins if the cards are on the table and a genuine effort to accommodate all interests is made.

13. Sensitive executives establish *quality-of-work-life programs,* which focus on making the working environment as agreeable as possible. Accomplishing this may include flextime, office landscaping (open-plan and free-form office design), day care, or job sharing. If an idea motivates employees, it's a good idea. After all, motivation is the name of the game.

14. A *life plan* is an extension of an exit plan and is similar in importance and treatment. Contrary to popular belief, all managers have a responsibility to be involved in the personal lives of their staff and to provide every possible support to help with personal goals.

———◆———

About 70% of the gross national product of most Western countries is accounted for by wages and benefits. People are the largest single corporate cost. They are more important than buildings, more important than machines —the latter can't even work without the former. As leaders, we cannot begin to motivate people until they believe that we value them more than our fixed assets.

The Most Powerful Motivators of All

In a study of 2,400 Canadian workers by Wyatt Company, 64% of those surveyed were content with their pay and 64% with their benefits. But only 40% felt that management treated them with respect and showed a genuine interest in their needs; and 71% felt that management poorly explained the reasons behind decisions. Particularly irritating to employees was that management made decisions behind closed doors. The same study among U.S. workers resulted in identical findings, except that only 50% were satisfied with their pay.

Another study (shown in Table 5-3) conducted in 15 countries by Louis Harris for Steelcase gives pause for thought:

Table 5-3   Office Workers Rate Their Jobs

Do you . . .	United States	European Community	Japan
find your work satisfying?	43%	28%	17%
feel proud of your company's products and services?	65	37	35
feel happy about your pay?	44	26	15
believe management is honest and ethical?	40	26	16
feel you can contribute significantly to the company?	60	33	27

Table 5-3   (Continued)

Do you . . .	United States	European Community	Japan
believe doing a good job greatly helps you to achieve your life's goals?	53	65	31
think management is sensitive to family needs?	35	19	21
try to do it right the first time?	67	40	33
work too many hours?	21	31	33
feel safe from layoffs?	56	56	50

Note the insecurity of Japanese workers, despite the much-vaunted notion of cradle-to-grave security.

In research we've undertaken for our clients, we've discovered three frequently overlooked prime motivators: **integrity, meaning,** and **time.** It is hard for most of us, steeped in our traditions of left-brained analysis, to wrap our arms around the idea that motivators can be "soft" just as easily as "hard." But increasingly—after the issues of money and benefits have been settled—people are concerned about these three intangible but vital benefits. Many people will switch their allegiance to organizations who stand by these precepts; they will even change their careers and life-styles or take a reduction in their standard of living. This is how they articulate their feelings:

Integrity: I want to know that the company's leadership is fair with suppliers and competitors, straightforward with unions, governments, and regulators, and open with employees. I want to know that managers don't play politics, that they won't say things about me behind my back that they wouldn't say to my face. I want to know that managers won't claim credit for the things that I have done well or blame me for the mistakes they made. I want to know that leadership is committed to high levels of mutual trust, respect, truthfulness, and fair dealing.

Meaning: I want to know that if I am not at work that my absence will be noticed; that what I do is important and makes customers feel better; that I don't just push paper around because it pleases some faceless bureaucrat at head office; that my work is relevant; and that if I wasn't around anymore, I would be missed.

Time: I want to know that the leadership of our organization will not turn me into a clock-watcher, that there will be a certain give and take about my schedule. I want to feel that I can work as long and as hard as I have to in order to be highly effective; likewise, if I need to take time for myself, I won't be told that I've used up all my holiday entitlement.

There is much evidence to support our findings. One of the most striking is a study commissioned by Robert Below, chairman of Heroic Environments. The study covered 2.4 million workers in 32 industrial sectors and was conducted by Chicago's International Survey Research. The findings showed that the top eight characteristics sought by employees from their work environment were as follows:

1. To be treated with uncompromising truth
2. To be trusted by one's associates

3. To mentor and be mentored unselfishly
4. To work in a climate receptive to new ideas, regardless of their origin
5. To be able to take risks for the organization's sake
6. To be given credit where it's due
7. To be able to behave ethically in an ethical organization
8. To work in a culture where people tend to consider the interests of others before their own

The new fuel of the motivated team is **values,** and the higher the octane, the better it will run.

———◆———

I am the people—the mob—the crowd—the mass. Do you know that all the great work of the world is done through me?

—Carl Sandburg

Chapter 6

A Team of Superstars

Great star, great director, great play, great cast.
You are authorized to get these without stint or
limit. Spare nothing, neither expense, time, nor
effort. Results only are what I am after. Simply
send me the bills and I will OK.

—Louis B. Mayer

When you're as great as I am, it's hard to be
humble.

—Muhammad Ali

*I*n order to win the game of building a superbly
balanced and high-performing team, we need a fundamental ingredient: a winning hand. Our trumps are the very
best talent available in the marketplace—superstars.

———————◆———————

Many years ago I worked for a company president
whose recruitment methods were interesting, to say the
least. He would take a candidate out for lunch, during
which he would watch to see whether his unsuspecting
guest used pepper or salt before tasting the food. He considered candidates who seasoned before tasting
unsuitable—he felt they were showing signs of compulsive
behavior and an unwillingness to plan ahead!

189

On other occasions the president would introduce himself to a candidate in the company's reception area and ask the visitor to follow him to his office. He would then proceed to bolt down the winding corridors at speeds that would have made Carl Lewis envious! If the candidate couldn't keep up, the CEO concluded that he or she didn't have the necessary stamina or drive. As a backup test, the CEO considered candidates' actions if they became lost en route: Did they return to the receptionist? Wander about the offices aimlessly? Ask someone for help? Use deductive reasoning to find the CEO's office? Apologize? Joke nervously? Or simply give up? Although these games may seem foolish, in fact they were very concrete tests of initiative and very effective screening techniques. Often, he could spot potential failures as soon as they stepped out of the elevator!

Another CEO I worked for would initially hire two senior executives for the same job—the winner of the ensuing competition was rewarded with the whole job!

Walter B. Wriston, the former chairman of CitiCorp, used a similar strategy to select a chief executive for the bank. He appointed three vice presidents—John S. Reed, Thomas C. Theobald, and Hans H. Angermueller—who competed for 2 years. On the basis of track record, results, and specialized talents, Reed got the job in the summer of 1984.

Some CEOs spend as much time interviewing the candidate's spouse as the prospective executive. They do this because they believe that the candidate's partner should be able to ask questions about issues like travel and schedule, especially in a two-career family of shared parental responsibility. Most successful executives need to maintain an intensive pace, and a leader with a collapsing marriage may not perform to the maximum.

Other CEOs will only hire executives with high academic qualifications, or those who attended a select educational establishment (these CEOs often being self-

taught, of course!), or those who have worked for an executive or a corporation personally known to the CEO.
Some CEOs will only hire people who have earned a college degree through night courses—the rationale being
that anyone who can do that has moxie!

We tend to look upon such idiosyncratic hiring
criteria as silly or out of date. What we seem to forget
is that organizations are run by *people;* that these people
spend more time with each other than with anyone else
in their lives; that they work very hard together during
their best years; and that it is more fun and much more
rewarding to work with stimulating and sympathetic colleagues. With these truths in mind, managers with moxie
use wider criteria than espoused by current management
theory, in their attempt to establish an environment in
which interpersonal chemistry can flourish—because it's
chemistry that makes a corporation "hot."

I have long since ceased to laugh at so-called idiosyncratic hiring practices, which have so often been responsible for bringing dynamic team players together. Instead,
I have copied and tried to perfect these techniques
whenever and wherever I could.

Putting the Right Person in the Right Job

When I first moved from Canada to England as the
greenhorn CEO of Manpower, I realized we needed a
financial director immediately if we were ever to control
the company's runaway finances. I searched long and hard
for a candidate who possessed both a chemistry to complement mine and skills for the job; I wanted the best,
and I was not prepared to compromise. Almost as an after-
thought, we ran an ad in the *Wall Street Journal,* which
elicited a response from a candidate (in Montreal of all
places) who proved to be the perfect choice. After flying
to Canada to meet him and his family, we hired him.

Although moving this executive to the United Kingdom, family and all, was enormously expensive, it was worth every penny—he was superb.

This experience taught me an important lesson: When searching for the ideal candidate, never despair or stop trying new techniques. In this case especially, with the CEO and his team in a tight spot, it is crucial that they can rely on the integrity and commitment of each other—and especially on that of the top financial manager.

This man and I worked closely together for 8 years and are still good friends. Someone once asked me why I hired him. My reasons were simple:

- ◆ I *liked* him and thought I could work well with him.
- ◆ Other members of the team, especially his peers, liked him and believed they would get along well with him.
- ◆ I trusted him implicitly.
- ◆ His track record indicated that he was very good at what he did.

Sounds almost too basic, doesn't it? But successful executives know that these are the qualities and characteristics of teammates on whom they can depend and with whom they will spend the majority of their waking hours.

One often hears the adage, You don't have to like someone to work with them. This is rational thinking carried to absurdity! It is absolutely essential that we get along very well with our working colleagues: How else can we tolerate each other, let alone respect each other and work together to shape the destiny of a great corporation? In short, cohesive and successful leadership teams are made up of people who get along, who are temperamentally and technically synergistic, and who enjoy and respect each other. Such teams can make any corporation work— as anyone who has worked with a successful, dynamic team can attest.

Take Edward and Peter Bronfman, nephews of the legendary Sam, who control a $95 billion network of companies from their Toronto base. Jewels in their corporate crown include interests in the Toronto Blue Jays, Brascan, Hees International, Great Lakes Group, Kerr Addison Mines, John Labatt, London Life, MacMillan Bloedel, Noranda, Royal Trustco, Trilon Financial, and numerous others. Trevor Eyton, a former corporate lawyer, is one of the Bronfmans' longest-standing executives and confidants. He has had a number of top assignments in the Bronfman empire and, until his appointment to Canada's Senate, was generally regarded as its top deal maker and a critical member of the inner circle. Eyton attributed the rapid growth of the Bronfman interests to "a bunch of people who are really quite unique." Describing the Bronfmans, Eyton observes that "they are not only my employers, they are also my partners and my very close friends." That attitude is nearly always present in fast-track corporate success stories.

THE LEADER AS BICYCLE OR LOCOMOTIVE

In an average year, 750,000 new businesses are started in the United States, over 2,000 every day, 3½ times the annual rate of 20 years ago.

Entrepreneurship is a wondrous thing. Creating and building a business. Turning customers on. Leading and motivating a pumped-up team to a shared vision of the future. These are the things that entrepreneurs find as much fun as you can have standing up with your clothes on!

A very high proportion of shiny new entrepreneurs are either people who have been fired from larger corporations or who have left them in frustration. People like Lee Iacocca who was fired by Henry Ford or H. Ross Perot who quit IBM. Canadians have followed a similar pattern. Ron Hume quit McGraw-Hill to found the Hume group and the *Moneyletter.* Harry Rosen quit Tip Top

Tailors to start his menswear group, which he later folded into Dylex. Many of these entrepreneurs think (usually quite correctly) that they can run a business better than their former employers.

In the beginning, entrepreneurial leaders are founts of innovation and creativity. But after a while, many reach a plateau. New ideas don't come as easily; the larger dimensions of the organization are unfamiliar and difficult to manage; and there is a growing need to deal with complex administrative requirements and communications issues. The entrepreneurial leader becomes increasingly frustrated. What has happened?

The problem is that the *bicycle* type of leadership is no longer adequate. Bicycles get their power from the back wheel; they *push* the vehicle forward. Although most organizations require bicycle leadership for a time, they cannot function this way indefinitely. At some point, they need a *locomotive* to pull them forward. They need leaders who *have been there before.*

Consider this: Can you remember being conscious of the Montreal Symphony Orchestra before Charles Dutoit became its conductor? Were you an avid fan of the Los Angeles Kings before Wayne Gretzky? Did you buy Remington razors before you heard of Victor Kiam?

What do these leaders have in common? They are "locomotive" leaders. They've *been there* before.

At a seminar I recently conducted, the owner of an insurance agency with sales of about $2 million asked me how he could increase his firm's sales to $5 million. I told him to hire a $5 million executive.

It's the same for any organization—a church, a school, a corporation, an orchestra, a not-for-profit organization, a hospital, or a government department. Sometimes, in order to go from *here* to *there,* we need outside help—someone who has been *there* before and knows what *there* feels like. An executive who has never been there will find it difficult to imagine what it takes to get there. But executives who have, already know what they must do. In fact, they stand *there* and draw the organization to them.

In playing a sport, it's easy to team up with a partner of matching skill. When you win, you get satisfaction —for a while. But when you team up with pros of undoubted superiority, you really challenge yourself. Over time you learn from them, match them, and perhaps eventually go beyond them. This is as true in the boardroom as it is on the tennis court. The conscious acquisition of executives who possess skills or talents superior to your own is one sure way to reward yourself and your team— because the sum of the team's potential will be enlarged.

Hiring a pro has a more practical side too. We all know how difficult it is for senior executives to find the time or the opportunity to improve existing skills or acquire new ones, because they believe their day-to-day tasks are often just too demanding. Valuing high-flying talent and being willing to learn is one of the finest ways to improve the team's collective pool of leadership. So when appointing a new executive, the leader with moxie asks, What can I learn from this person?

Committing to the Acquisition of Superstars

It's often said that successful executives have a considerable amount of luck. I don't believe it—luck is merely the ability to stand in the way of more opportunities than other people do. I prefer Woody Allen's philosophy: "If you want to be a success in life, just show up 80 percent of the time!" You accomplish this by being in more places than your competitors and looking more assiduously for opportunities than they do. Harvard professor Theodore Levitt is equally skeptical about executive good luck. He believes that "the best way for a firm to be lucky is to make its own luck. That requires knowing what makes a business successful." So it is with hiring good people. Paraphrasing Louis Pasteur, Hallmark's Irvine O. Hockaday, Jr., puts it like this: "Chance favors the prepared mind." As America's second largest printer, with sales of $2.5 billion produced out of five plants with 15,000 employees, Hallmark achieves a 44% share of the $5 billion U.S. greeting-card market—so Hockaday knows what he's talking about.

A properly directed corporation with a climate for success and the high morale generated by a finely tuned motivated team will naturally attract good people. But that's not enough. A corporate leader must keep the recruitment radar turned on at all times, so he or she can scoop up talented people whenever they appear. Finally, corporate leaders must agree to acquire only the *finest talent available,* the superstars, and make sure that the organization has the will and the budget to do so. As the old proverb reminds us, it's not the ships but the men who sail in them.

Although this approach might seem to encourage overhiring, it must be appreciated that these stellar talents are the builders of the corporation's future. Superstars have a natural commitment to building a corporation up to their own personal potential; they are locomotive leaders who stretch corporate performance to new heights. It follows, therefore, that underhiring is a terminal philosophy and overhiring a necessity for corporate success.

There is a corollary to the magic formula, superstars = dynamic corporate growth: It takes a lot of wisdom and courage to turn down anything but the best, especially when the pressure is on. But it's vital to hold out for superstars only. The day you allow hiring standards to slip is the day you stymie your company's future success.

The Talent Acquisition Plan (TAP)

Your corporation should have a drill for negotiating with and acquiring executives. Few management efforts are as important as recruiting superstars, so leaders should be thoroughly rehearsed in how to bring the players of their choice onto the team.

Here's a blueprint for a hiring strategy:

1. Determine how the contact will be initiated.
2. Spell out the terms of the appointment and the mission of the job; decide who will negotiate these.
3. Establish who will make the final hiring decision.
4. Set the limits of the negotiating parameters.
5. Determine the information requirements of the rest of the team regarding the progress of the search.
6. Determine which team members should interview the candidate(s).
7. Assign someone as mentor to the new team member for the initial employment period.

When you and your team agree on all the components of the hiring strategy, you will have designed, in effect, a **talent acquisition plan (TAP).** But you don't have to follow it slavishly. These seven steps should be adapted, when you and your team deem necessary, to fit the circumstances and the individual candidate. The TAP should recognize Simone Weil's advice: "Every being cries out silently to be read differently."

Remember too that top-quality talent is very hard to find; executives of this caliber are constantly turning down offers that are probably better than yours. There's no room for slip-ups in this quest; any mistake and your superstar will be attracted elsewhere.

Since talent *is* so scarce, it's essential to maintain a standing commitment to its acquisition—to be prepared to consider hiring first-rate people *any time.* This is not as reckless as it may sound, because superstars are always a good investment, the cost of a talented executive only being important in relative terms. What really counts is the quantum jump additional talent can make in the corporation's ability to create wealth—and therefore new opportunities for the business, its employees, and society.

———————◆———————

Linear Technology of Milpitas, California, is a good example of how superstars can contribute to a growing corporation. In 1984 it was estimated that less than 200 competent designers of linear integrated circuits were working in the United States; and industry experts considered only 12 of those to be stars. Half of those 12 were designing new circuits for Linear Technology—more than the combined total of the next three largest companies in the business (Motorola, Texas Instruments, and National Semiconductor). Tiny compared to its competitors (the largest of which enjoys annual linear-circuit sales of more than $200 million), Linear's first-year $10 million of sales displayed the moxie of its leadership team, which went on to build revenues exceeding $50 million (with profits of about 20%). Analysts predict a continuing growth rate for Linear of 20% per annum. As Linear's president, Robert H. Swanson, remarked, "This is one business where all you really need is people." (National Semiconductor apparently agreed. Shortly after Swanson left National to found Linear—taking with him four top circuit designers and seven key manufacturing, sales, and finance managers—his former employer hit the fledgling company with a lawsuit that was later settled out of court.) According to Swanson, his designers have been responsible for half the linear industry's most successful chips and design techniques and for many significant analog-circuitry products.

Consider another example. In 1986 Coleco Industries (of Cabbage Patch Kids fame) acquired Selchow & Righter, the U.S. producer of Trivial Pursuit, the hottest board game of the decade (which was invented by a trio of Canadians).

When Coleco made the acquisition, Trivial Pursuit was still romping away with record sales; nevertheless, in a few years, Coleco filed for protection from its creditors under the provisions of Chapter 11.

What happened? One of the most important reasons for Coleco's failure was that the company didn't acquire the entrepreneurial team behind Trivial Pursuit's success.

The former West Coast manager of Selchow & Righter, Tom McGuire, recalls the 12-month period when the company sold almost 15 million units of Trivial Pursuit. "It was insane back then," he said. "The numbers were ridiculous. It was hard to come back to reality." So he didn't.

McGuire set off to locate the game world's next Trivial Pursuit. Through his informal network, he learned of another Canadian who had invented a game called Pictionary that had sold over 6,000 copies in Seattle at $35 each. After testing the game on his three grown daughters, McGuire realized he had another winner.

With Pictionary in hand, he teamed up with former Trivial Pursuit production manager Joseph Cornacchia to form The Games Gang. The two began marketing Pictionary and were later joined by Doug McFadden, who had been Trivial Pursuit's marketer abroad. Sales took off, reaching almost $5 million in the first 6 months and $57 million in the following year. In its first 2½ years of business, The Games Gang racked up sales of $150 million, proving that there was much more than luck behind the team's phenomenal success with Trivial Pursuit. It then located its next American hit, a word-bluffing game called Balderdash that had been the number-one game in Canada for 2 years running. Learning from Selchow & Righter's past mistakes, The Games Gang has stayed lean, hiring just 16 employees, 9 of them salespeople.

———————◆———————

Once your team is committed to talent hunting, your principal criteria should be a candidate's **attitude** and **intelligence.** At Manpower, we believed that attitude and intelligence were *mandatory* qualities, because they were the only ones we couldn't teach: We could teach a new team member about our industry and its idiosyncrasies; we could teach functional responsibilities; we could teach job mechanics. But we couldn't teach flair, creativity, chutzpah, panache, passion, positive thinking, vision, ambition, and tenacity. And we couldn't teach raw intelligence. Nobody can. Over the years, research we conducted at Manpower showed that our most successful managers possessed:

♦ High problem-solving abilities
♦ High levels of physical and mental energy
♦ Very high levels of curiosity
♦ Very demanding needs for achievement
♦ High levels of empathy

Ed Booz, of Booz, Allen, & Hamilton, the internationally renowned firm of management consultants, said it all when he remarked, "You can reach any goal you want to if you just put the right [person] on the right job." The "right" person has the right attitude—"the right stuff"—and may or may not have the relevant technical skills. Robert Browning said, "Ah, but a man's reach should exceed his grasp, or what's a heaven for?" We need talented individuals in our organizations made of the right stuff, whose reach exceeds their grasp. After a certain point, we need leadership by locomotive rather than by bicycle.

Sources of Talent

Some of the best sources of talent are the most obvious. Although superstars are hard to find and catch, sometimes they are right under our noses—and we are, as Pogo said, "confronted with insurmountable opportunities."

PROMOTING FROM INSIDE
Curiously, many executives often overlook their own backyards when scouting for superstars. One of the best reasons for looking inside *first* is the motivational effect this has on employees. They know the company will not overlook their talents—and they will work all the harder to demonstrate their abilities. This is true for employees at all levels, especially those at the top.

Aside from the motivational effect on employees— which cannot be overstated—there are other good reasons to hire from within: The promoted employee will undoubtedly work exceedingly hard to deserve the faith shown by the company; and he or she may already possess the necessary task-related skills and certainly a knowledge of how the company works. In addition, a corporation that hires from within can fulfill enlightened social goals by developing its employees. This contributes to consistent and rapid personal growth, which translates into consistent and increased corporate performance.

When a vacancy occurs, announce it corporate-wide, to maximize employee awareness of both the opportunity and the company's expansion. The former aids in the search, the latter reinforces corporate self-esteem. The signal being sent is that the company is on the move and expressing its commitment to fellow team members by giving them the opportunity first.

RECRUITING FROM OUTSIDE
The reception area.   Any visitor to your company may be a potential candidate. Since all visitors pass through the reception area, it's a good idea to keep current copies of corporate publications for their perusal. This way you can declare the company's recruiting intentions and promote the organization at the same time. One way or

another, the guests in the reception area have an interest in your organization and its future. This interest may suddenly deepen when they realize your corporation is on the lookout for superstars. The advantage is that such visitors probably are familiar with your company already, either as suppliers, as customers, or even as competitors!

Other sources.   Friends and relatives of employees are important recruiting contacts. Because of their close relationship with employees, they have unique insight into the company's operating style, objectives, and potential—as well as the kinds of people who work there and are successful.

It can be a large network. Take Manpower, for instance, which employed 72,000 full- and part-time staff when I was president. Considering that most were married or supporting a dependent, 140,000 people were materially reliant in varying degrees on our company. In addition, we reasoned that each employee had at least one good friend with whom he or she might discuss work. This meant that Manpower directly touched the lives, materially or emotionally, of 210,000 people who had a vested interest in helping us to meet our continuing need for superstars.

We regularly reviewed our diaries, scanning every contact that we had made over the prior year, no matter how unrelated it might seem at first glance. In this way we hired a top union official as director of Manpower's union affairs; a peer of the realm to undertake public relations activities; and a college lecturer who became our planning manager. The rapid expansion of Manpower's franchise network was accomplished with the help of this technique; over half our franchisees were referred to us by existing franchise owners (to whom we paid an introductory bonus as well).

We also encouraged former employees to keep in touch, and they often suggested high-quality talent. Other valuable sources included banking contacts; accounting firms; and alumni, professional, and trade associations. Most of these groups shared a common interest with us— in some way their fortunes were intertwined with ours, and it was in their interests to send us superstars whenever they could.

You can increase awareness of the opportunities within your organization by creative use of the media. When I was at Manpower we had a contact at a major national financial paper, with whom we would review our senior openings as they occurred. A day or two later, an article would appear describing our corporate development, our future plans, and the career opportunities we were trying to fill. Unpaid media coverage like this is more valuable than paid advertising because it carries more credibility, doesn't have to compete with hoards of classified advertisements, and builds institutional pride at the same time.

The nature of first-rate corporations gives rise to other creative techniques for finding superstars. Often, for instance, "bunching" occurs at top levels: There are simply not enough top jobs for top candidates to move up into. If you successfully identify such executives, you have a shot at getting them when they become dissatisfied with advancement at their present company.

In addition, whenever Manpower hired key managers from prestigious firms, we asked them to recommend ten top executives (and others) who fit our attitude/intelligence criteria. Although most of these would be from the manager's former company, others came from various personal contacts. Each new list of executives became our target list—in one instance we hired four executives from the same firm.

We often found that when a company with whom we had a good working relationship was undertaking a major recruitment exercise, they would come to an understanding with us (and their candidates): They would offer us the opportunity to review any candidates that did not fit their immediate requirements.

Of course, executive search firms, classified advertising, and the many other traditional techniques are important additional recruitment devices and should not be ignored.

SOME TACTICAL POINTERS

At Manpower we paid a recruitment bonus to *anyone,* employee or otherwise, who introduced a candidate who was then hired. We paid the bonus in full 30 days after the candidate began work for us. As mentioned in the last chapter, recruitment bonuses are important in-company motivational tools. They're equally effective as image enhancers in the outside world. But we didn't stop there. We employed an old trick from the head-hunting business: We asked our friends. How many times has a headhunter diplomatically inquired whether you know of anyone who could fill a certain slot? This is a winning question in two ways: First, the person asked may be a candidate or may know of one. Second, he or she will tell others about the opportunity, thus continuing to build the corporation's image for you, if nothing else!

It is especially important to remember that the recruitment of executives is *the responsibility of the leadership team.* Superstars are simply too vital to a corporation's life to be handled by anyone else. You should *never* allow them to become the charges of the most recently hired trainee in the human resources department. Although staff departments have a useful role to play after the hiring negotiations are settled—they can arrange for family relocation, take care of payroll, and supply administrative support services, for instance—they are facilitators *only.* The responsibility for locating, acquiring, and nurturing superstars is simply not assignable to anyone but the leadership team.

The Talent Acquisition Team (TAT) and the Hiring Process

Say that you've come across a likely candidate. Before proceeding further, you must determine that he or she is really worth the effort of pursuit. You should let such candidates know that you intend to make discreet inquiries of contacts within their current and former organizations, of competitors and trade associations with whom they are connected, and of current industry opinion regarding them and their performance. The information you obtain from these inquiries will either confirm or deny a candidate's desirability for your organization.

Once you've identified an outstanding talent, enticing him or her is a complex tracking task, akin to securing a major sales contract. To pull it off, the leadership team needs to agree on its **talent acquisition plan (TAP)**, which then becomes the touchstone of the **talent acquisition team (TAT)**. This TAT group may be a standing unit or it may be formed for this specific task only. Depending on the business's size and preference, the TAT group may consist of the owner and manager of the company and the manager's secretary or the entire leadership team. Regardless—because the task is not assignable—the leader should direct the TAT group, the members of which should reflect the talents, skills, functional bias, and interests of the candidate.

The TAT group must agree on objectives, establish an operating plan, and assign responsibilities. Superstars are seldom looking for you—you, and lots of others, are looking for them. George Bernard Shaw could have had the top executive candidate in mind when he observed, "You think . . . that it is your part to woo, to persuade, to prevail, to overcome. Fool: it is you who are the pursued, the marked-down quarry, the destined prey." So recruitment strategy has to be good if you want to stand out from the crowd. The plan should include all of the currently known information about the candidate, what you still *don't* know about this individual, and how you're going to find out. You must consider things such as where the target lives and who in the TAT group best knows this environment. You also need to identify who on the team is most in tune with the candidate's background, skills, and interests. Other questions to be answered: Who in the TAT group is opposed to this appointment and why? What can be done to alleviate their concerns about the appointment? How should the TAT group play its strengths, especially its trump card, the CEO? Who will make the offer and what should it be? What will the TAT group do if the candidate turns the overture down? What is the best venue for initial and subsequent contacts? What paperwork do you need from the candidate? Whom else in the organization should the candidate see? Should the candidate visit the operations, and/or the head office of the company? Who will the candidate report to? You must weave the answers to all these questions into the TAP. Once agreed on, adhere to the plan until you have executed it.

The administrative steps for hiring superstars include such tasks as conducting any relevant tests, preparing the letter of appointment and the employment agreement, arranging medicals, and obtaining the necessary personal details that facilitate payment, tax deductions, and so forth. The human resources department should be advised of the TAT group's game plan but should remain independent of the search until the candidate has agreed in principle to the terms offered. At this point, you can hand the paperwork over to the human resources department for processing.

During the hiatus between acceptance and assumption of the new appointment, assign one member of the TAT group (preferably the one who has developed the best rapport with the candidate) to the role of the candidate's "buddy," or mentor. The buddy need not necessarily be the candidate's future manager.

Before acceptance, the candidate should have a frank discussion with a member of the TAT group about the negative aspects of the organization and the position under discussion, thus averting the danger of the candidate acquiring false expectations about the future. After the candidate has been hired, all personnel (including—and this is especially important—suppliers and clients) with whom the new executive will interact should have an opportunity to talk with him or her. This helps them "own a part of the decision"—very important, because their support in the early days of the new appointment may be crucial to its success.

After the appointment is confirmed, a designated TAT group member should visit the candidate's previous managers to conduct a formal review of technical and personal strengths, weaknesses, and idiosyncrasies. If this review elicits negative results, you can get out of the contract at minimal cost—but this is the last opportunity for doing so inexpensively. Obviously, the review takes place after the appointment is confirmed to avoid compromising the candidate.

Women in the Boardroom

Sir Winston Churchill was once asked whether he agreed with the prediction that women would rule the world by the year 2000. Churchill replied, "Yes, they will still be at it."

The modern reality, however, is that women are, consciously or unconsciously, still discriminated against in business, despite enabling legislation, an active women's movement, and much posturing about sexual equality. Although women make up 55.5% of the U.S. work force and 44.7% of the managers, professionals, and specialists, they account for less than 2% of the corporate officers of major public companies. A recent survey by *Fortune* magazine is even bleaker, putting the figure at 0.5%.

Discrimination on the basis of sex is a grave infringement of human and civil rights, but this is not the place to discuss those issues. In the business context, successful leaders now agree that discrimination is a serious managerial error, both a fiscal and a qualitative mistake. A fiscal mistake because companies that pass over women for top executive positions may often not be getting the best person for the job. Qualitative because many male executives still cling to the subjective view that women simply can't execute the top strategic responsibilities as effectively as men. This attitude amounts to executive irresponsibility, because the companies where these prejudices are practiced deny themselves access to a massive pool of high-quality talent. They will have to compete with sharper companies whose leaders, realizing that superstars are scarce and the competitive search for talent intense, will tolerate no impediment in their quest. As Evelyn Waugh has reminded us, "Instead of this absurd division of the sexes into masculine and feminine, they ought to class people as static and dynamic."

Because women are still so extensively discriminated against in business they represent an enormous reservoir of superstars eager for the opportunity to prove themselves in the catbird seat. As any enlightened CEO will tell you, the enterprising female executive more than earns her salary. It's not hard to understand why. Striving in a world of unfair odds, women must outperform their male counterparts. The result is that dollar for dollar, female executives are very often better value than their male competitors.

Psychologist Michael Maccoby, from Harvard's John F. Kennedy School of Government, has conducted extensive research into executive leadership. In his book *The Leader,* he describes attitudes toward women held by outstanding leaders as revealed by their Rorschach tests. (A Rorschach test involves a set of ten cards containing differently shaped ink blots. Subjects are asked to interpret the shapes in terms that reveal intellectual and emotional factors.) Maccoby's test results showed that the outstanding leaders he sampled (including Pehr Gyllenhammar, CEO of Volvo, who relies heavily on his wife's judgment) ''express a deep identification with women as well as men.''

All leaders should include women in their executive search efforts, while this (it is to be hoped) temporary bonanza lasts. Apart from the obvious rewards, such a policy makes good business sense: A corporation may gain an enviable reputation as an organization where women get a better-than-equal opportunity to demonstrate their skills and share corporate rewards. In the decade ahead, we are likely to see a surplus of ambitious and well-educated young female entrants into the job market. The challenge of how to assimilate them and fully use their talents must be addressed now.

Filling the Top Job: Management Succession

Much has been written about the need for leaders to groom their successors, either to minimize any negative impact on the corporation caused by their unplanned departure or to facilitate the smooth transfer of power following a scheduled one. However, except in a few of the top 2% of corporations—which can afford such luxuries—planning for succession is closer to pie-in-the-sky than to reality.

One of the reasons for this failure is the dichotomy of the leader's task. Entrepreneurs seek to assemble a team of talented, creative, action-oriented managers. Such entrepreneurial builders are in a hurry; they're creating something important to them; they're having fun and, it is to be hoped, making profits at the same time. They are not normally in tune with the idea of appointing a "number two" who will patiently wait in the wings until it's time to assume the crown.

In addition, members of the entrepreneurial team themselves are either content with their positions or have a burning ambition to lead their own teams. If the latter, they will not be content with an indefinite engagement as the understudy to the leading role. Moreover, any leader worthy of the title will not be an easy person to follow. As Shaw astutely observed: "The reasonable man adapts himself to the world; the unreasonable one persists in trying to adapt the world to himself. Therefore, all progress depends on the unreasonable man." And leaders with moxie are "unreasonable" in the best Shavian sense of the word.

Shaw's sapience is corroborated by the example of the late Dr. Armand Hammer, the autocratic and feisty chairman of Occidental Petroleum of Los Angeles, who went through six CEOs in 11 years. Hammer was not fazed by the musical chairs below him. "The people who built this company are still here" was his taciturn assessment. In Hammer's mind, who was number two mattered least of all. As Zoltan Mersei (a former Oxy CEO) put it: "Hammer doesn't give a damn, frankly, about who's president, because he is the boss, period." Executives like Zoltan Mersei and A. Robert Abboud (another former Oxy CEO) chafed under these conditions, their obvious competence constrained by what they rightly perceived as a holding pattern. After all, as Hammer said at the time, "There's not a deal made in this company that I have not made. I'm the chief executive and I intend to remain here as long as God will permit me." He was called from this life in 1990, and Ray R. Irani, an 8-year veteran with Oxy, succeeded him. Irani, a Lebanese-born holder of 150 patents who earned his doctorate from the University of Southern California when he was 22, plunged into his new job at

Oxy as if he'd been doing it all his life. Within a month of his appointment, he unveiled a $5 billion restructuring plan designed to slash the firm's heavy debt and refocus on its core operations in oil, natural gas, and chemicals. At $6.4 million, Irani ranks 27th on *Forbes* magazine's list of the 800 highest paid CEOs in America. And Oxy weighs in as America's 16th largest industrial corporation. As in so many other cases, fears about a succession crisis at Oxy were unfounded.

Like entrepreneurial leaders, the company's shareholders don't worry about succession either. They are primarily concerned with the corporation's long- and short-term performance. In 20 years, Hammer took a tiny company with eight played-out oil wells and fashioned it into one of the 20 largest corporations in America—a track record that's hard to argue with.

But some form of planning is prudent. Curtis L. Carlson, the 78-year-old founder and sole owner of the Carlson Companies, took precautions to mitigate the potential problems in a family-owned business. Carlson operates nearly 300 Radisson Hotels and Colony Resorts, almost 200 TGI Friday's bar/restaurants, and over 250 Country Kitchen restaurants; the Carlson Travel Network with over $5 billion in sales through 2,100 offices; a $900 million marketing and motivational services company; and a $400 million real estate portfolio. With sales clipping along at an annual compound growth rate of 21% during the last 5 years, no one is pushing for Carlson's early retirement (but since he's the sole shareholder, that isn't too likely anyway!).

Recently, Carlson underwent quadruple bypass surgery. Though he was back at work in just 3 months, the shock came as a warning to the rest of the family, who realized that one day they would have to run the business without its founder. Marilyn Nelson, the older of Carlson's two daughters, is senior vice president, director of community relations, and a board member of Carlson Holdings (she's also on the boards of Exxon, First Bank System, and U S West Communications). Her sister, Barbara Gage, is also a board member of the holding company; and Barbara's husband, Edwin (Skip) C. Gage, occupied the CEO slot for 7 years before being shown the door by his father-in-law. Says Carlson, "I'm not trying to run this company from the grave, but I want to make sure it can go on without the need to sell stock or sell out." So Carlson has established a procedure by which, after his death, each of his daughters can select a lawyer (acceptable to the other side) to represent her in the event of a dispute over the family business. If this process fails to resolve outstanding issues, they can go to arbitration presided over by a Minnesota state judge.

It is often more helpful to support, augment, and build on the strengths of founding geniuses than to be constantly sniping at and criticizing their weaknesses. It can be no accident that the five large retailers that have out-performed all the others through recent economic ups and downs, as well as the gut-wrenching changes that have occurred in retailing, are either run by such geniuses or by their family members. Dillard family members hold most of the top positions at Dillards; until his recent death, Sam Walton was chairman of Wal-Mart; a Fisher runs The Gap and Fisher family members own 40% of the stock; three of Nordstrom's four co-chairmen are Nordstroms and 40% of the firm's stock is held by family members; and Bernard Marcus and Arthur Blank, cofounders of Home Depot, are CEO and president respectively.

Research suggests that CEOs are notoriously poor judges of who should best succeed them. Indeed, pressing this responsibility onto CEOs can divert their energy from their real world: the corporate mission and corporate objectives. No, the best time to choose a successor is when one is required—and you should handle it in the same way as any other strategic talent search.

Management Manpower Planning (MMP)

So far, we have mainly concerned ourselves with the search for superstars at the top of the organization. But *all* good managerial talent searches are the result of careful planning. Knowing *when* and *what kind* of talent will be required is as important to a company's success as hiring the right people. In the corporate world, **management manpower planning (MMP)** is the name of the game. The general precepts of MMP were developed by Lawrence A. Appley, former president of the American Management Association.

In 1964, sales at Harris Corporation were $89 million and the company had 4,900 employees on the payroll. By the 1990s, sales were well over $3 billion, putting Harris solidly in the top 150 largest industrial companies in America, and there were more than 33,000 employees on the payroll. George S. Dively, former president and CEO of Harris for over 25 years, believed that the corporation would not have achieved this enviable record without MMP. In 1981 he said:

> Our manager talent was developed almost entirely from the inside and today's management positions are filled by individuals who are generally identified early in their careers, trained, and then supported in the performance of their responsibilities. . . . The future of Harris Corporation was not left to chance, and its record seems to support our overall planning philosophy in managing the business.

The leadership team at Manpower felt the same way. Once a year (more frequently if conditions demanded), we would retreat to an isolated location—as exotic as our fortunes would permit—to contemplate our future. Developing a management manpower plan was always an important part of this exercise.

The annual MMP session is the time to take inventory of existing human resources and to identify needs for replacement, addition, and succession. Such planning is vital because corporations are nothing without *people,* and corporate plans are worthless without a clear understanding of *who* will implement them.

In the Western world, corporations traditionally plan in 1-, 5- or even 10-year cycles. The reasons for this seem to be rooted in history, the company's culture, or the dictates of home office coordinators. In reality, the cycle for the successful implementation of a strategic plan is *the time it takes to coach and develop the skills of the manager responsible,* to the optimum level. If it takes 3 years to bring a new plant manager to the peak of his or her operating skills and performance, then 3 years should be the planning cycle for that plant. The reason for this is simple: If that manager leaves the company and unless the rest of the team is exceptionally strong, it may take up to 3 years to bring the operation back up to full speed again, excluding the time it takes to find a replacement manager. One could circle the globe with textbooks saying this isn't so and can be avoided—but in the real world, executives *do* leave suddenly, and it is damage control, not textbook theory, that leads to recovery. Management manpower planning is a tool that, at the very least, aids in damage control, and at best helps to form future human resource plans. It consists of five steps.

STEP 1: TAKING MANAGERIAL INVENTORY
Successful corporations maintain an up-to-date inventory of management manpower, including information about an employee's biography, career progress, experience, education, internal career aspirations, special skills, coaching undertaken, prior experience, income aspirations, successful projects undertaken, and best/worst working relationships; each file also contains copies of performance evaluations and reviews. In addition, the leadership team

maintains short profiles of all prospective senior-level appointees, together with action plans stating the position(s) that the appointees could take over (a) immediately, (b) with some coaching at short notice, and (c) with a crash coaching program and reasonable notice.

STEP 2: EVALUATING MANAGERIAL PERFORMANCE

Performance evaluation follows the establishment of a **position description** (the "memorandum of agreement") and **standards of performance** for each executive (see Chapter 7). Because of their subjectivity, **performance reviews** (or "progress reviews," as they are sometimes known) have always been a difficult leadership tool to use effectively. However, the leader and the person reporting directly to him or her should jointly develop the standards of performance; if these incorporate agreed-upon criteria for measurement and flow from a carefully designed counseling and professional development program, then much of this subjectivity can be eliminated.

The achievement of high performance in challenging and demanding executive positions is one of the most accurate indicators of future performance and potential upward mobility. Performance reviews should be regular (held at least twice a year); formal (that is, summarized in writing—where appropriate, by the appraisee—and signed by both parties); conducted in a congenial environment, without interruptions and distractions; and paced at the appraisee's discretion. The written record of the review should be quantitative as well as qualitative. It should also describe extenuating circumstances where necessary, so that future promotional reviews may also be objective. The language of the progress review should ensure that the information can be instantly understood by anyone not familiar with the appraisee but who may be required to play a pivotal role in future promotion decisions. Apart from the achievement of performance criteria, consideration should also be given to identifying opportunities for building on an individual's strengths and other developmental options, as well as recognizing personal growth since the last review and expected achievements to be accomplished by the next review.

There is a strange reluctance on the part of senior executives to provide this much-needed feedback. A recent study suggests that the higher you move up the corporate ladder, the less you are likely to receive feedback on your performance. Clinton Longenecker of the University of Toledo and Dennis Gioia of Pennsylvania State University found that even in organizations where corporate policy dictated that executives could not receive a salary increase without an annual review, only two out of five top executives who pocketed higher salaries received an annual review. Reasons: Presidents and other top executives think their subordinates are too high up the ranks to need them; they're too busy; they're uncomfortable providing them.

STEP 3: DEFINING MANAGEMENT MANPOWER NEEDS

The sensitive and subjective task of defining the requirements of future management manpower is a product of forecasting, of business and organizational planning. Qualitative future standards need to be regularly updated so that tomorrow's executive resources will match the corporation's anticipated needs. New markets, products, customers, services, corporate size, and programs may dictate a shift in qualitative executive requirements, indicating the need for reassignments and the addition or development of team members. The ALDO audit (described in Chapter 3) may also help identify future needs: Demographic changes; compensation trends; new business formations; downsizing; a shift in the demand for, say, financial executives; or changes in the output and emphasis of business schools may all affect a corporation's future manpower needs.

After gathering this information, the leadership team can synthesize the results and develop a statement of the **executive resource gap.** This shows the anticipated resource shortages that will impede the achievement of planned goals.

STEP 4: DEVELOPING EXECUTIVES

The executive resource gap indicates whether an organization should develop and promote existing personnel or institute a search for personnel outside the company. The first option, though preferable, often will not meet all the needs for top executives in a rapidly expanding entrepreneurial corporation.

Corporate executives have a responsibility to commit a major portion of the firm's resources to organizational development. In addition, employees have a right to participate in ongoing professional-development programs, designed with both their long-term interests and the company's in mind. Such programs, combined with a commitment to promoting from within whenever possible, reinforce positive corporate climate and corporate self-perception. This manpower strategy provides the executives needed to fill the gap and motivates employees at the same time.

Analysis and Benefit of Coaching and Development (ABCD).   At the end of this chapter, you will find the Thaler **Analysis and Benefit of Coaching and Development (ABCD),** which measures the value gained from coaching and developing employees. This allows you to see whether your efforts in this area have made any difference. From the results, you can decide what changes, if any, to implement.

STEP 5: FORMULATING MANAGEMENT CONTINGENCY PLANS

Team members sometimes leave at inopportune times. What do you do if a strategically important position is unexpectedly vacated? Of course, prevention is the first tactic, followed by an attempt to dissuade the incumbent from departing, or at least postponing the departure date. If none of these strategies work, it's time to look at the profiles of executives who can replace the incumbent, as delineated in the managerial inventory (step 1). Naturally, this inventory becomes outdated quickly and therefore should be overhauled regularly.

Keeping Up with the High-Flying Corporation

A permanent commitment to executive talent hunting and to obtaining only the finest talent available is necessary to maintain the heady pace of high-growth companies, be they big or small.

Take Timeplex, a manufacturer of high-tech electronic data communications. It achieved a 21.5% return on equity during its first 5 years and an average earnings per share of 25%. Its sales tripled during the same period to $37.8 million, and the firm turned in profits of $3.4 million. But this quick growth had its drawbacks. When asked to define his biggest problem, former owner and chairman Edward Botwinick cited the recruitment of enough *good new people:* "I knew we had to do something when I realized I was spending 80% of my time backstopping people who could not do their jobs adequately. Because of that, I couldn't do my job."

He decided to make recruitment his top priority, adding new people and a new level of management to the organization. But he said:

> Making that decision was a bitch. We were a close family. Three or four years ago, I knew everybody

on a first-name basis. I played tennis and softball with them, we went drinking together. But a lot of the people I used to see socially are now three or four levels down from me. I don't see them month to month, let alone every week. The facts simply are that some of the people who helped us to grow from $20 million toward $50 million are not adequate for future growth. They are marginally adequate now.

Botwinick had realized that he was presiding over a graying corporation, so he used an old and trusted technique: He hired a number of seasoned communications executives—locomotives—who had already managed the transition in other companies from $200 to $400 million in revenues and who would add their experience to the requirements of Botwinick's rapid-growth corporation.

My own experience at Manpower was the same. In the early days, I knew everybody—I even had keys to every one of our 11 offices, which I would visit regularly. But by the time we had established 100 offices— many of which were in any one of half a dozen countries in two hemispheres—just visiting each office annually became difficult!

We all made strong commitments to accelerate our learning and self-development so that we could keep pace with the intellectual and leadership demands of such rapid growth—because it's an inescapable law of business that growing companies have an insatiable and expanding need for superior executive talent. We were growing at an annual compound rate of 40%, but we couldn't "grow" our own new superstars at the same pace. Few companies can. Therefore, searching for superstars outside the company continued to be a top priority.

Experienced talent must often be recruited or enticed from larger, blue-chip corporations. Because such corporations provide excellent personal development and experience but limited opportunities for growth and creativity, many promising executives can be found languishing there. These men and women will jump at the chance to implement the ideas they have acquired from their big-company experiences.

The only hitch is that many of these executives are tied to their big corporations by golden chains; they are often overpaid, and matching their income packages is often out of the reach of smaller companies. But as we saw earlier, this problem is not insurmountable. If the challenge and creative opportunities of the new position can be demonstrated, the remuneration package can be "leveraged" so that the ultimate rewards are very substantial. Equity participation and junior stock-option plans, long-term equity purchase agreements, and incremental profit sharing are just a few of the many ways that smaller companies can sweeten modest remuneration plans.

From the leader's point of view, a rapidly growing corporation *cannot afford to pass up superstars,* regardless of the price. To do so spells a slowdown in growth, and perhaps even atrophy. The cost of hiring superstars and providing imaginative and lucrative payment-on-results remuneration packages as well as powerful psychic rewards are usually offset by the resulting higher productivity. The consequent lower levels of support costs and associated infrastructure add to the efficiency and effectiveness of the organization as a whole.

Paying in the top quarter of the market average is probably a useful benchmark when constructing a final remuneration package—but be flexible. Money, as we have discussed earlier, is not the only motivator—but it is one of the ways that ambitious and stylish executives keep score.

Finally, since hiring the finest talent available at every level is a non-negotiable objective, it follows that continuing with a vacancy is superior to filling it with someone who is mediocre. Great organizations never compromise their standards of recruitment; the watchword is, *Superstars or no one.*

———◆———

If a man is called to be a streetsweeper, he should sweep streets even as Michelangelo painted, or as Beethoven composed music, or as Shakespeare wrote poetry. He should sweep streets so well that all the host of heaven and earth will pause to say, here lived a great streetsweeper who did his job well.

—Martin Luther King, Jr.

Take away my people but leave my factories and soon grass will grow on the factory floors. Take away my factories but leave my people and soon we will have a new and better factory.

—Andrew Carnegie

WORKSHEET 6-1:
ANALYSIS AND BENEFIT OF
COACHING AND DEVELOPMENT (ABCD)

How can you measure the value of your investment in developing and coaching your team? Leaders who seek to justify their commitment to the professional and personal growth of their team members must continually answer this question.

Because there are few if any professional tools available that identify needed leadership and management skills, recognize current capabilities, define development needs, and measure the before-and-after effect of coaching and development programs, at Thaler we designed the Analysis and Benefit of Coaching and Development (ABCD). It answers three basic questions that help you determine the value of your investment in executive development.

1. How are your managers currently performing?
2. What are their development needs?
3. What progress have you made in closing any gap between your managers' current performance and their development needs via a recent coaching or development program?

IDENTIFYING THE CORE COMPETENCIES

There are only two people who really know the answers to these three questions: the people who display the greatest mastery in the task being measured—in this case the best managers in the organization—and their customers. So the first step is to assemble a small team consisting of your best managers and some of their most thoughtful and articulate customers, to form an ABCD team. Invite this group (made up of perhaps eight to ten people) to a working session whose purpose is to identify the ten most important **core competencies** or attributes, and their **relevance,** required by successful managers. The relevance ranking is deduced by ascribing a value between 0 and 10 to each of them. A competency of low relevance might be rated 0, an irrelevant core competency; a highly relevant competency will score a 10, a mandatory core competency. (In practice, there are seldom any "irrelevant" competencies.) The ABCD team must determine the value of each competency by consensus using Schedule I on page 225. The contributions of both the managers *and* their customers are equally valuable. In addition, it is vital to obtain the input of the chief executive and the senior human resources executive, both of whom should be members of the team and attend all the meetings. (See Figure 6-1 on page 227 for a sample ABCD format.)

RANKING THE CURRENT STATUS
OF ABCD-TEAM MEMBERS

After ranking the core competencies and their relevance for the function being evaluated, all ABCD team members rank each ABCD-team manager in terms of his or her *current status* for each core competency on a scale from 1 to 10. The team can work on this as a group, at first, so that discussion can clarify the issues. However, final evaluation should be made individually and anonymously, to avoid personalizing any critical assessments. These analyses should provide valuable feedback to the team and especially to the managers on the team.

DETERMINING THE CURRENT FINANCIAL
VALUE AND DEVELOPMENT NEEDS

The next step is to identify the **current total income** (base salary, benefits, overhead, and expenses) for each ABCD-team manager. Then total the current status of competencies for each and multiply the sum by the current total income. The resulting number determines the value being gained or lost by the organization for that manager being evaluated. (See Figure 6-1 for a sample evaluation.)

The current status column also indicates the competencies that a particular manager needs to develop further. List the recommendations for professional development in the section titled "Schedule II: Current Coaching and Development Needs" on page 226. This then becomes the working document for recording the development and growth of each manager as well as his or her increasing value to the organization.

REVIEWING THE PROGRESS OF
COACHING AND DEVELOPMENT PROGRAMS

Six months after a manager has received the benefit of the recommended coaching or development, the ABCD team should reevaluate his or her current status for the desired core competencies using identical methodology. Enter the new rankings in the **revised status** column and total them. (See Figure 6-1.) Multiply the revised status total by the **revised current total income,** which may have changed in the interim, to determine the **revised financial value,** which shows what proportion of the manager's total income is considered effective by the organization.

The Analysis and Benefit of Coaching and Development should be a permanent tool for each manager to gauge his or her own value and to work with the company to develop professionally and personally. Organizations should use the ABCD to measure every significant training, coaching, and development program to establish their value.

The ABCD can also be a significant tool in salary- and performance-review programs. But perhaps the most important benefit is its measurement of the effectiveness of *specific* coaching and development programs. In these cases, we recommend that you use the ABCD *before* the program and again about 6 months *after* completion.

SCHEDULE I: CORE COMPETENCIES FOR

_____

(Position Title)

	Competency	Relevance (0–10)
1.	_____	[ ]
2.	_____	[ ]
3.	_____	[ ]
4.	_____	[ ]
5.	_____	[ ]
6.	_____	[ ]
7.	_____	[ ]
8.	_____	[ ]
9.	_____	[ ]
10.	_____	[ ]

SCHEDULE II:
CURRENT COACHING AND DEVELOPMENT NEEDS

1. (*Name*) _____

   Competency: [_____]

   Current Status: [   ]   Desired Status [   ]

2. (*Name*) _____

   Competency: [_____]

   Current Status: [   ]   Desired Status [   ]

3. (*Name*) _____

   Competency: [_____]

   Current Status: [   ]   Desired Status [   ]

4. (*Name*) _____

   Competency: [_____]

   Current Status: [   ]   Desired Status [   ]

5. (*Name*) _____

   Competency: [_____]

   Current Status: [   ]   Desired Status [   ]

Figure 6-1   A Sample Format for the Analysis and Benefit of
Coaching and Development (ABCD)

Core Competencies for an ABCD Team Manager	Relevance Weighting	Current Status	Revised Status
1. Decision-making skills and judgment	10.00	6.00	8.00
2. Motivational skills	10.00	7.00	9.00
3. Knowledge of industry	8.00	8.00	8.00
4. Knowledge of top customers	10.00	4.00	6.00
5. Administrative ability	7.00	5.00	7.00
6. Political and diplomatic skills	7.00	6.00	8.00
7. Ability to listen	10.00	3.00	6.00
8. Ambition	9.00	6.00	5.00
9. Sensitivity	10.00	7.00	8.00
10. Fairness	10.00	7.00	10.00
	91.00	59.00	75.00

Current Total Income:	$60,000.00
Current Status of Competencies:	59.00%
Current Financial Loss:	$24,600.00
Current Financial Value:	$35,400.00
Revised Current Total Income:	$65,000.00
Revised Status of Competencies:	75.00%
Revised Financial Loss:	$16,250.00
Revised Financial Value:	$48,750.00
Percentage Growth of Value:	29.46%
Financial Growth of Value:	$17,676.65

Chapter 7

Delegation and Empowerment

Give a man a fish and you feed him for a day.
Teach a man to fish and you feed him for a
lifetime.

—Chinese proverb

*H*aving set the stage, we must get out of the
way. Highly motivated superstars thrive on vigorous
delegation and empowerment. The highest-quality decisions are made in organizations where power is diffused
and responsibility is moved to the lowest appropriate
levels.

◆

Recently I worked with a *Fortune* 500 company to
help it make major changes in their corporate culture. The
CEO was especially disturbed by the failure of a previously introduced "empowerment program," which had
reached an unfortunate impasse: Employees were saying,
"Thank you for empowering me. Now what would you
like me to do?"

Few concepts are more confusing or easily misunderstood than the frequently misused terms *empowerment* and *delegation*. Part of the problem is the mind-
numbing language that academics and researchers use to
define them. Writing in the *Academy of Management*

Review, Jay Conger and Rabindra Kanungo offer this snoozer as the definition of *empowerment:* "A process of enhancing feelings of self-efficacy among organizational members through the identification of conditions that foster powerlessness and through their removal by both formal organizational practices and informal techniques of providing efficacy information." *The Encyclopedia of Professional Management* defines *delegation* as: "The task of farming out one's work to one's subordinates and making sure that the subordinates successfully accomplish the projects or tasks thus assigned"—an underwhelming turn of phrase if ever there was one.

If you have stayed with me this far, you probably want to skip ahead. But hang in there, because despite the confusion surrounding the concepts of empowerment and delegation—and despite their misuse by a few buzz-word-toting power freaks in management—*they hold the secret of organizational and personal transformation.* As Herodotus said, "This is the bitterest pain among men, to have much knowledge but no power."

First, let's explode a few myths. Notwithstanding conventional wisdom, neither empowerment nor delegation can be taught. They are not things you "do" to people; neither are they "programs." They do not replace participative management, rather they depend on it; and if you want concrete results now, forget it; it can take up to 10 years to fully implement empowerment and delegation within an organization.

This is my definition of empowerment:

> *Trusting people and giving them all the information, training, encouragement, authority, and power they need to make the right decision for the customer.*

Delegation is simply a necessary ingredient of empowerment.

I want to emphasize that empowerment is *not* a managerial methodology or technique. Rather, it is a *philosophy*—a Lockean attitude—rooted in the principles of trust, respect, camaraderie, shared vision (the customer's need), and decentralization. It requires that authority *and* responsibility devolve to the organizational level and individual most appropriate for making *effective* decisions.

Regarding the connection between bloated bureaucracies, empowerment, and exceeding the quality needs of customers, Tom Peters has this to say:

> Employee involvement and Total Quality Management are not working in most places. . . . Sad to say, 15 years into the quality movement, the exceptions are just that. Yet many, if not most of the failures have all the trappings in place. Flags. Banners. Thousands of company copies of Deming's book. Thousands of hours put into statistical process control training. But no change of attitude. True empowerment is still a myth, a sick joke. Real TQM has little to do with the trappings preached by most of the TQM gurus—and everything to do with ethereal things such as trust, bone-deep belief in the dignity, worth, and talent of the individual. Moreover, TQM—and especially, to its everlasting discredit, the Baldrige-award criteria—blithely ignores the No. 1 stumbling block to achieving a true TQM environment: smashing, blasting, totally destroying the bureaucracy. Quite simply, unless all first-line supervisors are removed—now—there's no hope! So, too, with middle management. If you've got more than four layers of management in a billion dollar plus company, forget real TQM. Empowerment means letting the people close to the action get on with the show. When that happens, then apply your TQM miracle cures.

Figure 7-1   The Traditional versus The Empowered Organization

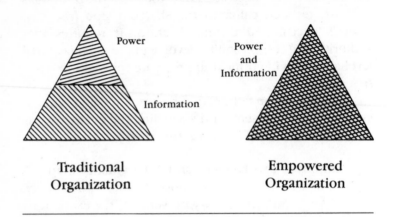

Traditionally, we find organizational power at the top. But we don't find the information needed to make the best decisions for the customer there. So we have power and the knowledge and understanding of customers in two very different parts of the organization. In a traditional department store, for example, an unempowered sales clerk must seek the approval of the store manager in order to issue a credit to an irate shopper. In a department store in which employees feel empowered, the sales clerk has the authority to act in the best interests of the customer. The two approaches are illustrated above in Figure 7-1.

Nordstrom, the Seattle-based chain of apparel stores, has perfected the new approach:

1. Coach employees thoroughly until they are ready to assume responsibility; when they are ready, *give it to them.*

2. Support employees who make decisions that, in their good judgment at the time, were in the best interests of the customer—even when their decision turns out

to have been flawed. Refrain from punishing; use the experience as a learning device.

3. Abandon any other "rules."

Figure 7-2 displays the entire contents of the Nordstrom's employee handbook, which runs to one 8-by-5-inch card.

Figure 7-2   Nordstrom Employee Handbook

WELCOME TO NORDSTROM

We're glad to have you with
our Company.

Our number one goal is to provide
outstanding customer service.

Set both your personal and
professional goals high.
We have great confidence in your
ability to achieve them.

Nordstrom Rules:

Rule #1: **Use your good
judgment in all situations.**

There will be no additional rules.

Please feel free to ask
your department manager,
store manager or division general
manager any question
at any time.

nordstrom

Reprinted by permission of Nordstrom, Inc.

Empowerment is an *approach,* a leadership style that shapes the overall management of an enterprise. The leader who empowers employees unlocks their potential by garnering their full contribution and stretching and teaching them through self-development. Empowerment is one of the most effective means for teaching the right-hemispheric arts of leadership: It encourages optimum individual and group contribution. Properly employed, empowerment helps to create high motivation and performance levels in successful organizations. Empowerment is *learning by doing.*

Authority, Responsibility, and Accountability

Some leaders find it difficult to square empowerment with what they see as their managerial tasks—in part because they believe the fallacious axiom that authority and responsibility must accompany accountability.

Authority is the power and the right to take appropriate action in a given situation. In general, we recognize two forms of authority: legal or nominal authority and "real" authority. **Responsibility,** in the corporate sense, refers to an individual's being answerable to a senior individual or group for the successful accomplishment of a task or tasks. Responsibility implies a willingness to accept an obligation for something. **Accountability,** which is often confused or used interchangeably with responsibility, means an unconditional obligation for the satisfactory execution of a task, regardless of who is actually doing it.

Although it is generally agreed that the levels of authority and responsibility possessed by every manager in an organization must be equal (the so-called parity principle), accountability does not form part of the parity

involved. Accountability for the performance of a corporation rests with its owners, usually the shareholders. It
follows therefore that accountability, unlike authority and
responsibility, *cannot be delegated*. Accountability is the
final mandate of the CEO as long as the CEO is the representative of the shareholders. Delegation of accountability
is tantamount to abdication and for this reason is uncon-
scionable. In some cases, it may even be illegal. But
nothing prevents the devolution of authority or responsibility except personal insecurity.

The insecure executive, who confuses giving power
with losing it, often suffers from a chronic need to
control others. During his incarceration in a Soviet
prison, Alexander Solzhenitsyn learned that as long as
he tried to maintain power over his captors concerning his food, health, or clothing, he was at their mercy.
But when he came to accept his powerlessness, their
power over him ceased and he became free. Observed
William Hazlitt, "The love of power is the love of ourselves."

David McClelland describes two kinds of power:
social power and personal power. The use of personal
power tends to be coercive, egotistic, callow, and self-
serving. Those who use it view people as *things,* pawns
to be manipulated in the pursuit of their own aims.
Abusers of personal power tend to lack self-esteem, lean-
ing toward autocracy and Hobbesian behavior. Social
power, on the other hand, is motivated by Lockean characteristics like justice, fairness, and equality and is more
frequently associated with serving the common good.
Leaders who skillfully deploy social power are self-
assured; they don't require dominance over others or
status to confirm their self-esteem; they are able to let go,
and they tend to gain genuine pleasure from the achievements of others. Yet all too often—and to the detriment
of the organization—management regards employees as

capable only of taking orders. The case of Twentieth Century Fox and Alan Ladd, Jr. is a classic example of this kind of tunnel vision and how to avoid it.

The People-First Organization

I used to believe that an organization's most important asset was its customers. Recently I have changed my mind; I now believe that employees are its most important asset. I've come to understand that customers alone cannot sustain an organization—they must be coupled with an inspired and motivated team. But dedicated employees *can* sustain an organization, because they will find the customers and delight them. In a finely balanced organization, the balance of emphasis should be 51% internal customer and 49% external customer.

Alan Ladd, Jr., former president of Twentieth Century Fox and leader of its motion picture division, produced *Star Wars,* the 1977 hit that became the second-greatest all-time box office draw in the industry's history. By his own admission, Ladd backed George Lucas, not *Star Wars* or Twentieth Century Fox. In 1979 he resigned from the studio, together with two of his close friends and leadership team members, over a major dispute with then-chairman Dennis C. Stanfill regarding the payment of bonuses to production staff. Ladd's management style supports the argument that it is *people* who create products and services, not companies; and leaders and managers depend on *people* for creative thrust and the execution of ideas. Ladd reflected:

> One thing that characterized us at Fox, which made us distinct from other companies, was that we ran it much like a family. Our personalities, thoughts and ideas intertwined. This is a business of collaboration; you'll find that among people who make films . . .

[T]he creative side is a business of input, discussion and attitude . . . [T]he creative process comes out of the chaos. No book can tell you how to make a good movie. All these involved people and all of their ideas make a movie.

Ladd could surely have said the same thing about any business. The essence of his philosophy is testimony to what I call the **goals/people/structure** model of organizational design and decision making. This model requires that leaders do as follows:

1. Establish the **goals** of the organization.
2. Identify the **people** with the best "fit" (their leadership skills, managerial strengths, and task-related talents) for the job (leadership, managerial, and task objectives and opportunities).
3. Develop an organizational **structure** to fit the assets and liabilities of the key players.

Big names like Richard D. Zanuck, Mel Brooks, and George Lucas follow Ladd from studio to studio—it's the man not the organization these superstars want to associate with. George Lucas said that the only reason he brought his film *Willow* to MGM was to work with Ladd. Zanuck felt the same way, observing, "Laddie's word is his bond." Because of this reputation, Ladd earns $3.2 million a year as head of MGM-Pathe and operates with an annual production budget of $125 million.

The people-first rule applies to *all* organizations, regardless of size. It comes naturally to those who are creative themselves; such right-hemisphere leaders encourage discussion and welcome the creative ideas of *everyone.*

OLD AND NEW ORGANIZATIONAL DESIGNS

The concept of empowerment can only flourish in an appropriately designed organization. However, much of the present design of executive and administrative work derives from the writings of Adam Smith and Max Weber, who defined the need to establish a division of labor in order to optimize the efficiency of capital and labor. All our organizational structures—functional, matrix, line, territorial, product departmentalization, divisional; brand-management based (pioneered by Procter & Gamble); strategic business units (SBUs; developed in 1971 by General Electric); and the decentralized, multidivisional structure (originated by Du Pont but exploited by General Motors)—are attempts to continue where Smith and Weber left off.

It's interesting to note that most of these organizational models derive from Chinese models established 5,000 years ago; incorporated into the canon law of the Roman Catholic Church 800 years ago; and adapted and developed over the years by the armies of the world. The term *line authority,* for example, describes the military chain of command in which a superior makes decisions that are relayed to a subordinate, who makes further decisions that are relayed to his subordinate, and so on down the line. The term *staff,* as in *staff authority,* derives from the stick or baton formerly carried by army officers as one of the supportive trappings of rank. In military and business terminology, staff authority provides administrative support to line authority. The ancient history of these organizational terms and their continued use demonstrate our failure to modernize our organizational thinking and therefore to fully exploit the potential of empowerment and delegation.

Indeed, the lack of development in organizational structure illustrates the degree to which our thinking has become stuck. Over the last 5,000 years, we've made wide-ranging advances and modifications in our thinking about people, about the goals we set for our organizations, and about how we achieve them. But we have made virtually no innovations in how we structure our organizations. Fundamentally, the same pyramid structure, if a little flatter, exists today as it did 5,000 years ago. And yet the human spirit cries out to be free from this tyranny.

Although many organizational theorists agree that structure should follow strategy, they haven't made the connection between organizational design and the changes in social expectations and in product and service innovation. Such changes are so rapid that, as Alan Ladd, Jr. has proven, only structures that are flexible, sensitive to change, and responsive to individual aspirations and contributions are relevant to today's environment. Organizational theorists Roger J. Howe and Mark G. Mindell classify today's employees as either "traditional" or "contemporary." Writing in *Management Review,* they observed:

> Motivating the contemporary employee requires a different form of management than is required to motivate traditional employees. Recognizing and adapting to employees who hold new work values is one of the greatest challenges facing managers today. In our increasingly complex society, people have more educational and developmental opportunities than ever. This in turn has helped create a whole new set of employee expectations. As a result, the traditional employee and the contemporary employee tend to hold markedly different attitudes towards work and organizational authority.

Figure 7-3 on page 240 summarizes the differences between traditional and contemporary employees.

The generalizations in Figure 7-3 apply as readily to the new breed of executive as they do to employees in general and make apparent our lack of appropriate organizational structures. We continue to focus on form rather than function—let alone people—and we seem to believe that the solution to the structural needs of tomorrow's organizations is more of yesterday's recipes, yet

Figure 7-3   Traditional Versus Contemporary Employees

The traditional employee displays more *loyalty and commitment* to the company than the contemporary employee.

Compensation has always been important to employees, but tends to be valued more as a consequence of performance by contemporary employees.

Contemporary employees are more concerned with organizational *recognition* than are traditional employees.

In contrast to traditional employees, contemporary ones have more desire to *participate in decisions* that affect them.

Traditional employees are more concerned with *job security.*

Contemporary employees value *communication* from management as to what's going on in the company.

Contemporary employees have short-term *goal orientation,* as opposed to traditional employees, whose orientation is long-term.

More than traditional employees, the contemporary group desires work to be *challenging.*

Contemporary employees are more concerned that their work be *worthwhile.*

Contemporary employees desire *developmental opportunities.*

Contemporary employees want their work to be *interesting.*

Contemporary employees want their work to be *creative.*

Traditional employees usually put their *work* before family and leisure; contemporary employees tend to place their priorities first with *leisure,* then family and work.

Source: Howe, R. W., and Mindell, M. G., "The Challenge of Changing Work Values: Motivating the Contemporary Employee," *Management Review,* September 1979. Reprinted with permission of the American Management Association.

another reorganization. We continue to do things backward: First, we articulate goals; then we define the structure to meet those goals; then we drop the appropriate people into the structure—goals/structure/*people*. But the goals/*people*/structure approach described by Ladd makes much better sense in today's environment. Sometimes an even more enlightened model may be called for—*people*/goals/structure. It works as follows:

1. First, add to your team the best people in the world, the superstars.

2. Next, agree on goals commensurate with the team's talents.

3. Finally, ask the team to design the structure to achieve those goals.

Here's how the enlightened approach might work: Two superstars, say, George Lucas and Alan Ladd, Jr., seek to work together because they admire each other's talent (*people*). They identify the ideas and desires they have in common and define one or more objectives (*goals*). Then they form an organization to reach their goals (*structure*). Figure 7-4 on page 242 illustrates the three approaches to structural organization.

At Manpower I felt more affinity, more respect, and more affection for the leadership team that we built than for any other group that touched my life with the exception of my immediate family. I understood then and I understand now just how important people are to the success of an organization. To this end, leaders with moxie strive to create a structure in which their team can best perform.

HOW TO LOSE SUPERSTARS

As we've seen, failure to give superstars their heads has been responsible for the creation of many entrepreneurial organizations. Several disaffected managers resolve to

Figure 7-4   The Three Approaches to the Structural Design
of Organizations

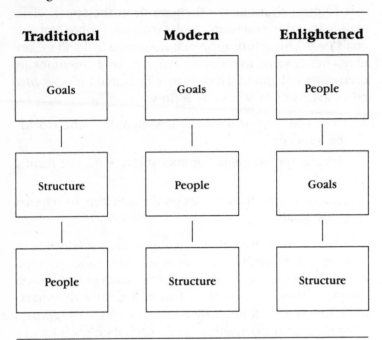

Traditional	Modern	Enlightened
Goals	Goals	People
Structure	People	Goals
People	Structure	Structure

leave their current employer, taking with them the projects they have been nurturing in the backs of their minds.
They develop a business strategy and build their own independent organization to accommodate and implement
their big ideas. This is the way that many startups in
California's famed Silicon Valley came about.

Steve Jobs and Steven Wozniak tried to produce their
new computer at Hewlett-Packard but encountered so
many obstacles that they left to start their own company
(which they called Apple because they wanted to be in
front of Atari in the telephone book). Tom Watson might
have continued to work for John Patterson, the autocratic
founder of NCR, if their working styles had been more
compatible. But Watson left NCR to found IBM, after

describing Patterson as "an amalgam of St. Paul, Poor Richard, and Adolf Hitler."

These are just two examples of big talent that got away because management was unable or unwilling to give bright employees enough leeway to exercise their creativity and talent—to *empower* them. These stories illustrate the need for a real shift away from the still-prevalent, non-productive, my-way-or-the-highway school of management. Continuing to pursue the goals/structure/people model instead of the people/goals/structure one is a sure way to lose superstars.

The lessons come hard. Hewlett-Packard and NCR, both exemplary companies in many respects, still live with the curse of these old errors.

That Hewlett-Packard should have fudged this opportunity is ironic, since it too was started by two men in a garage! Formed in 1939, it now employs 89,000 people and places 6th on the *Fortune* 500 list of largest industrial companies. Another U.S. high-tech company, Tektronix, founded in 1946, now employs 12,000 and is America's 279th largest company. These two companies and a handful of other high-flyers (including Fluke, GEC, Thorn EMI, Philips Industries, and Smith Industries) were the subject of a research project undertaken by the City University Business School in London, England. The investigators were trying to throw some light on the fact that some companies are better at developing new products than others. They found that companies typically fell into two categories: leaders and followers. *Leader companies* preferred organic structures, which were very difficult to chart and explain but which worked. The *follower companies,* on the other hand, favored mechanistic organization structures with very clearly defined job responsibilities. The researchers also found that leaders gave little direction to employees concerning the type of innovation they wanted, but followers spelled out what they wanted in specific product terms. From this, it's clear that empowerment and delegation are one half of the equation; the other half is innovation.

An open, trusting environment so pervades Herman Miller (the Zeeland, Michigan, designer and manufacturer of furniture systems) that supervisors encourage their employees to go over their heads; they cite this practice as one of the reasons for the company's success. The key values at Herman Miller of participative management, profit sharing for all employees, and open communication have encouraged employees to generate ideas that have saved the company $12 million during the last 5 years. Empowering employees in this way has earned Herman Miller a top position in many lists of most-admired corporations.

The role of leadership is to empower others by

1. Ensuring that the organization's structure continually reflects and enables management's primary purpose: to support the people who support the customer
2. Encouraging employees to make commitments, take risks, and volunteer creative suggestions for improvement, so that the company consistently surpasses the expectations of both its internal and external customers
3. Encouraging honest feedback by permitting employees to discuss how they feel, free from fear of reprisal or judgment
4. Talking straight to foster basic trust
5. Making work, as Noel Coward put it, more fun than fun and turning customers into fans

Delegation

A willingness to delegate is a precursor to empowerment. The act of delegation sends powerful signals to employees. The leader who delegates is saying: "I like, trust, and

believe in you. I know you will not let me down. I think
you have potential and I will help you to achieve it." The
employee reacts by thinking: "I like this. I'm challenged
and able to grow, which will help my career. I'm trusted.
I'll earn the faith placed in me."

When we fail to delegate, we send equally powerful
signals. We are saying: "You'll screw up; you can't be
trusted. Only I know how to do it best. You're not competent enough to assume new tasks or responsibilities."
And the employee thinks: "I'm being patronized. Instead
of being challenged, I'm not permitted or encouraged to
grow. There is no potential here."

Most of us owe the good breaks in our careers to
mentors—special people who cared about us and gave us
opportunities that stretched us, often before we were completely ready for them. They gave us big responsibilities
and helped us learn how to handle them; in short, they
delegated to us. And any of us lucky enough to be in this
position worked like crazy to prove our mentors right.

When I was 27, just such a mentor asked me to go
to Europe to turn around a struggling company with sales
of $1 million and losses of $350,000. That special person
was repaid with some of the best years and efforts of my
life. In just over a decade, we built that business into a
world-class outfit with sales of $100 million and profits to
match—and I retired when I was 40 and so did he!

Failure to delegate—the hallmark of the insecure
manager—leads to the demotivation of employees, driving out the brightest and best who believe that they can
start their own businesses or grow faster with another
company. Usually they are right, and your best employees
become your most formidable competitors.

Delegation—the hallmark of the secure leader—is
just another word for motivation: When we delegate, we
motivate. And building a motivated team is what leadership in successful organizations is all about.

If you want to start a revolution, leave this book open at this page in a prominent place so that your leadership team can learn the secret:

> *Delegation is another word for motivation!*

Pass it on!

Devolution of power and decision making leads to decentralization and is the natural condition of healthy organizations. Democratic and participative management reinforces high morale, generates high performance, frees top management for strategic activities, encourages managers to grow and develop, promotes managerial creativity and initiative, and allows decisions to be made faster, because those closest to the issues make them. Delegation without participation is **abdication.** Thus, participation is not a means to an end but rather a philosophy that provides people with the emotional and intellectual tools to get the job done and have fun.

As long ago as 1955, Robert Katz argued that the responsibilities of corporate leadership embrace significantly greater levels of conceptual thinking and much less technical skill than middle and supervisory management. The senior executive must have a holistic view of the corporation—that is, a right-hemispheric view—he or she must be able to integrate the circumstances and issues as well as the people involved. To do this effectively, leaders must delegate the responsibilities that are no longer appropriate to their mission. As they move from supervisory to senior executive roles, their focus on technical issues gives way to a more human and conceptual perspective. Figure 7-5 illustrates the principle involved.

Beyond the need to delegate is the need to distinguish between *real* delegation and *pseudo*delegation. The latter includes cosmetic delegation rather than full respon-

Figure 7-5   The Evolution from Supervisor to Leader

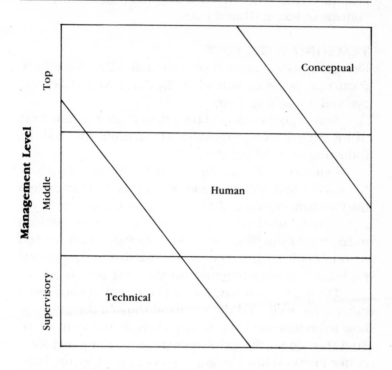

sibility; programs or projects that are almost certain to crash; disaster scenarios with a high degree of adverse political repercussions; boring assignments; and dangerous regional responsibilities. Executives should avoid these as well as any attempt to delegate accountability (which by definition *cannot* be delegated).

The delegator with moxie knows that when a task is fully delegated, the credit for successful execution is delegated too. Delegating the responsibility but not the glory is a sure way to demotivate people; but giving generous credit where it's due ensures a positive corporate climate and a motivated team.

TEACHING WITH LOVE

Delegation is a statement of respect and love for others. It can only be successful when the delegator has a caring eye and a teaching heart.

Years ago, James L. Hayes, then chairman and CEO of the American Management Association, told me the following story about delegation:

One day Fred was minding his lathe on the factory floor, as he had been doing every day for 35 years, when his foreman introduced him to a new employee.

"Fred, I want you to meet Carl. He's joined our team today. Would you please show him the ropes? He's worked on other lathes but never on your particular equipment. I'll leave you both together for the next few days."

During the first day, Fred and Carl got to know each other quite well, and the old hand showed the new one how to operate the lathe. Midmorning on the second day, Fred shut down the lathe, telling Carl, "I'm going for a coffee break. While I'm gone, you can start up the lathe on your own."

Fred left Carl staring at the machine. After a few moments, Carl pressed the red button that normally started the lathe, but nothing happened. He pressed the button again—still nothing. Scratching his head, he circled the machine looking for a second button or something that he might have overlooked. But he had no luck.

When Fred came back and found Carl bewildered and the lathe idle, he wanted to know why. "Well," said Carl, "I've tried everything. I've checked all the switches, the fuses, the belts, and the safety locks. We have power, lubricant, and coolant. I just can't seem to get it going!"

Hearing this, Fred approached the lathe, leaned on the red start button with all his weight, and gave the machine a solid kick. The lathe sprang to life.

Through this story we see the importance of teaching with love. When we teach someone the mere mechanics of what we know, we teach without love. As Carl might have put it, "He taught me all *I* know, but he didn't teach me what *he* knew."

As Jim Hayes explained to me, "When you love someone, you teach them the art of the job. When you tolerate them, you only teach them the technology." Delegation is the finest means by which leaders who love their colleagues enough to teach them properly transfer to them their skills, knowledge, and wisdom.

The necessity to make a decision is a tremendous teacher. With each occasion that requires executives to take action, their initiative and executive abilities are stretched and developed. With increasing autonomy, executives test their limits and improve their performance.

THE RESULTS OF ABDICATION

The balance between anarchy (the loss of total control) and efficient corporate performance is delicate. Steven J. Ross, chairman of Warner Communications (before the merger with Time), built sales at Warner's from $522 million to $4 billion in 10 years. This success stemmed largely from his philosophy of delegating complete control to division heads. However, Ross's commitment to total delegation backfired when he hired James J. Morgan (from the senior team at Philip Morris) to head Warner's Atari unit. Atari's fiscal 1982 profits of $323 million were followed by a loss of $539 million in 1983. Although much of this red ink was incurred before Morgan's era, Ross's hands-off management style, by his own admission, resulted in a lack of clarity about what was going on at Atari—which seriously compounded Atari's problems. At the time, Ross said that "the way a division is run is up to the CEO. This management philosophy has built this company." He also indicated that he had no intention of changing his decentralized management style. However, he admitted that communications and feedback at Atari were not functioning well and that Warner's needed to improve management strength at headquarters.

But it was too late. In July of 1984 Atari was sold for a mere $240 million in low-interest notes, forcing Warner to take a second-quarter loss of $425 million. The buyer was Jack Tramiel, who had built Commodore International, famous for its home computers. Tramiel immediately laid off 75% of Atari's U.S. staff, pointedly observing that "James Morgan is now taking a long holiday." Unfortunately, the fallout from uncontrolled delegation is usually counted in terms of human casualties.

COMMUNICATIONS AND FEEDBACK

As the Atari story demonstrates, one of the hazards of decentralization and delegation is a deterioration in communications and feedback. This deterioration can be overcome by formal and especially informal techniques.

The informal system of communication is often more effective and much faster than the formal. Commonly referred to as the "grapevine," it is generally seen as a negative influence because it so often transmits malicious gossip or distorted information—and it usually doesn't contribute to the achievement of corporate goals. Most executives try to ignore the grapevine, relying for communication on more conventional means. But if put to positive use, the grapevine can be invaluable.

By tracing all known personal links between senior management, the effective leader can discover the most sensitive sources for "input" and "output" and then draw up an informal communications chart. It will take only two or three phone calls to the appropriate input sources to introduce information into the system; the organizational tom-toms will do the rest—and do it faster than Federal Express!

Because the grapevine is subject to rapid and frequent changes, it needs constant updating. In addition, any attempts to silence it are doomed to failure. It's wiser to treat it with considerable respect and provide it with regular and nourishing information. If you starve it, it will create its own news—gossip and rumor—which can be quite harmful.

Because the grapevine is the most powerful communications force within any organization, it can be especially helpful during times of change or upheaval; for example, during acquisitions or the introduction of new technology or the expansions or closures of facilities. At these times, it will be hyperactive; you must make sure that you feed it accurate and timely information. The grapevine is also invaluable for correcting erroneous information; you can squelch a rumor in no time with the right word in the right ear.

Positive management of the grapevine is indispensable to feedback in an organization—and feedback is essential to successful decentralization and delegation. Enlightened leaders don't try to stamp out the grapevine, which they rightly see as an exercise in futility. Instead, they understand and harness its power to the advantage of the entire organization and its customers.

THE URGE TO CENTRALIZE

Today, corporate delegation is not an option; it's a necessity: No leader is clever enough to make all the decisions required in our increasingly complex world. If the leadership team does not delegate voluntarily, modern executives will force it to, and delegation will occur by default.

This is not to deny that in many corporations centralized power is still common. It usually indicates that the CEO has little confidence in the organization's executives. Or it suggests the reverse; that is, the CEO fears that their excellent performance will show up his or hers (a condition for which Professor C. Northcote Parkinson coined the term *injelititus*). Regardless of the cause, executives who cannot handle their fear of delegation are in the wrong job. And those working for them should find a more promising assignment, because the corporation in which the CEO makes all the decisions is ruining its most valuable asset: its leadership talent. It's only a matter of time before such an organization fails.

The tendency to centralize may be caused by two other factors: Either the CEO possesses a house-sized ego or a crisis disturbs corporate rhythm.

An ego in itself is not a bad thing—the world's most successful corporations are not run by shy, retiring wallflowers. But even so, such egos must be managed if the rest of the players are to exercise their talents and creativity. It's up to these players to demonstrate that they can achieve results through devolved decision making and at the same time make the CEO look great.

Crisis is another reason that leadership may favor centralized power. In times of crisis, centralization may be an appropriate short-term strategy. Often, when the collective fortunes of a corporation are temporarily in decline, people defer to a natural leader to get them safely through the storm.

In the United Kingdom, the turbulent economic period of the 1970s provided several recessions, national strikes, and other assorted economic traumas. During the worst of these crises, our leadership team at Manpower reverted to increased centralization. We consciously reorganized, reassigned senior executives, and changed the decision-making process to show our employees that we had adopted a take-charge approach. These were periods of discomfort for us, because centralization was foreign to both our values and our skills. As executives we were better at building and creating than hunkering down; and as soon as circumstances permitted, we reverted to our looser, decentralized style. Although our executive effectiveness was probably inferior during these periods, we were responding to our employees' instincts —which told them that democratic decision making was not the way to run a company caught between a rock and a hard place!

Empowerment

The number of people on Jack Welch's payroll exceeds the number who live in Tampa, Florida; or Newark, New Jersey; and together they earn more than the combined personal income of all Alaskans or North Dakotans. Jack Welch's company is General Electric, the fifth largest company in the United States. It makes everything from dime-store light bulbs to 400,000-pound locomotives and billion-dollar nuclear power plants. If it were a bank, it would be in the top ten, overseeing more credit cards than American Express, owning more planes than American Airlines, and second only in market capitalization to Exxon. But Jack Welch wants to make this colossus feel and act like a small business, powered by "speed, simplicity, and self-confidence." One of the paths on this journey is empowerment, or in GE parlance, "work-out." The future of GE, Welch says, is based on "winning by our ideas . . . not by whips and chains."

But what *is* empowerment? It is the sense that one has the power to make the necessary decisions affecting the major aspects of one's life or work. William C. Byham, author of *Zapp! The Lightning of Empowerment,* calls it "the psychological energy that activates us. When we really work hard and the day goes fast and we feel good about what we're doing, it's because we're empowered."

Empowerment is intoxicating. Ask any manager who's been deprived of real freedom and then tastes real power. Talented people who are unempowered are wasted—on themselves, their friends and family, their colleagues, and their organization. (The opposite is just as true—people who lack the skills and attitudes to be effective will not become so through empowerment.)

Powerlessness is the root of many major weaknesses in modern organizations: turgid decision-making processes, resistance to change, poor quality, poor customer service, low productivity, distribution tangles—all could be significantly improved by the antidote to powerlessness: empowerment.

But as with delegation, empowerment is not something one *does* to people; rather, it is a state of mind, a Lockean attitude to life and people.

Nor is it just another buzzword. In one form or another, the concept of empowerment has been around for centuries; during the 1960s and 1970s, its popularity grew. Social activists saw it as a way for people to take control of their destinies, especially those members of "out" groups (blacks, elders, the homeless, gays, single parents, environmentalists, and others who perceived themselves to be disenfranchised).

In my work, I am frequently asked by organizations to "install an empowerment program." But empowerment is *not* a "program"—it is a change of culture and values. And it takes time. Says Ed Lawlor, a professor of business at the University of Southern California: "It's a very long-term, hard process . . . it involves at least 8 to 10 years of activity and changing just about every piece of the management system." Harvard's Len Schlesinger, who is one of several academics helping GE to adopt a culture of empowerment, describes the efforts there as "one of the biggest planned efforts to alter people's behavior since the Cultural Revolution [in the People's Republic of China]."

Introducing the concepts of empowerment to an organization without a change in the cultural environment will almost certainly breed employee cynicism—a condition that might have been avoided altogether if management had refrained from introducing "an empowerment program." I have even seen a major organization introduce such a program with much ballyhoo while simultaneously laying off 600 employees!

Sam McLaughlin, who runs Pillsbury's new Green Giant plant in Wellston, Ohio, has successfully empowered his colleagues by establishing a series of self-directed work teams. He says, "Empowering people is simple. You need three things—visionaries to develop the talk; champions to walk the talk; and teachers to talk the talk."

Head of General Electric's audit staff Teresa LeGrand describes the effect of the culture change at her firm: "When I started 10 years ago, the first thing I did was count the $5,000 in the petty cash box. Today we look at the $5 million in inventory on the floor, searching for process improvements that will bring it down."

Like delegation, empowerment is more about enabling than doing; removing policies, procedures, and rules that stifle initiative; removing fear of reprisal for voicing honest opinions; eliminating controls and punishments. For these reasons, it is impossible for the control-oriented manager to embrace, because even though empowerment is more about turning executives into employees' coaches rather than employees' equals, such managers cannot grasp the notion that by giving away power, they gain power.

Jack Welch's approach is testimony to one mandatory condition—an empowered organization gets that way through the passion of the CEO. But even if the CEO and the leadership team are earnestly committed to the concepts of empowerment and delegation, their followers must share that commitment too. Executives who lack the necessary self-esteem and personal motivation will never become empowered; they will shun the risks and the responsibility, preferring to be "victims" rather than agents of change. Before empowerment can take place, everyone on the team must be encouraged to share the same vision: They must believe that they can make a difference, that they have choices, and that the power is theirs to claim.

THE UNIT-PRESIDENT CONCEPT

Of all the management models proffered over the years, one stands out as a simple, clear, and practical approach to empowerment. Called the **unit-president concept,** it is a wonderful blueprint for a perfect empowerment and delegation strategy.

The ultimate level of autonomy within the corporation is that enjoyed by the CEO. The best CEOs are successful because they treat their corporations as if they owned them. The unit-president concept assumes that ambitious and creative executives are keen to accept the same type of responsibility for their results as the CEO does for the corporation as a whole. The theory is that if all the organization's executives felt the same way about the businesses they ran—if they thought and acted like presidents—they might produce presidential results. Empowerment and delegation help people to feel as if they do own the unit or functional areas for which they are responsible; therefore, they are able to identify more closely with performance objectives and results.

To illustrate the effectiveness of this principle, I am reminded of one of Manpower's middle-management teams to whom we sold the unit they previously managed through a management buy-out. Some months later, I visited the "new" operation on a Saturday and found the new owners in. When I asked why they were working on their day off when they had never regularly done so before, the president (previously the branch manager!) reflected for a moment and then replied, "It never occurred to us to do so when we were working for someone else." This group fulfilled the promise that all sellers hope for in management buy-outs; they made more money for our company as franchisees than we had been able to make when they ran it as salaried managers. I spent much time with these newly minted entrepreneurs, trying to find the key to their present success in light of our earlier, less spectacular performance. I learned that there is no substitute for the feeling of ownership. Within an organization, the key to turning top managers into top producers is to provide them with the same freedom and status enjoyed by owner/managers. The unit-president concept is a vehicle for implementing this strategy. Its cornerstones are as follows:

♦ The CEO must be strongly committed to a decentralized structure, to a participative or consultative leadership style, and to the attitudes that lead to empowerment and delegation.

♦ The leadership team must genuinely want senior executives to achieve, to be creative, and to be imaginative in the execution of their responsibilities.

♦ All executives must be empowered to exercise self-supervision, self-control, and self-appraisal.

♦ All executives are considered to have failed if their employees need to ask what has to be done, whether they have the necessary authority, and whether they have met their goals.

The unit-president concept works on the principle that the clear definition of areas of authority and strong delegation create a **charter of freedom** within which executives may exercise their responsibilities in the manner most appropriate.

Figure 7-6 shows how the unit-president concept attempts to encourage *all* managers to think and act like presidents. The charter of freedom in the center of the square is synonymous with *autonomous responsibility.* The boundaries of each executive's responsibilities, labeled outside the square, are negotiated between the executive and his or her manager. That is, executives are *not* presented with job descriptions that tell them *how*

Figure 7-6   The Unit-President Concept

Duty Constraints:
Laws, Morals, and Ethics

Procedures

> **The Unit President**
> *(The Charter of Freedom)*

Plans

Information

Budgets

Memorandum of Agreement
(Position Description)

---

to discharge their responsibilities (common practice today); instead, within certain external constraints, they have complete freedom as to how they achieve agreed-upon objectives. This is called the **memorandum of agreement.** Some external constraints follow.

1. *Duty constraints: laws, morals, and ethics.* These include the laws of the country; the organization's statement of values; its moral and ethical code; its policies and procedures.

2. *Plan constraints.* These include annual plans established by the unit president, negotiated with and agreed to by his or her manager, and revised as necessary during the year; the statements of organizational and unit missions and objectives.

3. *Budget constraints.* These include the annual operating budgets, which have been negotiated and agreed on for the year (or other time period) between the unit president and his or her manager. These budgets may be revised from time to time during the course of the year.

4. *Memorandum-of-agreement constraints.* These include performance standards and limitations on authority.

5. *Procedural constraints.* These include the "rules of the game"—the agreed-upon, simplest methods for undertaking repetitive but important tasks and functions.

6. *Information-for-control constraints.* All executives need regular feedback to help them track actual results and compare these to desired goals. All executives in the team must cooperate in order to achieve their common objective.

One of the ambitions of the unit-president concept is to limit as much as possible the normative statements usually found in a memorandum of agreement concerning job content and the manner in which tasks must be undertaken. For example, it is not necessary to identify the authority that goes with responsibility. Unit presidents are automatically given *all* the authority required to undertake their responsibilities. It's only necessary to define the **negative authority standards,** which take the form of three questions:

> *Standard 1:* What can I do that does not require me to tell anyone?
>
> *Standard 2:* What can I do that requires me to subsequently inform someone?
>
> *Standard 3:* What can I do only after I receive permission?

THE MEMORANDUM OF AGREEMENT (THE POSITION DESCRIPTION)

Managers should always prepare draft memoranda of agreement before hiring so that they can think through the responsibilities to be delegated and be able to justify the new appointment financially and organizationally. The final version will of course be negotiated with the candidate after a hiring decision has been made. The best memoranda of agreement contain the following:

1. The objective or purpose of the job
2. The scope of the job
3. The main responsibilities and negative authority standards of the job
4. A statement and description of the main working relationships that are part of the job's routine
5. Standards of performance (these are mandatory in memoranda of agreement) that delineate the conditions that will indicate whether a responsibility is acceptably (but not necessarily well) done

Although sales or profit targets are standards of performance, they should be included in plans and budgets rather than in the memorandum of agreement. A definition of the means by which the executive may contribute to corporate goals outside his or her immediate functional responsibilities may be more meaningful.

I refer to the position description as a memorandum of agreement because I see it as a singularly personal and profound document, invested with great hope and mutual trust. Consequently, it should be given careful thought and enough uninterrupted time in which to negotiate. It should consist of verbs and nouns and, as far as possible, nothing else. It should be no longer than one page. It should incorporate an expiration date and should be revised annually following a personal review between the unit president and his or her manager.

Too Much or Too Little?

In Shaw's play *Major Barbara,* Undershaft, the old cannon maker, reviews potential career options with his 24-

year-old son, Stephen. First he asks if his son has considered literature or art. "No, I have nothing of the artist
about me," Stephen replies. "A philosopher, perhaps? Eh?"
Undershaft inquires. "I make no such ridiculous pretension," the young man says. His father suggests the army,
the navy, the church, or the law, but his son professes no
acquaintance with or interest in any of these. Exasperated,
Undershaft asks, "Well come! Is there anything you know
or care for?" "I know the difference between right and
wrong," declares Stephen. "You don't say so!" proclaims
Undershaft. "What! no capacity for business, no knowledge of law, no sympathy with art, no pretension to philosophy; only a simple knowledge of the secret that has
puzzled all the philosophers, baffled all the lawyers,
muddled all the men of business, and ruined most of the
artists: the secret of right and wrong. Why, man, you're
a genius, a master of masters, a god! At twenty-four, too!"

When executives delegate to and empower others,
they devolve some of their responsibility and authority
to them; they transfer power. Usually, empowered people
are, like Undershaft's son, quite clear about the big picture but a little uncertain about the details: They feel sure
that they can undertake their new responsibility as well,
and perhaps even better, than had been done before.
Therefore, sensitive and motivational encouragement as
well as appropriate coaching and professional development are required to achieve a successful transfer of
responsibilities.

Leaders and managers with moxie seldom commit
the delegated functions or tasks to paper, partly because
the memorandum of agreement should provide the
necessary controls between the two executive levels, but
also because it would be constraining: It would emphasize
details rather than the whole picture and box the
employee into a status quo, left-hemispheric rather than
an innovative, right-hemispheric perspective. Superior
performance requires a holistic view. The unit-president

concept is notable for its absence of written rules, which are sure inhibitors of vital flexibility. Finally, writing down delegated functions ignores the known fact that everyone has their own way of doing things. One of the big advantages of empowerment and delegation—beyond their value as opportunities for personal learning, growth, and development—is the chance they give executives to stamp their own imprint on an activity handled previously by another. This sense of "presidential ownership" fosters outstanding executive performance.

Unfortunately, many organizations display their disdain for empowerment and delegation by providing huge manuals, so that employees have an answer for almost every anticipated situation. There are two problems with this approach: First, no one can predict all eventualities; if they could, the manual would be taller than the World Trade Center; and second, such all-encompassing manuals are an insult to employees' dignity and self-esteem. Emerson observed, "Trust men and they will be true to you; trust them greatly and they will show themselves great." Executives who are comfortable with the concepts of empowerment and delegation find it better to err on the side of ambition than parsimony. In other words, delegating to and empowering others a shade in excess of their current capabilities is always better than staying within their reach.

A reluctance to delegate or empower is a notorious demotivator. A management style that favors underdelegating and underempowerment doesn't stretch an executive adequately and infers a lack of confidence. When you're surprised by the resignation of a promising key executive, chances are that you underdelegated and he or she felt underempowered. Most of my mistakes concerning empowerment and delegation, even today when I should know better, have been errors of parsimony rather than generosity. We have a natural tendency to underestimate the potential of others, often thinking, "How could someone who is my junior be capable of handling tasks better than I can when I have been doing them for years?''

But it is full-bodied commitment to empowerment and delegation that inspires people to rise to meet the scope of the job and the confidence placed in them. Well-motivated executives nearly always surprise their leaders by performing at quality and output levels beyond those required or anticipated. While this outcome may also depend upon the corporate climate, the Lockean leader believes that to err on the side of ambition, in the hope of encouraging outstanding performance, far outweighs the risk of encountering the Peter Principle.

Indeed, one of the highs for a CEO is the reflected glory that comes from vigorous empowerment and delegation, because in the empowered organization, there is rapid individual and group development of ability and professional stature within a leadership team. But if a managerial failure does occur, the Lockean executive simply tries again, sure in the belief that knowledge is one of the few gifts that can be shared with another without loss to the giver. Overdelegation and a vigorous empowerment style is the *finest* learning experience available to superstars, their corporate leaders, and up-and-comers, because positive learning experiences—which by definition mean alterations of behavior—result in improved personal and therefore corporate performance.

I recently heard about the chief executive of a fabulously successful *Fortune* 500 company who was asked by a journalist to share his secrets for successful decision making and leadership. After pondering the question for a minute, he responded, ''Leadership comes from good judgment.''

''How do you get good judgment?'' the reporter asked.

''From experience,'' came the reply.

Tenaciously, the reporter insisted, ''How do you get experience?''

"From bad judgments," said the CEO.

Owner/entrepreneurs are constantly exposed to such learning experiences, many of which probably seemed more like baptisms by fire at the time. But hindsight mellows even the most experience-hardened entrepreneur's view, and most will later attest to the value of learning about people in this fashion. Although costly mistakes are sometimes made, the richness of the lesson, the positive impact on future performance, the development of executive judgment, and the subsequent retention of talented executives will nearly always offset the initial cost.

An entrepreneur is often successful when first starting a new business because of an inherent ability to make many decisions quickly with a limited amount of information. But the **span-of-control problem** soon arises: As the work force reaches 100 or so, the entrepreneur *must* delegate, and even more important, he or she must empower, so that innovation *and* management grow hand in hand.

A corporate ethos that recognizes empowerment and delegation as both good leadership and the right of employees will, quite correctly, stimulate senior managers to submit proposals to the CEO, suggesting additional transfers of responsibility. Implementing such proposals not only develops the team but also allows the CEO to increase the amount of time he or she spends on strategic issues. Increased trust and good chemistry, so essential to the development of synergy in the leadership team, are the natural by-products of this type of leadership.

Finally, the appropriate climate for success, which is the parent of empowerment and delegation, leads to another vital ingredient of managerial moxie—**action.** As all successful leaders know, it's more important to do *something* than *nothing.* Almost any action that springs from commitment and vigor is better than none at all; almost anything will work if it has enough commitment and dollars behind it. Sun Zi has said, "Weak leadership can wreck the soundest strategy; forceful execution of even a poor plan can often bring victory." A "wrong" decision, so long as the leader and his or her team believe in it, will quite often work better than a "right" one in which the leader and team have no ownership.

An empowered team can make anything work. For example, during the Iranian revolution, communications between Manpower's management team in Iran and our headquarters in London were cut off. Our Iranian management, headed by Martin Dyas, was subjected to terrifying physical and psychological threats while assuming responsibility for the safety of our staff as well as the protection of the company's assets. Because communications between Teheran and London had been severed, the Iranian team had to make all decisions without any direction from corporate executives. We had no opportunity to debrief with them until the ordeal was over and they had successfully left Iran. All our employees were safe and our financial losses were nominal. Dyas led an empowered team and this, together with the force of circumstances, ensured that he and the rest of his management team rose to the demands of a very tough situation.

Delegation in the Multinational Corporation

It is imperative for the contemporary leader to redefine the nature of the modern corporation in terms of a "cooperative system" or a "federation of individual intellects" rather than a traditional hierarchical structure. Such sponsors of the decentralized corporation hold an abiding and deep belief in absolute empowerment and delegation.

Confident executives always assume that they have the right and the authority to undertake assigned responsibilities in the *manner* of their choosing unless specifically instructed otherwise. This is the unit-president concept in action. Though corporate accountability at Manpower remained squarely with the chairman of its U.S. parent, Mitchell Fromstein, he good-naturedly bestowed upon my leadership team the nickname "Manpower Cuba," because of our independent attitude and thirst for autonomy. And it was those two traits that drove the U.K. leadership team to build "Manpower Cuba" from insignificance to the highest profit producer in Manpower's worldwide organization. Tony O'Reilly enjoyed the same reputation for autonomy when he ran the U.K. operations of H. J. Heinz, which he did so independently and so well that the U.S. food giant gave him the president's job in Pittsburgh! Heinz earns $500 million on sales of more than $6 billion and over the last decade has averaged a 16.6% return on shareholder's equity—for which Heinz thanks O'Reilly with nearly $3.5 million in compensation. He is sufficiently independent to run a number of his own companies in Ireland, including Independent Newspapers, Fitzwilton, and Atlantic Resources (a Celtic Sea oil-exploration company).

Merrill Lynch food analyst William Maguire says that Heinz is almost "universally regarded as the best-run, best-structured of the major food companies." This kind of success is repeated in scores of successful and forward-thinking multinationals all over the world.

The unit-president concept is a management style well suited to a multinational company. In such organizations the parameters of the job should be agreed upon, the constraints negotiated, and the objectives set; after that, the local CEO and the leadership team must be left to get on with the job. CEOs who continuously turn in poor results would probably opt for a pink slip rather than be subjected to "marionette management," in which all important decisions are made by the head office.

Despite this obvious logic, senior international executives and shareholders are often nervous about transferring too much power to subsidiary heads. During my early days at Manpower, we were faced with a series of corporate catastrophes that had been caused by the unthinking narrowness of a former manager in the U.S. home office, who had required the company's subsidiaries to run by the book. As soon as we negotiated local autonomy, individual initiative, and a free hand, we were able to instill a sense of corporate personality that started us on the long process of building our own style. Our local style, in turn, shaped strategy, developed a climate for success, and built a motivated team.

The leaders of multinationals have two choices: (1) They can run their subsidiaries by the book (that is, follow the branch-plant mentality), or (2) they can empower their subsidiaries. If the latter doesn't work, the answer is to get a new CEO for that subsidiary. Of course, the trick is to hire the right leader in the first place, then follow the unit-president concept by giving the subsidiary the freedom to make its own decisions. Any CEOs who can't cut the mustard should be encouraged to find better uses for their talents elsewhere. For the CEO in a multinational subsidiary, the game is straightforward: Perform or make way for someone who can. Along with this accountability —and its two functional offspring, responsibility and authority—goes risk: to the organization, to its mission, and to the CEO who is associated with failure. A finely tuned risk/reward ratio is the essence of the delegated task and the empowered team.

What distinguishes Lockeans from Hobbesians is their love for and faith in others. Lockeans give away power, secure that people will honor the gift. Hobbesians, who hold people in such contempt that there is no faith or trust, keep everything—responsibilities, power, information, and opportunities—to themselves. It is the Lockean who holds the key to empowerment and delegation. Aspiring leaders should learn from a Lockean mentor; executives should work in Lockean organizations; and *everyone* should avoid Hobbesians.

———◆———

The great end of life is not knowledge but action.

—Thomas Huxley

Territory Defeats Synergy

—Sign hanging in the office of Marty Myers of Miller Myers Bruce DallaCosta, Inc., an advertising agency in Toronto

Chapter 8

Out-Sourcing

An expert gives an objective view. He gives his
own view.

—Morarji Desai

*I*t stands to reason that to become superb at
what we do best, we must stop doing those things that
others do better. We can achieve this by *out-sourcing*—
transferring the risk and execution of noncore functions
to specialized outsiders—so that the members of the
leadership team can concentrate their unique skills and
passions on their own areas of mastery—the organization's
core business.

◆

In Chapter 3 we reviewed the importance of defining the corporate purpose of an organization and especially its corporate mission. In reality few CEOs and their
leadership teams successfully clarify the overriding purpose of their organization and stick by it. But even those
that do may undermine their mission and their expertise
by becoming *internal* conglomerates. They find themselves providing printing, graphics, maintenance, security,
catering, transportation, medical services, tax and legal
advice, temporary staff, travel agency services, publicity
and promotion, and on and on. Why do so many corporations straddle an ill-fitting assortment of internal minicor-
porations that are incompatible with their core competencies, that are not part of the corporate purpose, and for

which they possess no managerial expertise? This chapter will try to answer this question and offer some practical suggestions for implementing a policy of out-sourcing within the corporation.

Why Organizations Internalize Staff Functions

Building a successful organization is never simple in the best of times. Then why do so many leadership teams pursue a policy of self-sufficiency that substantially increases fixed overhead?

There are five major reasons that spur most companies on this misguided path.

1. *Economy.* Executives mistakenly believe that the organization's use of a certain service is great enough to justify it becoming an in-house department. The three traditional approaches to implementing this policy are (a) the "green-fields" method—starting a new staff service from scratch; (b) the acquisition of a successful private company in the appropriate field; (c) the evolutionary method—management wakes up one day to discover the staff function has been there all along and has mushroomed into an uncontrollable and profit-famished giant.

2. *Quality.* Executives become exasperated with the deterioration of service from outside suppliers and decide to internalize the function.

3. *Security.* Management becomes paranoid or insecure, believing that the tasks involved have such critical security dimensions that outsiders cannot be trusted with them.

4. *Empire-building.* Bureaucrats and egocentrics wish to enlarge their power base and therefore their status. They develop a plan for going into a business that already thrives in the marketplace.

The bureaucrat's natural tendency is to measure power and authority in terms of the number of personnel supervised. Combined with ambition, this can lead to empire-building. Its modern antecedents can be found in the British army, during the apogee of British colonial rule. Because rank and pay were dictated by the number of men under an officer's command and because retiring officers were pensioned accordingly, a flurry of organizational expansion would occur immediately prior to retirement.

5. *Speed*. If you control the service from the inside, it will yield results more quickly than the equivalent, outside service, right? Wrong! As any jaded customer of an inside service knows, improving speed is merely a function of cost; if enough of an organization's scarce profit dollars are thrown at the staff service, its celerity can be improved. The catch is that comparable services, at similar or lower costs, are readily available externally—and without the administrative and managerial headaches!

Out-Sourcing

Out-sourcing is strategic *delegation* at the corporate level. It is becoming increasingly common. According to Yuji Furukawa of Tokyo's Metropolitan University, one-third of Japan's total manufacturing costs are accounted for by *out-sourcing,* a figure that he says has risen from 20% in the 1960s and will rise to 40% by the end of the century.

Out-sourcing is not restricted to the private sector; institutions and public corporations can take advantage of the approach too. A current example is the growing tendency for many U.S. and Canadian universities to contract the management of their bookstores to companies like Barnes and Noble or Brennan College Services. The University of Ottawa took a 51% interest in a joint venture with Brennan called Ottawa-Brennan. This marriage of convenience enabled the university to capitalize on the out-sourcing offered by Brennan while bypassing Canada's tough legislation (since relaxed) that was designed to prevent unrestricted foreign ownership of Canadian corporations.

Out-sourcing—the assignment of professional, service, and staff functions to specialists *outside* the company—can be achieved in a number of ways. It may involve transferring internal specialists to their own businesses and then hiring their services on an as-needed basis. Or it may include entering into contracts with the best specialists in the marketplace. Both techniques free the corporation's creative talents to concentrate upon their main mission. And to be truly successful, high levels of respect must exist between the organization and its outside source.

In 1969, the late inventor and entrepreneur extraordinaire Howard Head sold the famous ski company that bears his name to AMF for $4 million. Just before doing so, Head had begun designing and selling tennis rackets under the Head label. He subcontracted the manufacturing to Maark Corporation (near Princeton, New Jersey). After the sale of his company, Howard Head bought Prince Manufacturing, a company that makes machines that fire practice balls across the court for tennis buffs to hit. In due course, Head turned again to his reliable subcontractor Maark to produce his new, patented 110-square-inch racket. One year later, AMF acquired Maark. Unlikely though it might seem, Head and Prince rackets were then made by the same manufacturer, even though the rivalry between AMF/Head and Prince was as keen as anything on Wimbledon's center court! The arrangement endured, even while AMF/Head's market share was slumping and Prince Manufacturing was serving itself the leading market share. At the time, Prince was producing all the "oversized" rackets being sold, which helped to boost the firm's market share of all racket sales in North America to 35%. Meanwhile, one-time leader AMF/Head could only claim 21%. Although AMF/Head and Prince were competitors, the mutual subcontracting arrangement satisfied the needs of both companies—and at 70 years of age, Howard Head didn't intend to get into the manufacturing game! He just sold out again; this time to Chesebrough-Pond's USA. Even today, over 90% of all tennis rackets sold are not manufactured by the company whose name is on the product, but are out-sourced through subcontractors.

When Richard Branson left school in 1967 to start what would become Britain's Virgin Group, his first few record shops were noisy, cushion-strewn emporiums for teens and rockers. By 1991, Virgin's music sales in the United Kingdom alone had soared to $300 million. Virgin has evolved into an empire of 150 companies and 2,500 employees. Its businesses include popular-music publishing and recording, retail stores, book publishing, broadcasting, cable TV, videocassettes, film production, construction, heating systems, nightclubs, and a low-price airline (Virgin Atlantic, which flies the London/New York and London/Los Angeles runs at competitive prices).

Branson operates Virgin by four fundamental tenets:

1. *Commitment to cost control.* Virgin's head offices are several miles from London's high-cost, prestigious downtown City district.

2. *Entrepreneurship.* Virgin regularly establishes separate recording labels to keep management close to markets and artists. It provides venture capital for start-ups by employees and cuts the employee who runs the project into the action.

3. *Commitment to the core business.* Virgin remains focused on fulfilling the entertainment needs of trendy 15- to 35-year-olds who have substantial disposable income.

4. *Out-sourcing.* Branson believes in "buying not making." He and his team see themselves in the business of entertainment publishing, in all its forms. They find an idea and exploit it; they own no record-pressing plants; the cable TV division owns no TV hardware;

even the airline leases its planes, which Virgin Atlantic can sell back at the end of the first, second, or third year if it so chooses.

Additionally, Branson believes in limiting the size of each operation to about 80 people, each with its own director. When an operation exceeds this size, he empowers the director to spin off a new unit, in this way keeping each within the "tribal" configuration (see Chapter 2). His recipe for success is to develop an innovative concept, empower his leadership team, delegate the execution, and be there at the finish to help bring it off with a flourish. In this way Branson works on his strengths—his abilities to motivate people and to draw out their very best performance. This recipe has proved so successful that in 1992 Thorn-EMI made Branson an offer he couldn't refuse for the entertainment publishing division.

OUT-SOURCING A PROJECT

IBM is often cited as the paragon of U.S. corporations because of its rigorous and efficient internal culture as well as its marketing prowess, which has kept it at the top of the information-processing industry. Yet "Big Blue" did something very uncharacteristic to develop the IBM Personal Computer in 1980. The late Philip D. "Don" Estridge led a team of dedicated designers who worked 80 to 100 hours a week for over a year in conditions that were a far cry from their usual cozy corporate offices. Their new workplace was a converted warehouse with a leaky roof and an air conditioner that didn't respond to the demands of summer in Florida. But the innovation that contributed to IBM's success was more than just putting a bunch of bright guys in a Spartan building with hardly any windows. The microprocessor, the heart and soul of the PC, was designed and manufactured by Intel. The operating system software was especially written for IBM by Microsoft (at the time, a budding software manufacturer headed by a 27-year-old entrepreneur named William H. Gates III). And prior to launching the PC, IBM released classified technical details to outside suppliers, inviting them to write applications software and develop other IBM-specific support materials. IBM realized that out-sourcing the program-writing function was crucial to launching the new product as fast as possible. In doing so, the company launched not only a new product but a revolution. Douglas R. LeGrande, the former vice president of operations for IBM's entry systems division, stressed, "The decision [to publish the design] was fundamental to our success."

Only 3% of IBM's managers leave the company each year, including retirees. The culture that nourishes such low turnover includes the "outplan" concept in which as much as 7% of each laboratory's budget can be allocated to employees currently running separate units but empowered to be internal entrepreneurs who are not required to account for this funding until a potential new product has been identified. Once this spark is ignited, the entrepreneurship of outside sources is harnessed to fan the sparks into flames—marketable products and services. The IBM PC started life this way, as do 90% of IBM's new product lines.

Apple Computer in Cupertino, California, followed a similar approach. The cost to build an Apple II was $500, but $350 of that was out-sourced as follows:

Component or Service	Outside Supplier
Microprocessors	Synerteck
Other chips	Hitachi, Texas Instruments, Motorola
Video monitors	Hitachi
Power supplies	Astec
Printers	Tokyo Electric, Qume
Promotion	Regis McKenna
Software development	Microsoft
Product styling	Frogdesign
Distribution	ITT, Computerland

Today fully 90% of Apple's manufacturing costs are accounted for by bought-in components. Although Apple is a highly efficient manufacturer, its policy of outsourcing effectively classifies it as an assembler rather than a manufacturer.

North America's most effective companies got that way by exchanging scale for concentration; by dumping businesses and functions not germane to their corporate purpose. Take Minneapolis-based Honeywell. In terms of inflation-adjusted sales, it is a smaller company today than it was 10 years ago, but its earnings per share and dividends have doubled, and its stock has tripled in value. It is the world leader in its core businesses of manufacturing controls that regulate the light, temperature, air, and water flow in domestic and commercial buildings; process control equipment used by paper companies, oil refiners, and plastics makers; and commercial avionics equipment—all of which are linked by Honeywell's core expertise, the processing of input from electronic sensors. Honeywell has stripped away all other interests, including its computer business. The path has been expensive and rocky, but today, says Chairman James J. Reiner, "We can build something in the U.S., spec it in France, buy a part in Kuwait, and deliver it anywhere in the world."

An Out-Sourcing Policy

To implement a policy of out-sourcing, managers with moxie adopt the following criteria:

♦ Keep a lean and motivated team at the center—that is, thinkers, builders, and motivators, not support staff or facilitators.

♦ Beyond the leadership team, employ as few personnel as possible regardless of level or function, in order to keep the administrative bureaucracy slim.

◆ Contract out as many specialist functions as possible. This lowers the corporate breakeven point and keeps corporate options open (which allows you to take advantage of the finest talent available in the marketplace).

◆ Maintain and increase the quality and scope of corporate *profit* centers and reduce (or eliminate) the size and number of *cost* centers.

Adopting a corporate philosophy dedicated to outsourcing begins with an assessment of the cost/benefit relationship for *all* functional and staff areas. Robert Townsend even went so far as to suggest shutting down the whole purchasing department and reassigning the staff to more productive tasks. In his book *Up the Organization,* he observed that the purchasing department costs "ten dollars in zeal for every dollar they save in purchasing acumen . . . they'd probably hire Einstein and then turn down his requisition for a blackboard."

Even if he was stretching the point, it is still a good one. Townsend was suggesting that the competition between external, free-market entrepreneurship on the one hand and what amounts to internal corporate socialism on the other represents no contest. Furthermore, the job of selecting, cultivating, and managing relations with outside suppliers is best placed with operating executives rather than staff functionaries.

See Table 8-1 on page 278 to review the impact of out-sourcing on the performance of various companies.

Thomas Chan, managing director of Hong Kong-based Playmates International, is sanguine about running a lean organization. The manufacturer of Teenage Mutant Ninja Turtles employs 100 staff members who generate $530 million in sales and $156 million in profits. Success has been heady: 90% of American boys aged 3 to 8 own at least one turtle and the average has more than five in his toy box. From drab headquarters in Hong Kong's

Table 8-1 The Impact of Out-Sourcing

Company	Industry	Sales ($ million)	Number of Employees	Sales per Employee ($)	Industry Average
Lyondell Petrochemical	Chemical	6,508	2,250	2,892,444	212,381
Liz Claiborne	Apparel	1,755	6,028	291,141	64,869
Coca-Cola	Beverages	10,406	24,000	433,583	202,030
Whirlpool	Electronics	6,647	36,157	183,837	111,478
Kellogg	Food	5,199	17,239	301,584	223,584
Herman Miller	Furniture	869	5,770	150,606	103,800
Crown Cork and Seal	Metal products	3,080	17,205	179,018	123,038
Peter Kiewit Sons'	Metal products	5,087	23,000	221,174	123,038
Merck	Pharmaceuticals	7,824	36,900	212,033	147,553
Reader's Digest	Publishing	2,056	7,400	277,838	124,763
A. Schulman	Rubber and plastics	681	1,385	491,697	136,867
Hasbro	Toys	1,520	7,700	197,403	155,502
Time Warner	Entertainment	11,517	22,900	502,926	N/A
Turner	Entertainment	3,260	3,026	1,077,330	N/A
Reebok International	Athletic Shoes	2,175	1,334	1,630,435	N/A
Ford	Motor vehicles	98,275	370,400	265,321	130,265
Chrysler	Motor vehicles	30,868	124,000	248,936	130,265
General Motors	Motor vehicles	126,017	761,400	165,507	130,265

Kowloon district, Chan does business in a style that is in stark contrast to his U.S. counterparts. Chan points out, "Coleco had 1,000 employees when it went bankrupt. At one point, it had 75 vice presidents—we have 5 or 6 and they talk to me every day. At Worlds of Wonder [since filed for Chapter 11], the president's office was 3,000 square feet; mine is 150 square feet. If I ran Mattel it would make [profits of] $150 million, instead of $90 million." (Mattel turned down the Teenage Mutant Ninja Turtles as being too risky!)

THE WD-40 COMPANY

The president of the San Diego-based WD-40 Company, John Barry, says his organization "is really a marketing company, not a manufacturing company." At face value, this isn't earth-shattering news—but Barry has a deeper understanding of his business than most CEOs ever do. What his company is good at, they do; the rest they out-source.

WD-40 is a chemical/petroleum-based lubricant and rust and corrosion preventive that comes in a blue-and-yellow spray can. It works to penetrate metal and displace water. The name is an acronym for Water Displacement Formula No. 40, derived from its original use as a protectant for the skin of the Atlas missiles made by the Convair division of General Dynamics in the 1950s. General Dynamics workers started smuggling the blue-and-yellow cans home to free up jammed locks and rusty fishing reels. In 1961 when Hurricane Carla hit the Gulf Coast, the company began promoting WD-40 to industrial-parts distributors to spray on mechanical and electrical equipment to displace moisture and prevent corrosion. Then, during the Vietnam War, the company sent small sample cans of WD-40 to GIs there who found it a perfect protectant for their rifles and sang its praises when they returned home.

Its marketing message is so powerful that WD-40 has assumed almost mythical proportions. It can be found in

75% of U.S. households. Fishermen spray their bait with it, swearing that it helps their catch. Many sufferers of arthritis claim that their pain is relieved when they spray their joints with it (a claim discounted by the company).

According to a Nuclear Regulatory Commission spokesperson, when a California nuclear power plant had trouble with 4 of the 16 circuit breakers essential for the safe operation of the automatic-shutdown system, the problem went away with a squirt of WD-40. Publicity like that is the genius of a focused company.

How does the leadership team at WD-40 generate $21.4 million on revenues of $89.8 million? By focusing on core skills. WD-40's only manufacturing plant is in San Diego, where the secret ingredients are mixed in a single vat and then shipped in bulk by rail or tank wagons to five contract packagers in the United States and one in Canada, who put the product in cans, label them, and ship them to wholesalers and distributors.

Barry periodically considers internalizing some of these functions but in the end always rejects the idea: "Lots of people make a profit on WD-40. That's fine. I don't want their headaches," says Barry. What about diversification, acquisition, or development of other products to protect the company from being a one-product phenomenon? "We're already breaking all the Harvard Business School rules," says Barry. And he adds, "I don't believe in running out and buying another company that I don't know anything about."

The product is so successful that more than 250 imitators—including Borden, Du Pont, General Electric, Minnesota Mining & Manufacturing, and Pennzoil—have tried and failed to introduce me-too products. Despite these irritations, the company piles up annual compound-growth rates of 25%.

The salient characteristics of the WD-40 Company include the following:

1. Management intends to remain a one-product company as long as untapped sales potential exists.

2. With a staff of only 136, WD-40 racks up sales per employee of $670,000, compared to the *Fortune* 500 average for industrial companies of $154,604.

3. Management keeps manufacturing operations and costs to a minimum.

4. The company has used no debt since it went public in 1973.

A Guide to Staff Services

In 1989 Eastman Kodak of Rochester, New York, made a landmark decision: It sold its mainframe computers to IBM and asked the company to undertake its data processing. Kathy Hudson, Kodak's director of information systems, describes the logic: "IBM is in the data-processing business, and Kodak isn't. IBM runs our computer center as it's supposed to be run—except as a profit center rather than a cost center." The results have been dramatic: Kodak's capital spending on computers has dropped by 90% and operating expenses have declined by 10–20%. Enron has done the same thing, selling its computers for $6 million and transferring 550 Enron employees to the payroll of its out-sourcing supplier, EDS of Dallas (at over $6 billion, the largest computer-services out-sourcer in the United States). Enron's CEO, Jack Tompkins, says, "Our goal is to be the first natural-gas major. Nothing in that vision says we want to be a provider of information services." Enron hopes to save $20 million during this decade, which represents 20–24% of total computing costs. This pattern of out-sourcing will grow rapidly in the years ahead because staff services are distracting, drain an organization's profits, and demotivate its people.

There are two kinds of staff services:

1. Profit-center staff services
2. Cost-center staff services

The former are those that management has convinced themselves are capable of making money, someday ("If we build up our management-information department, we will be able to sell its services to outside organizations"). The latter are those for which even this pretense has been abandoned ("All well-run organizations need to have their own printing department").

PROFIT CENTER STAFF SERVICES

If the internal service is treated as a profit center, it is attempting to add value. The value it adds must come from its customers; that is, from its sister functions within the same corporate family. Consequently, profit-making staff services are predatory in nature: They compete for corporate profit, thereby posing a conflict of interest. In addition, managers often establish incompatible goals, such as maximum use of staff services *and* the reduction of overall department expenditures. Departmental contests ensue, as staff service managers scramble to cover their overhead and make budget by aggressively selling their services. Their reluctant customers, who are only to be found within the organization, are bullied into purchasing services that they suspect could be surpassed in quality, service, and cost-efficiency outside the organization. Apart from the debilitating loss of corporate strength caused by these contests, this is simply squeezing the fiscal balloon—nothing changes except the distribution of the contents. If the staff service has a charter that permits it to build volume by pursuing external customers, internal service will soon deteriorate because captive customers, who are prohibited from selecting alternative suppliers, will sink to second-class status. On the other hand, providing efficient, high-quality internal services is a thankless task: Internal customers will grumble that the silver-

platter service is overpriced in addition to being ineffi-
cient, avaricious, and run by parasitic incompetents—the
customary corporate perception of staff services.

The function can also be expected to assume the
form of an internal civil service, thereby offering a daily
validation of all of Parkinson's Laws. If the service fails
because of arbitrary market controls and criteria that
would never fly in the real world, the manager will be
fired, in order to "improve" the service. To make matters worse, senior management usually ignores the replacement costs, the aggravation, and the general demoraliza-
tion that results—thereby adding to the difficulty of
assessing the real costs of the function.

When the use of the internal facility is optional,
management achieves the worst of both worlds. The
organization will have gained nothing by the establishment of the facility. After all, the option to shop among
competitive suppliers existed in the marketplace *before*
the corporation went to the expense of creating this new
and hungry dependent.

COST-CENTER STAFF SERVICES

If the internal staff service is a cost center, it will be closely
managed and required to provide a service of maximum
quality and efficiency with a budget that has been pared
to the bone. This represents the corporate equivalent of
asking Martina Navratilova to throw a game—and invariably leads to poor service (no pun intended). The
facility's manager will claim that better service can be provided only if staffing and equipment are expanded. The
veracity of this claim lies at the bottom of a very deep
well because of the following:

♦ Cost analysis for the facility's services is rarely done
  on a project-by-project basis, so it is not really meaningful.

♦ The facility will have a large number of indirect and intangible costs having more to do with corporate culture and precedent than cost/benefit analyses.

♦ Because various levels of staff have access to the service, conflicting internal political objectives will blur the fundamental issues.

STAFF SERVICES AS A DEMOTIVATOR

Frequently, staff services managers (and sometimes those in operations as well) have a tendency to build empires, which act as a drain on the corporate coffers—another good reason to out-source such functions. This financial drain affects compensation too—a fact not usually lost on employees. Underperforming staff services are a good example of what Frederick Herzberg described as negative hygiene factors (discussed in Chapter 4). If employees see a staff service as a negative hygiene factor, they may be considerably demotivated: Because staff services drain an organization's profit resources (regardless of the service's quality), they obviously compete with employee compensation plans and reward systems. It's no coincidence that employee-suggestion programs target the elimination of staff services! Such competition does nothing to encourage corporate brotherly or sisterly love—another reason to use outside suppliers instead.

In addition to unwelcome competition, staff services create second-class employees: Others in the organization regard them, at best, as indifferent and, at worst, as corporate pariahs. In a focused, successful, and well-motivated organization, the folks who find and keep customers for life are the heroes. How can staff services employees compete or even be motivated in a corporate culture that does not respect or honor their contribution? Friction is the inevitable result.

Another advantage of out-sourcing is that it removes dead-end jobs. Although the argument is often made—perhaps with some merit—that not everyone seeks promotion, this is irrelevant to the well-motivated organization, in which every position should contain the potential for growth. Better to leave the routine jobs to specialists outside the organization, so that people within it can concentrate on pleasing customers.

Out-Sourcing as a Control on Cost and Quality

Results-oriented managers will naturally prefer out-sourcing to staff services in order to control costs and quality. It's too easy for the costs of internalized functions to be arbitrary *and* anonymous; they add unnecessarily to overhead, which undermines management's control over its budget. Quality can suffer too. But out-sourcing to successful and reputable suppliers not only enhances quality but provides the cachet of doing business with the best-known and most highly regarded professional services. Out-sourcing therefore fulfills several needs: It gets the job done well and cost-effectively; it is a good marketing device; and it can keep an organization out of trouble.

———◆———

With a payroll that mushroomed over the years to 72,000 full- and part-time staff but began with only a few hundred, Manpower needed a retail banking organization that had good service awareness; a major presence in all the markets and towns in which we had established operations or planned to; international connections; the ability to solve technical problems nonbureaucratically; sensitivity to the mundane but important personal requirements of our employees and customers; and the know-how to give us state-of-the-art technical advice. So we became customers of the National Westminster Bank at their prestigious flagship branch on Lothbury Street and grew with our big friend to maturity.

In those early days, we were such a shaky outfit that we paid our few employees in cash in sealed envelopes; but once our employees found out where we banked, they realized that we could and would be able to pay them. Over the years, we converted to biweekly checks and ultimately to electronic banking. Our self-confidence was considerable; we had no doubt that we would achieve our ambitious long-term goals. But we also knew that we would need the support of the finest outside services, in all sectors, to help us on our long journey and to give our employees and customers the same feelings of confidence.

The same philosophy should guide the selection of legal advisers. The trick is to hire the best generalist legal firm that can be found and add specialists if and when the need arises. It may be a sad admission but nevertheless a fact of life that heavy-duty names either faze the opposition or batter its resistance, thereby saving time and expense—both of which are in short supply for an organization on the move.

Financial advisers and specialists (audit, tax, acquisition, divestment, and international); banks (commercial, retail, and merchant as well as venture-capital supply); public relations (government lobbying, media relations, industrial relations, international contacts, publicity releases, and promotional writing); and advertising (institutional, divisional, product as well as recruitment, and dealer/franchisee acquisition) are good examples of the types of outside services where retaining the best is the *only* permissible approach. The best will of course cost more; but because they are the best, they will help you to grow by many times their cost.

RECESSIONS AND FIXED OVERHEAD

Recessions mandate cost cutting, but these economic downturns make it even tougher to cut back the fixed overhead of staff services; they develop strong resistance to pruning and are as tenacious as any other bureaucratic vine when their survival is threatened. And as we've seen, the superstars—the finest practitioners of professional services—are almost certainly not on your payroll but on their own: They are partners in leading firms in their field, successfully running their own independent businesses. Therefore, because ownership concentrates the mind, they will deal more effectively with the tough decisions necessary during recessions. In these circumstances owner-operated companies are the best kind to deal with because their relationship with the corporate customer will often reflect a better understanding of bottom-line issues than one can generally expect from a staff service manager, who is mounting a defensive campaign against a reduction of power and influence, untouched by the fire of corporate profitability.

OUT-SOURCING AND SUPERSTARS
As we've seen, superstars are essential to an organization's success. This is true for those on the outside as well as the inside. And once you realize that your company cannot and should not do everything—that it must concentrate on its core business—you will also see that even if you did decide to internalize, say, advertising, you could not attract advertising superstars. You could not convince them to work for you, pay them enough, motivate them adequately, pamper their egos, feed their genius, and offer them enough variety and stimulation to keep them excited about your widgets. Nor should you want to. Can insiders ever know as much, have the richness of experience, or accumulate the diversity of contacts and skills of the outside superstar? The relative merits of putting a top-flight corporate attorney on your payroll or retaining the finest law firm in town, which specializes in issues that concern you, seem beyond argument.

Both expediency and the pursuit of excellence therefore point to a policy of out-sourcing. The CEO looking in the marketplace for superstars in staff or professional services will quickly discover that it's impossible to hire the best specialist talent in *all* the different fields required by the corporation. The only way you will get Melvin Belli to work for you is to hire his firm.

OUT-SOURCING, CREATIVITY, AND INNOVATION
Creativity and innovation keep organizations on the cutting edge. But internalization of purchasing, value engineering, and estimating, as well as research and development facilities, must ultimately stifle creativity and innovation. The leading edge of printing is in printing companies, not yours (unless *it* is a printing company).

In 1980 Robert H. Hayes and William J. Abernathy wrote one of the most insightful articles ever to appear in the *Harvard Business Review,* "Managing Our Way to Economic Decline." In it they suggested that

> the real competitive threats to technologically active companies . . . arise from abrupt changes in component technologies, raw materials or production processes. . . . A company may find itself shut off from the R & D efforts of various independent suppliers by becoming their competitor. Long-term contracts and long-term relationships with suppliers can achieve many of the same cost benefits as backward integration without calling into question a company's ability to innovate or respond to innovation.

Companies that internalize a function take on the particular industry in an unfair contest: They simply will never be as good as an outside specialist, period.

It has often been argued that most corporate innovation is the result of borrowing, creatively copying, adapting, or improving upon existing ideas. Organizations usually accomplish this by studying and then duplicating the product, service, process, or approach that they admire; or alternatively, by luring an expert onto the team who possesses the appropriate intellectual property and

abilities. If a company uses large numbers of outside suppliers and services, innovation is more likely than with
in-house facilities, which tend to become introverted.
Because they lack diverse contacts and the resulting
synergistic enhancement, these functions and their
management become intellectually withered. Given this,
it's clear that wide use of outside sources refreshes the
intellectual and creative juices of an organization in almost
every way.

The Lego Corporation

Lego building kits delight 50 million youngsters in 129
countries, generating sales of $600 million and un-
protected by patent. The firm, still privately held, was
founded in Denmark in 1934 by Ole Kirk Christiansen
and today is run by his grandson, Kjeld Kirk Kristiansen.
Lego kits come complete with directions for building a
single unit, such as a spacecraft; Lego is also available in
a multiple-unit system (such as an entire space station).
Although there are 1,800 different Lego parts available,
these can only be assembled into 150 unique kits, as designed by the Danish manufacturer. But a fertile imagination and dexterity make the potential number of com-
binations almost infinite. The child's maxim is, *Lego ergo
sum,* or roughly translated, I build, therefore I am.

Lego is a good metaphor for the modern organization, which I call the **Lego corporation.** Leaders of a
Lego corporation motivate, maintain, and reward their
brightest talent, which is an organization's greatest asset
and the individuals of which can be likened to Lego parts:
Each component (individual) has an inherent design logic
that allows the builder (the leader) to combine it with
others into a comprehensible whole (the organization) that
is more than the sum of its parts. Talented hands reveal
the gestalt of Lego pieces—their natural tendency to
become whole, to complete themselves. This idea carries

over to organizational design: Talented managers create organizational forms that best complement the personalities, strengths, and skills of the individuals to achieve the corporate mission.

Directions for a Lego management kit follow:

♦ *First,* identify all the human "parts" required; that is, the particular talents, attitudes, and skills needed to make a project or an organization fly.

♦ *Then,* assemble those parts into a structure. The components, not their form, are the important thing. As you change direction, grow, or alter your strategy or goals, you will need different parts, some temporarily, others permanently.

The Lego corporation allows a great deal of organizational flexibility, providing the means to achieve an ideal fit between talents and tasks. As should be clear, the concept works best when outside sources are used to augment internal resources—when out-sourcing is an attitude rather than a process. The marketplace is rich in talents, and you can obtain the Lego parts you need from consulting firms, temporary-staffing services, professional firms like accounting and law firms, free-lance specialists, and internal employees on sabbatical or on temporary assignment outside the organization. In some cases, it may be even more practical to transfer entire functions to members of a Lego management team.

One example of this approach is Rank Xerox in the United Kingdom, which has provided several of the company's former senior executives with home computers and contracts to provide consulting services in their fields of expertise. Although this approach makes close supervision difficult because team members may be widely dispersed, it widens the field of choice and thereby increases the general caliber of accessible talent that would be unavailable in conventional organizations.

But the benefits of the Lego corporation are reaped only by a leadership team with a passionate belief in empowerment and delegation, because out-sourcing is the ultimate expression of empowerment: Out-sourcing is the empowerment not of a single individual but of a whole organization over whom we exert scant control. Top-quality talents—either individuals, teams, or organizations —work most effectively when they identify with and commit to the goals of the team leader but are empowered to take care of the details and the means by which they are to be achieved. Out-sourcing is the mark of leaders who are self-confident and secure—so secure that they willingly share power and glory with colleagues in other organizations.

The Supplier as Partner

The concept of *partnership* is an important one, and its adoption as a cornerstone of corporate strategy is growing. Today all of IBM's resellers are known within the company as "business partners." But the partnership must be *total*—good times and bad, bouquets and brickbats. When General Motors' Saturn division discovered that the radiators of their newly launched cars had been filled with faulty coolant—provided by their partner, Texaco—they recalled the 1,836 cars that had already been delivered, and instead of simply repairing them (the standard practice in an industry rife with recalls and glitches), they replaced them, at no cost to the owner. This action was totally consistent with GM's newly acquired passion for high quality. They also wrote a letter to all of Saturn's customers explaining that their partner, Texaco, was responsible. Said Alan Perriton, Saturn's director of materials management, "There should be a sharing of risk and reward." David Cole, director for the Office for the Study of Automotive Transportation at the University of

Michigan, adds, "Suppliers are increasingly asked to catch it on the warranty side." Of course, reputations were at stake all round: Texaco, anxious to protect its 16% share of the coolant market, rushed out a letter of its own, explaining that the error had been a freak accident. Texaco's Paul Weeditz gamely announced that his firm "will bear the costs associated with standing by our product."

Out-sourcing changes the rules of the game—partnership is a tango for two. Saturn is driving this point home by asking its suppliers to beef up their design, engineering, and quality standards in exchange for a long-term supplier relationship. But the upside is good for everyone: happier customers and more sales. In fact, Saturn dealers noticed a sales surge shortly after the recall and replacement because customers had heard the news: Saturn doesn't just fix faulty cars; it replaces them.

Building the Out-Sourcing Relationship

Shopping for suppliers on a regular basis keeps their prices sharp and exposes you and your team to new and competitive ideas in the marketplace. You should advise all suppliers that they must bid on your business as a matter of routine; no supplier relationship should depend on any criteria other than the quality and/or price of the services provided. For example, it's prudent and instructive to seek a minimum of three bids for your advertising account before you renew the contract with the present agency—no matter how long-standing the relationship. Motorola, itself a former winner of the Malcolm Baldrige National Quality Award, even requires its suppliers to apply for the award too.

In addition to regular bidding for your business with a clear understanding that suppliers keep your business as long as they keep earning the right to do so, you should regularly inspect your suppliers' offices and plants and talk with them frequently and at length about their plans, programs, current projects, philosophies, and attitudes. This way you'll receive a regular update on new ideas and developments in the relevant fields as well as a first-hand assessment of the management of both your existing suppliers and their competitors. The benefit to the outside supplier is that they keep your business if their standards grow with yours; they can also look forward to a long-term relationship with fewer competitors. Enlightened leaders now realize that the revolving-door approach to suppliers is unproductive. Instead, they favor a partnership that shares risks, pools resources, and deepens long-term ties.

The most important precept to remember about out-sourcing is that outside suppliers are *not* outsiders—they are family. They are partners, risk sharers, collaborators, and friends, with different interests but common goals: mutual growth, excellence, and the success of *your* customers. But because suppliers are often misperceived as outsiders, leaders sometimes forget that they need to be inspired and motivated—just like the rest of the family. Wise leaders romance outstanding performances from suppliers in exactly the same way they do from their employees: by treating them as members of the team— with integrity, respect, and honesty—by praising them, by including them and confiding in them, by celebrating their contributions and rewarding them fairly, by making them feel part of the family, and by sharing the glory of success.

By externalizing the risks as well as the tasks to which the organization's executives can bring no specific skill, the leadership team keeps its options open and costs down while being regularly apprised of state-of-the-art developments in specialized fields. The organization's leaders are freed up to apply their brand of managerial moxie to the things that they do well, the things defined in their mission statement. But even more vital to the greening of the corporation is the removal of bureaucratic baggage.

Internal staff and service functions attract bureaucrats; out-sourcing gets rid of them and allows the organization to breathe freely.

———◆———

Either dance well or quit the ballroom.
—Greek proverb

Who begins too much accomplishes little.
—German proverb

Chapter 9

The On Organization: Dedicated to Customers

Customers are the precious things; goods are only grass.

—Chinese proverb

Okyakusama
—"Honored guest" or "customer" in Japanese

*T*he great organizations are *on*. They are energized by a "visceral feeling of greatness" based on a customer-dedicated, service-driven philosophy that makes the customer a permanent part of the business.

◆

The show-business expression *totally on* means that an entertainer gave his or her very best; things couldn't have been better—the showperson and audience connected perfectly. Everyone knows when they are totally on—the people who give and the people who receive. Great corporations are the same; they are totally committed to making the customer (the audience) feel good. The ultimate goal of any high-flying leadership team is to fashion an **On Organization.**

The Disney Company is legendary for its commitment to its customers—it is the quintessential On Organization. Employees are cast members who are not on duty but "onstage"; Disneyspeak for taking a coffee break is "go offstage." Uniforms are "costumes," the personnel department is "casting," and customers are called "guests."

Every trash can at Disney World is painted to blend with the immediate scenery. Every piece of pavement is steam-cleaned and every window is washed daily. The shrubbery in heavily traveled areas is trimmed into the shapes of penguins, elephants, swans, and camels.

Once, when Walt Disney planned an elaborate $350,000 Christmas parade at Disneyland, his aides objected, believing that holiday crowds would come to Disneyland anyway. But Walt disagreed, saying, "We've always got to give them a little more. It'll be worth the investment. If they ever stop coming, it'll cost ten times as much to get them back."

Disney spends $1 billion on listening to guests and meeting their needs. This dedication fosters customer loyalty (60% of Disney's visitors return). Such success and a policy of promoting from within is a strong lure for job seekers. Each year Disney receives 70,000 resumes for 300 managerial openings.

The same commitment to quality that led Walt to gamble his future on *Snow White* lives today in all that the Disney Company does, with some prodigious results. For example, last year:

♦ More than 200 million people saw a Disney movie
♦ More than 1 billion people read a Disney book or magazine
♦ 395 million watched a Disney TV show every week
♦ 270 million bought Disney-licensed merchandise
♦ 212 million listened to Disney music

♦ More than 50 million visited Disney theme parks in California, Florida, and Tokyo

Hey, wait a minute—take the long view, concentrate on quality and training, listen to customers and treat them special, smile a lot and get rid of trash fast, promote from within, make employees feel good about their jobs, and keep the kids safe—what's so new about all this? Nothing, we've heard it before, but Disney *does* it: The Disney Company is a totally On Organization.

The Essence of the On Organization

Disney understands what many don't: *All businesses are service businesses,* whether they "make things" or "sell services." Either way, satisfying, or better still, *exceeding* the customer's perceived need—before, during, and after the sale—is the essence of the On Organization with a tightly focused corporate purpose. Unfortunately, too many companies are staff driven rather than customer driven: They serve organizational needs before all others and see themselves as providing a living and an ever-increasing income to their employees, regardless of the quality of the relationship between the company and its customers. The extreme version of this irrational thinking is the belief that government or some other fairy godmother will come to the rescue if the bottom falls out of the marketplace.

Meanwhile, customers see the level of service sinking. Most consumers can reel off ten ideas for making organizations more sensitive to their needs. When are waiters going to stop looking as if you'd left your brains at home when you walk into an empty restaurant without a reservation? When will food manufacturers call a truce in their war against consumers who valiantly struggle to open fiendishly clever packages? When will newspaper companies train carriers to hurl your favorite daily on the same side of the street as your house? According to a recent report from the Gallup-American Society for Quality Control, 15% of Americans "could not think of a single company whose name they associated with quality." The same survey reported that 61% of the respondents had experienced incidents of extremely poor quality (up from 51% in a similar survey in 1985). Of these, half complained and only 28% received satisfaction. It is not a major challenge to do better than this!

PUTTING THE CUSTOMER FIRST

Although Henry Ford was an engineering genius—he invented the moving assembly line—he was a marketing ignoramus. Between 1909, when he introduced the Model T, to 1926, he made no changes to the car. The phrase, You can have any color you want as long as it's black! best describes Henry's attitude to his customers. But in the mid-1920s, General Motors introduced the Chevrolet, which featured color, comfort, design, safety, and an up-to-date image. Although Ford frantically tried to copy GM, the Model T was doomed and so was Ford's primacy in the marketplace.

In 1958 Ford once again demonstrated its myopia with the ill-fated Edsel, a car that took 10 years and $250 million to develop—and that nobody wanted. Table 9-1 shows the number of foreign cars imported into the United States from 1948 to 1960 (by definition, *foreign* is synonymous with *small* during the period in question). Unfortunately, Ford did not perceive that the trend of buying smaller cars signaled a change in consumer tastes. Nor did it get the message from the consistent drop in the production of medium-priced cars that had been occurring since 1955. (See Table 9-2 on page 300.)

Ford's failure to respond to customers' changing wants and needs underscores the bottom line: The strategic and tactical determinant of *any* business is its

Table 9-1   U.S. Sales of Import Cars, 1948–1960

1948	28,047
1949	7,543
1950	21,287
1951	23,701
1952	33,312
1953	29,505
1954	34,555
1955	57,115
1956	107,675
1957	259,343
1958	430,808
1959	668,070
1960	444,474

Source: *Automobile Facts and Figures,* 1981 (Detroit Automobile Manufacturers Association), p. 5, compiled from U.S. Department of Commerce statistics. Reprinted with permission.

customers; that is, by definition *all* successful businesses are customer focused, without exception.

For an organization to focus on customers *effectively,* it must imbue every single employee, from the CEO to the receptionist, with the customer-first concept. This attitude represents an important breakthrough from perceiving the organization as a producer of things and seller of services to seeing it as one that finds and keeps customers for life by listening to them and meeting or exceeding their wants and needs. A recent Dow Corning message to its employees says it all: "We don't want you to work for us anymore. . . . We want you to work for our customers."

CUSTOMER-BASED COMPENSATION

To facilitate our clients' customer-first approach, my firm developed the concept of **customer-based compensation** (CBC; referred to briefly in Chapter 5). CBC

Table 9-2 U.S. Medium Car Production, 1955–1959 (units)

	1955	1956	1957	1958	1959
Mercury	434,911	246,626	274,820	128,428	156,765
Edsel	54,607	26,563	29,677		
Pontiac	581,860	332,268	343,298	219,823	388,856
Oldsmobile	643,460	432,903	390,091	310,795	366,305
Buick	781,296	535,364	407,283	257,124	232,579
Dodge	313,038	205,727	292,386	114,206	192,798
DeSoto	129,767	104,090	117,747	36,556	41,423

Source: 1973 *Ward's*, pp. 112–113. Reprinted with permission.

considers customers to be part of the organization's "family" and therefore includes them in reward decisions.

We base a CBC program on research conducted with a client's customers, who are asked to define what would constitute a "perfect 10" in customer service during the next quarter (or year). From this we develop a list of six to ten service and quality criteria, which our client uses not only to create a marketing plan but to work out a compensation program for *every staff member,* even those who do not directly interface with the customer. We push this concept even further when we ask the company's customers to evaluate the company's service, which in turn determines the compensation that our client's employees receive. In other words, CBC *empowers customers* by giving them a significant say in designing the service and determining the rewards to the organization's people. This represents a major breakthrough in modern leadership theory because it recognizes that the destiny of an organization depends on a partnership between customer and supplier, not just in terms of the company's transactions but in terms of its relationships and leadership. In other words, customer and supplier together guide the organization to a shared objective—exceeding the needs of the customer.

Many executives have difficulty empowering customers in this way: The old school wants to keep the power *within* the organization, failing to appreciate that giving the customer power results in greater power for the company. But when a customer ranks a supplier at 80% on the CBC criteria and bonuses are adjusted accordingly, everyone gets the message!

The Xeroxes, IBMs, and Federal Expresses are the companies that link their executive compensation plans to customer service and other "soft" measures; it's no coincidence that they're also the ones who win the Baldrige Award. When you are prepared to stake the outcome of your own pay on customer satisfaction, you are telling your employees and your customers that you are serious about meeting and exceeding customer needs.

CREATORS, PROTECTORS, AND SPENDERS

On Organizations have a preponderance of employees devoted to meeting or exceeding customer needs. But all employees fall roughly into three categories—*creators, protectors, and spenders*—not all of whom are customer centered.

Creators: The front-line team players who do something that makes the cash register ring. This group generally consists of operating staff and management (excluding their support personnel) who undertake marketing and customer-service activities. Their key activity is related either directly or indirectly to meeting or exceeding the needs of customers.

Protectors: These people perform a mixture of operational and staff activities. Protectors may be credit staff, accountants (but not usually), market researchers, recruiters, planners (occasionally), attorneys (occasionally), maintenance and security staff, and financial controllers. Protectors aren't responsible for creating new wealth but for protecting and maintaining existing wealth, which accrued from the earlier efforts of creators.

Spenders: These people make up any corporation's faceless bureaucracy, creating the fog that creators and protectors waste valuable time trying to penetrate. They comprise a cloud of anonymous accountants, clerical staff, form fillers, and functionaries with self-important titles like ''assistant to the president'' or ''senior vice president, international corporate affairs.'' These functionaries are not capable of or intended to make the cash register ring—they simply consume corporate wealth. They are the dependents of the creators, although they usually don't convey that impression.

In many staff-driven (as opposed to customer-driven) corporations, the swarm of spenders and protectors can eclipse the creators in numerous ways: They can get a bigger proportion of the wage bill and may enjoy more status, better facilities, higher salary levels, additional perks, and so on. To avoid this costly imbalance, leaders of On Organizations ensure the following:

1. Creators account for at least half of the total wage bill. After all, they carry the organization.
2. The earnings potential of creators *always* exceeds that of protectors and spenders by a considerable margin.
3. Although the On Organization celebrates all employees, it gives creators the highest internal and external status; it only honors protectors and spenders for helping to meet or exceed the needs of customers directly or indirectly.
4. Creators get the best facilities and they get them first.
5. Creators are the organizational elite, occupying the jobs admired by and aspired to by others.
6. The career fast-track is via the creator path.
7. *All* staff have an equal opportunity to assume creator tasks and responsibilities, thereby reducing internal class distinctions and competition.

You can easily recognize businesses that are out of balance on this score. They are the banks with only two tellers, who are frantically handling the customers lined up a block long while thirty stunned supernumeraries look on. Or the airlines whose "customer-service" staff vanish as soon as the loudspeaker announces an unexplained delay for the seventh time.

Not only should you avoid situations like the above, but you should go one step further. Although not all employees are creators, you should see that those who are not spend a majority of their time supporting those who are. All noncreator employees should feel that, in some way, they contribute to the daily corporate effort to make the cash register ring.

At Manpower, the costs of our marketing personnel were our second largest expenditure, after our costs for service personnel. We designed all customer-service coaching and media expenditures to reinforce the efforts and image of the people we sent out to work on our customers' premises. And we made sure that *all* staff— even those with minimal operational or customer-relations responsibilities—completed customer-service and sales courses and made customer-service calls.

We gave Manpower's customer-service function a high image. We treated our customer-service staff like aristocracy. Our customer-service staff who were field based had very strong links with their internal counterparts and enjoyed high financial rewards, responsibilities, and prestige. They had good collateral in the form of high-quality marketing materials and aids, and benefited from the very high level of camaraderie that prevailed among even those whose jobs involved customer contact. As individuals and as a group, our customer-service staff were highly respected by all their contacts, including those within the media, government officials, union leaders, or other companies in our industry. This high status profile was both cultivated and justified. They were the spokespeople for our company and could authoritatively inform any outside contact on most aspects of our business.

What Marketing Means

The "visceral feeling of greatness," as Theodore Levitt called it—so vital to corporate growth and success— cannot occur until the top team agrees on the meaning of the term *marketing*. Philip Kotler, one of North America's leading marketing gurus defines marketing as "the task of finding and stimulating buyers for the firm's output." Popular though this view is, it better defines selling than marketing, and the distinction between the two is important. Selling is a product-centered activity; it concerns itself with finding customers, with creating customer need for the corporation's products. Prevalent immediately after World War II, this philosophy is based on shortage. In the postwar automobile industry, for example, market conditions were such that customers could be scared up for any sort of car that a manufacturer could produce. But although these conditions have long since vanished, the product-centered mentality still prevails. A case in point is former Commodore CEO Jack Tramiel, who used to preach that "the job of marketing is to sell the products we give them . . . the job of engineering is to give marketing good products they can sell." Tramiel kept the marketing staff separate from the scientific and development specialists (they worked in different buildings). This attitude permitted scores of late arrivals in the computer industry to put Commodore, and later Atari (Tramiel's subsequent fiefdom), in the shade.

Increasingly, however, executives are subscribing to a middle-of-the-road definition that says that marketing produces "economic want-satisfaction" by matching consumer's needs and the resources of business firms. While it is true that equilibrium must eventually exist between corporate resources and customer needs, defining resources is unimportant until the needs of customers are identified. As we stressed in Chapter 3, the corporate mission is couched in terms of the needs the corporation seeks to satisfy; only when these are understood is it possible to assemble the structure, the resources, and talent necessary to meet them.

Recently, we were asked to help a client develop a new mission statement. During preliminary discussions, we learned that management had just completed a review of the organization's structure and was in the process of implementing wide-ranging changes. We innocently inquired whether they had asked their customers if these changes would help better meet their needs. Did they have any alternative suggestions? We found that the client had not consulted with the customer *at all.* The client had no way of knowing whether the changes would help the company meet or exceed the customer's needs.

When Ellen Johnson, leisure-products buyer for Canadian Tire, suggested to Rubbermaid that the company put some of its plastic containers inside a lunch box and sell it as an alternative to resource-hungry plastic and paper wrapping, a new product was born. Rubbermaid's product-development team, led by Scott Jennie, came up with Sidekick, an insulated "green" lunch box that holds three plastic containers (for a drink, a sandwich, and another item). The result: Rubbermaid's share of the $35 million lunch-box market doubled to 12%. To be sure, Canadian Tire is a demanding customer of Rubbermaid; but as in all successful collaborations, there is more to the relationship than simply supplier and customer: They are a team, sharing the goal of turning customers into fans and building a profitable and lasting association. For Canadian Tire, Rubbermaid is "family," and this helps the company to generate 30% of its sales from new products each year.

In another case, we were engaged by a financial-services client to help redesign the corporate structure. We found that this $100 million company was organized by divisions ranging in size from $80 million to under $1 million in annual sales. Many of these divisions did business with the same customers. When we shifted our focus away from the organization's structure to the customer, we found that 40 clients generated 80% of the business, with the largest producing $5 million in annual sales alone. Yet the senior executive looking after a $750,000 division was a vice president, while the senior executive looking after the $5 million account was a humble salesman! As we often do, we suggested that management reorganize by customer, scrapping the divisional structure, in order to achieve the purpose of meeting or exceeding the needs of customers. (This story has an interesting footnote. The perceived loss of status among the divisional vice presidents was so severe that an internal political power play forced the company to rescind its decision to reorganize. Thus, the company sent out a strong signal that personal power, prestige, and status were more important than the needs of customers. This organization couldn't walk its talk.)

The Chicago-based advertising agency Leo Burnett has always maintained a client-centered structure, which probably explains much of the firm's success. In a period of real declines in advertising expenditures and an increase in company mergers, Leo Burnett is distinctive: It is still privately owned; it has only 33 clients including 15 multinational accounts, compared with the hundreds of clients at many other agencies; and half of its largest clients have been with the agency for over 20 years. Tony the Tiger, the Jolly Green Giant, the Pillsbury Doughboy, and the Marlborough Man have been remarkably loyal to Burnett— so much so that the agency hardly ever pitches for new business and enjoys a reputation as Philip Morris's "Mr. Fix-it" (it saved the bungled campaigns of other agencies for the giant tobacco and food firm). Burnett achieves success by staying very close to its clients—getting to know them so well that the agency is in a position to extend its relationship into other divisions of their largest clients: In the past 5 years, Burnett has doubled its billings with hardly any additions to its client list. In America's 13th biggest ad agency, each account is personally supervised by a member of the board of directors—underscoring Burnett's belief that its most important assets are its clients.

As Peter Drucker has written:

It is the customer who determines what a business is. It is the customer alone whose willingness to pay for a good or for a service converts economic resources into wealth, things into goods. What the business thinks it produces is not of first importance —especially not to the future of the business and its success. . . . What the customer buys and considers value is never a product. It is always utility, that is, what a product or service does for him. . . . The customer is the foundation of a business and keeps it in existence. He alone gives employment.

The vital distinction being made here is the notion that we all *work for the customer,* from whom our paychecks originate, *not* for the company from whom we receive them. The distinction between selling and marketing is therefore more than a matter of semantics. In fact, selling is the *inverse* of marketing: It seeks to find a customer for a firm's products or services, whereas marketing seeks to *identify the consumer's needs* and then arrange corporate resources in order to meet or exceed these needs. It therefore follows that if the marketing function is undertaken with precision, the selling function is superfluous. Will Rogers had it all figured out: "Let advertisers spend the same amount of money improving their product that they do on advertising and they won't need to advertise it." But this would be a perfect marketing condition—and since hell will freeze over before we witness such perfection, profit-making organizations will continue to use selling as a tool.

But selling is becoming increasingly irrelevant. Network television shows us why. At the beginning of the 1980s, over 75 million Americans watched network TV, "worshipping at the flickering altars of the three pillars of the national electronic church," to quote Ken Auletta, author of *Three Blind Mice: How the TV Networks Lost Their Way.* The number of viewers still loyal to the major

U.S. TV networks has shrunk from 87% to 60% in the last decade, and average prime-time audiences have slipped from 24.1 million to 15.8 million in the same period. Research indicates that viewers can't recall the commercials and, worse, finding them irritating and offensive, they deliberately switch channels or mute their TVs to avoid them. We should hardly be surprised that people seek refuge from advertising when one considers that in North America we are each subjected to 3,000 marketing messages a day. In 1986, 64% of those surveyed by Video Storyboard Tests could name a TV commercial they had seen in the previous 4 weeks compared to only 48% in 1990. My firm's research has shown that viewers find the garish puffery of many TV commercials to be egocentric, often self-serving, and subliminally violent. Viewers cannot articulate why, but TV commercials "don't make them feel good." During our seminars, we run a selection of award-winning TV commercials from around the world, juxtaposing commercials that are noisy, ugly, violent, or aggressively competitive with those that are romantic, sensitive, caring, and beautiful. Seminar participants always remark that they "don't feel good" when watching the first category and "feel better" when watching the second. Our physiology and biochemistry, and as as a result our emotions, are adversely affected by self-serving, abrasive, hard-selling TV commercials. In short, such advertising turns people off, because it literally makes them ill. Says William Johnson, CEO of Heinz pet products, "For all but a few products, network TV no longer makes sense." The new marketing—listening to customer's needs and then designing products and services that will meet or exceed them—is done belly-to-belly with the customer, where the customer lives, works, and plays. Thus, selling is irrelevant to the On Organization.

The health of a corporation can be gauged by its dependency on selling. Healthy corporations are market oriented; they direct their organizational and managerial energy toward meeting or exceeding customer needs. Weaker corporations harness large sales forces to find consumers for the products or services they generate.

Given this, we must still decide where to place the function of marketing within the corporate structure and what the status of this function is.

THE CEO AS CHIEF MARKETER

Much of the focus in this book has been on the importance of the leader's role *inside* the organization. But successful leaders have responsibilities that extend to the *outside* as well: These pertain to the customer. The CEO must exert leadership skills in all areas, internal *and* external, where customer attitudes can be shaped to the mutual benefit of the consumer and the corporation. As Theodore Levitt realized:

> No organization can achieve greatness without a vigorous leader who is driven onward by his own pulsating will to succeed. He has to have a vision of grandeur, a vision that can produce eager followers in vast numbers. In business, the followers are the customers. To produce these customers, the entire corporation must be viewed as a customer-creating and customer-satisfying organism. Management must think of itself not as producing products but as providing customer-creating value satisfactions. It must push this idea (and everything it means and requires) into every nook and cranny of the organization. It has to do this continuously and with the kind of flair that excites and stimulates the people in it. Otherwise, the company will be merely a series of pigeonholed parts, with no consolidating sense of purpose or direction.

If the purpose of a business is, as Peter Drucker says, "to create a customer" (or as Levitt puts it, "to buy a customer"), then the responsibilities outlined by Levitt certainly are the CEO's primary responsibilities—they cannot be unloaded on the marketing department. Who better to tell the consumer about Remington razors, Wendy's hamburgers, or Chrysler cars than the CEO? Yet in the organizational structure, the marketing function is very often a staff activity rather than a line activity—and too many CEOs rarely consider that calling on the corporation's top customers is a critical part of their role.

But it is. An enlightened leader wants to get so close to customers that he or she does not need market research—the relationship *is* the research. Successful companies treat their largest customers as "family," maintaining and deepening the relationship to keep in touch with their clients' needs.

Shortly after Toyota launched the Lexus car in the United States, the company had to recall the vehicles for a warrantied adjustment. Prior to the recall, dealers made arrangements with every Lexus owner to personally pick up the car; they also offered replacement vehicles. In this way they turned a potentially damaging situation into an opportunity to deepen their relationships with their customers. Burger King uses an 800 number to keep a finger on the pulse of its customers. When the firm introduced recycled bags to 50 pilot stores, it received such a favorable response that it threw out its plan to move slowly (after market research confirmed its wisdom) and launched the program nationwide in only 6 weeks.

Since 20% of the corporation's customers will probably account for 80% of its revenues, the fortunes of the corporation are inevitably intertwined with those of its customers, so a good intelligence system regarding customer health and satisfaction levels is vital. With so much riding upon so few, the leadership team cannot afford to take a detached view. At Manpower, every single member of our leadership team, with no exceptions and regardless of functional responsibility, was assigned a "godparent" role to a core group of customers. In addition to the obvious benefits, this technique yielded a secondary bonus; because our customer-service staff worked with all our top executives, a valuable two-way communication process became a standard feature of internal development and feedback. For instance, the switchboard operator would also assist the account executive responsible for the client who was her former employer. We repeated the same pattern with every staff member. We never had to discuss our customers theoretically because someone in the organization had first-hand experience of them.

The CEO is not only the chief entrepreneur and chief marketer, but chief management developer as well. Keeping the leadership team close to the customer is a key component of the leadership role. In this way specialist staff executives—personnel, accounting, management information, planning, and finance, for example—are able to diversify their experience, collect field data, and expose laboratory-stage ideas to the customers' scrutiny. After all, it's the customers who are the ultimate judges of whether the ideas will work, and customer feedback can only sharpen your organization's relevance. For instance, at Manpower we often asked our director of finance to combine his customer relations skills (which he had learned with us) and his accounting knowledge (which he brought with him to the job) to the successful resolution of complex customer negotiations leading to a major contract. A qualified accountant, he is now the CEO of his own marketing and sales-promotion company.

EVERYONE IS A MARKETER
An opportunity is missed by many corporations when they don't encourage administrative staff to embrace marketing and customer-service roles. For many managers the idea that *every* employee in the business can and should play an important role in building the company's relationships with its customers is a new one, which often

gets short shrift in their left-hemispheric outlooks. But executives with moxie appreciate the potential contribution that every employee can offer in a company that is keen to acquire new customers, keep existing ones, and build a reputation that reinforces a corporate culture focused on meeting or exceeding the needs of customers. *Every* employee has the potential to contribute ideas that will improve service standards, upgrade and advance the company's products or services, win new customers, solve complaints, identify new markets, wean customers from other companies in the industry, and generally sharpen the company's performance edge.

From the first employment interview, *all* prospective employees should understand that an important part of their responsibilities will include the maintenance and development of customers. During that initial interview, applicants should be asked if they have any objection to assuming some, or even all, of the responsibility for being the principal ambassador to their former employer (if applicable). *Without exception,* employees who cannot enthusiastically accept these responsibilities in addition to their functional or specialized roles should be encouraged to work for other companies in your industry —where they will do you much more good!

Indeed, the involvement of all employees in the care and custody of customers is an important asset for every organization. The leadership team's responsibility is to exploit the synergy that exists between particular skills and experiences of employees (at any level) and specific customer or market needs. At Manpower, we maintained an inventory of the special interests, expertise, and prior experience possessed by every employee. For example, some of the managers and staff who had worked previously in the car industry were assigned to watch over our major clients in that field. These employees were involved in presentations, preparation of proposals and bids, and so forth. In another case, one of the managers in our human resources department who had previously worked for an international manufacturer of information-processing equipment was, for many years, responsible for the successful annual negotiations of our national sales agreement with a major client in that same industry.

THE MARKETING CONCEPT AND ITS CRITICS

Academics have recently taken to criticizing the marketing concept. Before discussing this further, a quick review of its history seems to be in order.

Peter Drucker credits Cyrus H. McCormick (1809–1884), the inventor of the mechanical harvester, with the invention of modern marketing. Others credit General Electric for publicly embracing the marketing concept in 1951 and, through its corporate reorganization, communicating the idea that the consumer is the strategic determinant of the corporation. Yet we have only to look at history to know this is inaccurate. The British East India Company (1660–1858) and the Dutch East India Company (1602–1798) marketed power, commodities, and natural resources around the globe and were so successful that they gained trading monopolies and administrative control of whole countries before they were disbanded. They and scores of other groups, before and since, have benefited from the identification and satisfaction of consumers' needs. It's the commonsense formula of business—nothing happens until somebody gets an order. Or as Robert Louis Stevenson wrote in *Across the Plains,* "Everyone lives by selling something!" The idea of marketing is not new—it's as old as our species. And its reported death in business-school marketing courses is, like Mark Twain's falsely reported death, greatly exaggerated.

But Drucker points out that the rise of consumerism —defending the rights of consumers—has proven that marketing is still more rhetoric than reality in many modern businesses. For this reason Drucker calls con-

sumerism the "shame of marketing." Even before the
marketing concept gets its 20th-century innings, we find
it is already being defined as obsolete!

Consumer groups like Ralph Nader's "Raiders" question the wisdom of meeting consumer demands if doing
so brings a wake of problems, such as waste disposal,
pollution, safety concerns, and other ecological and
environmental issues as the price to be paid by society.
But society and the consumer are not different people;
they are the same people in different contexts, and
sometimes one's increased standard of living may well be
another's environmental or safety issue. Consumerism is
contemporary democracy. Its effect on production and
the marketing concept in the years ahead will *increase*
not decrease. The message behind Adam Smith's dictum
in *The Wealth of Nations,* "Consumption is the sole end
and purpose of production," is as much the message for
leadership teams in the new millennium as it was in 1776;
it simply needs to be tempered to our times.

A second criticism of the marketing concept is that
it has damaged American business by leading to a dearth
of true innovation, because it distracts executives from
focusing on the product. This, the criticism goes, may
satisfy in the short run but will leave the organization
vulnerable in the long run.

There are two things wrong with this criticism. First
is the assumption that producers are better judges than
customers of what is best for the customer. The implicit
message is that consumers do not know that they need a
photocopier, fax machine, compact disc player, or a microcomputer until it is invented. But inventors frequently attempt to identify markets for their ideas and seldom invent
new products or services without considerable input from
the potential user. Indeed, Clarence Bird, the inventor of
modern frozen foods; Ray Kroc, the converter of the local
hamburger stand into the largest fast-food franchises
in the world; and Ole Kirk Christiansen, the Danish

carpenter who invented Lego—to name three random examples—all modified their ideas to suit customer needs.

When the governor of North Carolina complimented Thomas Edison on his accumulation of over a thousand patents and praised him as a great inventor, Edison demurred. "The only invention I can really claim as absolutely original is the phonograph."

"Just what do you mean?" the governor asked.

"Well," explained Edison, "I guess I'm an awfully good sponge. I absorb ideas from every source I can and put them to practical use. Then I improve them until they become of some value. The ideas I use are mostly the ideas of people who don't develop them."

The conversion of added utility for the customer into added value for the corporation is the most consumer-oriented of corporate behaviors and therefore a principal purpose of every business. Peter Drucker has pointed out that "because its purpose is to create a customer, the business enterprise has two—and only these two—basic functions: marketing and innovation. Marketing and innovation produce results; all the rest are 'costs.' " The arrogant assertion by some managers that consumers don't understand their own wants or needs is the commercial equivalent of the conceit, widely embraced by many politicians, that they can outsmart the voter. Fortunately, like voters, consumers vote with their feet: They beat paths to the doors of those companies that listen to consumers and use that feedback to get even closer to the customer—the organization that is totally on.

The second error in this criticism is the notion that consumer orientation is only good for the short term. Frequent innovation in a changing marketplace should not be confused with a short-term commitment to the customer. Describing Nike's habit of updating every running shoe that it sells every 6 months, Vice President Andrew Mooney says, "We're like the auto industry, constantly looking for new technologies to pep up the product." Nike's CEO Philip Knight elaborates by pointing out that the new ideas generated by Nike's exercise physiologists and mechanical engineers could enable the company to introduce new products for the next 3 years. In fact, the changes in Nike's product line every 6 months are part of its long-term strategy; the company grows in double digits every year, lists 800 shoes in its catalog for 25 different sports, and has built a long-term franchise with its distributors and consumers. It is clear that identification of consumer needs and wants is a short-, medium-, and long-term affair. But whenever management is motivated, compensated, and measured on the basis of short-term criteria *alone,* it's a result of executive incompetence, not of consumer-sensitive attitudes. (One way to avoid this is customer-based compensation.)

Some critics of the marketing concept ridicule its short-term concentration on such consumer-inspired products as new cake mixes, new-fangled potato chips, feminine-hygiene deodorants, and the pet rock. But focusing only on trivial results is not an intellectually rigorous criticism of the concept. By attending to consumer needs and desires, over 80% of the economic output of modern Western companies consists of information and services— certainly no trivial outcome. Satellites that provide better weather services; laser technology in communications and life sciences; new drugs that relieve pain and cure diseases; genetic engineering that leads to improved health; cheaper and more efficient air transportation; information-processing technology; the exploration for future energy sources; and hundreds of other enormous human advances testify to both the long-term nature of many consumer-driven corporate strategies as well as to a widely held corporate conviction that the consumer is right.

For those who still doubt the lock-step relationship between innovation and corporate success, a recent analysis by *Fortune* magazine showing the changes in the

Table 9-3   The Top Patent Winners in the United States

1980	1990
1. General Electric (U.S.)	Hitachi (Japan)
2. Bayer (Europe)	Toshiba (Japan)
3. RCA (U.S.)	Canon (Japan)
4. U.S. Navy (U.S.)	Mitsubishi (Japan)
5. AT&T (U.S.)	General Electric (U.S.)
6. IBM (U.S.)	Fuji Photo (Japan)
7. Hitachi (Japan)	Eastman Kodak (U.S.)
8. Westinghouse Electric (U.S.)	Philips (Europe)
9. Siemens (Europe)	IBM (U.S.)
10. General Motors (U.S.)	Siemens (Europe)

number of patents awarded to U.S. companies paints a remarkable—if not pretty—picture of the changes during the last decade. The results are shown in Table 9-3.

In 1980 62% of patents were awarded to U.S. corporations and citizens. By 1990 this figure had declined to 53%, and seven of the top-ten patent winners were not U.S. nationals.

RISK AND PATIENCE
A decade ago when Sony invented the Walkman, market research indicated that the portable tape player would sell poorly because it was unable to record. Since then Sony has sold more than 30 million Walkmans in the United States alone. The decision to go ahead with the Walkman was made personally by Akio Morita, Sony's chairman, and it was based on—how can we bring ourselves to admit this?—gut feeling. The Japanese constantly eschew traditional market research in consumer and packaged goods in favor of sending their chief executives into supermarkets to ask the "average" consumer simple questions like, What do you like about our cereal? Why did you just buy another company's product? How can we make our cereal better or differently?

In 1973 RCA earned $183.7 million on sales of $4.2 billion. In the 10-year period that followed, RCA posted a mere 2% profit on sales of over $67 billion. This lackluster performance was in part caused by a series of initiatives to meet consumer demand on a number of different fronts. RCA sank $2 billion pretax into mainframe computer technology; made heavy investments in high-resolution, low-cost TV research; and put $580 million into videodisc technology, which RCA then abandoned (pronounced by then-chairman Thornton F. Bradshaw as "a technological success but a commercial failure"). Many observers have criticized RCA for failures of marketing, but it was doing exactly what a marketing-oriented company should do: investing heavily in research that it hoped would result in bringing products successfully to market.

Creating products that will satisfy consumer needs is a risky business; we must learn to accept the fact that both failure and success spring from such endeavors. Staying power is important too—the videodisc has made a comeback since RCA abandoned it, prized by videophiles for its high resolution and sound quality. RCA had the right product but was overcome by impatience.

The U.S. health care industry is a $1.6 billion-a-day business, larger than the auto, aircraft, textile, steel, mining, and petroleum-refining industries combined. Although hospitals have long been the preserve of nonprofit, community, and government organizations (90%, as recently as 1979), today profit-making organizations account for 25% of all U.S. hospitals.

Two of the largest hospital management companies are Hospital Corporation of America (1990 revenues $4.7 billion) and investor-owned Humana (1990 revenues $4.9 billion), which runs 83 hospitals in 19 states. Why have these private companies grabbed so much business from the public sector? Because they identified and met customers needs. Humana was started in 1962 by two Louisville lawyers, David Jones and Wendell Cherry, with one Kentucky nursing home and $1,000 (borrowed).

Humana offers its "customer" (a word that many doctors at first found offensive) an assurance of quality at every stage of the health care delivery system. It has opened over 100 neighborhood clinics to provide simple medical treatments not requiring hospital facilities, with convenient hours (weekends and evenings) and locations (shopping malls and street corners). It provides insurance plans to companies and guarantees to keep employee medical-cost increases at the same level as the Consumer Price Index for 4 years (health care costs are currently rising at twice this rate). Humana claims 986,000 members enrolled in its health insurance plans, 63% of whom use Humana hospitals. It has been described as the lowest-cost health care company in the United States.

Good hospitals require good equipment. Industry sources estimate that U.S. hospitals will need to raise hundreds of billions of dollars during the 1990s. For-profit hospitals with good medical and profit performances can raise capital for these purposes by selling stock, an opportunity not available to the public sector, which must continue to rely on philanthropy and public handouts. In most fields, the public sector cannot continue to ignore customer needs in this manner. Like Humana, the alert marketer who can identify opportunity can create the only kind of enterprise worth building, the On Organization that profitably meets customer needs.

DOING IT BETTER: *KAIZEN*

In 1989 Xerox controlled only 7% of U.S. fax-machine sales while Japan controlled 66%—but it was Xerox that had introduced the first commercial fax machine 25 years earlier.

In 1947 the U.S. company Raytheon sold the first microwave oven; but today although four out of five American homes have microwaves, three out of four of the ovens were made in the Far East.

In 1979 American-owned companies built 80% of the autos sold in the United States. But in the following decade, U.S. car makers closed 13 of their North American plants while Japanese auto producers opened 11 new ones. The Big Three's market share dropped to 67%.

What happened? The Japanese quality movement happened—a phenomenon that owes much of its development to an American, W. Edwards Deming. The highest award for quality in Japan today is the Deming award.

Underlining the passionate commitment of Japanese management and their employees to quality is the concept of *Kaizen*. The *Kanji* characters that translate as *Kaizen* describe the Japanese concept of continuing improvement. In his book *Kaizen: The Key to Japan's Competitive Success,* Masaaki Imai describes *Kaizen* as "continuing improvement in personal life, home life, social life, and working life. When applied to the work place, Kaizen means continuing improvement involving everyone—managers and workers alike."

Everyone agrees that the genius of Western business is innovation and creativity. These two characteristics are the crown jewels of our commercial organizations. No one anywhere in the world can match our prolific output of inventions, innovations, and new twists or new uses for old products. We are driven by a constant search for change, replacement, newness. The Western way is to do it *differently.*

The Japanese (and increasingly the Oriental) way is to do it *better.* One senior executive from a major multinational corporation recently told me that his firm's Japanese competitors had so improved their manufacturing processes that they were now able to sell their products for the same price that it cost the American firm to *make* theirs. This famous American firm is now in a flat-out race to improve the quality of its manufacturing processes. Its survival depends on it.

The Japanese have extended and refined the notion of *Kaizen,* or continuous improvement, to an even higher level, which they call *Warusa-Kagen,* a term meaning "things that are not yet problems but are not quite right."

The story is told how Pentel, one of the largest manufacturers of stationery products in the world, introduced a mechanical pencil that had a cap on the end, which when removed and placed on the opposite end of the pencil could be used to push the lead out of the tip. A *Kaizen* team at Pentel asked potential customers how the pencil could be better. (Who else understands how to make things better than customers? Certainly not the engineers!) The customers told Pentel that the cap should click when attached to the other end, just like the caps of pens do. Of course, the engineers knew that this did not make the pencil a better product—but it did in the customer's perception. And since *perception is reality,* the customer's view is the correct one.

The result: The caps on Pentel products click, and Pentel does not regard its products as market-ready unless they click just right. It matters not that the click of the cap makes-no-never-mind to the performance of the pencil. But it makes a big difference to its marketing success, because the customer is reassured by the sound of the cap snapping on tightly. Such is the wonder of doing it better, or, as the Japanese call it, *Kaizen.*

In another case, a *Kaizen* team detected a minor problem on a ball-bearing manufacturer's assembly line. Bearings of different sizes were dropped from a hopper on the assembly line into the boxes that were eventually sold in stores. The entire process of production and packaging was automated. But customers were complaining that sometimes they got a box containing no ball bearings. This would occur once in every 100,000–200,000 boxes (a ratio that would satisfy most Western executives). Although the cost of replacing empty boxes after delivery was minimal, the *Kaizen* team convinced Pentel that inclusion of the empty box itself could seriously damage the company's reputation.

A *Warusa-Kagen* group originally suggested installing an X-ray system to detect the empty boxes, but they abandoned this idea because of its high cost. Then they came up with the solution: They installed a small fan at the side of the assembly line that blew the empty (and therefore lighter) boxes off the line. Later they upgraded the process by using pressurized air, which was readily available everywhere in the factory.

Such dedication to continuous improvement has helped propel the Japanese to their current world status in manufacturing. Nowadays, organizations with moxie have discovered that although they may be world class at innovating—doing it differently—they must also become as skilled at *Kaizen*—doing it better. This subtle difference propels outstanding organizations into a class of their own. It is not simply a Japanese idea; it is an *intelligent* idea.

THE TELEPHONE AND THE ON ORGANIZATION

Often, apparently insignificant details are crucial to an organization's image and success. One of the most crucial is the telephone.

Few companies fully understand the ambassadorial role of their switchboard operator or receptionist, who is actually a spokesperson for the organization. Because he or she is usually the first contact that real or prospective customers have with the organization, the image projected is important. This seemingly innocuous contact gives callers an impression of how their relationship with the company will progress.

When I first arrived at Manpower, our receptionist's telephone-answering style conformed to the dismal standards of most other companies. Accordingly, we completely revamped our whole telephone procedure by instituting new techniques and installing an entirely new system. We recruited top-caliber staff and paid them twice the previous levels of remuneration. Our new approach was to greet every caller with a cheery, "Good morning/afternoon. This is Manpower. May we help you?" and to answer all telephones within two rings. At first these modest changes brought on severe culture shock, which soon gave way to wonder and enthusiasm: Companies from all over the country complimented us on our company's pleasantly bold telephone-answering style and the improvement in our corporate image—and our employees sensed that this was not simply a cosmetic improvement but the beginning of a new era.

The opportunity for an On Organization begins when the telephone rings. Every employee's telephone manner and his or her attitude toward the telephone is therefore crucial for the success of modern organizations. Frequently, however, the telephone is used as a blunt instrument, alienating rather than winning customers.

Recently, I received a telephone call from a big shot, or at least from the big shot's assistant.

"Can I speak with Dr. Secretan?"

"Speaking," I replied.

"Just a moment please, Mr. Big Shot would like to speak to you."

I hung up. Mr. Big Shot was so obviously self-important and inconsiderate that he didn't hesitate to waste *my* time. But when my temperature returned to normal, I reconsidered; perhaps I had overreacted. So I called Mr. Big Shot back.

I was greeted with, "ABC Company, please hold," and then music (which on any other occasion might have been pleasant). An eternity passed before a voice came back on the line to ask me to whom I wished to speak. I asked for Mr. Big Shot. Click. More music. Another eternity. Finally, the switchboard operator came back on the phone: "I'm sorry, I can't find Mr. Big Shot, and his secretary seems to have stepped away from her desk for a moment. . . . " I hung up for the second time.

If any university ever offers me another teaching position, I shall propose a foundation course to replace Sociology 101. Telephone Techniques 101 will be mandatory for all students, regardless of discipline. Among other things it will teach the following basic rules:

1. Don't be a telephone snob. Place your own calls.

2. Never leave your desk without telling someone where you will be, so as not to waste everyone's time: the caller's, yours, your secretary's, and the receptionist's.

3. Be empathic. Use the telephone to create a good relationship between you and your caller.

4. Be innovative. Use the latest technology (call waiting, message forwarding, electronic mail, answering machines or services).

5. Provide a voice-mail message that informs and entertains. It should be so good that callers tell others to call you just to hear it. Coach those in your organization who are not natural communicators so that they can develop appropriate messages.

6. Call your own company from time to time and ask yourself how you would feel if you were a customer. If the experience is wonderful, publicly celebrate the switchboard operator as soon as you can; if it was horrible, coach some more.

7. Appoint a superstar to be responsible for the switchboard. Make sure that this person is a highly valued, well-paid ambassador with managerial responsibility for maintaining and improving the standards of telephone communications across the entire organization.

Digital Equipment in Finland provides its people with cordless phones. Although this is hardly state-of-the-art technology, it gives the employees autonomy and freedom. When you think about it, it's absurd to chain people to their desks with bits of electronic cable. By freeing employees in this way, Digital has enabled them to make or take calls wherever they may be: in the canteen, in someone else's office, or even outside the building.

At WordPerfect in Provo, Utah, you will encounter a new twist to the old-fashioned "all-our-lines-are-busy" message: "hold jockeys." These people have responsibilities similar to radio disk jockeys: They chat with callers, play soothing music, tell the time, read advertisements, and give up-to-the-minute traffic reports. With 13,000 calls a day, WordPerfect is attempting to deal creatively with the inevitable backups that occur (some lasting as long as 10 minutes).

Voice mail.   Voice mail sends a clear message to callers: We are a lean organization. We've decided that it is more important to save money than to spoil customers and other callers. As a result, we have invested in a piece of technological hardware that enables us to avoid the salary costs we would otherwise incur if we took a "high-touch" approach to our handling of the telephoning public.

Whether this decision is the right one or not may be moot. Having made it, however, the trick is to turn voice mail into a source of mastery instead of a source of irritation and inefficiency. Here are some tips.

Never force callers to make their first contact with your organization by voice mail. *Always* make customers' first connection—and therefore their first impression of your organization—a warm, friendly, human one. This contact should be charming; callers should be romanced by a congenial and efficient operator who asks whether they would like to be connected to the organization's voice mail in order to leave a message. The idea is to overcome the feeling of helplessness experienced by most callers when they are swept into the voice-mail vortex. A skilled operator *seeks callers' permission* before shunting them into the voice-mail system, thereby giving them a degree of control over their situation.

Thoroughly train an operator as the *manager* of telephone services and coach someone else to be backup. Remember to include in the training pertinent information about major customers, suppliers, and other key external contacts. The people you choose for this job should be intelligent, courteous, helpful, knowledgeable, and upbeat. Pay them well to reflect their importance to the company, as the first contact the public has with your organization.

Never subject callers to "radio-while-they-wait." Customers do not place long-distance calls to your organization in order to listen to commercials on your local FM station.

Coach *every* user in the techniques of recording their announcements. Pay particular attention to the articulation, tone, and rhythm of the delivery. Send them to voice classes if necessary, or consider selecting people from within the organization to grace voice-mail messages with their dulcet tones. Otherwise, customers may be dissuaded from placing multimillion-dollar orders by someone who unsettles them with a scratchy, whiny voice.

Make every recorded message upbeat and exciting. You want callers to enjoy your message so much that they call back just to hear it again. Use your imagination: include quotations, information about the company, poetry, music, and anything else that will engage the minds and hearts of callers. Show them that you care about them, using voice mail to distinguish your organization from the rest of the pack.

Don't recite long lists of options or include technobabble instructions about "pushing pound signs"—most people can't tell you the difference between a pound sign and a pound cake. Keep instructions simple. Most callers will not have completed a shorthand course, nor will they have notepads handy. Because they are unprepared, they will not easily remember or record lengthy instructions. It's easier to call a competitor.

Encourage individuals to change their voice-mail messages frequently during the day, giving specific information about their whereabouts and when they can return the call. They then must keep their promises—just as they would with their customers' delivery dates.

Introduce the following mandatory policy of logistics for every person with an extension:

1. Whenever employees are away from their telephone extension, they must inform the operator.

2. They must let the operator know how they can be reached at their temporary location.

3. They must brief the operator about expected calls so that he or she can greet callers appropriately. For example, "Mr. Jones was expecting your call but had to step out for 10 minutes."

Don't give the operator a collection of miscellaneous jobs. The one he or she has—managing corporate telephone communications—is too important to be diluted with extraneous work. Besides, if you've selected the operator properly, he or she will be overqualified for clerical work.

With these steps safely implemented, callers will overcome their yearning for high-touch contact and their deeply ingrained animosity toward high-tech voice mail, and you will have kept them as delighted customers.

Customer Satisfaction: Closing the Back Door

It's not only important to identify and then meet or exceed your customers' needs; you must also *keep* your customers, for life—which means you need a follow-up system to keep them satisfied. Think of an organization in terms of front and back doors. The front door is the development of new business; the back door is quality and service. Often, companies pull customers in through the front door but drive them out the back by poor quality or service. Even with a mediocre marketing strategy, many companies would be hugely successful if they simply closed the back door.

Research by the Washington consulting firm Technical Assistance Research Programs (TARP) showed that 90% of the customers unhappy with a company's service did not repurchase from that company; 54% of the customers happy with a company's service stayed with that company. In addition, each complaining customer tells 9 or 10 people about his or her experience. TARP went on to quantify the potential benefit that would accrue to companies that implemented vigorous customer-service programs: automakers, $142,000 over a happy customer's lifetime; appliance makers, $2,840 over 20 years; and supermarkets, $22,000 over 5 years (all in constant dollars).

A Harris study revealed that consumers believe service is worse today than it was 10 years ago. In fact, study after study shows that the consumer has become disenchanted with shopping. Yankelovitch Clancy Shulman, another firm that regularly takes the pulse of American consumers, found that 66% of consumers consider shopping for clothes frustrating and time-consuming; 47% of food shoppers feel the same way. An American Management Association study showed that a satisfied customer praises the company to 3 people while a dissatisfied customer beefs about the experience to 11 others.

Since 1980 J. D. Power Associates, of Agoura Hills, California, has compiled a customer satisfaction index (CSI) for the automobile industry. Each year Power sends a six-page questionnaire to 73,000 owners of current model-year cars and receives approximately 23,000 responses. Power sells the results to automobile makers, who use it to advertise (if they do well in the survey) or improve (if they do not). For years, the "customer-handling" component of the weighting in the survey accounted for 40% of the total score. Recently, it's been changed to 60% to reflect the shifting needs of customers.

Gun Dukes, who administers the survey, observed, "How [customers] are treated at the dealership has become more important to customers and should carry greater weight." The Malcolm Baldrige National Quality Award offers a potential score of 1,000 points of which fully 300, the largest share, are allocated to customer satisfaction.

Richard J. Chitty, customer-satisfaction manager at Lexus, uses Power's CSI and the average gross profit of dealers to determine the costs of customer dissatisfaction. The costs of poor service to each dealer, the firm calculates, is between $4,300 and $66,762 in lost gross profits. Adds Chitty, "That assumes the lost customer would only buy one more car. And it doesn't count the 200 or so friends each one talks to about the experience."

McDonald's Corporation built its business on the solid pillars of its corporate motto, Q. S. C. & V.: *quality* food products; efficient, friendly *service;* and restaurants renowned for their *cleanliness* and *value.* When quality and service are such obvious methods of leaving other companies standing, it is surprising that only a few corporate leaders seriously consider these as cornerstones of corporate success.

Philip B. Crosby founded Quality College, in Winter Park, Florida, dedicated to teaching managers how to achieve optimum quality in plants and offices. He admits, "Until recently people thought I was a madman. Now they think I'm a statesman." Sales at Quality College boomed to $84 million in 1991, and Crosby's book *Quality Is Free* has sold several million copies since 1979. Executives from such corporations as General Motors and IBM have attended programs at Winter Park; the General Motors executives were so impressed that they put down $4 million for a 10% stake in Quality College and took an option on another 10%. Crosby has since cashed in his chips to form a quality consulting company.

Table 9-4   The Low-Service/Margin Model

	Manpower	*Everyone Else*
Sales	100%	100%
Gross Margin	20%	25%
Expenses	30%	15%
Net Profit	(10%)	10%

If you were to stand in the front hall of most corporations, figuratively speaking, you would be flattened by the stampede of new customers being driven in through the front door. If you picked yourself up off the floor quickly enough and turned around, you'd probably see the same customers zipping out the back, without so much as a handshake.

In our early days at Manpower, we found that our gross profit margins were just over 20% of sales while our operating expenses were 30% of sales. Other companies in our industry enjoyed a gross margin of 25% of sales and expenses of 15%, resulting in net earnings of 10%. This is shown in Table 9-4.

The conventional wisdom in our business was to operate with financial ratios similar to those of the other players in our industry. However, our gross margin, expenses, and net-profit aspirations did not even match theirs, and we were trying to grow by cutting our prices. The result was the acceleration of our financial hemorrhage. The truth was that we were copying a bad recipe. We recognized that in order to regain our lost position in the market we would have to create distance between ourselves and the other players in order to improve our image with our existing and potential customers. What we needed before we perished altogether was the development of a distinctive competence and the creation of a market niche. Consequently, we resolved to make the

Table 9-5   The High-Service/Margin Model

	Manpower	*Everyone Else*
Sales	100%	100%
Gross Margin	40%	25%
Expenses	30%	15%
Net Profit	10%	10%

highest standards of service in the industry our hallmark. This helped us to formulate a conscious, long-term, strategic decision to alter the internal construction of our operating ratios to those shown in Table 9-5.

As Table 9-5 shows, we chose to elevate the image and quality of our company and its services by spending at *twice* the relative rate of other companies on service and operations. This required a realignment of margins to double their previous levels, a level that was now 60% higher than theirs. We achieved this through a price increase, a risky gamble but worth it considering that the alternative was almost certain extinction. Besides, this strategy of high margins coupled with exemplary service fitted comfortably with our newly defined corporate mission (described in Chapter 3). Over time, we were consistently 20% to 25% more expensive, on a unit-cost basis, than other companies, and sometimes much more. On the other hand, we had a service advantage. As Table 9-5 demonstrates, we could always outspend them on customer support, by as much as 2 to 1. This gave us a people edge; we could and did employ more and better people, and we were able to invest much more heavily in marketing, quality, customer service, training, and advertising than our competitors. We provided a no-hassle, money-back guarantee, because unlike those of other companies, our new margin policy was built to stand the pressure, even as our increase in service reduced this risk.

We built a culture within the company that rested on a self-perception of high quality and fair but higher pricing than other companies. This culture made us the leading company in our industry—and it helped us to maintain our reputation for being the very best in our business for 15 years. We addressed the market with a high-service/high-margin mentality: It took us 5 years to emerge from the swamp to market leadership.

Our service costs became our largest single expenditure item. Most companies put a lot of rhetorical weight behind the importance of service, but the mouth seldom matches the money. If service is the heart of a service business (and as we've said before, what business is not a service business?), then the only logical corollary is that the service personnel (the creators and protectors) must be the most numerous in the organization. The emphasis of the leadership team must be squarely behind this principle, financially and psychologically.

We made major investments in coaching and established continuing service-staff development programs. We instituted a rigorous recognition system. We rewarded employees through an appraisal system and profit-sharing programs. We honored local service teams and individuals with plaques and trophies for their service achievements; we presented outstanding-service awards at public events to which our customers were invited; and we associated high levels of customer service with high levels of esteem for everyone in the corporation, at every opportunity.

In addition, we instituted a major customer-service audit program. All our offices issued spot-check, service questionnaires to customers on a random basis; we sent another tier of questionnaires to local customers from the head office. We reviewed the results in regular quality-review meetings.

When hiring, we sought a high degree of inherent altruism, and we developed new tests and screening methods in order to discern this characteristic, which we felt was crucial: We needed to build on a strong, personal, latent affinity to quality and service. From this individual foundation, we sought to develop a keen sense of customer awareness in all new employees. A powerful, customer-oriented service business cannot be constructed upon weak foundations; every individual is a vital brick in its construction. This service culture ruled our actions: What was right for the customer was right for Manpower —for its reputation, its future, and its success, all of which we shared with our employees and all of which they helped to build, because their lives depended on it.

LISTENING TO THE CUSTOMER

A thorough knowledge of its customers and its market is a prerequisite for any On Organization. A company obtains such knowledge by *listening* to what its customers have to say about the company's products and services as well as those of the competition. Organizations must overcome their desire for homeostasis—for maintaining the status quo—to respond to customer feedback positively and quickly, because the customer is the *only* expert on what he or she wants. Let me give you an example.

What is the first name that comes to mind when I say, "I liked the razor so much, I bought the company"? Victor Kiam, right? The ubiquitous entrepreneur who liked his Remington razor so much he bought the company and then told us about it in countless TV commercials and then again in his book *Going for It!*

But one morning some months ago, as I stared at myself in the shaving mirror, I made a momentous decision: It was time to retire my old Braun electric razor, so I took myself off to the store.

My Braun had put in yeoman service over many years, and I had no intention of changing brands. But I thought I'd keep my prejudices to myself and let the expert do the talking. "Which electric razor do you recommend?" I asked Mr. Shaver Man.

"Well," he responded, "the Braun is a very good razor. It's made in Germany, and the company is a subsidiary of Gillette. But the razor we most frequently recommend is the Payer, made in Austria."

Now, I had never heard of a Payer nor had I ever seen an advertisement for one. Mr. Shaver Man proceeded to explain the comparative merits of the Braun and the Payer, making no bones about the fact that he favored the Austrian razor.

After much tire kicking, I decided to follow his recommendation, a decision that was sweetened by the fact that the shaver was being offered with a discount.

As Mr. Shaver Man wrapped my purchase, I asked him about Philips and Remington, the other brand names I knew. He grimaced, "The Philips doesn't give you a close shave."

"What about the Remington?" I asked.

"Hell of a salesman that Victor Kiam!"

"What do you mean?"

"The Remington is great when you buy it, but after you've had it for a few weeks, it falls apart. Poor quality, shoddy workmanship."

That did it. Mr. Shaver Man convinced me that I had made the right decision. This savvy shopper was not buying a razor that would fall apart 3,500 miles from home.

Later I got to thinking about Victor Kiam. In 1989 he said that "we can grow as long as we remember that quality is uppermost and that when you offer a consumer a product with a consumer benefit at a fair price, you can have success." He was in town recently as part of a speaking tour in which he lectured about how he had rebuilt the Remington business. I wondered if he knew what Mr. Shaver Man was saying about his products. And I realized that every organization has many Mr. Shaver Men. They are the surrogate salespeople without whose neighborhood charm, the nice things they say about us, their knowledge of our products, their goodwill, their attention to quality control, and their friendly customer service, no one would every buy anything at all. All those Mr. Shaver Men, from every industry and service, reinforce or alter the image of an organization.

Mr. Kiam, like all of us, should take better care of Mr. Shaver Man, because no multimillion-dollar advertising campaign can persuade me to buy a razor that Mr. Shaver Man is telling me will fall apart in a few weeks.

By listening to customers closely, Whirlpool identified which parts fail in older models, Vivitar modified a flash unit for its cameras, and Sony took only 3 months to redesign TV sets after learning that customers wanted to easily connect them to computers.

COGNITIVE DISSONANCE

One of the reasons that customers don't come back to companies that provide poor service is because, for most people, buying a lemon results in subconscious self-criticism, a phenomenon called **cognitive dissonance.** This concept was first articulated by Leon Festinger: "Two elements are in a dissonant relation if, considering these two alone, the obverse of one element would follow from another." Thus, for example, the information that Pepsi is better for you than Coke will be dissonant for you if you usually buy Coke. Regular smokers suffer cognitive dissonance when they learn that smoking is a lethal habit.

Cognitive dissonance has two effects:

1. Because dissonance is psychologically uncomfortable, a person will to try to reduce it and achieve consonance.
2. In addition to trying to reduce dissonance, a person will actively avoid situations and information that would likely increase it.

I'll use smoking to illustrate the three ways people seek to eliminate dissonance:

1. Change behavior: Stop smoking.
2. Change values: "I could just as easily die crossing the road as I could of lung cancer."
3. Change the environment: Provide incontrovertible evidence to refute the research.

The basis for the theory of cognitive dissonance is that people seek powerful justifications for their behavior. Applied to consumers, it follows that they not only wish to believe that they have purchased wisely, but they seek to minimize internal conflict. This is why it's so important to always communicate with customers in terms of *their* interests, demonstrating why they are making a smart decision when they buy our products and services. This is also why after-sales service is the secret to customer retention: Customers continually seek to justify their earlier purchases; they wish to feel that the reasons for their decisions are overwhelming and sound.

PAMPERING THE CUSTOMER

You simply cannot cosset a customer enough—unrestrained pampering brings customers back for more. Patrons of restaurants where the food is mediocre but the staff remembers their names and a special table is always available are walking testimony to the fact that good service creates a loyal following.

One of the ways that we pampered our customers at Manpower was through "customer weeks": Each week we targeted a specific customer, whom we exhaustively researched: the company's history, markets, personnel, financial performance, objectives, reputation, technology, problems, and its relationship with our company. We developed a plan for this customer that involved everyone in the company and included our objectives for that week. We circulated copies of the program to all managers; held briefing sessions with all staff at every level; assigned duties; and solicited additional comments and suggestions. Then we set aside a whole week for the red-carpet treatment: We invited the customer's key personnel to our head office and branches, where we made them all feel like VIPs. We presented our best face to them and took note of all brickbats and bouquets. The following week, we did it all over again with another customer. Such close contact with our top-priority customers kept us abreast of their needs and desires. In this way we were able to satisfy them, often tailoring services to their specifications or developing entirely new services.

John Deere and Company has a similar program for getting close to its customers. When Lloyd Pettersen, a farmer from Truman, Minnesota, ordered one of the largest combines made by Deere, the company invited Pettersen and his wife on an all-expenses-paid visit to the plant to watch his machine being built. Much advance internal publicity presaged the visit. Posters appeared with such teasers as "Where is Truman, Minnesota?" and "Who is Lloyd Pettersen?" By the time the Pettersens arrived, the whole factory was keyed up for their visit. Many of the factory's workers and management chatted with the visitors and thanked them for their business. The company videotaped the whole exercise for use in training Deere's 5,000 employees. At the end of the harvest season, Deere invited Pettersen back to the plant, again at company expense, to talk with employees about his experiences with the combine.

In this type of exercise, everyone wins: The employees identify with the customer; the customer feels good about the company's interest in him and becomes a goodwill ambassador. Moreover, the company often gets a repeat customer—Lloyd Pettersen bought a second machine shortly afterwards!

Getting close to the customer has many benefits for the On Organization. In Deere's case, although the warranty period has doubled during the last 5 years, warranty costs have declined by 40% in the same period.

THE CUSTOMER AS FAMILY

It is traditional to think of customers as third parties—individuals and companies "out there" with whom we do business. But they should not be out there, they should be "in here," with us, on our team—they should be "family." When we consider customers in this way, our perspective changes. Although we treat everyone well, family gets our very best attention and consideration. We know each other in the family better than we know other folks. We trust family members, and we don't take advantage of each other.

One of the great benefits of this familial relationship is the effect it can have on corporate research and development. Capitalizing on customers' creativity is one of the most obvious and least practiced methods of maintaining and strengthening the loyalty of existing customers and creating new ones. Many leaders with moxie ask key customers to design new products or services that their company can provide to them in the future. The Pillsbury Bake-Off is a good example of this approach. Using certain Pillsbury products, contestants submit recipes for evaluation. Pillsbury publishes the winning submissions and awards prizes. Originally designed as a public-relations device, the program is now a major corporate activity; Pillsbury judges tens of thousands of entries annually. This strategy has resulted in several new products, a completely new line of cake mixes, and a number of variations to another line of mixes.

Service industries are an especially fertile source of user-initiated ideas. One example is the development of software initiated by users who subsequently sell the rights to the manufacturer. IBM has even developed an "installed user program" department to coordinate the acquisition of user-developed programs.

Customers should be participants and partners in the development of products and services. It helps if their relationship to the organization is symbiotic, like family.

Achieving Critical Mass in the Marketplace

If you are a small, struggling corporation in an immature industry, as we were at Manpower, the goal of market coverage assumes major proportions. As in most industries, we knew that the first company to saturate the market would lead the industry. A leader that develops an effective distribution and delivery system with a minimum of hassle will find it much easier to consolidate its position and keep its large customer base.

The principles of cognitive dissonance and good customer service play an important part in this outcome. People like to do business with successful people; and often, success is symbolized for the customer by speed, local presence, and a lack of bureaucratic hassle. When corporate and individual customers hear about the success of their suppliers, they bathe in some of that reflected glory. This "halo" effect reinforces their earlier decision to purchase from the company and improves the probability of their doing so again.

In an organization's early days, pursuit of a customer base to achieve critical mass is crucial to long-term success. It should be an overarching goal in the formative period of any corporation. It can't be said enough: The first well-managed company to achieve complete market coverage is in the best position to win the most customers.

The Coca-Cola Company demonstrates this concept vividly. Coke has dominated the soft-drink industry for most of its 100-year history with an impressive 40% of the $44 billion U.S. market, virtually no debt, and a $2.3 billion overseas business that enjoys fabulous gross margins. Robert C. Goizueta, Coke's chairman, cranked up a breathless marketing pace, introducing four new colas in less than one year. Observers point out that in the past, Coke's "power has derived more from sheer size than savvy marketing." Although industry-watchers see a change to a more innovative, marketing-oriented strategy, Coke's market position has enabled it to plan its new marketing strategies without immediate fear of displacement by PepsiCo, the soft-drink industry's number-two company, hot on Coke's heels with a 30% market share. Such regal privilege belongs to the market leader.

Speed: The Next Edge

In the modern marketplace, the service edge has traditionally been achieved through product differentiation (innovation, uniqueness, utility value), cost, quality, or service. But a new dimension is emerging that may prove to be the hottest market trend of the future—speed. It will be a distinguishing feature of On Organizations in the 1990s.

In this new age of timeliness, Is it faster? will be the question constantly on managers' lips, because *faster* will mean *more advantageous and more profitable.* In every On Organization, speed will be a key element of market strategy: Can we make it faster? Can we deliver it faster? Can we get paid for it faster? Can we give the customer a refund faster? Can we innovate faster? Can we turn our inventory over faster? Can we get customers through the checkout faster? Can we communicate with each other faster? Can our suppliers ship to us faster?

Nike, the Beaverton, Oregon, firm, has become the world's leading sports-shoe designer and marketer (but not manufacturer, since it out-sources all manufacturing to Korea, Chile, and Thailand). One of the reasons Nike is the industry's major player is its recognition of speed as an edge. Its strategic program "Nike Next Day" embodies the promise that it will fill merchants' orders within 24 hours. One North Carolina distributor recently remarked, "I deal with 100 other vendors. Nike is *the* standard in the industry."

Since the early 1980s, Federal Express, the global overnight-package deliverer, has identified each package it handles with a bar code that is scanned at various points on the way to its destination and networked to a mainframe computer. The system has been so successful that FedEx now provides its high-volume customers with on-line access to the parcel-tracking system. Another demonstration of FedEx's commitment to meeting its customers' need for speed was the acquisition of a fleet of snowplows, painted in the firm's colors, parked near their Memphis runways. Federal Express bought the equipment in 1988 after an unusual snowstorm in Memphis played havoc with its landing and takeoff schedules. The fleet of plows is used an average of one night every 2 years, but as an executive from FedEx pointed out, "When we need it, we really need it." Federal Express spends $200 million every year teaching techniques to employees to improve the speed and effectiveness of their delivery to customers. By doing so, FedEx continues to keep the top spot in its industry.

More and more, speed is the critical factor that distinguishes the marginal business from the best-of-breed in every kind and size of organization. Arthur, Ontario, is a little village located about 70 miles from Toronto (it's so small you could probably drive through it without noticing). Although only 1,800 people live there, out-of-the-way Arthur is home to one of Canada's most successful retailers.

"When people first come to Arthur, they're always surprised when they see my store," says David Kozinets, owner of Sussman's Men's Wear. "It beats anything in Toronto in terms of choice, quality, service, and sheer size."

Kozinets has every reason to feel proud. Sussman's of Arthur has just undergone its sixth major expansion in 12 years. A small-town giant, the store now stretches continuously for 250 feet along the main street. It boasts 27,000 square feet of retail space packed with over $3 million in stock. What is the largest independent men's clothing retailer in Canada doing in the boonies of Arthur, Ontario? About $9 million in annual sales, that's what!

This impressive sales volume is the result of an aggressive business-building campaign over the years by Sussman's in the significant surrounding population areas. "The advertising began several years ago, after a fire nearly destroyed the store," David Kozinets explained. "Following the fire, we turned catastrophe into opportunity by launching a giant fire sale and advertising it widely. We were amazed by the high level of customer response, and as a result, we permanently increased our advertising expenditures to where they now stand. All of our advertising dollars are spent on print media."

The advertising flyers announce the wide choice available at Sussman's: all the world's leading brand names, a selection of men's and women's wear, over 4,000 suits, 2,000 sports coats, 5,000 pants, and 10,000 shirts. Sussman's exemplifies David Kozinets's philosophy of offering quantity *and* quality. Sales of one type or another are a regular attraction to draw new customers to the clothing cornucopia.

Once inside the store, customers are treated to standards of service unfamiliar to most of us. The staff of 70 is motivated to operate like a customer-pleasing machine.

Salespeople enjoy a generous commission program and are encouraged to keep themselves abreast of the latest styles and trends.

The last time I shopped at Sussman's I tried on a suit. Roger Gibson, one of Sussman's star salespeople, told me, people, told me, "The pants look a little baggy in the rear. Slip them off for a moment." He whisked them away and disappeared. Upon his return he said, "Try them on now." Where had he gone? What had he done? They fitted perfectly! What else could I say but yes after he had hacked a chunk out of the seat of the pants? I felt as if I already owned them! Then Gibson offered to alter the cuff length while I waited. Later I peeked behind the doors where my pants had been transformed. An in-house sewing staff of five was performing on-the-spot alterations. The Toronto department stores think they are breaking speed records when they suggest that you come back in a week to pick up your altered pants. But David Kozinets has listened to what customers really want: speed, and at Sussman's you get it *now*.

As Ben Franklin observed, "Time is money," and like real estate, they don't make it any more. As we move from a decade of extreme materialism to a period in which we place higher value on the quality of our lives, we are willing to pay for product and service differentiation, quality, service, and *more time*. The first airline to introduce simultaneous front and rear passenger loading will attract a flood of new customers. Hotels that eliminate checkout hassle will scoop the market. Car manufacturers that eliminate "key fumble" will win consumer's hearts. Cities that end traffic gridlock will prosper. So will computer-software writers who can get users up and running quickly. The opportunities are enormous. As the Mad Hatter in *Alice's Adventures in Wonderland* said, "If you knew Time as well as I do, you wouldn't talk about wasting it."

Technology and the On Organization

The development of the best service standards and programs in an industry takes a huge financial and human investment, together with enormous attention to the technical detail of the operating systems: A corporate culture cannot be built overnight. But given enough time, energy, and dollars, it can be done. If the corporation makes imitation of its standards a difficult, demanding task that requires, say, a minimum of 2 years of development, its market leadership is assured. Leaders must keep the corporate intelligence system sharp, so it can provide timely warning when others are working on a new service system. Meanwhile, with a 2-year lead and a new generation (the Mark II version) of the service programs already on the drawing board, a customer-focused leadership team can continue to deepen and refine the existing service structure and programs. The maintenance of such a lead, a good intelligence-gathering network derived from the ALDO audit, and a cool confidence (but not complacency) in existing high standards of service ensure security for the market leader.

But even equipped with this strategy, the marketplace still remains fickle and full of surprises. In the mid-1960s, traditional theories of new-product cost and learning were swept aside when Bruce Henderson, the founder of the Boston Consulting Group, introduced the notion of the **learning curve** (or experience curve), illustrated in Figure 9-1 on page 346. First applied to the airframe industry, the learning curve concept is based upon three assumptions:

1. The amount of time required to complete a task or produce a unit will be less for each time the task is undertaken.

2. Unit time will decrease more slowly as experience increases.

Figures 9-1, 9-2, and 9-3

The Learning Curve   *The S Curve*   *The U Curve*

3. This process will follow a predictable pattern, such
   as an exponential formula.

But the economy has since changed. Theories like
the learning curve—based on a manufacturing economy—
are often irrelevant in an information economy; and
nowadays the rush to market of new services and products makes their predecessors obsolete faster than ever
before. The learning curve has been replaced with the *S*
curve, which holds that as each new technology climbs
to maturity, another technology will have started, at a
higher level of efficiency, that will eventually take over
just as the first technology reaches its maximum payoff.
(See Figure 9-2.) Studies have revealed that the impact of
economies of scale is modest over time when compared
with the impact of innovation. In the microcomputer industry, software advances; the rapid, successive appearance of 8-bit microprocessors, then 16-bit, 32-bit, and
64-bit microprocessors; RISC technology; and the like
have led to Gertch's Law of Technology: "You get twice
as much for half the price every 6 months." This means
that the leading corporation has a very small amount of
time in which to make its mark and its fortune. Only
high levels of investment in research and development,

especially in service industries, can prevent an organization's obsolescence.

Harvard's Michael Porter has conceived the notion of the *U* **curve** (shown in Figure 9-3). The horizontal dimension represents market share and the vertical represents return on investment. Companies that have created a highly specialized product or service through intensive research (at the curve's upper left-hand) may enjoy better than average margins, even though their market share is small. The low-cost, high-volume giants of a service or product sector, on the other hand, may achieve the same thing through their economies of scale (at the curve's upper right-hand). It is the companies in the middle, without the clout of size or the appeal of specialized expertise, that will be the losers in the modern marketplace. The lessons for profit margins and technological leadership are chilling and clear.

Being "On" in Tough Times

No small amount of courage is required to run an On Organization. But less is needed than you might think, because On Organizations have a lot of friends—their customers. Your customers don't want you to go out of business any more than you do; your futures are intertwined.

The first signs of recession usually send chills of panic through the ranks of management, and down-sizing usually occurs in the training and advertising departments —in the muscle that most firmly supports service and quality rather than in the administrative fat. It's easy to discontinue investing in people and promotion, because these are "soft" expenditures. They are simple to ax and their retention difficult to justify when the going gets tough. Yet this is *the very moment* when you should accelerate these expenditures, not cut them. When threatened by recession, is it less critical to find new customers and retain existing ones through superb service? Of course not. Yet this is precisely when faint hearts in the board-rooms junk their investments in promotion and coachings. But this tendency presents an advantage to the On Organization.

By investing rather than paring, the On Organization can wean customers away from those companies that panicked, thereby minimizing the effects of the business downturn. This can be more easily accomplished if the corporation can rely on its friends for support during tough times while going after new business. The corporation that follows this plan will emerge from the recession stronger and with its programs still intact. Moreover, its customers are even better friends now—everyone went through the fire together!

Shortly after Federal Express completed its billion-dollar merger with Flying Tiger, Hurricane Hugo tore across the Carolinas and decimated the company's fleet there. Hot on the heels of this disaster came the San Francisco earthquake, which knocked out the Bay Bridge, halting deliveries across the bay. Then Alaska's Mount Redoubt volcano erupted, causing a giant dust cloud that grounded five of the company's 747s in Anchorage. It seemed there would be no end to these trials when the coldest Christmas in 50 years came to Memphis, the firm's U.S. air-transport hub, bursting water pipes that damaged vital computers. And this was in just 5 months!

Even though these inconveniences lopped 80% off the quarter's profit, Federal Express didn't trim its service and quality. It did just the opposite, by investing its dimin-ished profits in another quality initiative. The need to con-stantly improve service, defined at Federal Express as "all actions and reactions that customers perceive that they have purchased," doesn't respect economic downturns or inclement weather. Service is a neverending, bone-marrow-deep, perpetual passion within On Organizations.

Another compelling reason for keeping a steady
course during a recession—besides the obvious one of
not wasting previous investments—is the **zero-sum opportunity** that recessions offer for winning new customers. The term *zero-sum* derives from game theory. In
a zero-sum game between A and B, what A wins, B loses.
Checkers, two-man blackjack, two-person poker, and
chess are examples of two-person, zero-sum games.
Each game ends with one person having a score of
$+y$ and the other of $-y$. The size of the "pot" is y, and
a value is assigned to y depending on the game being
played. In the soft-drink industry, for example, y is a total
annual market with low yearly growth and sales hover-
ing around $20 billion with per capita consumption at
40 gallons. If Coke increases its market share by 2%,
the rest of the industry loses the same amount. If this loss
is evenly distributed among the rest of the players, the
pain, though unpleasant, may be bearable. If the 2%
increase in a finite market share were to come from the
Mountain Dew brand (current market share 1.9%), that
brand would have to fold. Gains in market share, therefore, are not just your gains; they are the losses of others,
and invariably, those losses hurt. The weakest player is
easy prey in the zero-sum game, and the corporate strength
gained through an increase in market share is always
drained from the former strength of another player. The
result is that the gap widens exponentially. For example,
if both A and B start with 10 each, they are even. But if
A gains 5, its position is being understated if it is merely
described as being better by 50%; A is now *three times*
the size of B. This may give A sufficient strength to
take over B. When a recession is at its height, players
will fold. It stands to reason that this is the time to accelerate investment in people and in meeting customer
needs.

The *S* Zone

A recent article in the *Wall Street Journal* suggested that "service providers treat customers similar to the way they as employees are treated by management. In many such organizations, management treats employees as unvalued and unintelligent. The employees, in turn, convey the identical message to the customer."

Motor Cargo, a Salt Lake City-based carrier, initiated a voluntary quality program that went far beyond the traditional boundaries. Keith Avery, coordinator of Motor Cargo's employee-involvement team, says, "We feel there is a relationship between job performance and the respect that management extends to individual employees—a linkage that, unfortunately, is not as widely recognized as it should be in the trucking industry." The initial focus was not to solve problems but rather to address the self-esteem of employees. Explains Avery, "That way, each person's attitude begins to bolster his or her teammates, and positivism spreads systemwide."

> Outstanding customer service is the direct result of high employee self-esteem. Poor service is the direct result of low employee self-esteem.

What is high self-esteem, why is it an important component of the On Organization, and how is it fostered? Back in 1943, Abraham Maslow, the father of modern organizational psychology, suggested that "all people in our society have a need or desire for . . . self-esteem . . . soundly based upon . . . the desire for strength, for achievement, for adequacy, for confidence in the face of the world, and for independence and freedom."

We all have a powerful and constant need to feel good about ourselves. Overmanagement of employees undermines their self-esteem, which results in the deterioration and eventual destruction of the quality of service given to customers.

Let me give you an example of how it works. Recently, I called the president of one of my publishers with some very good news. I had heard that a top publishing-industry executive was leaving his current employer. I thought my publisher would be interested in talking to this outstanding individual and perhaps snapping him up. But when I called, I was told that the president was "involved with budgets this week and only taking calls from internal people."

In organizations with this attitude, pursuing "the system" (for example, the annual budgeting process) is more important than communicating with customers, the people responsible for the paychecks! The means (preparing budgets) is more important than the end (satisfying customers' needs). Customers can easily detect the low regard in which they are held by such organizations and will articulate this opinion by giving their business to the competition.

I think successful organizations enjoy a perfect balance between indulging the needs of employees and indulging the needs of customers. Most enlightened organizations know that customers and employees are their two most important assets, but a balanced commitment to the two is essential. Excessive indulgence of the customer will result in runaway costs that eventually leads to insolvency. Excessive indulgence of employees leads to the same wilderness but by a different path. The organization that achieves perfect balance resides in the corporate *S* (for *symmetry*) zone.

In asymmetrical organizations managers focus upon doing things right, controlling assets, reaching short-term organizational goals, and following the "rules." In such environments neither employees nor customers can satisfy their constant need for a sense of self-esteem.

In symmetrical organizations leadership in the *S* zone focuses on doing the right things, developing people, and creating a vision that enables them to be proud and fulfilled as humans. In symmetrical organizations employees with a highly developed sense of self-esteem attract customers who become infected with the positive attitude engendered by the corporate culture.

GREYHOUND LINES OF CANADA

John Munro believes that companies should be dedicated to the needs of the customer. He invested his passion for customers in the airline industry; then in creating Helijet, a highly successful helicopter service between Vancouver and Victoria; and then in Vancouver's Tourism Operations where, as its director, he overcame the post-Expo slump in tourism.

He then moved into the number-two job at Calgary-based Greyhound—the folks that keep telling us to leave the driving to them. Six-and-one-half million Canadians follow this advice every year.

Although the bus industry had been declining since 1982, Greyhound decided to invest $15 million in new coaches in 1989 and the same amount in 1990. Their aim: to offer a friendly, safe, and clean service to their customers.

As John Munro settled into his new job, he called all the regional vice presidents together to share his vision of Greyhound's position in the marketplace and his passion for customer service. He asked them to develop a comprehensive and imaginative program that would surprise and delight Greyhound's customers.

Over the next few months, he visited Greyhound locations across Canada, finding only minimal progress. So he again called all the vice presidents together and gave them a number of suggestions about how the company could improve its customer-service standards.

"For example," he said, "I would like the washrooms to be so clean that we would even find them enjoyable enough to eat in." As these words passed his lips, he thought for a moment and then added, "In fact, that's such a good idea that I'm going to institute the program, right now. Starting next month, we will eat once each month in one of the company's washrooms in Canada—and we won't tell anybody which washroom it's going to be."

Over the next few months, a steady stream of photographs began pouring into John Munro's office. They showed managers in fancy dress eating dinner at candlelit, linen-covered tables—in the company's washrooms.

One year after this shift in corporate culture was begun, the number of female passengers on Greyhound had risen from 51% to 61%—exactly capturing the market segment that John Munro had targeted—and total passenger revenues increased by 15.9%.

Leadership and customer service come together when the leadership team succeeds in achieving a level of "buy in" that reaches a critical mass in the organization.

———◆———

The arguments for creating the On Organization are overwhelming. In a study of 20 corporate finalists in the Malcolm Baldrige National Quality Award, the U.S. General Accounting Office found that companies that increased their levels of quality achieved a growth in their market share by an annual average of 13.7%; saw the number of complaints drop by 11.6%; and saw customer satisfaction grow by 2.5%—while staff absenteeism and turnover declined.

In their book *The PIMS Principle,* Robert Buzzel and Bradley Gate showed that the top 20% of companies delivering superior quality experienced an average return on investment of 32% and a return on sales of 13%, whereas the bottom 20% limped along with a mere 12% return on investment and 5% return on sales.

Being an On Organization doesn't cost money—it makes money.

————◆————

Be realistic—demand the impossible.

> —Sign hanging in the office of
> T. J. Rogers, founder and CEO
> of Cypress Semiconductor, San Jose,
> California

Chapter 10

Inside the Corporate Cockpit: The Dials

> There is always an easy solution to every human problem—neat, plausible, and wrong.
>
> —H. L. Mencken

*W*e will accomplish nothing if we continue to cling to the old-fashioned practices of *overmanaging by numbers.* The leader with moxie gently steers the corporation with the judicious aid of a few delicate and critical dials.

------◆------

Are you not amazed by the complexity and sheer volume of the paperwork generated in many organizations? Do senior executives really need all this information? What do they use it for? Do they have enough time left for their most important, right-hemispheric activity: inspiring and motivating their employees and finding and keeping customers—for life?

Early in my career, I worked for a CEO who insisted on receiving a monthly package of bound computer printouts so voluminous that they stood in a pile on his office floor that rose higher than his chest; and this pile was replaced *every month!* These were the monthly statements of our corporate subsidiaries in all four corners of the globe, yet he rarely consulted the printouts, preferring to either ask someone or consult his desktop computer whenever he needed some relevant numbers. I later realized that he was associating the amount of information he possessed with his status in the corporation, a common mistake among executives whose management style inclines toward the mechanistic (characterized by rules and regulations, more appropriate for routine and monotonous work) rather than the organic (characterized by freedom and less supervision, more appropriate for creative and innovative work). To me it looks like confusing heat with light. In order to impress their peers, such executives characteristically surround themselves with the trappings of status from the Information Age—the latest electronic toys that they never use and the urgent phone calls that they conspicuously receive on their cellular phones in unlikely public places!

Why do many managers feel a sense of security in the quantitative approach to management? Perhaps because our culture favors the left-hemispheric thinking first cultivated in our schools and universities and then reinforced by our corporate models of success.

A joint study of senior executives in *Fortune* 500 companies by the Graduate School of Management at UCLA and Korn/Ferry International found that 43% of the managers surveyed had graduate degrees. MBAs accounted for 18% of these degrees, 20% of which had been obtained from Harvard. According to the study, the average *Fortune* 500 executive had never worked for more than one employer. Twenty-eight percent had come from backgrounds in finance or accounting, 31% from professions such as law or engineering, and only 19% from sales or marketing. The survey further indicated that 60% of those who had risen from the ranks were now functioning as "superaccountants," and 30% of the former "professionals" were managing through application of their technical (left-hemispheric) training. Sadly, only 27% of those who had risen from sales were functioning as super-marketers. With the pseudoscientific bias prevalent in these organizations, it's not surprising that the marketing contingent tends to drift from its right-hemispheric focus to emulate the majority.

In a celebrated *Harvard Business Review* article entitled "Managing Our Way to Economic Decline," two Harvard professors, Robert H. Hayes and William J. Abernathy, argued that

> to an unprecedented degree, success in most industries today requires an organizational commitment to compete in the marketplace on technological grounds—that is, to compete over the long run by offering superior products. Yet, guided by what they took to be the best principles of management, American managers everywhere have increasingly directed their attention elsewhere. These new principles, despite their sophistication and widespread usefulness, encourage a preference for (1) analytic detachment rather than insight that comes from "hands-on" experience and (2) short-term cost reduction rather than long-term development of technological competitiveness. It is this new managerial gospel, we feel, that has played a major role in undermining the vigor of American industry.

By means of this gospel of pseudoscience, corporate directors ensure that managers, to quote Hayes and Abernathy again, "keep the faith on a day-to-day basis by insisting that as issues rise up the managerial hierarchy for decision, they be progressively distilled into easily quantifiable terms." In other words, the prevailing philosophy among upper-echelon executives is to increase analytical skills, produce copious amounts of quantitative data, and to do it according to formulas that have been enshrined for decades. They hold this philosophy because it largely explains how they themselves rose to the top—through diligent immersion in quantitative obscurantism. The wonder is not that most executives don't change jobs in an effort to test and develop their creative potential; the wonder is that the companies they run produce any new products or services at all.

All this is in striking contrast to the super successful Japanese, with whom the rest of the industrial world is forever being compared. Describing the period of Japan's most rapid economic growth, UCLA's William Ouchi pointed out that "the status of accounting systems in Japanese industry is primitive compared to those in the [United States]. Profit centers, transfer prices, and computerized information systems are barely known, even in the largest Japanese companies, whereas they are commonplace in even small [U.S.] organizations."

Ouchi has suggested that the Western approach is left-hemisphere dominated because "Western management seems to be characterized for the most part by an ethos that roughly runs as follows: rational is better than non-rational, objective is more nearly rational than subjective, quantitative is more objective than non-quantitative, and thus quantitative analysis is preferred over judgments based on wisdom, experience, and subtlety."

Finding out how to *control* our organizations, directing them toward improved performance in the marketplace, has become an imperative of modern management. What *is* this thing called "control"?

Control Systems

I like to compare the controls in a business to the fascia that houses the large array of electronic dials in the cockpit of a commercial airliner. Because the pilot's time and attention are vital, only the most critical operating dials are built into the cockpit configuration. Nothing is there that does not need to be. We should use the same criterion for controls on our organizations.

In an organization, *controlling* is determining what is being accomplished, evaluating performance, and proposing any corrective measures necessary to help executives guide performance according to plan.

Our corporate control systems often seem more concerned with the following:

Organizational politics

Appearing to be smarter or more important by gaining access to *more* information rather than *better* information

Exerting pressure on others to accept conventional wisdom and conform to the bureaucratic procedures it produces

Defending a strategic policy

Impressing the board, fulfilling statutory requirements, and dressing up the quarterly and annual reports

Amassing information with which to beat someone over the head

To make matters worse, these control systems frequently leave management befuddled because they either yield unexpected and undesired results, called the "Hawthorne effect," or encourage employees to beat the system rather than to attain goals. (The Hawthorne effect was named after the famous studies conducted in the 1930s by Elton Mayo and Fritz J. Roethlisberger at Western Electric's plant in Hawthorne, California, in which the productivity of assembly-line workers increased with each improvement of their working environment—and with the removal of each improvement too! It seemed that the introduction of human relational skills had more effect than technical and coercive expertise.)

Most of us have been the victims of attempts to bamboozle with figures. For example, not long ago the Boy Scouts of America discovered that they did not have as many members as they thought. Their membership drive had inadvertently prompted some of their field people to exaggerate the enrollment numbers.

In another case, a major multinational client of mine became very committed to the concept of "self-directed work teams." The manager of its North Carolina plant championed this philosophy and became a corporate hero because of the resulting remarkable gains in productivity and quality at her facility. My client had reams of figures and analyses documenting this phenomenal success. Some time later, though, I discovered that the North Carolina plant manager had left the company. Apparently, she had confirmed Lincoln's old adage that "figures can lie and liars can figure." One of her employees had rebelled, letting management know that the data was bogus.

In my own organization, we announced a reduced emphasis on our blue-collar, industrial services and an increased emphasis on our white-collar, office services. The idea was to reduce our dependence on a service that we believed was declining in demand and shift our resources to one we believed our customers wanted. Shortly after, we began receiving reports that showed the white-collar services were growing rapidly and blue-collar services were shriveling. This, we were sure, confirmed the high quality of our strategic decision making—until one day a licensee returned from a trip to the West Coast and told us that many of our offices had simply reclassified the old clunker as the new hot rod. We'd been "had"; the magical effects of our planning had more to do with crafty accounting than creative marketing.

These examples show the futility of control systems that don't really measure performance. Without the judgment of a leader, control systems can never put an organization, a strategic business unit, or a profit center on the right track.

A long-standing managerial conundrum is that there are so many business variables, so many ways in which a business could go off the rails, and so many possible "right" solutions that the opportunities for measurement are virtually infinite. Reacting to this, insecure executives often oppress their team with trivial measurement criteria that are exasperating, demotivational, and just plain useless. Even if there were a computer large enough to identify all the variables and measure the effects of all the potential interactions, the successful direction of businesses would *still* depend on a handful of vital measurements that actually facilitate decision making.

Drucker has pointed out that control systems must satisfy seven specifications:

1. They must be economical.
2. They must be meaningful.
3. They must be appropriate.
4. They must be congruent.
5. They must be timely.
6. They must be simple.
7. They must be operational.

The Control Process

Trust, which must exist among all members of a successful leadership team, is simply the ability to predict a colleague's response to most given situations. Trust is an inherent characteristic of people with a Lockean outlook. Drucker's description of control systems that work reflects a preference for the Lockean over the Hobbesian leadership style. A leadership team that is strongly committed to a Lockean, decentralized philosophy is likely to control the organization through **exception reporting** and a reliance on managerial integrity. Often called "no-surprises management," this approach is one in which managers negotiate and then agree on performance standards, trusting each other to report the exceptions the moment they notice a warning light in the cockpits of their respective operations. In such cases, the guideline is, *No exceptions, no reporting.* Exception reporting has the obvious advantages of minimizing the waste of energy while maximizing team spirit by building mutual respect and unclogging the lines of communication.

But we can take this idea further. If we want to build on our successes, we should highlight *successful* exceptions. The tendency is to focus only on the negative exceptions—but if we want to learn how to do more of what we do well, why not produce a monthly report that highlights our successes, so that we can identify and replicate them?

As we saw in Chapter 4, the Lockean philosophy enriches an organization's culture, quickly becoming a strong positive feature of the statement of values from which corporate climate derives. Operating plans and strategic plans are developed accordingly. When they are complete and have been approved, a careful review takes place to identify those *critical few conditions* that will exist when the plans have been fulfilled. These conditions are described for the organization as a whole and for each profit center or operating unit within it; these become the performance standards. Next, *all* possible methods for measuring whether these conditions exist are identified and then sifted to arrive at the *vital few controls* that will be used to monitor progress against the plan. The monitoring process itself is best left in the hands of the operations executives, but the information it yields will be used by the unit and operations executives *together* to determine whether corrective action is necessary. If correction seems to be called for, then a new plan may be needed. If not, then continued efforts to fulfill the objectives of the original plan are probably in order.

Of course, quantitative analysis has its place. But many leadership teams rely on it too much, forgetting that *corporate* performance is really *human* performance.

Information gathering and performance assessment, then, are the lifeblood of an effective, Lockean control system. How is information gathered? How is performance assessed? The following techniques have worked best for me:

1. Eyeballing
2. Critical-ratio analyses
3. Value-added accounting
4. Human-resource accounting

Used in combination, these four practices give top management all the information they need to control the organization, often without having to produce or interpret traditional financial statements and balance sheets.

EYEBALLING

There is a very old story of a man who saw two bricklayers at work. "What are you doing?" he asked the first bricklayer. "I am laying bricks," the workman replied. Turning to the second bricklayer, the man asked, "And what are you doing?" "I am building a great cathedral," said the second. The story illustrates that there are as many interpretations of the same activity as there are individuals interpreting it. But which description is the most accurate? If you were assigned to obtain a report on the progress of this project, what would your impressions be? How would you quantify them? Whose information would you deem the most accurate? From the statements proffered, would you learn more about the project or the people?

At some stage in our careers, most of us encounter "creative reporting" by someone who wants to project a more attractive picture than the truth. And when this occurs, we are at a grave disadvantage if we haven't formed our own picture of the organization and kept it current through on-the-spot observation. Why? Because we've made no effort to understand why people in general, and our people in particular, behave the way they do.

The philosopher Kenneth Boulding has pointed out that all human behavior is conditioned by internal images of the world, images that begin to accumulate while we are still inside the womb and continue to build up through the experiences of a lifetime. Because we automatically use these images to evaluate all incoming information, they can have three effects on behavior: They can reinforce it, revise it, or revolutionize it.

For example, imagine that it's a late afternoon in January and you see all the lights go on in your office building. Since you know that at this time of year and at this time of day the lights routinely go on, your image of reality is not disturbed and you take no action. This is the first effect; your image is *reinforced*. But if all those lights suddenly go off, your image of reality warns you that something is wrong. You must revise your current behavior—you will go home, call an electrician, or take some other action. This is the second effect, *revision* of behavior. But if you were to discover that owing to some unforeseen cosmological disturbance, electric lighting is no longer possible, you would act to restore the world to its previous order (by finding an alternative power) or create a new order. Whatever your reactions, your image of reality will be changed, and your behavior will change dramatically as a consequence. This is the third effect, *revolutionizing* your outlook and therefore your behavior.

Without internal images no human being can function. However, because images incorporate values as well as facts, people often filter the facts through their beliefs to reinforce their values.

Corporate control systems that put senior executives at the end of an information chain operate rather like a game of "telephone"; the messages that go in one end barely resemble those that come out the other. Each person within an organization has images; to confirm them, everyone filters and reshapes information before passing it on. Thus, corporate executives who base their picture of corporate reality solely on information designed and relayed by others give themselves no opportunity to formulate or update their own picture—so how can they possibly create strategies to meet new challenges from the marketplace? Having made themselves hostages of "facts" that have gone through much human handling, they have no way of interpreting events or behavior inside or outside the organization. It is obvious that without solid information and sound judgment no so-called leader can control anything. In addition, the "facts" are a matter of interpretation; are we laying bricks or building a great cathedral?

The oldest means of avoiding faulty interpretation of information is personal observation—*seeing for oneself.* The great historical leaders always visited the outposts of their empires, both to see things for themselves as well as to boost the morale of those who did the real work. Modern leadership teams need to apply the same tactics and for the same reasons. I call this process **eyeballing;** it is the only effective way to assess what is *really* being done, by whom, when, why, and how well. Testing corporate climate—reviewing opinions firsthand and taking the pulse of local operations—is the only way for leaders to keep their feet on the ground, a useful place for them to be in customer-focused, market-driven organizations.

But you should eyeball with a sensitivity to the needs of the local leadership team members, who are likely to be far closer to the numbers relating to their own operations than is a team of accountants from the head office. Because you want your visit to elicit feedback and augment morale, you should use it to observe and learn, not to issue instructions or criticize. Take advantage of one-on-one opportunities that your visit offers—the look in a local manager's face will often tell more than any financial statement. Ask a local branch manager if head office is doing everything possible for the local team to create new customers and compare the answer with the one given by head office staff! *Listening* (with the eyes as well as the ears) is the senior manager's primary and most reliable control system; you can augment direct feedback with quantitative data later, if necessary. It has been observed that we have been given two eyes, two ears, and one mouth; we should use them in the same ratio.

In some of our strategy workshops with clients, participants work in groups during which only one person is permitted to speak at a time. The current speaker has sole discretion over who shall speak next, and each participant must summarize what each speaker has said and offer a succinct statement of the speaker's recommendations. Almost without exception, participants tell me that they are exhausted by the end of the day. We simply are not used to listening, and when we do so we find it to be hard work, especially if we are trying to do it well. For the most part, we think that listening is simply "not talking."

Thomas Peters and Bob Waterman gave us the term *MBWA*—"management by walking around," which is similar to eyeballing. Most successful executives have always made it a policy to keep close to the operating end of the business.

———◆———

One of the first things that we did to turn around the ailing operations of Manpower in the United Kingdom was to visit each unit to see what people did and to find out what *they* thought ought to be done and how they would help our leadership team to do it. With their advice and personal offers of support, together with their realization that for the first time head-office executives were actually interested in their opinions, half the job was already underway!

Establishing office locations that were easily accessible to our employees provided us an important competitive advantage. By flying my own light aircraft at lunchtime and rush hours over cities in which we wished to establish future locations, we were able to eyeball the direction and volume of the flow of pedestrian and vehicular traffic. We analyzed this information together with the aerial photographs we took and then used the data to determine ideal site locations. Traditional, formal market research would have cost more and probably have been worth less!

Shortly after we started to get things sorted out, our management team was assigned the Middle East operations, which were having problems similar to ours in the United Kingdom. During my first visit to Tel Aviv, I was invited to debrief with the local manager at Ramlah jail where, following his disagreement with the Israeli government, they had invited him to be its guest—eyeballing in that situation gives the essence and flavor of problems in a way that no report can! A year or so later, our reputation for problem solving in trouble spots earned us the responsibility for another one—the African territory, which included our ongoing operations in South Africa. My unsympathetic views and those of my colleagues about the local politics and our organization's role in the country were fairly well known, but we made sure that our first visit was an opportunity to eyeball *only,* to exchange ideas with the local managers and talk to people of all persuasions so that we could make our own assessments.

In the Middle East and Africa, we were able to design strategies that brought about the results hoped for by management, clearly demonstrating that eyeballing is an

excellent way to gather information and that good decisions cannot be made without firsthand involvement. Had
we relied exclusively on briefings by staff specialists or
the highly biased reports of local managers, or had we
acted like Hobbesian auditors—stalking the halls, asking
irrelevant questions, and generally irritating and demoti-
vating the local executives—we would have failed to
appreciate the difficulties of doing business in these
politically sensitive countries and so failed to overcome
them.

George Cohon is an advisory director of the most
successful fast-food business in the world: He is president
and CEO of McDonald's Restaurants of Canada and the
man who put the Big Mac onto Moscow's Pushkin Square.
I once asked him how crucial to the success of his business
eyeballing was. He was unequivocal: "People who don't
believe in it or who think you do less of it as your company grows aren't in the real world. I had the original franchise for McDonald's for Eastern Canada. In 1970 I
swapped my 23 stores for shares in the parent company
and I don't think of myself any differently now—I still
think I own the company!" Cohon has used this
philosophy to guide his firm to mouth-watering levels of
success over 20 years. He adds: "You've got to stick to
the basics. When we opened the London [Ontario] store
in 1968, I'd walk in and if I saw a table dirty, I'd clean
it. I'd do the same thing today. And I still spend 70–80%
of my time visiting stores."

If the leadership team members want to know what's
going on in the business they're running—and they
should—then this is their *personal* responsibility. "On"
leaders inspire "on" employees. Together they raise the
level of passion about pleasing their customers to create
an On Organization in which no one is too senior or too
busy to get his or her hands dirty. Close contact with local
operations should not be seen as a tiresome chore best
left to the journeyman managers. Mouth-to-ear, ear-to-

mouth, eye-to-eye, hand-to-hand communication that's
purposely free from political "smoke" is the leader's link
to reality; it's where the rubber meets the road and where
successful leaders like George Cohon spend a lot, if not
most, of their time.

CRITICAL-RATIO ANALYSES

An old Persian proverb allows that, I murmured because
I had no shoes, until I met a man who had no feet. Four
centuries before Christ, Chuang Tzu advised us that
"if we say that a thing is great or small by its own standard of great or small, then there is nothing in all creation which is not great, nothing which is not small."
Numbers are the same; until compared, they have little
meaning.

The relativity of numbers is expressed colorfully by
Alexander B. Trowbridge, president of the National
Association of Manufacturers: "A billion seconds ago, it
was 1951. A billion minutes ago, Jesus was alive and walking in Galilee. A billion hours ago, no one walked on two
[legs] on earth. And a billion dollars ago was 10.3 hours
in Washington, D.C." Numbers are *always* meaningless
until they are related to something. Knowing that Canada
has one of the highest per capita levels of national debt
of any industrialized nation is a yawner. But people wake
up if it is explained this way: Each family owes $60,000;
the national debt grows by $1,000 per second; and each
year the government's operating surplus is wiped out
three times by the interest due. Notice that each of these
figures is comprehensible, is related to another figure or
index—a *ratio*—and is described in terms that are personal, that regular people can relate to. That's what makes
numbers come alive.

A **ratio** is the numerical relationship between two
numbers. Executives use ratios to interpret ongoing events
and trends. But before looking at ratios in detail, it is important to establish some background:

♦ Managers with moxie use all accounting statements *to confirm what they already know.* The operations executive who relies on others to tell him or her what is going on is lost: No accounting department or centralized management information system (MIS) is either equipped or responsible for piloting the plane. The map is not the territory. There is no way that one department in an organization can integrate all the bits and pieces into a coherent, intimate picture of the business as a whole. Alone or in combination, departmental personnel cannot acquire the gut understanding of the interactions among *all* the elements—finance and accounting; the logistics of supplies, pricing, distribution, facility utilization, and plant scheduling; legal, industrial, governmental, public, community, and shareholder relations; research and development; customer preferences; future market trends—because no such multitalented paragons exist at any level within the organization.

♦ Financial statements are most useful when they are produced within several days of the period measured. Otherwise, they are equivalent to yesterday's newspapers. Smart leaders don't waste money on elaborate analyses of history.

♦ Locally developed, zero-base budgets with a bottom-up perspective help managers achieve a sense of "ownership of the numbers" and a clear understanding of what is behind them. Managers who inherit the plans of others and simply add a percentage to prior-year actuals are dealing in mathematics, not leadership.

♦ Costs are ranked in order of importance. Like many other service companies, 60% of Manpower's costs were labor costs. The balance were mainly attributable to marketing, communications, recruitment, and property. Any detailed analysis was concentrated on these few critical items, because they had the greatest impact on our cash flow and profitability.

♦ The *bottom line* is usually taken to mean profit, but profit includes many noncash items like depreciation, receivables, work-in-progress, inventory, and so on. In reality, cash flow is the pure measure of a company's financial health. Working to a *planned* cash-flow budget leads to improved control of the business in terms of the *actual* cash flow. Most business failures are the direct result of underfinancing. This is usually a surprise to managers, who don't understand that you can make a profit but still go broke because of inadequate cash flow. These people are watching the wrong dials! The use of cash flow as a regular corporate benchmark would eliminate a shoal on which organizations frequently founder. You would do well to remember that *profit is a goal but cash flow is a need.* An old banker's saying is blunter still: Happiness is a positive cash flow.

Selecting the key ratios. Before the leadership team members establish the format of any financial statement, they should determine their preferences and requirements for the ratios that will be included. Number crunching is a waste of executive time and can normally be done best by those who produce the information. If it can't, beware: "It can't be done" is a signal that the wrong people have been asked to do the job. The producers of all aspects of MIS must have a can-do attitude and be sensitive to the prevailing customer-focused philosophy of the On Organization, providing regular improvements in content and format.

Though many managers pay lots of attention to quantitative analysis techniques, they often have a poor grasp of the possibilities of ratios and frequently will not admit to being ratio-illiterate. To put matters straight, the list on page 375 defines some of the key ratios most often used by management. Table 10-1 shows how these ratios are usually derived.

Table 10-1 Frequently Used Financial Ratios

Ratio	Formula	How Expressed
1. Liquidity Ratios		
Current Ratio	$\dfrac{\text{current assets}}{\text{current liabilities}}$	Decimal
Quick Ratio (Acid Test)	$\dfrac{\text{current assets} - \text{inventory}}{\text{current liabilities}}$	Decimal
Inventory to Net Working Capital	$\dfrac{\text{inventory}}{\text{current assets} - \text{current liabilities}}$	Decimal
2. Profitability Ratios		
Net Profit Margin	$\dfrac{\text{net profit before taxes}}{\text{net sales}}$	%
Operating Profit Margin	$\dfrac{\text{profits before taxes and before interest}}{\text{sales}}$	%
Gross Margin	$\dfrac{\text{sales} - \text{cost of sales}}{\text{net sales}}$	%
Return on (Assets or) Investment (ROI)	$\dfrac{\text{net profit before taxes}}{\text{total assets}}$	%

Ratio	Formula	Unit
Return on Equity	$\dfrac{\text{net profit after taxes}}{\text{average equity}}$	%
Earnings per Share	$\dfrac{\text{net profit after taxes}}{\text{average number of common shares}}$	Absolute $ per share
Productivity of Assets	$\dfrac{\text{gross income} - \text{taxes}}{\text{equity}}$	%

3. Activity Ratios

Ratio	Formula	Unit
Inventory Turn	$\dfrac{\text{net sales}}{\text{inventory}}$	Decimal
Net Working Capital Turn	$\dfrac{\text{net sales}}{\text{net working capital}}$	Decimal
Total Assets Turn	$\dfrac{\text{sales}}{\text{total assets}}$	Decimal
Fixed Assets Turn	$\dfrac{\text{sales}}{\text{fixed assets}}$	Decimal
Average-Collection Period	$\dfrac{\text{accounts receivable}}{\text{sales for year} + 365}$	Days
Accounts-Payable Period	$\dfrac{\text{accounts payable}}{\text{purchases for year} + 365}$	Days
Cash Turn	$\dfrac{\text{cash}}{\text{net sales for year} + 365}$	Days

continued . . .

Table 10-1 *(Continued)*

Ratio	Formula	How Expressed
Days of Inventory	$\dfrac{\text{inventory}}{\text{cost of goods sold} \div 365}$	Days
Price-to-Earnings Ratio (P/E)	$\dfrac{\text{market price per share}}{\text{earnings per share}}$	Decimal
4. Leverage Ratios		
Debt-to-Assets Ratio	$\dfrac{\text{total debt}}{\text{total assets}}$	%
Debt-to-Equity Ratio	$\dfrac{\text{total debt}}{\text{total stockholder equity}}$	%
Times Interest Earned	$\dfrac{\text{profit before tax and interest}}{\text{interest charges}}$	Decimal
Cost of Fixed Charges	$\dfrac{\text{profit before tax} + \text{interest} + \text{lease changes}}{\text{interest charges} + \text{lease obligations}}$	Decimal
Current Liabilities to Equity	$\dfrac{\text{current liabilities}}{\text{equity}}$	%

Key Ratios

Liquidity ratios: These show to what extent current assets are adequate to pay current liabilities and pay off debts without liquidating inventories.

Profitability ratios: These express earnings as a percentage of various components of the capital used in the business.

Activity ratios: These incorporate various measures of the organization's effectiveness in using its resources.

Leverage ratios: These measure the return on the owners' financing in relation to other sources of finance.

Making good use of the ratios.   You need to carefully identify the ratios that are relevant for your particular organization and then use them with considerable judgment. For example, in service businesses—where labor costs are the principal expenses and investment and where there is little investment in capital equipment, plant, inventory, or facilities—return on capital employed, return on equity, or return on investment have little meaning, because service is not capital-intensive. Return on labor costs, return as a percentage of gross margin, or gross margin yield per employee may all be examples of more relevant ratios.

In the previous chapter, the example showing the 100:40:30:10 relationships between sales, gross margin, expenses, and profit was used to demonstrate the *high-margin/high-service philosophy* in action. This gave us at Manpower a measure of performance against the other companies in our business, who usually conformed to the 100:25:15:10 model. In the example, we saw that these ratios were important to corporate strategy. At Manpower we considered them critical factors or indications of favorable shifts in direction or performance.

One of the most important of these was the daily sales report, which we produced for each location, by service, measured in absolute units and money. Since the essence of Manpower's service was the sale of employees' time (this is true for most service businesses), the ratio between the hours billed to our clients and the hours expended by management and operations staff during the same period represented a key measurement criterion. Our ideal was a ratio of 1:20 (although this differed from market to market). If the ratio climbed to 1:25, it meant that our employees were overloaded, warning us that customer service would soon deteriorate, which is highly dangerous in a service business and the reason that we produced this information daily. Experience had taught us that although a 1:25 ratio was more profitable in the short-run, in time the resulting short-cuts in service levels would result in customer defections. On the other hand, if the ratio sank to 1:15, we could safely assume that our managers and operating staff were functioning well below capacity. Continuation of this performance for any appreciable length of time would eventually produce red ink, because we were not billing enough hours to cover our operating salaries and normal overhead, let alone produce acceptable profits. In this way we had created a sensitive feedback loop that could predict what would later be confirmed by our financial statements.

The critical ratios of a business are the metaphorical equivalent of the cockpit controls for an airline pilot: The information contained in those dials means nothing until it is related to something. Strange though it may seem to nonflyers, it is very easy to fly upside down without realizing it if you are in a fast aircraft in a dense cloud. In an emergency even the most tranquil pilot will be unlikely to accurately estimate the implication of a sudden, unplanned, 45-degree dive; but the artificial horizon relates the attitude of the aircraft to the horizontal axis,

and the critical nature of the aircraft's status is signaled
to the pilot's subconscious. So it should be with corporate
leaders—which is why I call the control documents the
dials. In a service business, the balance sheet is of marginal
significance compared to other operating controls because
the dials of the balance sheet are not nearly sensitive
enough to steer such a business. For example, between
December 1973 and January 1974, a mere 30 days, Manpower's U.K. sales plunged to half their prior levels, due
partly to the oil embargo and partly to an incipient recession that had not been obvious (or in any event, had not
been picked up by our ALDO audit). But traditional financial and balance-sheet information would not have
predicted these shifts in market demand either.

Productivity ratios are the key to improving profit
growth in a service business, and "pilots" of successful
businesses must be highly selective about which operating
dials are to command their attention, what relationship
exists between the outputs of the different dials, and what
specific action should be taken to respond to each change
in each of the dials' readings.

At first sight, some ratios may appear a little off-the-
wall. But no ratio should be dismissed out of hand until
its relevance has been investigated and its accuracy tested.
Let me illustrate the point with an extreme example, the
theory of *burgernomics* devised by the *New York Times*.
The general idea of burgernomics is that if floating exchange rates prevailed in all major countries, then all identical products would sell for approximately the same price.
The way to implement the theory is to visit a McDonald's
restaurant for lunch in a sampling of major world capitals.
The price of a Big Mac, a small order of french fries, and
a small soft drink should be the same (assuming that no
internal differential pricing system exists). At one stage
during the summer of 1983, John Lute of Toronto's
respected financial weekly the *Financial Post* reported

that the Big Mac Index, converted to U.S. dollars, showed the following price discrepancies:

Paris	$3.82
New York	$3.39
Tokyo	$2.62
Frankfurt	$2.57
London	$2.52
Toronto	$2.40

This analysis would indicate that the Canadian dollar was farthest out of line with the prevailing foreign exchange rates—a 35% revaluation would not have been out of order. Revaluations of 22.7% for the yen, 24% for the West German mark, 25.7% for the pound sterling, and 29.2% for the Dutch guilder, respectively, were also indicated. The French franc was the basket case; it had already been devalued on several occasions since the election of the Mitterand government, but the Big Mac Index indicated that a further 11.3% devaluation was still required. Silly, you say? Try it sometime and you will quickly acquire a new respect for idiosyncratic ratios! Looking at the same data for 1990 offers some revealing insights (notice the revised rankings):

	1990	*1983*
London	$2.98	2.52
Tokyo	$2.81	2.62
Frankfurt	$2.57	2.57
New York	$2.25	3.39
Toronto	$2.04	2.40
Paris	$1.42	3.82

VALUE-ADDED ACCOUNTING
Value added may be defined as the difference between the sales revenue of an organization for a period and the cost of all bought-in materials, components, and services. Bought-in materials include all raw materials and com-

ponents. Bought-in services include rent, property, legal, advertising, public relations, accounting, consulting, banking, catering, cleaning, and others purchased from outside sources. The difference is the *vaue added,* which may be apportioned as shown in Figure 10-1.

The combination of positive cash flow and adequate value added in any for-profit organization will ensure its continuation as a viable commercial enterprise.

The real worth of an organization to its shareholders, creditors, lenders, owners, employees, and community is its current ability and future potential to generate income for these interested claimants. A value-added statement shows this income for the organization as an entity and how it has been divided among those who have helped to create the wealth—for this wealth is created by users and suppliers external to the organization as well as those internal to it. Table 10-2 on pages 380–381 shows Barlow Rand's fiscal 1983 value-added statement.

Figure 10-1   The Value-Added Pie

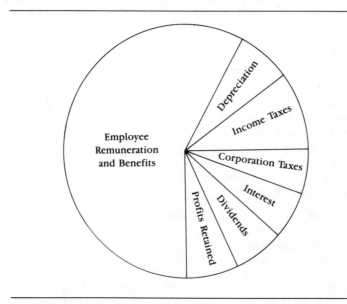

Table 10-2   Barlow Rand Limited: Value-Added Statement, Fiscal 1983

Value added is the wealth the group has been able to create by purchasing, processing, and reselling products and services. This statement shows how this wealth has been distributed to those responsible for its achievement.

	1983 R million	%	1982 R million	%
Group Turnover	7797.6		6462.8	
Net Cost of Products and Services	5597.3		4555.5	
Value Added	2200.3	100	1907.3	100
Applied to the following:				
Employees' Salaries, Wages, and Other Benefits	1152.2	52	954.1	50
Government Taxation	269.1	12	254.4	13
Providers of capital:				
Interest on Borrowings	157.2	7	148.2	8
Dividends to Outside Shareholders	88.9	4	84.2	4
Dividends to Shareholders of Barlow Rand Limited	105.6	5	99.1	5
Retained in the group for future growth:				
Depreciation	202.2	9	149.0	8
Retained Profit in Holding and Subsidiary Companies	225.1	11	218.3	12
	2200.3	100	1907.3	100

Table 10-2   (*Continued*)

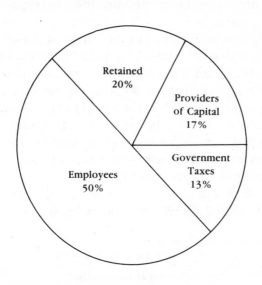

Although all the claimants of an organization usually hope for a constant rate of increase in the return from their claim, they seldom appreciate that this must be the corollary of increased wealth creation (which is the same thing as value added). For this reason, value-added measures are a more relevant and immediate indicator of corporate health and, along with cash flow, a more useful corporate objective than profit. Although profit measures define what *has* happened, they don't let you steer the organization. Hence, measures of corporate performance that are tied to profitability are also frequently off base.

Indicators like return on investment (ROI) can only be computed after profits have been established and are therefore nearly always produced at a stage when senior management has already moved on to more immediate issues and time periods. ROI is also a weak measuring device for most service companies. The ROI in a futures trader's business may be astronomic, but bankruptcy may be just as close as it is for a manufacturing business with a dismally low ROI. Another weakness of these types of controls is that they are very susceptible to manipulation and interpretation. Return on investment, return on equity, and earnings per share can all be manipulated by changing (1) depreciation policy; (2) the amount of goodwill and the book value of assets in the balance sheet; (3) intercompany charges and transfer pricing; and (4) accounting periods or practices. Changes in the ratio of return on value added are more difficult to play around with and are a powerful indicator of changes in the corporate growth vector. Return on value added (ROVA) may be expressed as

$$\text{ROVA} = \frac{\text{net profits before tax}}{\text{value} \times 100\%}$$

This corporate pulse taking is more meaningful to a leadership team when it is produced quickly or, better still, as a result of reasonably accurate estimates of anticipated performance.

The Barlow Rand value-added statement shows how the value added has been shared among the claimants on the business. Value-added statements can be designed to show how much value added was reinvested by way of depreciation (replacement, maintenance, and addition of assets) and how much became retained earnings (for future expansion of the business). This eliminates the "smoke" inherent in most corporate accounts and also indicates the leadership team's attitude toward and provision for the future.

Finally, a value-added accounting system is an essential ingredient of good employee communications programs as well as remuneration programs that enable an appropriate proportion of the wealth created to be shared among employees. Corporate leaders who truly believe that human assets are the most important components of a successful organization will make it easy for employees to access the relevant accounts so that they can see how they contributed to the organization's wealth. By recognizing the importance of value added as an indicator of corporate health and by reinforcing that recognition through the use of value added as a basis for remuneration, we are focusing on the drivetrain of the business. As Hayes and Abernathy said:

> The key to long-term success—even survival—in business is what it always has been: to invest, to innovate, to lead, to create value where none existed before. Such determination, such striving to excel, requires leaders—not *just* controllers, market analysts and portfolio managers. In our preoccupation with the braking system and exterior trim, we may have neglected the drive trains of our corporations.

HUMAN-RESOURCE ACCOUNTING

Perhaps we have arrived at a time that calls for better means to measure the way we compensate ourselves. By the end of the 1980s, the average CEO of a U.S. manufacturing company was earning 119 times more than the average worker in America. In Japan, where output per worker during the decade rose three times faster than in the United States, the average CEO earned just 18 times more than the average worker. Is there any objective way to determine what is fair, equitable, or rational? **Human-resource accounting (HRA)** may be the appropriate tool for this and many other tasks in our search for ways to define the value of human capital.

Taking another angle on the costs of human capital, Aetna Life, the Hartford-based insurer with nearly 20,000 employees, reckons that its annual turnover expense is over $100 million and that most of this is the cost of bringing new employees up to speed. Very few organizations have the will or the expertise to obtain this kind of data, let alone do anything about it.

The late Eric Flamholtz, former professor at the graduate school of management at the University of California, may be considered the father of human-resource accounting (or human-asset accounting, as it is sometimes known). In his book *Human Resource Accounting,* he defined HRA as "measuring the costs incurred by business firms and other organizations to recruit, select, hire, train and develop human assets . . . measuring the economic value of people to organizations . . . [and] accounting for people as organizational resources for managerial as well as financial accounting purposes."

Human-resource accounting assesses the human assets of an organization and measures the change in the condition of those assets over time. It is an approach born of the people-first philosophy—which is the golden thread of this book and the heart and soul of successful organizations. If the largest single expense and asset of an organization is its intellectual inventory, why then do we not recognize the need to take stock, update, maintain, service, retool, and account for the appreciation and depreciation of those precious assets? Perhaps the pious utterances of CEOs in their annual reports about the depth of the shareholders' debt to their most important asset, the work force, is hokum. If these utterances were genuine, why wouldn't the organization make an effort to measure and assess these assets, without which that organization would be a mere phantom?

> If the human assets of the organization are the most important ones, why aren't they on the balance sheet?

Imagine what would happen to an organization if each year all profit-center managers were invited to bid for the services of all employees, not just the most valuable ones, within an organization—a sort of free-agent system modeled after the North American bidding system particularly prevalent in baseball and football. A real value would be placed upon each employee that would, in all probability, be remarkably different from the value currently placed upon him or her by management. What would happen to the employees nobody bid upon? Perhaps a better partnership between management and employees would emerge, leading to a closer working relationship and the provision of professional development, coaching, and training to improve their market value.

You'll find a set of worksheets titled "Human-Resource Accounting: Key-Person Replacement Cost" at the end of this chapter. You can use it to develop your own human-resource accounting system. HRA is often criticized for being obtuse and esoteric in its procedures. But the purpose of the concept and the spirit behind it matters more than the methodology. Awareness of an organization's human dynamics is the important issue. After a careful review of the literature on the subject, almost anyone can establish an HRA system and develop a human-resource-value index. Using models similar to those contained in Figures 10-2 and 10-3 on pages 386 and 387, it is relatively simple to establish an initial value and the replacement costs of your organization's human resources and then use a human-resource-value index to track them over time.

The difficulty most likely to be faced by the CEO will be convincing traditional accountants with over-developed left hemispheres that human-resource accounting has any worth at all and that conventional accounting models can be bent to fit its principles. Once these resistances have been overcome, the next task is to make

Figure 10-2 Model for Measurement of Original Human-Resource Costs

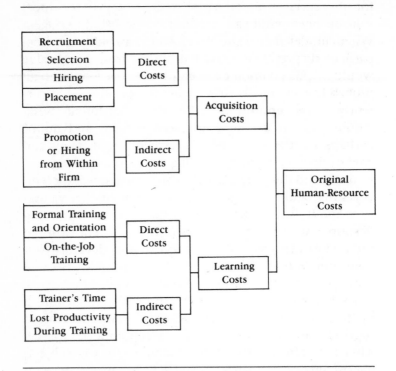

Source: Eric G. Flamholtz, "Human Resource Accounting Costs," *Human Resource Management,* Copyright © (Spring 1973, John Wiley & Sons.) Reprinted with permission.

the management accounts reflect the costs and values of the human assets on a timely and regular basis.

Managers with moxie realize that because human assets are the principal tangible asset of an organization—representing the key to future success—they are too valuable not to be accounted for. This realization motivates the rest of the players, who will take such accounting as a sign that their leaders prize them highly enough to establish a way of making their value known. As a leading

Figure 10-3   Model for Replacement of Human-Resource Replacement Costs

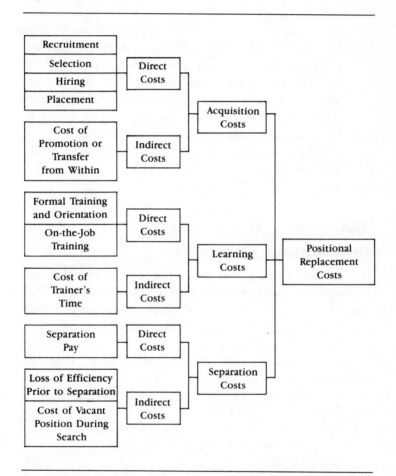

Source: Eric G. Flamholtz, ''Human Resource Accounting Costs,'' *Human Resource Management,* Copyright © (Spring 1973, John Wiley & Sons.) Reprinted with permission.

theorist of the humanistic approach of leadership development, the late Rensis Likert, pointed out:

The major source of the present-day apathetic and hostile attitudes of not only blue-collar workers, but also white-collar employees and supervisors, is the kind of management that focuses on short-range results—the kind of management that commonly used accounting methods fail to encourage and reward. But when current financial reports are accompanied by dollar estimates of the change in the value of the human organization for the same reporting period, the kind of management that builds more productive human organizations will be fostered, because such management creates the will to work and at the same time contributes to employee health and satisfaction.

Speed, Simplicity, and the Number Crunchers

How number crunchers view the world and the left-hemispheric perceptions that result for them is charmingly illustrated by the story of Charles Babbage, the 19th-century mathematics genius who invented (among other things) the speedometer, the cowcatcher, and what was to become the high-speed digital computer (which he called the "Analytical Engine"). It seems that he wrote a letter to the famous English poet Alfred Lord Tennyson:

> Sir, in your otherwise beautiful poem
> "The Vision of Sin" there is a verse
> which reads
> > Every moment dies a man
> > Every moment one is born
> It must be manifest that if this were
> true, the population of the world would be
> at a standstill. In truth the rate
> of birth is slightly in excess of that
> of death. I would suggest that in the

next edition of your poem you have it read
  Every moment dies a man,
  Every moment $1^1/_{16}$ is born . . . .
I am, Sir, yours, etc.

Organizations with prevailing left-hemispheric cultures tend to overcomplicate the control functions and
to overanalyze trivial quantitative detail. According to
General Electric's former vice chairman Lawrence Bossidy,
the goal of getting closer to GE's customers and pleasing
them more depends on the company's ability to increase
speed in every facet of the business and to reduce complexity, or more positively, to increase simplicity. Says
Bossidy:

> We found that complexity is often the by-product
> of insecurity. People who are unsure of their worth
> in an organization tend to surround themselves with
> complexity to make their functions seem more dif-
> ficult and sophisticated than they are—and them-
> selves more valuable because of their ability to
> penetrate the fog that they themselves generate.
> Those who know their worth because of their vis-
> ible achievements in the real world rather than on
> the artificial turf of bureaucracy act and speak with
> simplicity.

But even in an enlightened organization like GE, finding the appropriate measurement tools still challenges the
leadership team. Bossidy pointed out that at GE

> We measure our businesses on cash flow—even
> though that sometimes leads to an unintentional
> squeeze being put on suppliers and customers. We
> also measure our businesses on head count—even
> though that sometimes causes us to ignore or
> penalize customers. We have to find enlightened ways

to measure key performance results, ways that do not kill the new corporate culture that we are trying to midwife.

The cockpit fascia presented to leaders by insecure managers confuses and sometimes even impresses—but rarely informs. Flying the corporate machine is better accomplished when the dials are few, simple, of high quality, and sensitive to the environment.

————◆————

To be in hell is to drift, to be in heaven is to steer.

—George Bernard Shaw

WORKSHEET 10-1:
HUMAN-RESOURCE ACCOUNTING:
KEY-PERSON REPLACEMENT COST
WORKSHEET*

Position _____ Name _____

Estimate made by _____ Date _____

Cost Classification	Estimated # of Hours	Unit Cost per Hour	Total Cost
A. Recruitment Cost			
1. Internal screening	_____	_____	_____
2. Personnel Department time	_____	_____	_____
3. Acquiring Department time	_____	_____	_____
4. Agency/search fees			_____
5. Advertising			_____
6. Interview travel expenses			_____
7. Testing/evaluation	_____	_____	_____
8. Other	_____	_____	_____
9. Totals	_____	_____	_____

Cost Classification	Estimated # of Hours	Unit Cost per Hour	Total Cost
B. Acquisition Costs			
1. Personnel Department time	_____	_____	_____
2. Payroll administration costs	_____	_____	_____
3. Acquiring Department time	_____	_____	_____
4. Moving expenses			_____
5. Temporary living expenses			_____
6. Agency/search final fees			_____
7. Physical/medical			_____
8. Relocation compensation			_____
9. Other	_____	_____	_____
10. Totals	════════	════════	════════
C. Separation Costs			
1. Loss of morale, incumbent	_____	_____	_____
2. Loss of morale, department	_____	_____	_____

Cost Classification	Estimated # of Hours	Unit Cost per Hour	Total Cost
3. Loss of efficiency, incumbent			_____
4. Loss of efficiency, department			_____
5. Severance payments			_____
6. Outplacement			_____
7. Legal and professional fees			_____
8. Competitive threat or advantage taken			_____
9. Other	_____	_____	_____
10. Other	_____	_____	_____
11. Totals	════════	════════	════════

D. Orientation Training Costs

1. Trainer's time	_____	_____	_____
2. Trainee's time	_____	_____	_____

Cost Classification	Estimated # of Hours	Unit Cost per Hour	Total Cost
3. Time of others directly involved	_____	_____	_____
a.	_____	_____	_____
b.	_____	_____	_____
c.	_____	_____	_____
4. Training/course fees			_____
5. Other	_____	_____	_____
6. Totals	=======	=======	=======

E. On-the-Job Training Costs

	Estimated # of Hours	Unit Cost per Hour	Total Cost
1. Trainer's time	_____	_____	_____
2. Trainee's time	_____	_____	_____
3. Time of others directly involved	_____	_____	_____
a.	_____	_____	_____
b.	_____	_____	_____
c.	_____	_____	_____

Cost Classification	Estimated # of Hours	Unit Cost per Hour	Total Cost
4. Suboptimal output of trainee			_____
5. Training/course fees			_____
6. Other	_____	_____	_____
7. Totals	==========	==========	==========
TOTAL REPLACEMENT COST	_____	_____	_____

WORKSHEET 10-2:
THE MANAGERIAL MOXIE INDEX (B)

At the beginning of *Managerial Moxie* you completed the Managerial Moxie Index (A). After reviewing the essential concepts contained in this book, you will have developed a mental picture of the entrepreneurial culture that you would like your organization to possess—the kind of motivational leadership with which your team can inspire and motivate employees and find and keep customers for life. The result will be an entrepreneurial synergy that leads to organization-wide mastery.

To prepare an agenda for your next leadership team meeting, answer the questions below.

1. If you were to ask ten different colleagues the purpose of your organization, what answer would you like them to give?

   _____

   _____

2. By what date will your team have prepared a definitive corporate mission statement, an ALDO audit, a statement of values, and a vision statement? What will be the key elements?

   _____

   _____

3. a. In your company, "What is it like around here?"

   _____

   b. "How would you like it to be around here?"

   _____

   c. How will you ensure that the answers will be the same for both questions?

   _____

4. How can you ensure that you and your colleagues will become rich if you and your team consistently turn in outstanding results for your organization?

_____

_____

5. How will you obtain and with whom will you negotiate *all* the authority *and* responsibility you feel you need to meet your work goals successfully?

_____

_____

6. By when will your memorandum of agreement be revised so that it is covered thoroughly on one page? Who will be responsible for achieving this?

_____

_____

7. Who will be responsible for reviewing and providing proposals for your company to out-source services like catering, cleaning, printing, temporary staff, and security to specialized firms?

_____

_____

8. a. Who will conduct a review of your staff to determine the relative numbers of sales, marketing, and service staff (creators and protectors) compared to administrators (spenders)?

_____

_____

b. What is your initial view of an ideal *spenders/protectors/creators* ratio for *your* organization?

_____

9. What are the names of your top 20 customers? How much business did you conduct with them last year? What is the name of the key buyer? By when will you have visited them all? How often will you meet them all each year? By when will every member of your organization become personally responsible for at least one customer?

	Name	Volume	Key Contact	Next Visit
1.				
2.				
3.				
4.				
5.				
6.				
7.				
8.				
9.				
10.				
11.				
12.				
13.				

14. _____   _____   _____   _____

15. _____   _____   _____   _____

16. _____   _____   _____   _____

17. _____   _____   _____   _____

18. _____   _____   _____   _____

19. _____   _____   _____   _____

20. _____   _____   _____   _____

10. Who will be responsible for ensuring that all future
monthly operating statements will be limited to five
concise pages or less and delivered to you within
5 working days of your month-end? By when will this
be accomplished?

_____

_____

    This is not meant to be a complete list of the components
of managerial moxie but rather a "starter kit" that represents
your kick-off agenda. Your responses above should be completed with the benefit of the data you provided in the
Managerial Moxie Index (A). This will help you to develop a
partial statement of your organization's strategy, building on
a truly Lockean, double-dominant–hemisphere, entrepreneurial
leadership style.

> *From here, there are no limits.*

Chapter 11

The Greening of the Corporation

The large organization is loose organization. Nay,
it would be almost as true to say that organization is always disorganization.

—G. K. Chesterton

*A*pplying all the components of managerial
moxie results in the greening of a gray organization—
once again it feels as it did during the early entrepreneurial
years: vibrant, exciting, fun, innovative, effective, and
sharp. This is an organization that is *managed with moxie.*

◆

The story is told of a lost and weary traveler in
Ireland who asked a local resident for directions. He was
told: "If I was goin' there, I wouldn't start from here." And
so it is with great corporations—if you're going to build
one, you wouldn't want to copy most existing models.

General Motors is the largest corporation in the
United States, with sales approaching $130 billion. It
employs over 750,000 people, about equaling the populations of Memphis, Tennessee; Vancouver, Canada; or Man-
chester, England—or the state of Montana. If it were a
country, it would be the size of Sweden or Switzerland.
Most of us can't comprehend the logistics of an organization like this; the leadership of people in such monster
configurations is beyond the personal reach of the average

executive. Imagine doubling Switzerland's market share or writing integrated job descriptions for all the residents of Montana!

A nationwide poll conducted by the American Council of Life Insurance found that only 17% of those surveyed believed that the nation's large corporations had been responsive to the needs of the public. From this we might conclude that consumers are no more impressed with large corporations than are their employees.

In terms of the numbers of employees and inflation-adjusted sales, profits, assets, and cash flow, the decline of the megacorporation is well under way. Measured by these criteria, many of the largest companies in the world are already smaller today than they were 10 years ago. And as many writers and researchers have pointed out, the national and international mass markets have become outmoded notions. Consumers are more selective now than in the past and are more given to exercising their individual preferences. In light of these trends, smart megacorporations are reducing their internal mass. Even such giants as Coca-Cola and McDonald's, who constantly seek growth, are doing so through a confederation of ownership and structural interests; they now subcontract much of the supply side of their businesses and conduct significant portions of their retail operations through franchises and distributors. As a result of structural shifts like these, many large corporations are being replaced while others are slowly but surely passing into the annals of history.

As we have demonstrated, the techniques of managerial moxie can be used by the giant corporation as well as the small company. But the fact remains that although big companies wield significant economic clout, they are dwindling in number, frequently displaced by smaller, entrepreneurial firms where it is more customary to see the techniques of managerial moxie in action. Yet megacorporations need managerial moxie just as much as, if not more than, their smaller cousins if they are to be rejuvenated.

As we saw earlier, the paradox is that as successful companies grow and mature many of them slowly lose their "green" and become "gray." The antidote is to reverse the process by returning the corporation to its former green condition—**the greening of the corporation**—to the days of corporate youth, when the organization was fun.

At Manpower we strove valiantly to retain our entrepreneurial style but it was often beyond our grasp. Like most corporations that move rapidly through the five phases of the corporate life cycle, Manpower soon developed a bureaucratic will of its own. Notwithstanding our commitment to remaining lean, we eventually embraced such large-company trappings as a fully fledged personnel department; job and salary levels; company cars assigned by rank; computer systems designed to fit the needs of the data-processing specialists rather than the customers; financial reports produced to suit the system instead of the needs of the users; and an inexorable and unhealthy shift in the ratios between creators, spenders, and protectors.

Though there are ways to make the transition with managerial moxie, the transition itself is as certain as death and taxes. Among many examples of corporate evolution is the experience of Mitchell Kapor, founder of the hugely successful Lotus Development Corporation. During the first half of 1984, Lotus doubled its staff to 600 employees, and Kapor admits that fighting the creeping bureaucratization was tough. He found that his laid-back management style had to change; the weekly meetings to which all employees were invited to hear about company developments, meet new employees, and get answers to questions became unmanageable. New systems and procedures crept into the company to replace the previous informality. In the battle to protect Lotus's unique character, Kapor introduced a new corporate-philosophy statement covering such issues as the dignity of the individual, ethics, and even the maintenance of a sense of humor. To keep the entrepreneurial motors revved, Kapor acquired Daniel

Bricklin's Software Arts for $5 million; formed an engineering and scientific products division; hired software-industry guru Robert Frankston; and rehired Jonathan Sachs (who wrote the code for Lotus 1-2-3); bankrolled three former employees to form Arity Corporation and another group of ex-employees to establish Iris Associates; and formed a joint venture with Intel to expand the memory capacity of personal computers. But in the end the task overwhelmed Kapor, and he walked away from the corporate offspring he had created to found a new one, ON Technologies.

Entrepreneurial executives like Kapor are trying to do more than simply build successful corporations. As Harvard's John Kao has pointed out, "There is an interest in creating social value inside their corporations." Kao regards Lotus as an example of a business expressing 1960s' values through a modern organization.

The New Meaning of Work

In 1916 the French management theorist Henri Fayol wrote that "the interests of one employee or group of employees should not prevail over that of the [organization]." At the time, this was one of a number of Fayol's revolutionary ideas that together became known as the *administrative-theory movement*. Fayol's principles were an example of the theoretician attempting to catch up with reality—in this case the newly arrived, large corporation. Nowadays the difficulties that many large organizations face demonstrate that, like Fayol's dated theory, they are in need of modification.

New technology, changing social attitudes (especially those concerning work), shifting values, the globalization of business, and the permanent white-water conditions of the business environment comprise the anvil on which our corporations are being reshaped. The nature of organizational hierarchy has changed dramatically since the management theorists of the 1960s offered their bromides. The future promises an even faster pace of change. Over two decades ago, Robert Townsend advised us: "In the best organizations people see themselves working in a circle as if around one table. One of the positions is designated chief executive officer, because somebody has to make all those tactical decisions that enable an organization to keep working. In this circular organization, leadership passes from one to another depending on the particular task being attacked—without any hang-ups."

In his whimsical way, Townsend was urging us to learn new styles of interaction and to remove the status consciousness that has dogged our executive hierarchies. The warning was clear, even then: Don't put people in little boxes. But if you must draw an organization chart, always draw it in *pencil*. Better still, draw a chart like the one in Figure 11-1 or the one in Figure 11-2.

In any event, we are better educated today than in the past. As a consequence, we don't need the close supervision and instruction formerly prevalent in factories and offices, hence the widespread elimination of middle-

Figure 11-1   The Customer-Driven Organizational Chart

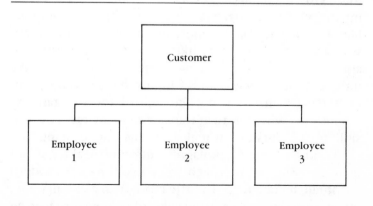

Figure 11-2   The Circular Organizational Chart

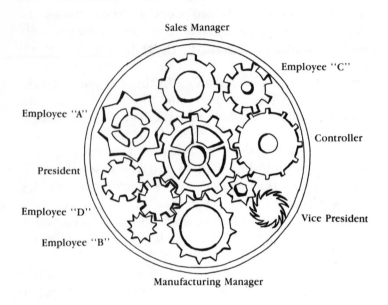

Sales Manager

Employee "C"

Employee "A"

Controller

President

Employee "D"

Vice President

Employee "B"

Manufacturing Manager

management positions in so many countries. The result is that a growing number of modern corporations are replacing the traditional *pyramid* structure with one that looks like an *hourglass.* But the most advanced companies work with a structure that looks like a *snowman,* consisting of a small core at the top, which represents the organization's unique competencies, and a highly decentralized, empowered organization within each of the freestanding operations, which in turn transfer as many tasks as possible to the outside through rigorous out-sourcing.

Another organizational revolution is sneaking up on us in the way we approach work itself. As the modern corporate leviathan, born little more than a century ago, moves into decline, swirling gales of changes are tearing through the fabric of corporate life and rearranging the meaning of notions like the "firm" and "work." Our social values have changed drastically since World War II and in particular over the last 20 years. There is a general disenchantment with *bigness*—with big business, big government, big countries, with oligarchies and monopolies of most kinds. This is not surprising because for many people *work* has become a four-letter word (a statement I make with intended double meaning).

We sometimes forget that we use the term *work* in a relatively new way. When a Native-American Blackfoot left for a hunting foray, there is no record of him saying to his wife, "Good-bye, honey, I'm going to work now. I'm going to hunt a deer." Nor does there seem to be any written evidence that any of the 12 apostles, Attila the Hun, Alexander the Great, or Hannibal had a compelling urge to "go to work."

In fact, I have searched through tons of data and historical references for the first usage of the term *going to work,* and the earliest reference I found was in the last decade of the 16th century. Shakespeare may have been the inventor of the phrase *to go to work.*

The term *work* is derived from Old English and an earlier Gothic word, *wuerc.* The current dictionary definition is "exertion, usually with painful or strenuous effort." But *work* didn't acquire this current, negative connotation until about 400 years ago, when it was first used to describe the act of going somewhere to do something in exchange for rewards that could be converted into food, shelter, and clothing.

Going to work is therefore a recent invention, and for most people, it fails to inspire. I haven't checked with them personally, but I doubt that Magic Johnson, Madonna, Wayne Gretzky, or Woody Allen think in terms of "going to work" every day.

Kahlil Gibran described work as "love made visible" and pointed out that "he alone is great who turns the voice of the wind into a song made sweeter by his own loving."

People are inspired to do what they do well by the love they feel for what they do, by the people they do it with, and by their reasons for doing it—what I described earlier as mastery, chemistry, and delivery. If we love what we do, if we love the people that we do it with, and if we love the reason that we do it, do we still call it *work?* (For more on "work," see my *The Way of the Tiger: Gentle Wisdom for Turbulent Times.*)

I have chosen to write, consult, and teach, all of which I try to do as well as I possibly can. I never seem to think of writing, consulting, or teaching as work. In fact, I often cannot tell the difference between when I am working and when I am playing.

Walt Disney once said, "Do what you do so well that others will pay to see you do it again." Shouldn't we *all* feel the same way about our work? Shouldn't one of our life's ambitions be to give of ourselves with a passion to whatever vocation we love, so that we no longer consider it to be work but joy? Should we not all feel as Noel Coward, who said, "Work is more fun than fun"?

In their book *Take This Job and Love It,* Dennis Jaffe and Cynthia Scott quote Tarthang Tulka, a Tibetan Buddhist teacher, who said, "Caring about our work, liking it, even loving it, seems strange when we see work only as a way to make a living. But when we see work as a way to deepen and enrich all our experience, each one of us can find this caring within our hearts, and waken it in those around us, using every aspect of work to learn and grow."

Love is a four-letter word too, and the greening of the corporation cannot occur until people love the work that they do, the people that they do it with, and the reason for doing it—mastery, chemistry, and delivery.

Much of today's work requires brain, not brawn; it's work that does not need to be done on location in an office or a factory but can be done at home, and not necessarily between 9:00 A.M. and 5:00 P.M. Work—usually meaning paid, 5-days-a-week employment—can mean part-time work, paid unemployment, volunteer activity, contracted services, bartering, home piecework, and self-employment.

Many sales representatives and technicians no longer "go to work" but work from home, with the aid of a car telephone and a home computer. Companies like Tupperware and Avon Products pioneered alternative work styles that appeal to people who value independence and flexibility. In recent years these firms have been joined by new giants like Amway, Mary Kay Cosmetics, NSA, Quantum Health, and Shaklee Chemical as well as the new phenomenon of network marketing and many companies from the new information technologies and service sectors—all of which contribute to the expanding pool of the independent self-employed.

The world of U.S. finance offers another illustration of the changing nature of work. Finance "boutiques" are forming at unprecedented rates (they raised $12 billion for investors by 1988). These boutiques are run by self-employed teams of financial specialists, many still in their 20s, who advise their clients on such subjects as futures, options, tradeable mortgages, foreign-exchange strategy, commodity trading, and collateralized mortgage obligations. As long as these boutiques do not have more than 14 clients, they are not required to register with the Securities and Exchange Commission. Mortgage companies, banks, and pension funds are increasingly doing business with these new entrepreneurs, who have opted to trade in their 9-to-5 jobs with the big brokers and banks for incomes of $200,000 and more. The rise of finance boutiques helped to increase the incidence of self-employed in the U.S. finance industry by 12%, compared to a rise of only 5% for all Americans.

The trend to self-employment is growing in all the industrialized economies. In 1900 nearly half of all

Americans worked on the land and were considered to be self-employed. By 1930 the number of people who were self-employed declined to only 20% of the U.S. work force, and this decline continued until 1970, when the proportion was only 7%. But by 1980 the U.S. Census showed that the trend had reversed and the number of self-employed in the United States had risen slightly to 8%. Then the numbers took off. By 1990 28% of the work force—34 million workers—worked from their homes; this was an astonishing increase of 29% from the previous year alone. In Canada three-and-a-half million people work from home. Of these, 34% do so to supplement their traditional day jobs; 37% run full-time, home-based businesses; 9% telecommute; and the remaining 20% bring work home from their regular jobs. According to Douglas Gray, president of the Toronto-based National Home Business Institute, 40% of North Americans will work from home by the end of the century.

The message is clear: The idea of "going to work" is undergoing a fundamental structural change. If it weren't for the money, many people wouldn't do it.

The greening of the corporation will be achieved when the work environment feels as much like the place an employee would *choose to be* as possible. These are the environments employees seek when they switch to self-employed status.

———————◆———————

An example of a green organization that provides such an environment is Biogen N.V., a Swiss industrial-science firm whose shareholders include Inco of Toronto and Schering-Plough of Madison, New Jersey. Started in 1981 by a group of eminent academic and industrial scientists led by 1980 Nobel prize winner Dr. Walter Gilbert, the firm employs 170 staff, representing 21 different

nationalities. There are 38 chemists, biochemists, micro-
biologists, and other scientists on the payroll, who would
normally be found in the bureaucratic recesses of universities or large scientific companies like Hoffman-La Roche
or Ciba-Geigy.

When he was president and chief scientist of Biogen,
Dr. Julian Davies would cycle the 2 kilometers separating
the company's two laboratories, where he frequently chatted in different languages on a first-name basis with the
staff. Biogen is still run with the freedom of a university
research establishment but with financial incentives that
encourage turning scientific discoveries into new products
for doctors faster than the drug industry has been doing
up to now. Biogen encourages its scientists to provide innovative genetic engineering services, like DNA sequenc-
ing and protein assays, to outside companies in order to
avoid any possibility of monotony creeping into their
routine. It allows its scientists to undertake their own
research for as much as 20% of their time and to work
when it suits them and their experiments. In order to
facilitate this, the laboratories are available to the staff 24
hours a day. Biogen also encourages individual research
links with universities; the company's scientists often
share their most difficult problems with their academic
colleagues. This practice is generally unheard of in most
large companies, which regard such two-way exchanges
with extreme paranoia (yet Dr. Davies could recall only
one breach of confidentiality). Biogen tries to simulate
the conditions of self-employment by using techniques
like a monthly wine-and-cheese party for the whole staff,
lucrative remuneration schemes, an emphasis on intellectual stimulation, the attraction of some of the finest talent
in the world, and an informal, unregulated style.

The path has not always been smooth for the fledg-
ling biotechnology company. Gilbert, who was Europe's
first bioentrepreneur, left Biogen in 1984. Other senior
people, who found the management culture too radical,

have been defecting to newer competitors; new investment capital has become tougher to raise, resulting in a
reduction in the firm's large list of research projects. But
something must be working! There are only two biotechnology companies in the world larger than Biogen; the
company has signed a joint agreement with BASF, the West
German chemicals giant, to develop an anti-cancer drug;
and when the company advertised for 6 scientists, it
received almost 900 applications! The results are promising—Biogen has been granted a broad patent for alpha
interferon, touted by many as a cancer-fighting drug with
extraordinary potential.

Managed Opportunism

Although it may seem hard to believe, big business as we
know it today is little more than 100 years old—just three
generations of managers. A century is a trifling time in
the evolution of humanity and knowledge, so it should
come as no surprise that we still have much to learn about
running our corporate behemoths properly.

The area in most urgent need of resuscitation and
regeneration, of course, is big business's oppressive
bureaucracy. A few years ago, a poll of 3,981 of Ontario
Hydro's 25,000 employees was published in *Hydroscope*,
the corporation's in-house newspaper. Of those surveyed,
52% felt that good performance had no bearing on promotion, and 60% felt that the giant utility took no action to address the wasted and duplicated effort in their
jobs. When Hydro's manager of human resources was interviewed about the survey by a reporter from Toronto's
Globe and Mail newspaper, he snapped defensively,
"What do you think the results would be if we asked the
same questions of *Globe and Mail* employees?" Most of
the results would be the same in any large organization,
the manager asserted. He went on to point out that in the
minds of those surveyed, most of the featherbedding

occurred in departments other than their own. All this inspired the *Globe and Mail* reporter to write one of those headlines that we all wish we had written: "Workers at Hydro enjoy their jobs—so much so that they apparently do many of them more than once."

Management's myopic attitude toward employee morale in large companies and its defeatist and unimaginative belief that employee dissatisfaction is a natural condition of large organizations tend to be self-fulfilling prophecies. The result is widespread organizational inertia and employee demotivation.

What is needed to green the corporation—to revitalize organizational entrepreneurship—is what I call **managed opportunism.** This term is not a euphemism for organizational anarchy but rather denotes the systematic identification of opportunities, the definition of how those opportunities may be exploited, and the controlled implementation of plans to do so. This is the opposite of conventional bureaucratic postures, which tend toward risk avoidance and problem solving instead of solution finding. The entrepreneurial cultures that *do* prevail in modern organizations are the result of managed opportunism.

General Electric's effort to successfully transform its organizational culture is captured in the remarks of James Meehan, an engineer who helped build GE's European semiconductor business and led a small group that developed a low-cost appliance motor. Later transferred to mastermind GE's push into robotics, Meehan observed of GE's developing entrepreneurial emphasis: "You get a sense that you own the business. What that means is that you're going to spend a lot less time worrying about whose toes you're going to tread on and much more time worrying about how you're going to move that business forward." That's the attitude of a large-corporation executive with managerial moxie!

Redesigning the Organization

As a reflection of the trend toward shaping the organization to the needs of the individual, some corporations no longer build facilities that will accommodate any more than 100 people. Canada's Magna International employs 6,000 people who produce some 2,000 different automotive components for the North American auto industry from some 50 separate locations in Canada and 5 in the United States. New factories created by the company generally employ no more than 100 people, and the company's CEO and founder, Frank Stronach, believes that this philosophy has been the principal driving force behind Magna's annual compound growth of 30% (from $31 million in 1974 to $2 billion in 1991). Like many modern leaders, Stronach believes that large units increasingly seem to fail as effective delivery systems for the social, psychological, and spiritual needs of a majority of the population. As a result, they also fail to make money.

The late Wilbert L. Gore, founder of W. L. Gore & Associates, held the same philosophy: The firm limits the size of its plants to about 200 employees. Said Gore, "It takes more investment to build new plants . . . but this is offset by the overall performance of the firm."

At F. Kenneth Iverson's Nucor (the company that pioneered the minimill steel industry), the story is the same—a dedication to simplicity and a sensitivity to the needs of the people who make Nucor their home away from home. Nucor has only three bureaucratic tiers between the CEO and the shop-floor steelmen. Its corporate leadership team is made up of a small group, and management salaries are pegged the same as those of production employees, to productivity and profitability. There are none of the traditional executive perks like company cars, aircraft, or executive dining rooms (if Iverson is buying, visitors often end up at Phil's Deli across the street from Nucor). "We're trying to eliminate the hierarchy of man-

agement," says Iverson. Many other modern entrepreneurial executives like Iverson share Balzac's view that
"bureacracy is a giant mechanism operated by pygmies."

The activities of Derlan Industries, a Toronto-based
company started by Dermot Coughlan in 1985, span the
aerospace, specialty manufacturing and engineering, and
construction businesses. Spread out across North America,
the organization's combined revenues are approaching
half-a-billion dollars—but there are only 16 people in the
head office.

Even elephants can dance. Percy Barnevik, chairman
of Asea Brown Boveri (ABB), has decentralized his
240,000-person enterprise into 4,500 profit centers
operating 1,200 different businesses with an average of
only 50 employees in each one. And the functions of
6,000 head office staff are now handled by just 150 people
based in a modest building opposite the main train station in Zurich!

The flat structure has arrived, and corporate leadership teams are redesigning the future. Debbie Fields, president and cofounder of Mrs. Fields Cookies, runs her
700-branch organization without a field management
structure. The largest mining company in the world, Britain's RTZ, employs 72,000 people and has 80 subsidiaries
reporting to its chairman, Sir David Birken. Alvin Toffler
has written about the "pulsating unit," like the U.S. Census Bureau, which "pulses" back and forth between centralized and decentralized organization as circumstances
demand. With the aid of computer networks, bureaucrats
can monitor hundreds of profit centers, leaving the leadership of these organizations where it belongs, in the
operating units.

In addition to the growing tendency toward organizational simplicity and design, enlightened corporate leaders
are monitoring employees' growing demands relating to
social values and work environment and are quickly set-

ting new standards in how their corporations address them. Environmental psychologist Franklin Becker categorizes offices as either **P-places** (people places) or **O-places** (object places). *P*-places are highly individualistic and celebrate individual differences and diversity. "*P*-places make good tools for knowledge workers," says Becker, "while *O*-places are like rusty saws, gears without grease, dull knives. They create friction, irritate, chafe, and thwart. They sap energy rather than release it. . . . You can recognize an *O*-place the moment you walk in. Is there a human imprint? If you cannot find one, that office is unlikely to be a good work place."

But changes are coming more slowly in other areas. While I was escorted around a bank recently, my host proudly showed me the new automatic teller machines and the pristine area in which they were housed. Its sterile display of steel, plastic, chrome, Formica, PVC, and polished granite gleamed in the neon lighting. When I asked the bank executive how many of the materials used in the area she would like to have in her own home, she blinked at me sheepishly. The truth is that the graying of the corporation occurs when it is designed to fit the bureaucratic requirements of the organization, rather than the individual needs of people—expediency and efficiency instead of a caring sensitivity—even though people *want* their work environments to feel the way they did when the corporation was green.

Entrepreneurial Leaders

Nearly every corporation enters the marketplace as a growth company with an entrepreneurial engine, which is the entrepreneur—a person who synergistically combines intelligence, motivation, vision, risk, innovation, leadership, mastery, artistry, skill, and craftsmanship to build and inspire a team—of customers as well as employees. This team evolves into a new enterprise; that is, an organization. As Emerson said to illustrate the critical importance of the founding entrepreneur: "An institution is the lengthened shadow of one man."

No one has ever provided an incontrovertible analysis of the *exact* nature of the entrepreneur, although David McClelland, the famous Harvard researcher, probably came closest to doing so. McClelland worked for 30 years to solve the Rubik's Cube of modern motivational theory: What drives the enterprising personality? He arrived at the following nine conclusions:

1. *The Need for Achievement:* Entrepreneurs seek to accomplish corporate goals embodying *moderate* risks. The need for achievement is what principally motivates entrepreneurs.

2. *The Desire for Responsibility:* Entrepreneurs want to use their own personal resources, in their own way, to achieve their goals. They hunger for accountability and glory, which to them are personal trophies. Entrepreneurs will function as team members, providing it's *their* bat and ball!

3. *Moderate-Risk Preference:* The enterprising personality is not a gambling one. Just as entrepreneurs eschew goals that offer no challenge, they are not high rollers either. They prefer to set goals that require a high level of exertion and skill but that, by stretching a little, can be met.

4. *Definition of Success Potential:* Entrepreneurs do not shoot from the hip. They prefer to study the facts carefully before formulating and implementing strategies. If facts are not readily available, entrepreneurs will fall back on their not inconsiderable self-confidence.

5. *Motivation by Feedback:* Entrepreneurs need constant feedback, be it positive or negative. Such feedback stimulates improved levels of performance.

6. *Energy:* True entrepreneurs aren't lazy. They are active, mobile, and concerned about time even while creatively pursuing innovative methods for accomplishing tasks.

7. *Forward Thinking:* Entrepreneurs are often positively engaged in planning and thinking ahead; they are dreamers and seekers.

8. *Organizing:* Entrepreneurs create order out of chaos (a right-brain activity). They are considerably skilled at organizing people, resources, and tasks to achieve goals. They are objective—preferring, for example, efficiency over nepotism.

9. *Money:* To the true entrepreneur, wealth and income are merely ways of keeping score (as Vince Lombardi put it), rather than ends in themselves.

Entrepreneurs want independence and control over their work environment, what psychologists call **locus of control.** This term describes the degree to which people need to control the world around themselves. *Externals* are people who believe that luck, fate, and the power of others are the factors that will most dramatically influence their lives. *Internals,* on the other hand, believe that destiny is within their own control and that they have the power to determine events. High-achieving entrepreneurs are internal types; they need to experience independence and achieve mastery.

In 1980 when Jacob Rothschild was ejected from the family bank, N. M. Rothschild & Sons, by his cousin Evelyn de Rothschild, he was a financial outcast. An external might have reacted defensively by shoring up his position and moving into a safe banking environment using the family name and personal connections. But not an internal like Jacob Rothschild.

In 4 years he built Charterhouse J. Rothschild into London's largest British investment-banking group, with assets of $675 million and 1983 profits of close to $50 million. In February 1983 Rothschild partnered Sir James ("Jimmy") Goldsmith (who owned Diamond International in the United States, France's Générale Occidentale, and Britain's Cavenham) in a daring raid on St. Regis, the lumber and paper company. They purchased shares at $36 and unloaded them shortly after for $52. The new company managed investment funds for the wealthy and the public offerings of high-tech companies, handled arbitrage contracts, arranged leveraged buy-outs, ran a merchant bank, and owned a brokerage and a life insurance company and a variety of other companies as well.

But even Rothschild's will to succeed was insufficient to make it happen immediately. Difficulties within Charterhouse J. Rothschild and the failed merger negotiations with Hambro Life resulted in the sale of the merchant-banking division, Charterhouse Japhet, to the Royal Bank of Scotland for $170 million. But this kind of setback doesn't deter an internal either. With a war chest of over $600 million and substantial liquidity, the balance of the business, renamed J. Rothschild Holdings, plc, refocused on risk arbitrage deals and leveraged buy-outs. Jacob Rothschild is living testimony to Winston Churchill's observation that "the optimist sees opportunity in every danger; the pessimist sees danger in every opportunity."

THE CORPORATE ENTREPRENEUR
Corporate entrepreneurs insert the entrepreneurial wire brush into the clogged arteries of large organizations. They're vital to successful organizational renewal. There are four main types of corporate entrepreneurs:

1. *The Maverick:* A curious, probing adventurer, who often uses the newest technology and/or innovative approaches to shake off the constraining shackles of the establishment and delights in tilting at corporate windmills.

2. *The Conscience:* Only obeys those rules requiring candor and truth. Frequently embarrassing bureaucrats by telling it like it is, the conscience often chastens the corporation and creates breakthroughs in values.

3. *The Visionary:* The corporate mover and shaker. This man or woman gets people to go for ideas that no one else can. By doing so, the visionary changes the corporation's product line, its market scope, and its destiny and culture.

4. *The Guru:* Serene and apolitical, self-aware and aware of others, enlightened and liberated, this type brings a new perspective to bear on old issues and ways of thinking about the world. Gurus frequently ask such devastating questions as, Who said so? Why? Just because we have always done it this way, why do we have to keep doing so?

In relation to the corporation, entrepreneurship is like Sattinger's Law: It works better if you plug it in. Many managers in large corporations rely heavily on what has gone before to help make decisions about the future. But this approach does not always provide appropriate solutions to pressing strategic issues.

When we ran into a legislative tangle with the British government, our U.K. management team at Manpower began an intensive review of options, but most of these were modifications of previous ideas. When we pulled in Dennis Stevenson of the Specialist Research Unit, an outside consultancy, he played the roles of guru and visionary. He would ask us what-if questions and check us when he felt we were relying too much on historical practices. Gurus must be exceptionally intelligent so that they can grasp unfamiliar ideas quickly; they must be neutral about the outcome of a particular decision so that they can be rigorously objective; and they must be very creative.

Frustrated with Manpower's growing corporatism, I tried another experiment. Sensing some restlessness in our field organization, I made a series of eyeballing visits to our branches to listen to and learn from employees about their concerns, about how they felt about the company, its policies, and their careers. I then compiled these concerns into a guide with suggestions on how to deal with them. I had the guide printed in the format of the *Little Red Book of the Sayings of Mao Zedong* and circulated it anonymously within the company. The suggestions were often used, and after a while, new ones began to be added.

BURR AT PEOPLE EXPRESS AIRLINES

Donald Burr, the former founder and CEO of now defunct People Express, described the vision that he originally held for his new company with the zeal of a missionary. During the heady days of this extraordinary corporate experiment, he said:

> This is not some old company refurbishing itself, it's a brand-new idea in brand-new clothes. This is not a social experiment. It's a hard-driving capitalist business. We want to maximize profits, and we want to do very well at that. But we can find a better way to do it, a way that is more friendly and more conducive to people getting out of life what the hell they're trying to get out of it. You don't just want to make a buck. You want people to become better people.

Burr took advantage of the 1978 Air Deregulation Act to start People Express in an abandoned, rat-infested terminal in Newark, New Jersey, with three used Boeing 737s purchased from Lufthansa. The single airliner grew to a fleet of 61, the staff from 250 to 4,000, and the profits from zip to $23.5 million in just 4 years. People

Express became the tenth busiest airline in the United States, carrying 1 million passengers a month on its 332 daily flights to 24 U.S. cities and the daily London/Newark run. Newark International Airport became so congested that it was one of six U.S. airports where peak-hour flights had to be capped by the Federal Aviation Administration. The company's rapid success moved Eastern Airline's chairman Frank Borman to observe that his own airline's "future is jeopardized . . . if we do not stunt the growth of People Express."

The company was organized and managed to serve each employee as an individual. Each one owned shares, participated in the decision-making process, and enjoyed a large measure of freedom to perform tasks. The corporation was organized into four functions: (1) people, (2) finance and administration, (3) marketing, and (4) operations. These were then subdivided into activities essential to the smooth running of the company, such as scheduling, baggage handling, air crew, and accounting. Since all employees managed an activity or task, they all sported a managerial title. What other airlines called a flight attendant for example, People Express called a "customer-service manager." Six managing officers provided the general direction and leadership within each functional area, and team managers liaised with the general managers and the managing officers. Employees set their own goals within the corporation's objectives (which they helped to establish) and measured their own performance. They were not monitored and their personal task achievement and performance was largely the result of their own initiatives. The result of these unique organizational structures was that People Express enjoyed operating expenses that were half the level experienced by the rest of the airline industry, and some of its fares were just one-quarter of those of other airlines.

By way of contrast, Pacific Express Holdings, racked by high operating costs and losses of $38 million on sales of $78 million during 1982 and 1983, filed for protection under Chapter 11. The same fate befell Braniff and Air Florida, and even Continental, Republic, and Western were close to extinction. In fact, losses in the U.S. airline industry from 1981 to 1983 totaled $1.2 billion. People Express, on the other hand, boasted many young employees who were the wealthy owners of corporate stock. The company was the focus of many studies by scholars, reporters, and competitors from all over the world and by investment analysts seeking sound, long-term equity opportunities in the fastest-growing airline in U.S. history. As Burr pointed out, "Most companies organize themselves around structures and policies that force employees to serve the company—but [at People] people *are* the company." Burr developed a real example of the people/goals/structure organizational approach discussed in Chapter 7.

But even though Donald Burr was right, he was ahead of his time. He flatly denies that his experiments were a failure. His innovative management practices were "the most successful part," he contends today. He adds that if he were to do it all over again, the only things he would do differently would be to implement a frequent-flier plan and strengthen his team with more experienced airline-industry executives.

Intrapreneuring

A growing organizational trend is to use the services of an **intrapreneur,** an independent expert in entrepreneurial techniques and approaches who works *inside* a corporation to encourage entrepreneurial attitudes and working methods. Although intrapreneurs may be found working directly for corporations, they are more usually independent consultants. Examples of intrapreneurship companies include Gifford Pinchot III's New Directions

Group; the corporate-venturing program set up by Mel Perel within SRI International at Menlo Park; The Tom Peters Group established by Thomas J. Peters (of *In Search of Excellence* fame); Innotech of Trumbull, Connecticut; and John Luther's Development Agency, a division of Marketing Corporation of America. These efforts provide a new entrepreneurial spirit *within* a corporation—from *outside* it.

Canada's Labatt Brewing Company pushed this concept even further when it hired "boardroom iconoclast" Iain Baxter. Baxter's sole assignment during a 40-hour week was to act as a sounding board and to provide non-traditional opinions of corporate ideas. Baxter was invited to all the board meetings and had unlimited access to all corporate records. He worked directly with everyone from Labatt president Sidney Oland to workers on the assembly line. How did Baxter see his role? He said, "I was brought in to be a catalyst. I am here to deal in paradoxes and analogues. My role is to let people pick my brain and to generate ideas."

The urge to introduce outside talent into the corporation is a relatively new trend that has shown a recent spurt of growth. *Fortune* magazine estimates that in 1973 U.S. businesses spent $1 billion on consulting services. By 1983 the figure had ballooned to $3 billion, and by 1991 it was at $6 billion in the United States and $25 billion worldwide. Obviously, it is not just a North American phenomenon. Intrapreneurship has been adopted by Siemens of Germany; Oxford Instruments of Britain; ABB, Volvo, and L. M. Ericsson of Sweden; Elf Aquitaine of France; and Furukawa Electric of Japan. The trend toward moving overhead from inside to outside the corporate structure (out-sourcing) and the purchase of the best external talent available is a positive indication of an entrepreneurial resurgence in modern business.

The Informal Economy

The economic structure of Western societies is also being altered by the growth of the so-called informal economy, the underground exchange system that is believed to account for a growing and substantial proportion of the GNP in many countries.

The **informal economy** is the individual's response to the crisis of the mass economy. As the mass economy declines, individuals turn away from the formalized procedures of economic participation, particularly high taxes, because they perceive them to be punitive and unfair. In other words, they are trying to escape the decline of the economy by creating small, local, more controllable economies around them. A powerful incentive for small-business owners to take their businesses underground is the prevailing rates of turnover tax levied on all goods and services supplied in Europe, Canada, and several other countries. Known as value-added tax in Europe and the Goods and Services Tax in Canada, it is not hard to see what people are trying to avoid:

Country	*Rate of Tax*
Denmark	22.0%
Ireland	21.0%
Italy	19.0%
France	18.6%
The Netherlands	18.5%
United Kingdom	17.5%
Portugal	17.0%
Belgium	17.0%
Greece	16.0%
Germany	14.0%
Luxembourg	12.0%
Spain	12.0%
Canada	7.0%

In the United States, the informal economy is currently estimated to account for as much as 15% of the GNP. Its total worth worldwide has been estimated at more than the entire GNP of France. In New York City alone, the estimated loss to the municipality is estimated at $1 billion. Names for the informal economy vary: The Germans call the phenomenon the "shadow" economy. In Italy, where it accounts for 30% of GNP, it is known as the "submerged" economy. In France the "travail au noir" has reached such epidemic proportions that 50% of French cement cannot be traced to formally recognized construction sites. In Brazil the informal economy accounts for over $100 billion annually, or about a third of the gross domestic product (GDP); in Argentina it accounts for 40–50% of reported GDP. Even Russia may cede as much as 20% of its GNP to the country's "second" economy.

The trend is slowly moving to the large corporation. For a membership fee of $10,000, Univex of New York will arrange corporate bartering links so that members can trade their products or services with member buyers. Members include Ampad, Emery Worldwide, Holiday Inns, and Polaroid. The International Reciprocal Trade Association of Atlanta, Georgia, reports that more than 175,000 companies are linked through 400 barter networks in North America. In 1990 these companies traded $175 million of goods and services, up 100% from the previous year.

Future Corporate Species

Economic shifts like these lead one to speculate that only four types of organizations will dominate our lives during the remainder of this century. For descriptive purposes I have called these corporations Mammoth Inc., Bee Inc., Beaver Inc., and Mole Inc.

MAMMOTH INC.
Small-scale shipbuilders, steel companies, oil companies, and utilities are seen about as frequently today as the passenger pigeon, because there are some industrial processes that will always require scale and mass. However, in the future all mammoth corporations will be highly productive and capital- and brain-power–intensive, rather than labor-intensive.

As a result of sophisticated computer-assisted design and manufacturing techniques, Mammoths will be able to tailor their products to individual requirements and tastes. The few jobs in these enterprises will be very well paid and those holding them will assume significant task responsibilities.

Businesses expected to hold Mammoth status include automobile, oil, lumber, chemical, steel, and textile industries, as well as the major services such as railroads, communications, and airlines. The signs of this trend are already evident. During the 1980s the U.S. steel industry invested $2.5 billion annually, about 8.5% of sales; cut capacity by 30%; and shed 58% of its work force to about 164,000. It now takes 5.3 worker-hours to make a metric ton of cold-rolled steel—44% fewer than 10 years ago, outdoing Germany's 5.7 and Japan's 5.6. But the transition to the new manufacturing is painful: The Big Six of U.S. steel (Armco, Bethlehem, Inland, LTV, National, and USX) still lose $28 for each $430 ton of steel they ship, and the auto industry has followed a similar pattern. In just 6 years of former chairman David Roderick's stewardship, USX alone shed 100,000 jobs. Since 1983, steel production has been cut by half to 16.5 million tons a year, and four out of seven plants have been shuttered. In 1982 it took 11 hours to make a ton of steel; today it takes one-third of that. The steel and coal industries of the United Kingdom and most other industrial countries have also shed tens of thousands of jobs.

The $20 million Apple Computer plant in Fremont, California, employs just 300 people, and only 200 of these are involved in manufacturing. The plant can turn out 500,000 Macintosh computers a year (that's one every 27 seconds). The labor cost of making these 450-part machines is just 1%. One Japanese company runs a 43-meter-long assembly line at which just six operators produce 2 million calculators every month. At a Texas Instrument plant in Lubbock, Texas, the introduction of computer-integrated manufacturing has enabled TI to reduce the manufacturing time of solar-powered calculators to just 20 minutes. After a $500 million refurbishing, General Electric's locomotive manufacturing facility at Erie, Pennsylvania, can now turn out a 2,500-pound locomotive frame in 16 hours, as opposed to the former time of 16 days.

BEE INC.
These enterprises will include large, labor-intensive activities, especially those that are service oriented, like training, education, health, social, and penal services. Bee workers will swarm over a large functional area. Altruists will find the work highly stimulating and satisfying but not very well paid. For this reason Bee enterprises will be the least efficient of the four types of organizations.

BEAVER INC.
These entrepreneurial organizations will account for the largest number of wage and, more frequently, fee earners. Beaver organizations will include profit-making, charitable, and not-for-profit enterprises. These corporations will be divided into small units, and the workers, who will work in teams, will enjoy a large measure of independence and mobility. Their tasks will be lucrative, so they will enjoy very high levels of achievement and satisfaction.

This sector will be highly flexible, extremely productive, and exemplified by franchising and network marketing, which will continue to command a growing share of all consumer spending and growth in the Beaver sector. According to the Washington, D.C.–based International Franchise Association, franchising now accounts for over one-third of all retail sales. Adds Leonard Swartz, managing director of Arthur Andersen's franchise consulting practice, "A lot of intelligent, experienced, and motivated people out there do not want to be at the mercy of a large corporation anymore. For them franchising is a way to take all that experience and make it work for them." Employees from "sunset" industries have begun to react the same way, seeking new career opportunities in Beaver enterprises. This trend is well under way; for example, although during the last decade the old-line manufacturing companies shed 100,000 jobs in New England alone, these losses have been partly offset by the creation of 50,000 new jobs in the small electrical and electronics businesses that cluster around Boston's Route 128—a famed Beaver territory.

MOLE INC.
The people who work for Mole organizations live underground, although they're fairly visible. Workers for Mole Inc. simply don't want to be bothered with the organizational and hierarchical tedium found in most traditional employment settings. Many moles will be retirees augmenting their fixed pensions with cash received for babysitting, gardening, handyman tasks, and arts and crafts. Others will be professionals and artisans pursuing a different set of values and alternative life-styles. People in today's informal sector will also be part of the future Mole group, because it will be difficult to distinguish between paid employment and the leisure activities of Mole workers. Like Beaver workers, the majority of Mole types are entrepreneurial personalities.

Large corporations are generally characterized by a lack of managers with moxie. As we saw earlier, this is often caused by the dichotomy between the needs of the entrepreneur and the needs of the large, organized bureaucracy. Nevertheless, the big company still needs managers with moxie. If these managers won't come to the big companies, in the future the big companies will have to go to them. Mammoths and Bees will enter into alliances with Beavers and Moles. General Electric has shown how this can be done. With sales of $58 billion, profits of $4.3 billion, and a research budget of $3.5 billion, GE could finance almost any internal venture it desired. Instead, when it wanted to get into biotechnology, it spent a trifling $3 million setting up a team of 15 scientists in a separate company called Biological Energy Corporation. Terence McClary, GE's vice president in charge of General Electric Venture Capital Corporation, says that most of the specialists for this type of work "are stifled in a corporate environment. . . . We want to get them into one where they can be more creative." When Biological Energy was ready to build a pilot plant, GE didn't fund it directly but instead raised $10 million in outside venture capital, to give the Beaver company an even greater sense of independence.

The Role of the Unions

The relevance of the union movement in such atomized work conditions is up for grabs. What does a member of the underground economy need with collective bargaining, pensions, holiday and sickness benefits, worker decision making, or political strikes?

Unions have realized the majority of their objectives and have served their purpose, by and large, very well. They have achieved their gains through a firm control over membership. But union leadership, like much corporate management, has been slow to appreciate the new sense of independence felt by many workers in their changing attitude toward work and authority. The top-heavy structure of most unions and inadequate ALDO audits have led to their outdated objectives. This has prevented them from meeting the new aspirations of their members. Their bureaucratic approach has alienated management as well. Robert Noyce, the cofounder and vice chairman of Intel, one of the leading companies in the semiconductor industry, told congressmen at a hearing of the Joint Economic Committee, "First names and success sharing are as essential to our productivity as executive dining rooms and unions are antithetical."

When YKK, the world's largest zipper manufacturer, came to Macon, Georgia, in 1974 to build a $15 million plant for 90 employees, there was an immediate clash of cultures. When the Japanese company's management underestimated the need for its team to master the English language, insisted that employees wear uniforms, and mandated evening social gatherings (intended to encourage a convivial atmosphere of teamwork), the American workers responded by calling in the United Cement, Lime and Gypsum Workers Union to represent them. YKK management reacted by setting up a personnel function staffed by Americans from within the firm (which scrapped the uniforms) and handed over the day-to-day management to American nationals. Ten years later the union was voted out, and today YKK operates 11 plants in Macon, employing 825 American and 50 Japanese on long-term contracts.

Western Union International employees had been organized by the International Brotherhood of Teamsters for 40 years when, in June 1982, MCI Communications bought the company from Xerox. Like most of the former Bell System's competitors, MCI had steadfastly avoided union organization and thus enjoyed a 10% labor-cost advantage over its unionized competitors. But when it took over WUI, it found that the employees were paid average wages and benefits of $19.31 per hour, were entitled to a pension that permitted them to retire on full pay once their years of service and age added together exceeded 75, and were entitled to an annual bonus that equaled 110 hours of normal pay. In addition, in the view of MCI executives, several hundred employees were surplus to the acquired company's requirements. In an effort to address these issues, MCI managers put a number of concessions to the union, which resulted first in an 11-week walkout and finally in the hiring of replacements. As Daniel Kane, president of Teamsters Local 111 at MCI remarked, "I think they very cleverly have gone through this to get rid of the union." Throughout the world, cases like this are occurring in every sector of the economy. Unions are finding that they are ill prepared to deal with the new attitudes of more pragmatic, modern leadership teams and that the trade-off for fighting to protect hard-won entitlements is an erosion of membership, influence, and status for the union movement as a whole.

Modern, Lockean managers—committed to a human resources management style that emphasizes the dignity of the individual, fair working conditions and rewards, good communications, and employee participation—will hasten the end of unions as we know them. When modern executives permanently distance themselves from the exploitive practices of an earlier era, the union movement is left with a policy vacuum and an urgent need to redefine its future role.

One important option available to the union movement is to act as a balancing factor between the parochial interests of government, employees, and corporations. Because of growing government involvement in business, corporate leadership teams spend more time dealing with government regulators. In a growing number of cases, unions and management have found that they have a common interest in this area. As a result, in the future, corporate leaders can be expected to enlist the support of labor leaders in order to bring extra clout to common threats and issues; for example, when government action may adversely affect an entire industry or the future of an individual company.

Another approach is the use of enlightened marketing to attract industry and therefore new jobs for members. Frank (now Lord) Chapple's Electrical, Electronic, Telecommunications and Plumbing Union (EETPU) paved the way in Britain by signing no-strike deals with such companies as Inmos, Optical Fibres Technology, Sanyo, and Toshiba. These contracts guaranteed that all disputes would be settled by binding arbitration rather than walkouts. This innovative approach inverted the traditional process of organizing membership and helped to make the United Kingdom the principal beneficiary of Japanese investment in the European Economic Community. Previously, union certification resulted when a work force cast a specified majority of ballots in favor of unionization. However, no-strike deals secure the agreement of management first and the work force second; they effectively exclude competing unions. In Britain, union membership has declined by two-thirds from its high-water mark of 12 million in 1980. Keen marketers like EETPU's leaders know that innovation in a declining market is one approach to survival and that listening to the customers (the members) is essential. This is what members want. They also want more education and training. In response to the needs of its member-customers, the EETPU began providing practical and theoretical courses in its industrial education college and based two fully equipped mobile education vans at each of its regional offices to deliver courses to 12 students at a time at plants and hotels throughout Britain. Corporations get a bargain too; the EETPU charges employers about half the rates of education specialists.

Enlightened unions everywhere are discovering that an educational partnership with business is a route to their own resurgence, because by building the skills of their members they are helping to keep the country competitive, their members in work, and their membership dues flowing. Professional development is not only a key to achieving an edge in the organization of tomorrow but also in winning the hearts and minds of employees, for there is a growing realization that we have all somehow been cheated on our journey to the affluent society. John Gatto, a seventh-grade teacher in Manhattan and the winner of New York City's 1990 Teacher-of-the-Year award, described how his students spend their 168 available hours each week. (See Table 11-1.)

During most of this time, Gatto's students—like most others throughout America—are under constant surveillance, have no private time or space, and are disciplined if they try to assert individuality in the use of time or space. Gatto's students are left with a mere 9 hours in which to learn how to fashion a self and grow up. According to the Children's Defense Fund, one American student drops out of school every 8 seconds, and each year 700,000 young students graduate who cannot read their diplomas.

Table 11-1   Breakdown of How Seventh-Graders Spend Their Time

	Number of Hours	*Balance*
Available		168
Sleeping	56	112
Watching TV	55	57
Getting Ready	8	49
Attending School	30	19
Homework	7	12
Eating	3	9

These students enter the American work force with very meager opportunities to shore up their inadequate work skills:

Public Spending on Employment and Training Programs as a Percent of GDP

Sweden	1.7%
West Germany	1.0%
Britain	0.7%
France	0.7%
Spain	0.7%
United States	0.3%

Consider the implications of these two sets of data together: Young people gain too little from their education and then are unable to redress their inadequate work skills later in life. This is why the greening of the corporation will also be achieved by following the lead of organizations like CitiCorp, Coca-Cola, Exxon, General Electric, IBM, Levi Strauss, Motorola, RJR Nabisco, Sears, and Xerox, which are pouring over $2 billion into educational causes, some 10% of which is going directly to the public education system. Educating our work force is not for "them" to do but for *us* to do. Louis V. Gerstner, chairman and CEO of RJR Nabisco, has committed $30 million to Next Century Schools, a corporate program that awards grants to "china breakers" who will "stand the [education] system on its head." David Kearns, former CEO of Xerox and later U.S. undersecretary of education, has called for "canny outlaws, system beaters, and responsible rule benders" to take risks and join the effort to reform the education system.

Kathryn (Kitty) Hach (pronounced *hawk*), chairman and CEO of Hach Company (a maker of water-analysis equipment, employing 820 staff in Loveland, Colorado), rejects 70% of the 2,100 job applications she receives each year "because applicants cannot write a complete sentence." So Kitty Hach plows 9% of the firm's $21 million payroll into professional development and employs three full-time teachers to provide 10,000 hours of remedial teaching and skill-based courses in 42 different programs, including Business Writing and Writing Skills for Second Language Employees. Kitty Hach does not attribute all of her firm's results to her commitment to professional development, but she's on a 7-year profit streak and employee turnover is down from 11% to 7%. Something's working.

The EETPU's Eric Hammond calls his union "the most responsible, realistic, representative, and modern trade union in Britain today." He believes that the future of the union movement in his country will be achieved through "cooperating with companies and contributing to their prosperity." If the future of the union movement is to be determined by the customer, then the EETPU is on the right track; recent polls show that 62% of the rank-and-file membership is in favor of no-strike deals, underlining Hammond's belief that "the key to winning our battle is to convince employees and managers that they need trade unions."

Collaboration with management through entrepreneurial attitudes and collective approaches is also beginning to pay off for some unions. General Motors and Ford have both established agreements with the United Auto Workers to set up new-venture funds that are jointly managed to develop nontraditional businesses to create new jobs for auto workers displaced by demanning. British Steel, Britain's state-owned steel company, owns a subsidiary whose purpose is to create jobs for members of the work force following the closure of a steel plant. Such proactive unionism is being studied and pursued by the enlightened managements of several labor unions in the industrialized countries.

Organized labor now addresses red-blooded private enterprise, long the ideological enemy of the union movement, with a new pragmatism. The Israeli labor federation, the Histadrut, is now the largest private-sector employer in the country. After years of difficult union management relations, Eastern Air Lines' employees purchased 25% of the company and three of its unions had seats on the board, taking special responsibility for decisions on pricing, scheduling, and capital expenditure. Many argue that the demise of Eastern might have been avoided through an even greater sensitivity to the advice of its unions. The United Steelworkers have reversed their traditional opposition to employee ownership and are now developing programs that help members acquire plants that would otherwise close. Lynn Williams sounded more like the president of USX than of the USW when he observed that the entrepreneurial spirit had "contributed enormously to the success—the material success—of this society." Williams has pointed out that the proactive stance of unions and their involvement in the decision-making process in corporations having the appropriate entrepreneurial urge could "inject a new dynamism and a new creativity into our whole society."

Managerial moxie has been a rare ingredient in most Western labor unions in the postwar era. Outmoded management thinking has failed to recognize union members for what they are: customers who are in the market for ideas as well as products. Instead, the old guard has continued to prescribe yesterday's bitter medicines for ailments that were cured long ago. But managerial moxie is as relevant to a union as it is to a commercial enterprise, because a union *is* a commercial enterprise.

Corporate Venturing

When Air Products & Chemicals, a major producer of synthetic fuels, was hit with the oil-price collapse, it sought diversification opportunities. But as Stanley Morris, general manager of technical diversification, pointed out, "For a company of our size to get involved in new businesses is not easy. . . . It is much harder than adding to existing lines." So Air Products called in SRI International of Menlo Park, California. With its help, Air Products set up an independent venture group to commercialize an extraction-processing technology for the food industry. Apart from the benefits of the specific market opportunity, Morris viewed internal venturing as a means of "replicating situations in start-up companies. . . . We hope we can develop a fleetness of foot that otherwise would not be possible."

When Compaq Computer introduced its first laptop model in 1986, it needed a breakthrough design for the hard disk drive. Though it first considered building one itself, it turned instead to Conner Peripherals, helping to finance the new Silicon Valley firm, which was already designing the kind of disk drive Compaq needed. Said Compaq CEO and cofounder Rod Canion, "We worked so closely with Conner that they were literally an extension of our design team. We got all the benefits but weren't tied down. If another company had come along with a better drive, we'd probably have bought from them as well." Apart from the benefits that come from the entrepreneurial infusion generated by corporate venturing come the advantages of out-sourcing—if the leadership team has made the philosophical leap of faith needed to relinquish absolute control over everything. "Vertical integration is the old way of doing things," says Canion. "The way to succeed in the 1990s is to be open to technology from anywhere in the world." Compaq buys most of its components in this way rather than producing them itself. One of its largest component suppliers is Toshiba—which to the uninitiated might seem like Goldilocks having a date with the Big Bad Wolf.

The U.S. machine-tool industry has been suffering from a long decline caused largely by a lack of new-product development. This situation encouraged Acme-Cleveland, a leading supplier in the field, to take a tack similar to Compaq's. It has acquired equity positions in several entrepreneurial companies with such diverse interests as laser systems, computerized graphics, and robotics, in order to "bootstrap" itself to a level equal to or above its competitors.

Another approach is the **strategic alliance.** This describes a special relationship entered into between major corporations and outside start-ups. These coalitions are similar to those between sharks and pilot fish: Each helps the other to achieve their mutual objectives. The potential mutual benefits hoped for by partners in strategic alliances have encouraged such giants as AT&T, Control Data, General Instrument, IBM, Lubrizol, Monsanto, Olivetti, NCR, and Tektronix to form strategic alliances of their own. The start-up gets the benediction of a "big name" and all the prestige that goes with it; the big company gets access to new technology, entrepreneurial attitudes, and spin-off products.

But if the original purpose of a joint venture is a speedy financial return or technological breakthrough, chances are it will be disappointing. According to a study of 118 corporate venturing deals (or strategic partnerships, as they are sometimes called) by Stockman and Associates, of Greenwich, Connecticut, the most profitable strategic alliances take place between large and small companies based on contractual relationships and owe their success to decentralized management. Says Jennifer Blei Stockman, "The blue suits of corporate America don't relate well to the blue jeans of the entrepreneurs."

Some large companies use equity compensation as a method of securing high performance and exclusivity from entrepreneurial suppliers. The supplier (an executive recruiter, for example) charges a reduced fee and takes the balance in equity warrants, which may be exercised when the client company's stock is at a higher standing. This arrangement is another way to plug into entrepreneurial expertise and form a strategic alliance.

SAVING ENTREPRENEURSHIP FROM THE BUREAUCRATS

A different approach to innovation is more commonplace. While running part of Time and Life's television subsidiary, Michael Garin thought to himself that at 32 he "was too young to be paid a high salary and be unhappy. I figured that if I didn't leave then, I'd be chained to a big corporation forever." In 1978 he founded Telepictures, a TV program syndicator; the firm went public in 1981. In 1983 Telepictures grossed revenues of $71 million and generated profits of $6 million, putting it solidly in the top-three U.S. distributors of first-run programming. The entrepreneurial loss to Time came at a bad moment. The $3 billion conglomerate had just blown $47 million on *TV-Cable Week*, $86 million on the *Washington Star*, $25 million on teletext, and $70 million on subscription TV! Telepictures later merged with Lorimar, becoming Lorimar Telepictures, which was acquired by Warner Communications, which in turn became Time Warner.

Some alliances fail to live up to their promise. Take Exxon, where early alliances gave rise to the sobriquet, put a tiger in your tank and a turkey on your board. Exxon pumped $600 million of its $63 billion of assets into Office Systems, a division of Exxon Enterprises, a venturing group set up by Exxon in 1963, from which it never made money. In 1984 Office Systems lost $70 million, as much as its entire sales for the year. Between 1963 and 1980, when Exxon halted its venturing policy, Exxon Enterprises seeded some 50 different ventures through internal research projects, acquisitions, venture capital, and portfolio investment. Office Systems became the 22nd venture abandoned when Exxon management announced that it was for sale. Even though Office Systems subsidiaries such as Qyx, Qwip, and Vydec produced facsimile machines, word processors, and the first electronic typewriter and embarked on promising research into voice synthesizers, optical data transmitters, voice-to-data translators, and flat displays, the ultimate promise was never met. "Every move had to be reviewed and approved by oilmen who just didn't understand the industry" was how one former Office Systems manager explained the sad saga.

Putting entrepreneurship to work in a large corporation requires a few brave people willing to accept and take risks, people who are prepared to adopt fresh, creative ideas drawn from the right hemisphere. Risk is an inevitable component of change, and the leadership teams of most corporations may resist change for several reasons, not the least of which may be their psychological and emotional conditioning. The latter may lead managers to a risk-averse style that precludes experimenting with anything new and to seek rapid paybacks on any new ideas that are tried. Managers who have no prior experience with product or service innovation may be awed by the consequences of failure. If left-hemispheric thinking prevails, new ventures will certainly wither on the vine. They *must* be planted in the rich soil of a right-hemispheric corporate culture because entrepreneurial change is a prerequisite to the greening of the corporation and therefore for corporate survival. Indeed, entrepreneurial leadership may be characterized as the ability to define and capitalize on change.

Even if the leadership team is persuaded to accommodate a modicum of entrepreneurship, the realization of its potential may be stunted by a lack of staying power. Corporate executives in North America have traditionally been concerned with quick fixes and short-term paybacks, relying upon innovation to produce a money spinner.

NOURISHING CORPORATE VENTURES

Corporate venturing is a twist on the out-sourcing theme discussed in Chapter 8 and can have an external or an internal bias. Some of the *external* options available to the corporation wishing to pursue new ventures include the following:

♦ Creating a venture-capital subsidiary
♦ Management buy-outs with retention of minority interests
♦ Joint ventures and partnerships
♦ Franchising and licensing

Some *internal* options include the following:

♦ Establishing venture-management divisions
♦ Transferring employees from the payroll to a fee-for-services structure
♦ Establishing majority holdings in employee spin-offs
♦ Establishing incentive schemes that enable research-and-development teams to take investment positions resulting from their discoveries
♦ Establishing equity-participation plans for employees and managers who introduce new products or services or who negotiate innovative new deals for the company

Corporations that are serious about harnessing every potential source of creative talent to their advantage look upon the formation of corporate ventures as a method of

acquiring entrepreneurial talent

shortening the time between the development and the commercial exploitation of new products and services

heightening the corporation's profile and prestige

gaining privileged access to new technologies and markets

infusing the corporation with new entrepreneurial spirit

generating long-term capital gains

benefiting from the "osmosis effect" of applying new technology to existing products or service lines

At Manpower an executive who had worked with me for a number of years appeared to be burned out, so we sat down and talked about it. At the time we were floundering in a sea of real estate management problems and casting about for a solution. This seemed like a good opportunity for our executive. Relinquishing his position with our company, he became a consultant to us. We negotiated a fee for his services and gave him all our property problems to solve. After several mutually beneficial years, he had sorted out many of the problems, restored order to the functional area, and savored the sweet taste of entrepreneurship. Impressed by his new track record, we gave him the opportunity to turn around one of our weaker branches. To sweeten this, we offered equity leading to 100% ownership and signed a contract that required us to put up the working capital, which he agreed to repay, together with compensation for the goodwill and assets acquired, out of future earnings. Ten years later this Manpower franchisee continues to go from strength. But there is a sweet irony: The franchisee did so well, he sold it back to the company again, which now operates it as a branch.

The out-sourcing of staff services and research-and-development functions has many imaginative possibilities. Many major corporations—among them Dow, Du Pont, Exxon, Kodak, Philip Morris, FMC, General Foods, General Electric, W. R. Grace, Johnson & Johnson, Minnesota Mining & Manufacturing (3M), and Xerox—have developed very successful new ventures. But corporate venturing was first popularized by 3M and Du Pont in the United States in the late 1960s. At one stage, almost a third of *Fortune* 500 companies practiced some variant of corporate venturing, but by 1980 many of these companies had abandoned their attempts to induce internal entrepreneurship.

Researchers have found that, despite such notable exceptions as 3M, Monsanto, GE, Ralston Purina, Xerox, and British Petroleum, corporate-venture groups fail primarily because of a lack of long-term corporate commitment. Lack of follow-through is usually caused by changes in top management, in corporate objectives, or in fiscal health. The majority of ventures either die a slow, painful death or are extinguished quickly during a traumatic corporate upheaval. Ralph Biggadike of the University of Virginia has undertaken extensive research into start-ups sponsored by large corporations. His findings show that, on average, new corporate ventures experience *severe* losses for the first 4 years and therefore require patience and continuing support from their champions during their nursery years—neither of which they are likely to get from their corporate parent. As Richard Onians of Monsanto puts it, "Executives expect venture groups to produce a good idea every Monday morning and [the executives] get disappointed when they don't."

Yet the spoils for the innovative organizations that emulate the managerial moxie of smaller, entrepreneurial firms are handsome, and the perseverance of the few stalwarts who took the long view has borne fruit. As David Bradley, one of the designers of IBM's famed PC computer, points out, "If you're going to compete with five men in a garage, you have to do something different." IBM did just that and rushed from a standing start to market leadership in the microcomputer industry in under 3 years.

The U.S. Small Business Administration has pointed out that small businesses have pioneered *2 ½ times* more new products than large companies. A study by the American Electronics Association has shown that companies 5 years old or less produced *100 times* more jobs than companies that had been established 20 years or more. It is this zest for innovation and *Kaizen* that is lost in the graying corporation.

If "sunset" industries like steel, chemicals, textiles, and heavy engineering and manufacturing are to enjoy a rebirth as a result of a rapid improvement in productivity, they will have to promote internal venture organizations to produce innovative products and services for the parent. In addition, they will have to call on entrepreneurial organizations like Intel (the inventor of the microprocessor, the miniature brain of all computers) and Unimation (the world's first manufacturer of industrial robots) to develop the products and skills they currently lack. (But being hugged by a bear can knock the wind out of you: Until Unimation was acquired by Westinghouse, it was the world leader in industrial robotics, but since then it has suffered a serious decline, and its very future is in doubt.) Rather than set up their own manufacturing operations, NCR, Burroughs, and Prime Computer have been realizing the benefits of outsourcing by buying work stations from Convergent Technologies (itself a 1979 start-up put together by Bill Hambrecht of the venture-capital firm Hambrecht & Quist).

The speed of introducing new products or services to the market can be accelerated by entrepreneurial and small-company approaches, as Gellman Research Associates pointed out in a study showing that small companies bring a product to the market in 2.2 years compared to 3.1 years for large companies.

Corporate venturing is an important method of adapting the large corporation for the modern marketplace, but it can only be done with the energetic support of right-hemispheric leaders who can run interference on behalf of corporate entrepreneurs, keeping them apart from their nemesis, the left-hemispheric manager.

The Footprint of the Owner

Many managers have felt that they could run the companies they worked for better than the existing occupants of the executive suite. The 1980s was *the* decade for putting such dreams into practice. Leadership teams and insiders collaborated to buy out the companies for which they worked, companies that had lost their entrepreneurial flair but which these teams believed could be turned into hot-shot corporations once again. Some investment firms (such as Kohlberg Kravis Roberts and Forstmann Little) specialized in management buy-outs (also called leveraged buy-outs, LBOs, a name derived from the high leveraging that characterizes the deals). Despite many disappointments, they have frequently fulfilled the aspirations of their architects. For 25 years, Winchester Rifles was a money loser for its parent, Olin, until 1981 when it became the new U.S. Repeating Arms Company. Purex bleach, Ray-O-Vac batteries, Congoleum flooring, McCulloch chain saws, Gibson greeting cards, Harley-Davidson motorcycles, Remington electric shavers, Dr. Pepper soft drinks, and Chris-Craft boats are some of the most famous brand names to change hands through management buy-outs in recent years. It is estimated that 500 such buy-outs took place from 1979 to 1984 (300 in the last year alone) and that the value of these transactions has ballooned from $500 million to $13 billion. For many, the investment is paying off; the value of the equity invested by Kohlberg Kravis Roberts in private companies has grown by 62% every year. Prudential Insurance invested $2 billion in the financing of management buy-outs since the early 1960s; Prudential's average return on these investments has been 4% more than the return achieved on single-A corporate bonds purchased at the same time.

One of the main appeals of the management buy-out is the transformation of attitudes. Seasoned, experienced executives, who know what is wrong with the business, itch to get their hands on the decision-making levers. They are invigorated by owning a piece of the action and the challenge of making it work. In other words, management buy-outs spell *motivation*, and investors know that a highly motivated management team enhances the climate for success. Bill Lawson and eight members of management put up only $250,000 of the $45 million purchase price to acquire 25% of the equity of Universal Electric from a subsidiary of Inco of Toronto. Two years later, the company had already retired $9 million of its $34 million debt, and Lawson exuded optimism: "I can't tell you how excited we are. The company's performance has improved incredibly, because everybody's working so damned hard . . . and the reason is that they've all got a piece of the action now."

In 1979 when Victor Kiam purchased the Remington shaver division from Sperry Rand of New York to form Remington Products of Bridgeport, Connecticut, he took out a bank loan of $14.5 million and negotiated a 15-year agreement with Sperry to pay back $10 million. The bank loan was paid off in 12 months and Sperry's debt was retired in 3 years. When Kiam took over, he found sales of only $47 million and employee morale so low that stopping talented executives from leaving was his first priority. Kiam put all the employees into profit-sharing and incentive plans; he admits that although "the base salaries are lousy . . . the total earnings if we're successful are great." Despite the arrival of many new competitors, by 1984 sales had risen to $160 million, and one out of two electric shavers sold in the United States are now Remingtons, up from one out of five in 1979.

The management buy-out trend has spread across the globe like a brush fire. Britain has enjoyed a phenomenal number of management buy-outs in the last 15 years. The trend has been facilitated by 60 new venture partnerships with a combined capital of £300 million and an unlisted securities market that financed 200 companies in its first

3 years. Two large financial groups that were nationalized by France's Mitterrand government, Compagnie Financière and the Paribas Group, established subsidiaries to put money into promising new ventures, with special emphasis on management buy-outs, a phenomenon then unknown in France. The two companies even had to push for changes in legislation in order to pave the way for their new ideas.

Implementing Managed Opportunism

Greening the corporation with managed opportunism requires large doses of managerial moxie; fresh, right-hemispheric leadership and thinking will most likely take place if the following occur:

♦ Responsibilities and guidelines for a regenerative or innovative approach are clearly defined and agreed on in advance. The establishment of corporate purpose is required to achieve this and will include a clear definition of corporate mission, a statement of values, a measurement of the strategic gap through the use of the ALDO audit, and a vision statement.

♦ The leadership team accepts the strictures of a long-term payback period, relying on a few, relevant dials in the corporate cockpit.

♦ Senior management views the entrepreneurial process as beneficial rather than the latest flavor-of-the-month being peddled by an idiosyncratic fad freak. The establishment of a climate for success by the CEO will enhance the success ratio of the people in the organization and therefore the projects they are working on.

♦ The individual entrepreneur is given the freedom to make his or her mark on the venture. Nearly all successful ventures are started by a leader with a high profile and a very personal management style. The leadership team must make a rigorous commitment to hiring superstars, never settling for mediocrity, and then must empower them to make their own decisions with their own teams using their delegated authority.

♦ Staff supports rather than obstructs the entrepreneur, who is protected from bureaucrats by being assigned a champion (an executive who will run interference for him or her).

♦ Wherever possible, those functions and services for which the corporation does not possess a distinctive competence are out-sourced to specialists, so that the company can concentrate on what it does best.

♦ Entrepreneurial results are rewarded in proportion to the venture and to the result. Reward, in the form of equity, capital gains, and other leveraging techniques, is the stuff that turns on the entrepreneur. Remember Samuel Goldwyn's epithet, "We're overpaying him but he's worth it." Motivation—using every motivator in the book, both psychic and material—is the key.

♦ Management sets aside a budget for the entrepreneurial effort and then gets out of the way. Empowerment of the team and delegation to the lowest level where a competent decision can be made are essential.

♦ The leadership team is tolerant of mistakes; as Samuel Johnson said, "He that hath much to do will do something wrong." Above all, don't punish, or worse, fire people for failing: They may have to fail a thousand times in order to succeed just once—the search for a cure for cancer being a case in point.

♦ The leadership team remembers that investment is the key to innovation and pays close attention to what the customer is trying to say. Being totally "on" and building relationships with current and would-be customers will do more to ensure a payoff for entrepreneurial initiatives than pulling the plug on a project that fails to meet some arbitrary financial criteria.

♦ Managers keep in mind that good ideas aren't necessarily obviously *good*—it's tougher to call the plays in advance. (As Mark Twain observed, "A man with a new idea is a crank until the new idea succeeds.") Assessments of corporate success should avoid the criteria of outmoded management theories or number-crunching formulas.

♦ Management forsakes the what-are-we-going-to-lose? mentality. Instead, it asks what the organization can afford to lose and realizes that it must invest. These attitudes address the fulfillment of customer needs.

♦ The emphasis is placed on riding up the growth curve of new products and services and allowing the competition to slide down the declining curve of mature products and services that it has been defending; the necessary intelligence for this strategy being updated through regular use of the ALDO audit.

♦ Management does not consider huge markets for new products or services to be the holy grail; most of the fastest-growing entrepreneurial companies expand by building perceived niches in the marketplace.

♦ Less emphasis is placed on doing it "right" (that is, according to the book) and more emphasis is placed on doing the *right thing*. Plans and approaches should be "loose-leaf," not copied from the policy manual (this also calls for a cultural shift from left- to right-hemisphere).

♦ Managers are courageous about maintaining satisfactory gross profit margins. Nearly all the fastest-growing companies enjoy margins that are much larger than those of their competitors who are expanding their market share by price cutting.

———♦———

I started this book with a plea for *fun*. Businesses don't work unless they are fun. People are the same— they don't "work" unless they are having fun either.

Professor C. Northcote Parkinson (of Parkinson's Law fame) used to recall a story about a British government minister during the post–World War I years. Young civil servants were forever bustling in and out of his office with urgent secret papers and serious looks on their faces. The minister would thank them and ask for the papers to be left on his desk, saying to the young man as he reached the door:

"Oh, one thing, Mr. Davenant."

"Sir?"

"Remember Rule Six."

"Yes, sir, of course."

Then, arrested by a thought, the young man would turn in the doorway to ask, "But excuse me, sir. What is Rule Six?"

"Rule Six is as follows: Don't take yourself too seriously."

Mr. Davenant would thank the minister, assuring him that he would keep his advice in mind, and then be seized by another thought:

"But, sir, what are the other rules?"

"There are no other rules."

———◆———

Not every end is the goal. The end of a melody is not its goal, and yet if a melody has not reached its end, it has not reached its goal. A parable.

—Friedrich Nietzsche

Bibliography

CHAPTER 1

Chopra, Deepak. *Perfect Health.* Bantam, 1990.

Chopra, Deepak. *Quantum Healing.* Bantam, 1990.

Cousins, Norman. *Head First.* Dutton, 1989.

de Bono, Edward. *Lateral Thinking—A Textbook of Creativity.* Penguin, 1977.

Deutschman, Alan. "The Trouble with MBAs." *Fortune* (July 29, 1991): 67–80.

Franklin, Jon. *Molecules of the Mind.* Dell, 1987.

Guinness, Alma E., ed. *ABC's of the Human Mind.* Reader's Digest, 1990.

Hutchison, Michael. *Megabrain.* Ballantyne, 1986.

Kuhn, Thomas S. *The Structure of Scientific Revolutions.* 2nd ed. University of Chicago Press, 1970.

Magrath, Allan J. "Born-Again Marketing." *Across the Board* (June 1991): 33–36.

Restack, Richard M. *The Brain.* Warner Books, 1979.

Restack, Richard M. *The Mind.* Bantam, 1988.

Sperry, R. W. "Brain Bisection and Consciousness." In *Brain and Conscious Experience,* edited by J. Eccles. Springer-Verlag, 1966.

Teilhard de Chardin, Pierre. *The Future of Man.* Harper & Row, 1987.

Teilhard de Chardin, Pierre. *The Phenomenon of Man.* Harper & Row, 1975.

For additional reading about brain-hemisphere theory and research, see Robert Ornstein, *The Psychology of Consciousness,* 2nd ed., Harcourt Brace Jovanovich, 1977; Sally P. Springer and Georg Deutsch, *Left Brain, Right Brain,* W. H. Freeman, 1981; Sid J. Segalowitz, *Two Sides of the Brain: Brain Lateralization Explored,* Prentice-Hall, 1983; and Jaquelyn Wonder and Priscilla Donovan, *Whole Brain Thinking,* Morrow, 1984.

CHAPTER 2

Ansley, Mary Holm. "Successful Firms Are Leanest, Study Says." *Toronto Star* December 16, 1984): B1.

Davis, Stanley M. "Entrepreneurial Succession." *Administrative Science Quarterly* (December 1968): 402–416.

"Employees Have Little Faith in Top Management." *Across the Board* (January/February 1991): 5.

Forrest, Diane. "Fifty Ways to Run a Company." *Canadian Business* (July 1991): 57–68.

Greiner, Larry E. "Evolution and Revolution as Organizations Grow." *Harvard Business Review* (July/August 1972): 37–46.

Haire, Mason. "Biological Models and Empirical Histories of the Growth of Organizations." In *Modern Organization Theory,* edited by Mason Haire, 272–306. Wiley, 1959.

"Office Workers Rate Their Jobs." *Fortune* (November 4, 1991): 14.

Secretan, Lance H. K. "Five Ways to Stay Hungry." *Canadian Business* (January 1985): 121–135.

Steiner, George A., and John B. Miner. *Management Policy and Strategy.* 2nd ed., 85. Macmillan, 1982.

Tart, Charles T. "Extending Mindfulness to Everyday Life." *Journal of Humanistic Psychology* 30, no. 1 (Winter 1990): 101–106.

Therrien, Lois. "McRisky." *Business Week* (October 21, 1991): 34–52.

Wise, Deborah C. "Steve Jobs vs. Apple: What Caused the Final Split." *Business Week* (September 30, 1985): 32.

CHAPTER 3

Ansoff, Igor H. *Strategic Management.* Wiley, 1979.

Cohn, Theodore, and Roy A. Lindberg. *Survival and Growth: Management Strategies for the Small Firm.* American Management Association, 1974.

Drucker, Peter F. *Management: Tasks, Responsibilities, Practices.* Harper & Row, 1974.

Faltermayer, Edmund. "'The Deal Decade' Verdict on the 80's." *Fortune* (August 26, 1991): 58–70.

Friedman, Milton. "The Social Responsibility of Business Is to Increase Its Profits." *The New York Times Magazine* (September 30, 1970).

Hall, R. H. *Organization—Structure and Processes.* Prentice-Hall, 1972.

Hunt, Pearson. "Fallacy of the One Big Brain." *Harvard Business Review* 44, no. 4 (1966).

Kastens, Marritt L. *Long Range Planning for Your Business.* American Management Association, 1976.

Kouzes, James M., and Barry Z. Posner. *The Leadership Challenge.* Jossey-Bass, 1987.

Labich, Kenneth. "The New Crisis in Business Ethics." *Fortune* (April 20, 1992): 167–176.

Leontiades, Milton. *Strategies for Diversification and Change.* Little, Brown, 1980.

Mintzberg, Henry. "The Manager's Job: Folklore and Fact." *Harvard Business Review* (July/August 1975): 49–61. Also, a list of 96 suggested readings can be found at the end of Henry Mintzberg's excellent article, "Policy as a Field of Management Theory," *Academy of Management Review* (January 1977): 88–103.

Musashi, Miyamoto. *The Book of Five Rings.* Overlook Press, 1982.

Newman, William H. "Shaping the Master Strategy of Your Firm." *California Management Review* (Spring 1967).

O'Toole, James. *Vanguard Management.* Doubleday, 1985.

Secretan, Lance H. K. *The Way of the Tiger.* Thaler Corporation, 1990.

Shostack, G. Lynn. "Banks Sell Services—Not Things." *The Bankers Magazine* (Winter 1977): 40.

Steiner, George A. *Strategic Planning.* Free Press, 1979.

Steiner, George A. *Top Management Planning.* Macmillan, 1969.

"We Don't Want You to Work for Us Anymore." *Across the Board* (June 1991): 5.

"When the Bubble Burst." *The Economist* (August 3, 1991): 67–68.

"Why Sports Didn't Pay at Ralston Purina." *Business Week* (July 4, 1983): 54–55.

Yi, Cheng. *The Tao of Organization.* Shambhala, 1988.

CHAPTER 4

Boettinger, Henry M. "Is Management Really an Art?" *Harvard Business Review* (January/February 1975).

Covey, Stephen R. *The 7 Habits of Highly Effective People.* Simon & Schuster, 1989.

Deal, Terrence E. *Corporate Cultures.* Addison-Wesley, 1982.

De Pree, Max. *Leadership Is an Art.* Doubleday, 1989.

Drake, John D. *Special Study No. 77, 5.* Presidents Association, 1982.

Drucker, Peter F. *Management: Tasks, Responsibilities, Practices.* Harper & Row, 1974.

Dumaine, Brian. "Creating a New Company Culture." *Fortune* (January 15, 1990): 127–131.

Farnham, Alan. "Who Beats Stress Best—And How." *Fortune* (October 7, 1991): 72–86.

Gardner, John W. *Self-Renewal.* Norton, 1981.

Garfield, Charles A. *Peak Performance.* Jeremy P. Tarcher, 1984.

George, Claude S. *The History of Management Thought.* 2nd ed. Prentice-Hall, 1972.

Hoerr, John. "A Company Where Everybody Is the Boss." *Business Week* (April 15, 1985): 58.

Jaffe, Dennis T., and Cynthia D. Scott. *Take This Job and Love It.* Simon & Schuster, 1988.

Killian, Linda. "Hamburger Helper." *Forbes* (August 5, 1991): 106–107.

Klemmer, Jim. "They See You Loud and Clear." In *Global Management 1991: Annual Review of International Management Practice,* 215–217. Canadian Management Center, 1991.

Kotter, John P. *Harvard Business Review* (May/June 1990): 103–111.

Labich, Kenneth. "Hot Company, Warm Culture." *Fortune* (February 27, 1989): 74–78.

Leavitt, Harold J. *Corporate Pathfinders.* Dow Jones-Irwin, 1986.

Lunding, F. J., George L. Clements, and Donald S. Perkins. "Everyone Who Makes It Has a Mentor." *Harvard Business Review* (July/August 1978): 89–101.

Mee, John F. "A History of Twentieth Century Management." Ph.D. diss., Ohio State University, 1959.

Morgan, Gareth. *Creative Organization Theory: A Resource Book.* Sage, 1989.

Ott, J. Steven. *The Organizational Culture Perspective.* Brooks/Cole, 1989.

Peace, William H. "The Hard Work of Being a Soft Manager." *Harvard Business Review* (November/December 1991): 40–47.

Plachy, Roger J. "Leading vs. Managing: A Guide to Some Crucial Distinctions." *Management Review* (September 1991): 58–61.

Rosener, Judy B. "Ways Women Lead." *Harvard Business Review* (November/December 1990): 119–125.

Senge, Peter M. *The Fifth Discipline.* Doubleday, 1990.

Sonnenfeld, Jeffrey. *The Hero's Farewell.* Oxford University Press, 1989.

Taylor, Frederick W. *Scientific Management.* Harper & Brothers, 1911.

Vaill, Peter B. *Managing as a Performing Art.* Jossey-Bass, 1989.

Wren, Daniel A. *The Evolution of Management Thought.* The Ronald Press Company, 1972.

Zinn, Laura. "Whales, Human Rights, Rain Forests—And the Heady Smell of Profits." *Business Week* (July 15, 1991): 96–97.

CHAPTER 5

Blake, R. R., and J. S. Mouton. *The Managerial Grid.* Gulf Publishing, 1964.

Carroll, S. J., Jr., and H. L. Tosi, Jr. *Management by Objectives.* Macmillan, 1973.

Cattell, R. B. *The Scientific Analysis of Personality.* Penguin, 1965.

Claude, Inis L. *Swords into Plowshares.* Random House, 1970.

Colvin, Geoffrey. "How to Pay the CEO Right." *Fortune* (April 6, 1992): 60–69.

Crystal, Graef S. *Executive Compensation.* AMACOM, 1978.

Fisher, Anne B. "Morale Crisis." *Fortune* (November 18, 1991): 69–96.

Haire, Mason. "The Concept of Power and the Concept of Man." In *Social Science Approaches to Business Behavior,* edited by George Strother. Dorsey Press, 1962.

Herzberg, F. *Work and the Nature of Man.* World Book, 1966.

Hilborn, Cathy. "Workers Crave Respect, Participation." *Profit* (November 1991): 9.

Hyatt, Joshua. "Words from the Wise." *Inc.* (June 1991): 50–62.

Ishihara, Shintaro. *The Japan That Can't Say No.* Touchstone, 1992.

Likert, Rensis. "Motivation: The Core of Management." *American Management Association.* Personnel Series, no. 155 (1953): 3–21.

Likert, Rensis. *New Patterns of Management.* McGraw-Hill, 1961.

McClelland, David C., and David H. Burnham. "Power Is the Great Motivator." *Harvard Business Review* (March/April 1976): 100–110.

McGregor, D. *The Human Side of Enterprise.* McGraw-Hill, 1960.

Manger, Gary, and Veronica Salinger. "Demilitarizing Our Minds." *Corporate Management* (Australia) (April/May 1990): 78–80.

Maslow, Abraham H. *Motivation and Personality.* 2nd ed. Harper & Row, 1970.

Miles, Raymond E., Lyman W. Porter, and James A. Craft. "Leadership Attitudes Among Public Health Officers." *American Journal of Public Health* 56, no. 12: 1990–2005.

"New Ways to Pay." *Economist* (July 13, 1991): 69.

Parkhouse, Gerald C. "An Interview with Niccolo Machiavelli." *Business Horizons* (May/June 1990): 3–5.

Richards, M. D. *Organizational Goal Structures.* West, 1978.

Sites, Paul. *Control, the Basis of Social Order.* Dunellin, 1973.

Whyte, W. F. "Culture and Work." In *Culture and Management,* edited by R. A. Wabber. Irwin, 1969.

"Workers Prize Privacy." *Across the Board* (March 1991): 6.

There appear to be two authors who might claim title to Theory Z: Laurence Foss, "Managerial Strategy for the Future: Theory Z Management," *California Management Review* 15, no. 3 (1973): 68–81; and William Ouchi, *Theory Z: How American Business Can Meet the Japanese Challenge,* Addison-Wesley, 1981.

CHAPTER 6

Appley, Lawrence A., and Keith L. Irons. *Manager Manpower Planning.* AMACOM, 1981.

Bernstein, Peter W. "Armand Hammer's Other Collection." *Fortune* (September 8, 1980): 47–48.

Ellis, James E. "Curt Carlson Keeps It All in the Family." *Business Week* (September 30, 1991): 76–77.

"Finding Your (Female) Mentor." *Executive Edge* (May 1990): 4.

Garland, Susan B. "How to Keep Women Managers on the Corporate Ladder." *Business Week* (September 2, 1991): 60.

Levinson, Harry. "Don't Choose Your Own Successor." *Harvard Business Review* (November/December 1974): 53–62.

Maccoby, Michael. *The Leader.* Simon & Schuster, 1981.

Marvin, Philip. *The Right Man for the Right Job.* Dow Jones-Irwin, 1973.

Miller, Gordon Porter. "Recognizing and Keeping the People Who Will Win for You." In *Global Management 1991: Annual Review of International Management Practice,* 211–213. Canadian Management Center, 1991.

Murray, William A. "What Price Management Education?" *Dun's Review* (March 1979): 104–106.

Neilson, Eric H. "The Human Side of Growth." *Organization Dynamics* (Summer 1978): 61–80.

"Women in Management and Their Influence on the Facility." Research summary from Herman Miller Inc., September 1989.

CHAPTER 7

Bossidy, Lawrence A. "Why Do We Waste Time Doing This?" *Across the Board* (May 1991): 17–21.

Brokaw, Leslie. "The Enlightened Employee Handbook." *Inc.* (October 1991): 49–51.

Byham, William C. *Zapp! The Lightening of Empowerment.* Edited by Jeff Cox. Development Dimensions International, 1990.

Chandler, A. D. *Strategy and Structure.* MIT Press, 1962.

Charan, Ram. "How Networks Reshape Organizations for Results." *Harvard Business Review* (September/October 1991): 104–115.

Collins, Eliza G. C. "When Friends Run the Business." *Harvard Business Review* (July/August 1980): 87–102.

Dalton, D. R., W. D. Todor, M. J. Spendolini, G. J. Fielding, and L. W. Porter. "Organization Structure and Performance: A Critical Review." *Academy of Management Review* (January 1980): 49–63.

Davis, R. C. *The Fundamentals of Top Management.* Harper & Brothers, 1951.

Drucker, Peter F. *Management: Tasks, Responsibilities, Practices.* Harper & Row, 1974.

Encyclopedia of Professional Management. McGraw-Hill, 1978.

Hodge, J. B., and H. J. Johnson. *Management and Organizational Behavior.* Wiley, 1970.

Howe, Roger J., and Mark G. Mindell. "The Challenge of Changing Work Values: Motivating the Contemporary Employee." *Management Review* (September 1979): 51–55.

Katz, Robert L. "Skills of an Effective Administrator." *Harvard Business Review* (January/February 1955): 33–42. (A timeless and instructive article, and still part of the subconscious of many leaders.)

Kizilos, Peter. "Crazy About Empowerment?" *Training* (December 1990): 47–56.

Koontz, H., and C. O'Donnell. "The Functions and Authority of the Manager." Chapter 3 in *Principles of Management: An Analysis of Managerial Functions,* 5th ed. McGraw-Hill, 1972.

Peter, Laurence J., and Raymond Hull. *The Peter Principle.* William Morrow, 1969.

Peters, Tom. "On Achieving Excellence." *TPG Communications* (January 1992).

Prahalad, C. K., and Gary Hamel. "The Core Competence of the Corporation." *Harvard Business Review* (May/June 1990): 79–91.

Stewart, Thomas A. "GE Keeps Those Ideas Coming." *Fortune* (August 12, 1991): 41–49.

Straub, T., and Stan Kossen. *Introduction to Business.* Kent, 1983.

Sweeney, Neil R. *The Art of Managing Managers.* Addison-Wesley, 1981.

Thompson, Arthur A., Jr., and A. J. Strickland III. *Strategic Management: Concepts and Cases.* 3rd ed. Business Publications, 1984.

CHAPTER 8

Alster, Norm. "In Fighting Trim." *Forbes* (June 10, 1991): 48–51.

Dumaine, Brian. "The Bureaucracy Busters." *Fortune* (June 17, 1991): 35–50.

Fuhrman, Peter, and Peter Newcomb. "A British Original." *Forbes* (December 9, 1991): 43–44.

Hayes, Robert H., and William J. Abernathy. "Managing Our Way to Economic Decline." *Harvard Business Review* (July/August 1980): 67–77.

"How the PC Project Changed the Way IBM Thinks." *Business Week* (October 3, 1983): 43.

McKay, Shona. "A Boardroom Iconoclast." *Maclean's* (September 19, 1983): 58.

Stewart, Thomas A. "Brain Power." *Fortune* (June 3, 1991): 44–60.

Therrien, Lois. "Honeywell Is Finally Tasting the Sweet Life." *Business Week* (June 3, 1991): 34.

Townsend, Robert. *Up the Organization.* Michael Joseph, 1970.

Treece, James B. "Getting Mileage from a Recall." *Business Week* (May 27, 1991): 36–37.

Wilson, John W., and Judith H. Dobrzynski. "And Now the Post-Industrial Corporation." *Business Week* (March 3, 1986): 60–63.

CHAPTER 9

Albrecht, Karl. *At America's Service.* Dow Jones-Irwin, 1988.

Auletta, Ken. *Three Blind Mice: How the TV Networks Lost Their Way.* Random House, 1991.

Armstrong, Larry. "Who's the Most Pampered Motorist of All?" *Business Week* (June 17, 1991): 62 D-E–62 H-E.

Bell, Martin L., and William Emory. "The Faltering Marketing Concept." *Journal of Marketing* (October 1971): 37–42.

Bennett, Roger C., and Robert G. Cooper. "Beyond the Marketing Concept." *Business Horizons* (June 1979): 76.

Bennett, Roger C., and Robert G. Cooper. "The Misuse of Marketing: An American Tragedy." *Business Horizons* (November/December 1981): 51–61.

Brehm, Jack, and Arthur Cohen. *Explorations in Cognitive Dissonance.* Wiley, 1962.

Brokaw, Leslie. "The Mystery/Shopper Questionnaire." *Inc.* (June 1991): 94–97.

Buzzel, Robert, and Bradley Gate. *The PIMS Principle—Linking Strategy to Performance.* Free Press, 1987.

Crosby, Philip B. *Quality Is Free.* Mentor (New American Library), 1979.

Drucker, Peter F. "Japan: New Strategies for a New Reality." *Quality Digest* (December 1991): 48–55.

Drucker, Peter F. *Management: Tasks, Responsibilities, Practices.* Harper & Row, 1974.

Enis, Ben M., and Keith K. Cox. *Marketing Classics: A Selection of Influential Articles,* xi. Allyn & Bacon, 1977.

Festinger, Leon. *A Theory of Cognitive Dissonance.* Stanford University Press, 1957.

Guaspari, John. *I Know It When I See It.* AMACOM, 1985.

Guaspari, John. *Theory Why.* AMACOM, 1985.

Gubernick, Lisa. "Our Products Have No Shelf Life." *Forbes* (June 10, 1991): 94–95.

Harris, John. "Dinnerhouse Technology." *Forbes* (July 8, 1991): 98–99.

Hippel, Eric von. "Get New Products from Customers." *Harvard Business Review* (March/April 1982): 117–122.

Imai, Masaaki. *Kaizen: The Key to Japan's Competitive Success.* Random House, 1986.

Imai, Masaaki. "Kaizen Wave Circles the Globe." *Tokyo Business Today* (Japan) (May 1990): 44–48.

Kiechel, Walter. "The Decline of the Experience Curve." *Fortune* (October 5, 1981): 139–146.

Koselka, Rita. "Fading into History." *Forbes* (August 19, 1991): 70–71.

Kotler, Philip, and Sidney J. Levy. "Broadening the Concept of Marketing." *Journal of Marketing* (January 1969): 10–15.

Landler, Mark, Walecia Conrad, Zachary Schiller, and Lois Therrien. "What Happened to Advertising?" *Business Week* (September 23, 1991): 50–56.

Levitt, Theodore. "Marketing Myopia." *Harvard Business Review* (July/August 1960): 45–56.

McKenna, Regis. "Marketing Is Everything." *Harvard Business Review* (July/August 1991): 26–36.

Main, Jeremy. "Is the Baldrige Overblown?" *Fortune* (July 1, 1991): 61–65.

Maitel, Shlomo. "Thinking Ahead Backward." *Across the Board* (June 1991): 7–9.

Maitel, Shlomo. "When You Absolutely, Positively Have to Give Better Service." *Across the Board* (March 1991): 8–12.

Rapoport, Anatol. *Fights, Games and Debates.* University of Michigan Press, 1974.

Rosenbluth, Hal. "Tales from a Nonconformist Company." *Harvard Business Review* (July/August 1991): 26–36.

Schiller, Zachary. "At Rubbermaid, Little Things Mean a Lot." *Business Week* (November 25, 1991): 70 D-E.

Schlesinger, Leonard A., and James L. Heskett. "The Service-Driven Economy." *Harvard Business Review* (September/October 1991): 71–81.

Sellers, Patricia. "Winning Over the New Consumer." *Fortune* (July 29, 1991): 113–126.

Sewell, Carl. *Customers for Life.* Doubleday, 1990.

Tomczyk, S. Michael. *The Home Computer Wars.* COMPUTE! Publications, 1984.

von Neumann, John, and Oskar Morganstern. *Theory of Games and Economic Behavior.* Princeton University Press, 1953.

CHAPTER 10

Boulding, Kenneth E. *The Image: Knowledge in Life and Society.* University of Michigan Press, 1956.

Burns, T., and G. M. Stalker. *The Management of Innovation.* Quadrangle, 1962.

Cammann, Cortlandt, and David A. Nadler. "Fit Control Systems to Your Managerial Style." *Harvard Business Review* (January/February 1976): 65–72.

Dearden, John. "MIS Is a Mirage." *Harvard Business Review* (January/February 1972): 90–99.

Drucker, Peter F. *Management: Tasks, Responsibilities, Practices.* Harper & Row, 1974.

Flamholtz, Eric G. *Human Resource Accounting.* 2nd ed. Jossey-Bass, 1985.

Hayes, Robert H., and William J. Abernathy. "Managing Our Way to Economic Decline." *Harvard Business Review* (July/August 1980): 67–77.

Hekimian, James S., and Curtis H. Jones. "Put People on Your Balance Sheet." *Harvard Business Review* (January/February 1967).

Henkoff, Ronald. "Cost Cutting: How to Do It Right." *Fortune* (April 9, 1990): 40–49.

Likert, Rensis. "Human Resource Accounting: Building and Assessing Productive Organizations." *Personnel* (May/June 1973).

Meyers, Bruce G., and Hugh M. Shane. "Human Resource Accounting for Managerial Decisions: A Capital Budgeting Approach." *Personnel Administrator* (January 1984): 29–35.

Ouchi, William G. *Theory Z,* 42–43. Avon, 1982.

Pendrill, David. "Introducing a Newcomer—Value-Added Statement." *Accountancy* (December 1977): 92–94.

Peters, Thomas J., and Robert H. Waterman, Jr. *In Search of Excellence.* Harper & Row, 1982.

Peters, Tom. "Letting Go of Control." *Across the Board* (June 1991): 14–18.

Richman, Tom. "Mrs. Fields' Secret Ingredient." *Inc.* (October 1987): 65–72.

"Scrambling to the Top." *Economist* (September 7, 1991): 21–24.

Sussman, John A. "Making It to the Top: A Career Profile of the Senior Executive." *Management Review* (July 1979): 15–21.

Terry, George R., and Stephen G. Franklin. *Principles of Management,* 422. Richard D. Irwin, 1982.

Woodruff, R. L. "Human Resource Accounting." *Canadian Chartered Accountant* (September 1970): 156–161.

For an extensive review of the literature concerning human-resource accounting, including an annotated bibliography of 113 works, see Gary Blau, *Highlights of the Literature: Human Resource Accounting,* Work in America Institute, 1978. See also Albert P. Amiess, "Human Resource Accounting in Industy," *CA Magazine* (Canada) 114 (August 1981): 113–118; M. J. Mee, "Tasks of Human Asset Accounting," *Accounting and Business Research* (England) 13 (Winter 1982): 42–48; Stephen A. Mascove, "Further Investigation into Human Resource Accounting," *Virginia Accounting* 35 (March 1983): 25–31; Angelos A. Tsaklanganos, "Human Resource Accounting: The Measure of a Person," *CA Magazine* (Canada) 113 (May 1980): 44–48; and Clark E. Chartain, "Evolution of Human Resource Accounting," *University of Michigan Business Review* 31 (January 1979): 16–23.

CHAPTER 11

Calish, Irving G., and R. Donald Gamache. "How to Overcome Organizational Resistance to Change." *Management Review* (October 1981): 21–50.

"Can Giants Live Happily with Midgets?" *Across the Board* (April 1991): 6.

Cetron, Marvin, and Owen Davies. *American Renaissance.* St. Martin's Press, 1989.

"Corporate America Invents the In-House Entrepreneur." *Economist* (February 23, 1985): 67–68.

Dumaine, Brian. "Is Big Still Good?" *Fortune* (April 20, 1992): 50–60.

Fast, Norman D., and Stanley E. Pratt. "Individual Entrepreneurship and the Large Corporation." In *Frontiers of Entrepreneurship Research,* edited by Karl H. Vesper, 443–444. Babson Centre for Entrepreneurial Studies, 1981.

Gatto, John. "Our Children Are Dying in Our Schools." *New Age Journal* (September/October 1990): 62–100.

Gibran, Kahlil. *The Prophet.* Heinemann, 1979.

Gilder, George. *Microcosm.* Simon & Schuster, 1989.

Gordon, Leon. "1992: Demolishing the Tax Frontiers." *The London School of Economics Alumnae Journal* (Spring 1992): 22–24.

Grossman, Stephen R., and Margaret J. King. "Eagles, Otters, and Unicorns: An Anatomy of Innovation." *Journal of Creative Behavior* 24, no. 2 (2nd Quarter 1990): 75–98.

Handy, Charles. *The Age of Unreason.* Harvard Business School Press, 1991.

Hawken, Paul. "The Ecology of Commerce." *Inc.* (April 1992): 93–100.

Hawken, Paul. *The New Economy,* 114–115. Holt, Rinehart & Winston, 1983.

Hecht, Maurice. "Real Managers Don't Need Theories Anymore." *Executive* (January 1984): 32–35.

Jaffe, Dennis T., and Cynthia D. Scott. *Take This Job and Love It.* Simon & Schuster, 1988.

Klingenberg, Ronna. "Decision Making and the Forces of Change." *Management Review* (December 1979): 13–16.

Lundberg, Craig C. "On the Usefulness of Organizational Rascals." *Business Quarterly* (Winter 1969): 7–13.

McClelland, David C. *The Achieving Society.* Free Press, 1967.

Main, Jeremy. "A Golden Age for Entrepreneurs." *Fortune* (February 12, 1990): 120–124.

Mintzberg, Henry. "The Effective Organization: Forces and Forms." *The Sloan Management Review* (Winter 1991): 54–55.

Nussbaum, Bruce, John W. Wilson, Daniel B. Moskowitz, and Alex Beam. "The New Corporate Elite." *Business Week* (January 21, 1985): 58–73.

"The Office Personalized: The Home of the Soul." Research summary from Herman Miller Inc., September 1989.

Peters, Thomas J., and Robert H. Waterman, Jr. "In Pursuit of Excellence . . . How the Best-Run Companies Turn So-So Performers into Big Winners." *Management Review* (November/ December 1982): 8–16.

Pinchot, Gifford, III. *Intrapreneuring.* Harper & Row, 1985.

Shapero, Albert. "The Displaced, Uncomfortable Entrepreneur." *Psychology Today* (November 1975).

Teilhard de Chardin, Pierre. *Toward the Future.* Harcourt Brace Jovanovich, 1975.

Toffler, Alvin. "Breaking with Bureaucracy." *Across the Board* (January/February 1991): 17–21.

Townsend, Robert. *Up the Organization,* 125. Michael Joseph, 1970.

Weiner, Johnathan. *The Next One Hundred Years.* Bantam, 1990.

Woodward, Herbert N. "Management Strategies for Small Companies." *Harvard Business Review* (January/February 1976): 113–121.

For further innovative ideas about the future and the meaning of work, see Charles Handy, "Through the Organizational Looking Glass," *Harvard Business Review* (January/February 1980): 115–121; Norman MacRea, "The Coming Entrepreneurial Revolution: A Survey," *Economist* (December 25, 1976): 41–44, 53–58, 60–65; Paul Hawken, *The Next Economy,* Holt, Rinehart & Winston, 1983; and John Naisbitt, *Megatrends,* Warner Books, 1984.

Index

Gage, Barbara, 212
Gage, Edwin C. (Skip), 212
Game theory, 349
Games Gang, The, 199
Gap, The, 212
Garin, Michael N., 440
Gate, Bradley, 354
Gates, William H., III, 125, 275
Gateway 2000, 37
Gatto, John, 434
GEC, 243
Gellman Research Associates, 445
General Dynamics, 168, 279
General Electric, 26, 30, 76, 238,
   253, 255, 318, 389–390, 413,
   428, 430, 435, 443, 444
General Electric Venture Capital
   Corporation, 430
General Foods, 443
General Instrument, 439
General Motors, 41, 76, 169, 238,
   298, 318, 330, 401, 436
   Saturn Division, 291
General Portland Cement Company,
   58
Générale Occidentale, 419
Genius, defined, 152–153
Gerstner, Louis V., Jr., 435
Gibran, Kahlil, 407
Gibson Greeting Card, 446
Gilbert, Walter, 410
Gillette Company, 335
Gioia, Dennis, 216
Glass, David, 136
Globe and Mail, Toronto,
   412–413
Goals, 60–61
Goals/people/structure organization
   design, 237, 241
Goizueta, Robert C., 341
Goldsmith, Jimmy (Sir James), 124,
   137, 419
Goldwyn, Samuel, 449
Goodwill Games, 140
Gore, W. L. and Associates, 131–132,
   414
Gore, Wilbert L., 1, 131–132, 414
Grace Corp., W. R., 443
Gracián, Baltasar, 149
Grapevine, 250–251
Gray, Douglas, 410
Great Lakes Group, 193
Greenberg, Robert Y., 169
Greenpeace, 63
Greeters, 135
Greiner, Larry E., 30–37
Gretzky, Wayne, 194, 407

Greyhound Lines of Canada,
   352–353
Growth
   five phases of, 30–37
   paradox of, 24–25
GTE, 170
Gyllenhammer, Pehr, 209

H. J. Heinz, 129–130, 266, 309
Hach Company, 435–436
Hach, Kathryn, 435
Haire, Mason, 40–41
Hallmark Cards Inc., 196
Hambrecht and Quist, 445
Hambrecht, Bill, 445
Hambro Life, 419
Hammer, Armand, 210
Hammond, Eric, 436
Handy, Dan, 116
Hanson, Lord, 124
Hansson, P. A., 7
Harley-Davidson, 446
Harris Corporation, 213
Harris, Louis, 184
Harvard Business Review, 31, 122
Harvard Business School, 120, 126
Hawke, Bob, 138
Hawthorne effect, 359
Hawthorne studies, 120
Hayes, James L., 248
Hayes, Robert H., 11, 288, 357, 383
Hazelwood, Joseph, 166
Head, Howard, 272
Hees International, 193
Henderson, Bruce, 345
Herman Miller Inc., 244
Heroic Environments, 186
Herzberg, Frederick, 168, 284
Hewitt Associates, 173
Hewlett-Packard, 242–243
Hidden economy. See Informal
   economy
Hierarchy of needs, 151
High margin/high service concept,
   330–334
Hiring, 200
   from within, 201
   and screening techniques, 189–193
   standards for, 196
Histadrut, 437
Hitachi, 318
Hobbes, Thomas, 149
Hobbesian perspective, defined, 149,
   153
Hockaday, Irvine O., Jr., 196
Hoffer, Eric, 23
Hoffman-La Roche, 411